KU-262-653

FURTHER STUDIES *for* SOCIAL CARE

Caroline Holden

Carolyn Meggitt

Dawn Collard

Chrissie Rycroft

Hodder & Stoughton

A ME[MBER OF THE HODDER HEADLINE] GROUP

Wiltshire College

115100

A catalogue record of this publication is available from the British Library.

ISBN 0 340 655267

First published 1996

Impression number	10 9 8 7 6 5 4 3
Year	2000 1999 1998 1997

Copyright © 1996 Caroline Holden, Carolyn Meggitt, Dawn Collard, Chrissie Rycroft

All rights reserved. No part of this publication may be reproduced or transmitted in any form or by any means, electronic or mechanical, including photocopy, recording, or any information storage and retrieval system, without permission in writing from the publisher or under licence from the Copyright Licensing Agency Limited. Further details of such licences (for reprographic reproduction) may be obtained from the Copyright Licensing Agency Limited, of 90 Tottenham Court Road, London W1P 9HE.

Typeset by Wearset, Boldon, Tyne and Wear.
Printed in Great Britain for Hodder & Stoughton Educational, a division of Hodder Headline Plc, 338 Euston Road, London NW1 3BH by Scotprint Ltd, Musselburgh, Scotland.

CONTENTS

ACKNOWLEDGEMENTS

The authors would like to thank the following for their help and advice during the preparation of this book: Hilary Dickinson and Michael Erben for exercises on issues of disability; Richard Kember for contributing a case study; John Mitchell, Kent Social Services, for the interview on his role as European Development Officer; Pat Evans for the article 'A Very Special Baby'; Peter Murray for advice and materials relating to the history of social policy. Dawn Collard would like to thank the staff at the National Institute for Social Work Library for their help.

Our special thanks go to our families for their support and encouragement.

For the reproduction of copyright material, the publisher would like to thank the following: Fig 1.1 Richmond College; Fig 1.5 Colin Wheeler; Fig 1.6 Jane Salvage/Butterworth-Heinemann Ltd; Fig 2.1 John Cole/Impact; Fig 2.2 Sam Tanner/Photofusion; Fig 3.11 Rachel Morton/Impact; Fig 3.20 John Almond/GDBA Holidays; Fig 3.22 Sally Greenhill/Sally & Richard Greenhill Photographers; Figs 4.1, 4.5, 4.6 Range/Bettmann; Fig 4.2 Mary Evans/Sigmund Freud Copyrights: courtesy of W.E. Freud; Fig 4.3 Range/Bettmann/UPI; Fig 4.4 OSU Photo Archives; Fig 4.10 William Vandivert, Dennis, MA, USA/Scientific American; Fig 6.1 Mary Evans Picture Library; Fig 6.2 Hulton Deutsch; Fig 6.6 European Parliament; Fig 7.1 Stan Eales/Grub Street.

The extract reprinted on page 46 from *Mustn't Grumble* by Lois Keith, first published by the Women's Press Ltd, 1994, 34 Great Sutton Street, London EC1V 0DX, is used by permission of The Women's Press Ltd.

Every effort has been made to trace copyright holders of material reproduced in this book. Any rights not acknowledged here will be acknowledged in subsequent printings if notice is given to the publisher.

1

ETHICAL AND LEGAL ASPECTS OF HEALTH AND SOCIAL CARE

Ethical and legal issues are central to health and social care. The special nature of the caring relationship means that professionals will frequently be required to make decisions which have important consequences for the health and well being of clients, such as determining the allocation of finite resources or weighing up the competing needs and rights of individual clients and the wider community. In reaching these decisions professionals will be guided both by specific legal obligations and duties and by certain agreed ethical principles. However, it is important to realise that although ethical and legal principles may overlap, sometimes they will *not*, and practitioners will need to reach judgements which seek to balance the competing requirements of law and ethics.

This chapter first addresses the important ethical principles and concepts which inform health and social care, and then goes on to consider the legal framework within which practitioners must operate. Examples of potential conflict are provided, together with an opportunity to apply ethical and legal principles to typical care-work situations.

ETHICAL PRINCIPLES AND PERSPECTIVES

What is ethics?

'Ethics' or 'morals' – the terms can be used interchangeably (Warnock 1987) – have for thousands of years been the subject of study by philosophers and others. Some of those who study ethics take a theoretical approach and try to understand what morality is about and why human beings have moral systems at all. This is known as *meta-ethics*. Others have been more concerned with what is known as *normative ethics* or the practical application of morality. Here philosophers have attempted to understand the moral rules which govern social life and to suggest how best we can live together.

One method that can help to make sense of ethical problems is the *thought experiment*, which creates an artificial situation that allows us to see clearly some of the basic rules and assumptions of our moral system. A famous example of a thought experiment is the 'Trolley Problem' (Foot 1978). You are standing on a bridge overlooking a railway line and can see that an empty railway trolley (an old-fashioned one as seen in many old American films) has broken loose and is careering down the track. You see that the track forks: on the left a small girl is playing on the track; on the right there are five children playing. You realise that the trolley is going to the right and is going to kill the five children, who appear oblivious to its approach. You are too far away to warn the children, but there is a lever beside you on the bridge. You cannot stop the trolley with the lever but you can switch the track so that the trolley will head for the little girl instead. This will mean that only one child is killed rather than five.

ACTIVITY

In small groups discuss whether it is morally permissible for you to pull the lever.

Now imagine that you are a doctor with six patients, five of whom will die without immediate organ transplants. The sixth has a non-life-threatening illness, and has tissue which is compatible with that of your other five patients.

ACTIVITY

Decide whether it is morally permissible to kill patient number six in order to save the lives of patients one to five.

It is quite likely that you reached different conclusions in these two cases.

ACTIVITY

In pairs, try to identify the morally significant differences between them.

Our *moral intuition* seems to tell us that in the first case it was permissible to pull the lever in order to save lives, but that in the second case it is not permissible to kill in order to save lives. Why might this be?

The motivation in the two cases appears to be different. In the trolley example, the intention is simply to save as many lives as possible, and although you know your action will kill a child, this is not your reason for acting. In the second case, you appear to take someone's life deliberately. However, when you operate on patient number six, perhaps you do not *intend* to kill him (see the 'Doctrine of Double Effect' below) – instead, your sole intention may be to *save the lives* of your other five patients. The death of patient six is an unfortunate side effect of an otherwise morally well-intentioned act. Nonetheless, it seems likely that you are still not satisfied. Perhaps the real difference here is that pulling a lever is in itself a morally neutral act (it is only in its consequences that it can be good or bad) but people have a right to their own body, and whipping out someone's internal organs without their permission is clearly a violation of this moral right, so that whatever your *intention*, this act cannot be morally justified.

Hopefully, this exercise will have enabled you to realise a number of things about our 'ordinary morality', including the following:

1 We can all recognise moral issues.
2 As members of a particular society, we share (at least some) moral beliefs and intuitions.
3 Disagreement seems to be an important element of morality.

ETHICAL THEORIES

There are many ethical theories or perspectives which, as we have suggested, try both to explain what morality is and to identify how we can behave morally. Two important but very different theories are explained here: *Consequentialism* and *deontology* or *duty ethics*.

Consequentialism

Consequentialist theories hold that the rightness or wrongness of an action depends entirely upon the effects which that action has – that is, on its consequences. One kind of consequentialism is *classical utilitarianism* which says that we must always act so as to promote the greatest happiness of the greatest number. In any situation, the morally right action will be whatever brings about the most pleasure or happiness or most decreases suffering or unhappiness – or both. It is important to note that on this view nothing is morally wrong or morally right in itself: actions can only be judged as good or bad in the light of the *consequences* which they bring about. Utilitarianism says that we must not give greater weight to our own happiness or that of those closest to us, but must consider the interests of all human beings equally as this promotes the greatest happiness of the greatest number. This may seem a very 'democratic' approach, but it also means that the interests of the minority will always be sacrificed to those of the majority.

ACTIVITY

What would you see as the major criticisms of the consequentialist approach to moral problems?

Deontology or duty ethics

Deontological theories hold that there are certain acts which are right in themselves and thus always morally required; or, more frequently, that there are certain acts which are always morally wrong even as the means to morally praiseworthy (good) ends. The word deontological derives from the Greek *deon* meaning duty and is frequently contrasted with the teleological (*telos* means goal) approach to morality of consequentialism.

One famous deontological theory was put forward by the philosopher Immanuel Kant. For Kant, a moral action is one that is performed out of a sense of duty – it is the motivation (the reason) for action which is important, not its consequences. Kant believed that as rational beings we have certain duties which are absolute and unconditional, whatever the consequences, such as: we ought never to lie, or to commit murder. To act in accordance with moral duty, we must only do things which it would be acceptable for everyone else to do. This is known as the 'universalisability principle', and is something like the Golden Rule of Christian ethics: 'Treat your neighbour as yourself.' Kant also says that morality requires us always to respect individuals (persons) as ends in themselves ('sovereign wills') and never treat them as means to be sacrificed to some greater end. That is, we must respect their *autonomy*.

ACTIVITY

Explain simply, in your own words, how the consequentialist and deontological approaches differ.

Here are two more thought experiments:

Two people are trapped in a burning building. One is a leading cancer researcher and the other is her cleaning woman. A man comes onto the scene and attempts to rescue them. However, he finds that he can only save one because of the degree of smoke and damage to the building. He must therefore decide who to save and who to leave to die. The man is the son of the cleaner.

ACTIVITY

Assume that the man is a consequentialist. Who would he save and why? Do you agree with his decision? If not, why not?

After many years of research a new and effective vaccine has been developed against a major childhood illness. However, extensive testing has indicated that 1% of all children who are vaccinated will experience severe (but not fatal) side effects. It is not possible to screen all children in advance to identify those likely to be affected.

ACTIVITY

Would a consequentialist go ahead with a mass vaccination programme, and if so, why?

Acts and omissions

Many moral systems make a clear distinction between acting, on the one hand, and omitting, or failing, to act on the other. Deontologists, for example, would say that there is a big difference between the moral rule which says 'Do not lie' and the requirement 'Tell the truth.' They do not believe that the two are equivalent in moral terms, or that the former entails (i.e. logically leads to) the latter. This means that if we actively lie, then we have behaved immorally, but that if we fail to tell the truth, we have not.

For consequentialists, acts and omissions *are* equally important morally. As we saw above, if the moral worth of actions is to be judged in terms of their consequences, then the failure to prevent an act with harmful consequences is no less morally wrong than actually performing the act in question ourselves.

ACTIVITY

For consequentialists lying and failing to tell the truth amount to the same thing. Do you agree?

ACTIVITY

Consider the following two thought experiments and decide whether you think it is morally justifiable to distinguish between acts and omissions in these cases.

1 James Smith stands to gain a large inheritance if anything should happen to his 6-year-old cousin, Tom. One evening whilst Tom is taking his bath, Smith sneaks into the bathroom and drowns the child. He arranges things to look like an accident.
2 John Jones stands to gain a large inheritance if anything should happen to his 6-year-old cousin, David. One evening whilst David is taking his bath, Smith sneaks into the bathroom, planning to drown the child. However, just as he enters the bathroom, Jones sees David slip, hit his head and fall face down into the water. Jones is delighted; he stands by, ready to push the child's head back under if this is necessary, but it isn't. With only a little thrashing about, the child drowns all by himself, 'accidentally', as Jones watches and does nothing.

(Adapted from Rachels article in Singer 1986)

It seems likely that in these examples you found no real moral difference between the *act* of Mr Smith and the *omission* of Mr Jones, but in other more realistic cases you may well feel justified in distinguishing morally between the two, as in the following examples:

1 Nurse Susan Jenkins has been requested to fit cot sides to the bed of a patient who has returned to the ward from the operating theatre, and to leave them in place for 24 hours. However, on locating the cot sides, Nurse Jenkins finds that she cannot fit them properly, so, being in a hurry, she attaches them in a rather haphazard manner – although she knows this is dangerous – and leaves the ward. Later the patient falls out of bed and sustains an injury.
2 Nurse Susan Jenkins checks on a patient who has recently returned from the operating theatre and finds that her cot sides have not been fitted properly by another nurse. She intends to report the matter to the ward sister but fails to do so before the patient falls out of bed and sustains an injury.

Is Nurse Jenkins equally responsible for the harm caused to the patient in each of these cases? If not, why not?

The Doctrine of Double Effect

Deontologists can also make use of the Doctrine of Double Effect which says that where there are two (or more) foreseeable outcomes to an action, the individual will not be held morally responsible for the negative outcome where this was not their intention (refer back to the Trolley Problem). For example, where a doctor foresees that saving the life of a mother in labour may also mean the death of her baby, the doctor will not be held morally responsible for this death because it is only a side effect of the *intentional* action to *save the mother's life*.

ACTIVITY

Do you think that consequentialists would accept the Doctrine of Double Effect? If not, why not?

KEY ETHICAL PRINCIPLES AND CONCEPTS

Many people are unaware of particular ethical theories or perspectives: what they are much more familiar with are the specific ethical rules or principles we use in everyday ethical decision making. It is important to realise, however, that few, if any, of these principles are *moral absolutes*: in each situation we face, we must decide which principle is most important. At times we may find it hard to reconcile conflicting demands, and we will find ourselves in a *moral dilemma* where we are faced with difficult moral choices, as the following section explains.

Rights, obligations and duties

In some ways moral rights can be understood as *freedoms*: the *freedom to do* something, or *freedom from* something. By contrast, as we have seen, *moral duties* and *obligations* (the terms are often used synonymously) can be understood as the opposite: as the *requirement* to do something. Many moral (and legal) obligations and duties arise in direct response to the rights possessed by others. For example, your right to freedom is balanced by my duty not to interfere with you; your client has a right to confidentiality, and you have a duty to respect that confidentiality. For deontologists, of course, moral duties *must* be discharged whether or not there are any corresponding rights.

LEGAL RIGHTS AND DUTIES

Unlike moral rights, obligations and duties, legal ones are publicly acknowledged and legally enforceable, e.g. the right not to be discriminated against in employment. However, although an attempt has been made here to separate ethical and legal issues formally, in practice they are often difficult to distinguish, and health and social care workers will face many situations where both legal and ethical rights, duties and obligations come into conflict.

The following moral principles can perhaps best be understood as the expression of certain rights, obligations and duties.

Autonomy

Autonomy means, literally, 'self-rule' and refers to the degree to which an individual can think, decide and act independently. For many, respect for the autonomy of the individual is a key goal of ethical practice. The thought behind the high regard afforded to autonomy is the uniqueness of each individual human being and the belief that to remove from the individual the opportunity for *self-determination* (the ability to make their own decisions and act on them) is fundamentally to compromise their humanity. Respect for the autonomy of the individual provides some protection in cases where the needs and wishes of the majority may override those of the individual or minority.

ACTIVITY

Suggest why respect for autonomy is such an important ethical goal.

Independence

Linked to autonomy is the concept of *independence*, the idea that we are most fully human when we can decide for ourselves what we want and can achieve it without dependence upon others. Independence is freedom to do something. For many health and social care workers, enhancing the independence of their clients is an important aim of professional practice.

ACTIVITY

One group of people historically denied the right to full independence are those with disabilities. Conduct some research into what measures people with physical disabilities feel would enhance their independence.

However, full recognition of and respect for the autonomy and independence of the individual patient or client is not always possible or desirable. In the case of small children, for example, we recognise that their rational faculties are not developed sufficiently for them to play a full role in major decisions about their own lives; or it may be that an individual has learning difficulties or is suffering from mental illness and is not fully capable of exercising their autonomy. In such situations the principles of autonomy and independence may be supplemented by the principle of *protection from harm*.

Protection from harm

All health and social care workers have an explicit moral as well as legal duty to protect vulnerable patients and clients from harm and always to act in their best interests (and in the

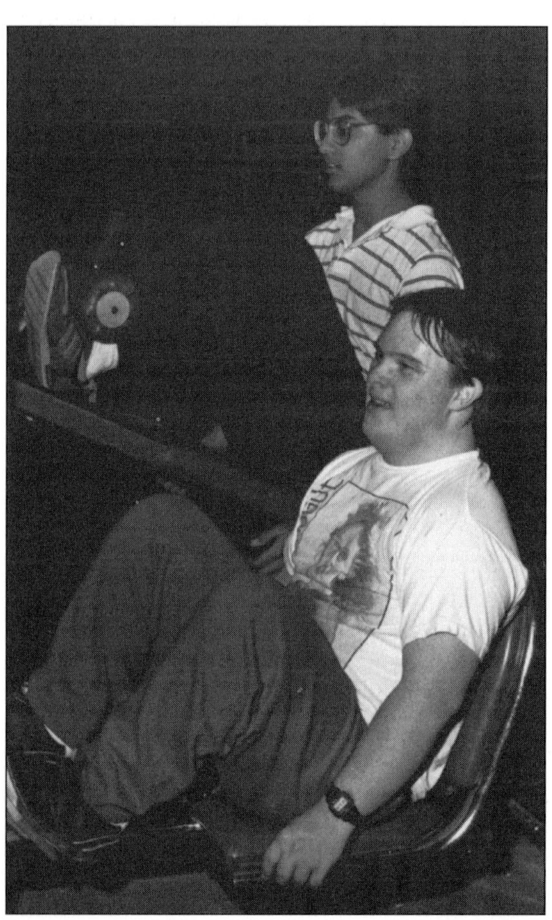

Figure 1.1 At Richmond College, independence is enhanced through partnership between mainstream and special-needs students

best interests of those to whom the clients themselves may pose a threat). This is sometimes known as a *parentalist approach*, that is, the practitioner acts towards their clients or patients as any good parent would.

POTENTIAL ETHICAL CONFLICT

Ethical conflict can occur between the right to autonomy and independence and the duty to protect from harm. For many vulnerable people, the exercise of autonomy and the enjoyment of independence is inevitably going to lead to the risk of harm. However, the necessity, indeed the right, to take such risks is explicitly recognised by agencies who work with vulnerable people, as the following statement of values makes clear (italics mine):

> Each person should be valued as a member of society and as an individual with needs and wishes which should be respected. In all cases each person should be enabled to make informed choices and to take *reasonable risks* in all areas of their life.
>
> *(Adapted from a statement by The Independent Development Council for People with Mental Handicap)*

What health and social care workers must do is to assess and manage potential risk but without unduly curtailing the freedom of the individual.

ACTIVITY

1 Why is it important to be allowed the freedom to take risks, even where harm may result?

2 What steps can child care workers take to balance children's need to become independent, with the need to protect them from harm?

Paternalism

In contrast to parentalism, the principle of *paternalism* is more authoritarian. This holds that decisions can frequently best be taken on behalf of others by those who have the best interests of those others at heart and who are in possession of all the facts. In a medical context this may take the form of the 'doctor knows best' view. This principle will result in a denial of the patient's autonomy and right to play a full part in decisions about their treatment but will be justified by the belief that patients cannot possibly be as well informed as their doctor and can therefore make no useful contribution to decision making.

POTENTIAL ETHICAL CONFLICT

Some argue that paternalism is never ethically acceptable because it fundamentally violates the right to autonomy and independence, but others believe that sometimes it is necessary when working with those who are vulnerable or in danger of harming themselves or others. One way of understanding this is to say that it may be morally permissible to violate someone's autonomy in order to preserve it for the future. A consequentialist would say that paternalism is always justifiable where it increases happiness or minimises suffering.

The following extract illustrates very clearly the problems which can result when the demands of paternalism and autonomy and independence come into conflict.

> INTERFERING MOTHER BARRED BY COURT
>
> A youth with cerebral palsy won a unique High Court ban yesterday when Mr Justice Johnson, a Family Division judge, granted an order restraining the 18-year-old's mother from interfering with his rights . . .
>
> Steven, the judge said, suffered from cerebral palsy, spastic quadriplegia and speech and learning difficulties but was a mentally capable adult.
>
> Steven's adoptive parents had had a child of

their own but it had died when a few months old.

'After the death of their own baby, the joy of these parents in this adoption can easily be imagined,' he said. 'Their expectations were shattered when Steven was about a year old and was diagnosed as having cerebral palsy' . . .

Their local authority became involved in 1985 . . . because of the mother's 'fiercely over-protective attitude to Steven,' the judge said . . .

'She exercised an increasingly close and intimate control of Steven's life . . .

'She would keep him from school, saying he was ill, when doctors said he was not. She would make excuses such as it was too cold, to avoid Steven having showers that were necessary.'

She made it impossible for him to have any semblance of social life and prevented him from developing his full potential, physically, socially, emotionally and educationally.

In the end, Steven was taken into care. In June, just before the care order was due to expire on his 18th birthday, he went to court seeking an order preventing his mother from running his life again by interfering with his right to live where and with whom he wanted.

Granting that order, the judge said that . . . 'On the facts as I have found them . . . There seems to me to be a real risk of infringement of Steven's freedom.'

(From an article in the Guardian, *14 July 1995)*

ACTIVITY

1. If you were a social worker with involvement in this case, what steps would you have taken to try to avoid the necessity of a court case?
2. In what situations do you think it might be justifiable to adopt a paternalist approach?

Respect for persons

Respect for persons is another very basic ethical principle, and it requires that we take into account the rights and wishes of all those affected in a particular situation. No individual, however autonomous, can demand treatment or services without reference to the needs of others or without reference to the opinions of those charged with their care. Likewise, even where the rights of one individual must clearly be given priority, respect must still be shown for others involved.

POTENTIAL ETHICAL CONFLICT

It is clear that respect for persons is likely to conflict with other ethical principles, including those of autonomy, independence and protection from harm. There are many situations where such conflict can occur in health and social care practice, both in the community and in institutional settings, where the needs and wishes of individual clients or residents must be weighed against the needs and wishes of those around them. Two examples follow:

Child protection

The harmful consequences of the physical and sexual abuse of children are now widely recognised, not least in the Children Act 1989 which makes the rights of children 'paramount'. Subsequent guidelines to social workers have further emphasised the importance of intervention by social services in suspected cases of child abuse.

However, concern has recently been expressed both by families and by the Department of Health that the goal of protecting children from harm has been prioritised above other important principles and has in some cases, in fact, *contributed* to harm, as the following extract by Rachel Downey illustrates:

CHILD PROTECTION

Teri's eldest daughter Jane told her teacher she had been sexually abused by her mother's partner . . .

Although the police rapidly concluded there

was no case to answer and both Teri's daughters were allowed to continue living at home, the family was the subject of a detailed seven-month investigation by social workers.

Teri claims social workers seemed to actively encourage the rift which grew between her, Jane and younger sister Jill . . .

'We lost control of our lives and were bogged down in a system we didn't understand, caught in a morass of oft-repeated jargon. There was a dearth of information, a conspiracy of silence, which increased our apprehension and rendered us impotent,' says Teri.

Jill sensed the vulnerability and became insecure, confused and afraid. She started having nightmares . . . Jill even began answering the phone with the question: "Are you a social worker?"

A child psychologist concluded that Jill had never been abused but was suffering considerable stress from the investigation. Teri says her partner, John, who underwent treatment for depression before the allegation, suffered repeated panic attacks from recurring nightmares because of his arrest and temporary incarceration in the police cells . . .

She claims a social worker told John that he was not their concern and that if he committed suicide as a result of the additional stress, it would merely confirm his guilt. Three months into the investigation, Jane opted to move in with foster parents.

Teri says she allowed Jill to be abused, not by any one individual, but by the very system designed to protect her. Jill began 'cutting up' – taking the skin off her arms and legs with the edge of a coin and engraving patterns on herself with pins. She cut her wrists; took overdoses and had to be hospitalised; she inhaled solvents, stole from home and was eventually arrested for shoplifting. Consequently she now has a criminal record . . .

After the Cleveland child abuse scandal in 1987, which prompted the 1988 *Working Together* guidelines, the pendulum swung from accusing social workers of doing nothing to outrage at their interventionist role in families's lives. Now philosophies are shifting again to take into account the rights of families in the child protection process.

(Community Care, *20–26 July 1995)*

ACTIVITY

1 Explain what went wrong in this case, and suggest how the goal of protection from harm *could* have been reconciled with the duty of respect for persons. What other ethical principles appear to have been overlooked in this case?

2 What general difficulties do child-protection workers face in attempting to balance the needs and rights of children with those of parents?

Elders and their carers

Demographic changes (specifically an aging population), together with an increased emphasis on care in the community, have served to highlight the needs and rights of millions of dependent elders in Britain. An appreciation of the scale of elder abuse and 'granny dumping' has added to this.

At the same time, however, there has been a belated official recognition of the needs and rights of Britain's seven million informal carers in the form of the Carers (Recognition and Services) Act 1995. Whilst legislation such as this is obviously welcome, as Thomas and Wall point out (1992), there is now increased potential for conflict between carers and users:

These two developments now find themselves on a possible convergence course where both carer and cared-for have growing notions of their rights which may be in conflict with one another. If we now have to take account of the carer's rights the question will arise as to whether this can be done at the expense of the rights of the cared-for person. In other words, is this a new ground for removing the rights of autonomy from an elderly person? As in the past we have compulsorily detained people who put others at physical risk . . . will we in the future be able to compel elderly people to, say, attend a day centre three days a week, even if they do not wish to go, simply because we wish to uphold the rights of the carer to some respite from their task?

(Thomas and Wall, 1992)

The particular concerns of one social services department are outlined in the following article:

The 'Carers' (Recognition and Services) Act . . . [has paved] the way for the statutory right of carers to have their needs assessed. While it is a milestone for carers' organisations and a partial recognition of their long-running argument that most care in the community is given by relatives and friends, some local authorities view the prospect of assessment with trepidation . . .

Barbara Wilson, principal officer for physical disabilities in Tower Hamlets social services department, [says] that the potential for conflict between meeting service users' needs and those of their carers is likely to be heightened . . .

'This can occur when the carer needs respite care, but the user often doesn't want this to happen. In practice we tend to offer respite care where it's clear the carer needs this in order to continue caring, otherwise they could end up being clients as well,' says Wilson.

She suggests actual or potential conflict could be handled better if there were separate assessors for the client and the carer, especially if both parties had access to independent advocates . . .

No-one has a simple answer to problems thrown up by the potentially differing interests and needs of clients and carers. But Wilson emphasises that it is vital to understand the often complex and emotionally-charged relationships of carers and clients, otherwise services could be offered which suit neither.

One care manager, who asked not to be named, says there can be dangers in offering home care assistance which might imply criticism of the carer or, worse still, that they are being supplanted by social services staff. 'In reality, a lot of carers may prefer to continue to give personal, and often intimate care to their loved one, and only want help from social services with things like laundry and cleaning, or maybe a sitting service or some other respite care,' she says.

(Community Care, *20–26 July 1995)*

ACTIVITY

In the light of the statutory recognition of the needs of carers, explain how respect for persons and the rights to autonomy and independence may come into conflict within informal caring relationships. Suggest how social services could deal with this potential conflict whilst still aiming to support both elder and carer.

Persons and human beings

Some moral philosophers argue that the requirements of morality relate only to *persons*, not to *human beings*. This may seem confusing because we often think of 'human being' and 'person' as synonymous terms. However, in the sense in which the terms are used within law and ethics, human beings are only persons if they are rational and self-conscious and have the ability to fully exercise *moral agency*. Some philosophers believe that some animals, such as higher apes and dolphins, may count as 'persons' whereas some human beings may not. This is of course a very controversial claim, not least because it means that many of those we automatically think of as persons, such as severely brain-damaged adults, would seem to lose their moral status, and that foetuses, which are not conscious or rational, would seem to warrant no moral consideration at all. However, others, including many of those opposed to abortion, believe that foetuses are 'potential persons' and as such must be granted full moral status.

ACTIVITY

1 Carry out some research into the status of foetuses in law. Do they count as 'persons'?

2 In small groups discuss the consequences for health care policy of making a formal distinction between persons and human beings.

The sanctity of life

The belief that life is intrinsically valuable or sacred is a widely held moral principle. Most people think it wrong to kill most of the time, and this is reflected in laws throughout the world which prohibit indiscriminate killing. However, the principle of the sanctity of life is in fact rather ambiguous. For example, it does not necessarily mean that killing is always wrong; many people believe that sometimes overriding moral principles such as self-defence make it right. Others say that only the life of *persons* is sacred, and that where someone has lost or has no consciousness or self-awareness, objections to killing do not apply. For others again, life is only sacred where a person has a desire to live, or where they have a certain quality of life.

POTENTIAL ETHICAL CONFLICT: EUTHANASIA

Euthanasia or 'mercy killing' illustrates clearly the potential ethical conflict between the principle of the value or sanctity of life and other ethical principles we have considered. A number of surveys have shown that doctors regularly receive requests for (voluntary) euthanasia, and that a sizeable number have carried it out. See, for example, the following extract:

The first comprehensive study into the scale of euthanasia in Britain, to be published tomorrow, indicates that more than 1 in 10 doctors have taken measures to end patients' lives at their request . . .

Positive steps to shorten a patient's life is known to be widespread, being regarded as acceptable if it is a side-effect of the treatment, invariably pain relief. But the significance of the study is that it shows that, even where doctors could defend their actions on the grounds that they were merely trying to relieve pain, the intent had been to shorten the patient's life to end the suffering . . .

(From an article in the Independent, *20 May 1994)*

ACTIVITY

Explain how doctors could make use of the Doctrine of Double Effect to justify their actions here.

However, the legal position is clear. The law makes a distinction between acts and omissions and holds that *active* euthanasia must be treated as murder or manslaughter. However, *passive* euthanasia by means of the withdrawal of life support from patients who are in the Persistent Vegetative State (PVS) has been sanctioned by the courts on a number of occasions. For patients who are not in PVS: although therapeutic treatment may be withdrawn (patients have a right to refuse treatment), palliative care (nursing care and nutrition) may not.

Whilst strongly opposing active euthanasia, the British Medical Association does counsel against artificially keeping individuals alive at all costs. They recognise that there are limits to care.

ACTIVITY

Discuss what the limits to such care might be. For example, should premature babies undergo very expensive major surgery when the odds against survival are high? Consider what factors should play a part in such decisions.

Supporters of euthanasia include consequentialists who do not recognise the act – omission distinction. Many feel that actively taking the life of someone who is in pain can be more humane and 'moral' than letting them die slowly. Others believe that sometimes other moral principles must take precedence over the sanctity of life, as the two following extracts make clear:

Now that the law allows suicide, it is difficult to explain why it should object to assisted suicide and that is what voluntary euthanasia is. Allowing voluntary euthanasia is an increase in options and is to be welcomed by anyone who values self-determination. Of course such an increase in options brings risks, but the way to think about it must be from the starting point of personal autonomy. We must think about the circumstances in which we want to live and the range of choices we want to have available to us. The question is one of risk analysis.

(Adapted from an article by Janet Radcliffe Richards in the Guardian, *16 May 1995)*

Opponents of euthanasia claim that, with modern methods nearly all pain can be controlled and that euthanasia is a sign of medical failure. However a recent survey suggests that this may be wide of the mark. It found that the main reason for expressing a wish to die was not pain but a fear of becoming dependent upon others. Requests for euthanasia may then indicate not that patients are giving up in the face of suffering but that they are positively asserting their desire to control events.

(Adapted from an article in the Guardian, *30 November 1994)*

ACTIVITY

What moral principles are identified in these two extracts in support of voluntary euthanasia? Do you agree that they may override the principle of the sanctity of life?

Opponents of euthanasia include some who are opposed even to the passive euthanasia of patients who are P.V.S. For them, the principle of the sanctity of life means that life must be preserved at all costs. Many such opponents, however, are more concerned about the consequences of legalising active euthanasia. Their main fear is that if the direct taking of life were to be legalised, this would lead to a relaxation of our general prohibition on killing. This would mean that it would become easier to kill disabled children who failed to reach an arbitrary 'quality of life' threshold, and that it would be easier for families to force elderly relatives to 'choose' to die. Some evidence to support this view can be found in the following (already-cited) study:

The study also showed, however, that while spouses were less likely to feel that it would have been better had the person died earlier, other carers were more likely to say that an earlier death would have been preferable – partly because they found caring more burdensome than spouses. Dr Doyle of a hospice in Edinburgh believes that the pressure for euthanasia reflects an increasingly warped sense of social values. 'We put such high store on employment and economic capability that if someone has none of these things . . . they feel a burden. Patients who are dying feel they are no longer valued and needed. The answer lies partly in reaffirming a person's worth despite their illness – in being rather than doing.'

For Dr Addington-Hall, coauthor of the study, 'there is an intractable conflict between the rights of the individual to take their own life and the consequences for other people who don't want to go down that path. It is very hard to see a position where people who really want euthanasia can be [given it] without putting pressure on others who don't.'

(Adapted from an article in the Guardian, *30 November 1995)*

What ethical principles are being suggested here as of greater importance than those of autonomy and independence?

ACTIVITY

In July 1995, two sets of parents sought permission to allow their severely disabled children (Thomas Creedon and Ian Stewart) to die. Carry out some research into these two cases and identify the particular arguments for and against euthanasia in each case.

If you wish to explore the issue of euthanasia further, you might like to contact pro- and anti-euthanasia pressure groups for information on their respective positions. There are also a number of useful (but sometimes distressing) video programmes which outline arguments for and against active euthanasia and which consider the consequences of its decriminalisation in places such as the Netherlands.

Maintaining confidentiality

Health and social care professionals have both a legal and moral duty to maintain confidentiality, that is, to respect privileged information which has been given by, or about, patients or clients. Maintaining confidence is linked to autonomy and respect for persons as well as to the moral requirement of *promise keeping*.

POTENTIAL ETHICAL CONFLICT

Sometimes, however, the duty to maintain confidence may conflict with other equally important principles, such as the duty to protect others from harm, or respect for (other) persons.

ACTIVITY

Suggest two health and social care situations which may present dilemmas between these three principles.

Consent

Like confidentiality, the requirement to gain consent is both an ethical and legal principle (see p. 1), and it too is explicitly linked to autonomy and respect for persons. To have regard for people, we must take into account their wishes and seek their permission where we need to undertake actions which may infringe their autonomy and individual rights. Sometimes there are particular problems in gaining consent, for example where there are intellectual barriers to communication.

ACTIVITY

In such cases, what other moral principles must also be considered?

Truth telling

Truth telling is a basic moral principle in our culture; it is something we teach children as they grow up, and something which is widely punished if violated. If you think back to the deontological and consequentialist theories, you will perhaps guess that deontologists think that telling the truth is a moral duty which must be observed whilst consequentialists would say that we should tell the truth whenever the consequences of doing so are more favourable than the consequences of *not* doing so.

POTENTIAL ETHICAL CONFLICT

Certainly, health and social care workers will frequently find themselves in situations where it is not immediately clear that telling the truth should take precedence over other equally important moral principles, such as respect for confidentiality or protection from harm. The following article provides an example of such an ethical conflict in the context of the treatment of HIV and Aids:

People who are unaware that they have HIV seem to live longer than those who know and are treated. This finding challenges the increasingly stated medical view that patients should know they are HIV positive as early as possible so that they can seek treatment.

However, researchers say it is still important that people know their HIV status so they can take measures not to spread the virus. Doctors at St Mary's Hospital, London, led by Mark Poznansky, looked at 436 patients treated for Aids between 1991 and 1993. The patients had different types of illness, with those in the 'ignorance group' having a dangerous but treatable form of pneumonia, while those who knew of their condition had more wasting Aids symptoms. Among those who knew of their infection before Aids developed, 194 patients died over the study period compared to 56 from the group who were ignorant of being HIV positive.

(Adapted from an article in the Guardian, *14 July 1995)*

ACTIVITY

In the light of these findings, are health workers justified in not revealing diagnoses to their patients? What ethical principles must they consider in reaching such a decision?

Equality

Equality is another frequently espoused moral principle, but it can be understood in many different ways. As it is mostly used in ethical discussions, it refers to the view that all human beings are fundamentally of equal worth: whatever our sex, race or colour, we are all of the same value. The usage of equality with which health and social care workers will be most familiar, therefore, is that of *equality of opportunity* and *equality of treatment*.

However, it is certainly not the case that such equality has been extended to the whole population. Comprehensive anti-discrimination legislation has yet to cover people with disabilities, and there are still occupations where individuals may be dismissed purely because of their sexuality. In a number of high-profile cases, lesbian and gay service personnel have challenged this discrimination as a violation of civil rights. Recently, however, a junior health minister has called on health care professionals to ensure that all lesbian and gay patients are treated equally and their partners accorded the same rights as all other close relations:

TORY MINISTER PRAISES GAY 'RICHNESS'

The gay community yesterday received its strongest support yet from a Conservative minister when John Bowis repeatedly condemned prejudice against homosexuality and tacitly acknowledged that gay couples constitute family units.

Praising the 'richness that lesbian and gay people add to our society', the health minister's comments prompted warm applause at a conference organised by the mental health charity Mind and gay rights groups . . .

Concentrating on the gay and lesbian community's experience of the health service, Mr Bowis attacked those who saw homosexuality as a mental illness.

He said: 'I do not believe loving or sexual feelings are mental aberrations to be suppressed . . . I do not believe society should be judgemental about what for an individual is a fact of nature.'

He called on health care workers 'to recognise a same sex partner as the next of kin' – giving them the same access and information as a spouse.

(From an article in the Guardian, *22 June 1995)*

ACTIVITY

Suggest how hospital staff can help to ensure that lesbian and gay patients are treated equally.

ACTIVITY

Equality of treatment requires that all patients and clients have equal access to information. Investigate how your local health and social care providers ensure that information about treatment and services is communicated to all users. Consider in particular the needs of ethnic minority users.

Equity

It is important to distinguish equality from *equity* or *fairness*. To treat people equitably is not always to treat them equally. Whereas equal-opportunities legislation requires all people to be treated in the same way, the principle of equity recognises that people have different needs and that responses may have to be tailored to the requirements and circumstances of particular individuals. For example, as many studies have shown, poor people in Britain (and elsewhere) have a greater need for health care than those who are better off. In trying to achieve equal levels of health, it may be necessary to create *unequal* access to health care services to ensure that those who need care the most receive it. To treat people with different needs in the same way (i.e. equally) may be to treat them inequitably.

ACTIVITY

Identify those types of health and social care provision which are delivered on an *equitable* rather than an *equal* basis. Is this morally justifiable?

Justice

Justice is another central ethical principle, and few people would disagree that it is worth upholding. Justice can also be understood as *fairness*; as ensuring, for example, that where people violate agreed codes of conduct and are to be punished, this is done in a fair way or in a way which is 'just'; or that where resources are allocated, this is done equitably. The problem here is that, morally and politically, not everyone can agree on what constitutes justice. This is certainly the case with, for example, criminal-justice legislation: some people believe that justice is served by rehabilitating offenders, whilst others believe that it will only be served by longer prison sentences or the reintroduction of capital punishment.

Frequently, in terms of criminal law, justice will and must compromise those other moral rights which the criminal has forfeited, such as the right to freedom, independence and autonomy.

POTENTIAL ETHICAL CONFLICT: THE RATIONING OF HEALTH CARE

One area of health and social care in which concerns about equity and justice are prominent is that of the rationing of health care. This is, of course, a contentious political issue, with many people arguing that, in Britain, if public health care were better funded the rationing of treatment would not be necessary. However, even the 'architect' of the National Health Service (NHS), Aneurin Bevin, recognised 50 years ago that there would be some mismatch between resources and the demand for care: 'We never will have all we need. Expectation will always exceed capacity. This service must always be changing, growing and improving. It must always appear inadequate' (Davey and Popay 1993).

Some therefore argue that if resources are finite, then it is important that health care be allocated in a just and equitable way. In response to this, a number of methods have been advocated, each of which makes use of different ethical principles. One approach, first adopted in Oregon in the USA, is to consult the public and ask them to rank treatments in order of priority. Such an

Table 1.1 Priority rankings of health services in Hackney n = 322 – 335

	1 Essential %	(no.)	2 Very important %	(no.)	3 Important %	(no.)	4 Less important %	(no.)	Mean	Rank
Treatments for children with life-threatening illnesses (e.g. leukaemia)	71	(239)	22	(74)	6	(19)	1	(3)	1.361	1
Special care and pain relief for people who are dying (e.g. hospice care)	53	(177)	30	(102)	15	(49)	2	(7)	1.660	2
Medical research for new treatments	50	(160)	26	(85)	19	(60)	5	(17)	1.795	3
High-technology surgery and procedures which treat life-threatening conditions (e.g. heart/liver transplants)	45	(149)	31	(101)	16	(52)	8	(25)	1.856	4
Preventive services (e.g. screening, immunisations)	40	(133)	31	(104)	23	(75)	6	(19)	1.940	5
Surgery to help people with disabilities to carry out everyday tasks (e.g. hip replacements)	22	(73)	43	(144)	32	(107)	3	(10)	2.162	6
Therapy to help people with disabilities carry out everyday tasks (e.g. speech therapy, physiotherapy, occupational therapy)	27	(91)	31	(105)	37	(122)	5	(15)	2.183	7
Services for people with mental illness (e.g. psychiatric wards, community psychiatric nurses)	21	(69)	33	(109)	41	(137)	5	(16)	2.302	8
Intensive care for premature babies who weigh less than one and a half pounds and are unlikely to survive	29	(95)	27	(89)	25	(83)	19	(163)	2.345	9
Long stay care (e.g. hospital and nursing homes for the elderly)	20	(65)	39	(126)	28	(90)	13	(44)	2.348	10
Community services/care at home (e.g. district nurses)	24	(78)	30	(99)	31	(104)	15	(48)	2.371	11
Health education services (e.g. campaigns encouraging people to lead healthy lifestyles)	14	(45)	18	(60)	26	(85)	42	(137)	2.960	12
Family planning services (e.g. contraception)	11	(36)	14	(46)	25	(82)	50	(163)	3.138	13
Treatments for infertility (e.g. test-tube babies)	8	(25)	9	(31)	34	(114)	49	(160)	3.239	14
Complementary/alternative medicine (e.g. acupuncture, homeopathy, herbalism)	7	(23)	11	(35)	18	(59)	64	(207)	3.383	15
Cosmetic surgery (e.g. tattoo removal, removal/disfiguring lumps and bumps)	4	(14)	7	(24)	13	(41)	76	(245)	3.596	16

Source: Bowling, A. (1993), *What People Say About Prioritising Health Care*, London: King's Fund.

exercise has also been undertaken in the UK by Dr Ann Bowling who asked a representative sample of 350 people in Hackney, London to rank 16 treatments according to whether they thought they were essential, very important, important or less important: see Table 1.1 on p. 16 for her findings.

ACTIVITY

1 Can you think of any general moral principles which could justify this particular allocation of treatments?

2 Are there any rankings that you strongly disagree with? Give your reasons.

3 Why do you think that no treatments were ranked as unimportant?

Another approach to the rationing of health care is the QALY (Quality Adjusted Life Years) formula. Using this method, treatments are ranked according to their costs and weighed against the projected increase in life expectancy and quality of life they will bring about. This means that patients will receive treatment only where the long term benefit is deemed to outweigh the cost.

Critics argue that this approach discriminates against people requiring continuing care and favours those needing immediate, one-off procedures. It may also fail to give sufficient priority to preventative health measures.

Other shortcomings of the QALY method of rationing health care are highlighted by the Medical Research Council:

Since such measures are affected by average life expectancy, they may discriminate against those sectors of society who already have a lower life expectancy. If applied rigorously . . . they would favour whites over blacks, upper social classes over lower and women over men (as well as young over old). The choice of determinants of resource allocation is not in itself simply an issue in economics, it is primarily an ethical question.

ACTIVITY

Investigate the QALY approach and assess the validity of these criticisms.

There are many ethical principles which could be used to govern the allocation of health care resources. The following are some suggestions:

- *Need:* those in greatest need should get help, regardless of age, cost of treatment etc.
- *Merit:* those who deserve it most should get help – this would mean that those whose illness is 'self-inflicted' (e.g. smokers with lung cancer) would not be treated.
- *Welfare maximisation (utilitarian)*: resources should be allocated so that the maximum number of people benefit. This could mean that very expensive procedures such as organ-transplant surgery or kidney dialysis may be excluded altogether.
- *Random allocation:* some argue that as all the above principles would exclude some patients from treatment in advance, the fairest system would be a 'lottery' where all have an equal chance of 'success'.

ACTIVITY

1 Identify arguments for and against each of the above as principles for the allocation of health resources.

2 Which principle do you think was adopted by the judge in the following case who upheld the medical decision to deny further treatment to a young girl with leukaemia?

CANCER GIRL LOSES FIGHT FOR TREATMENT

A father yesterday lost his fight for NHS treatment for his 10-year-old daughter, who is dying of an acute form of leukaemia . . .

The landmark Appeal Court decision has, in effect, sanctioned rationing in the health service. The Cambridge Health Authority argued the £75,000 could be better spent on other patients since further treatment had a low chance of success and could even kill the child.

As the father was led away from the Appeal Court looking dazed and close to tears, the family's lawyer, Michael Sinclair, said that an appeal to the House of Lords would be considered . . .

The father, who cannot be named for legal reasons, had been told in January that his daughter had six to eight weeks to live. The Cambridgeshire family wanted further treatment at a hospital in London.

The Appeal Court ruling by three of the country's most senior judges said Cambridge Health Authority had acted rationally and fairly in denying the sick girl treatment. They ruled it was not for courts to interfere in such circumstances with the way health authorities made medical judgements on funding . . .

The British Medical Association said the case of Child B, as she was described in court, raised fundamental issues of how health care resources were rationed in the NHS. 'Doctors have a duty to society to ensure that health care expenditure is based upon medical knowledge and the clinical judgement that flows from that. But it is unacceptable to suggest that a doctor can be forced to offer a treatment which he or she thinks is medically inappropriate because a patient demands it.'

(From an article in the Independent, *11 March 1995)*

ACTIVITY

Arrange for a speaker to talk to your class about ethical issues in health and social care. Ask them to explain how practitioners attempt to resolve problems both individually and as members of a team.

THE LEGAL FRAMEWORK OF HEALTH AND SOCIAL CARE PROVISION

The law refers to the set of rules by which a society regulates the behaviour of its members. In the case of health and social care, it provides a complex legislative framework which confers legal rights, duties and obligations on both service providers and users.

Sources of law

There are three main sources of law:

1 *Custom or common law.* This is law based on accepted ways of doing things, on 'custom and practice' which go back many centuries. The Duty of Care, which is of particular concern to health and social care practitioners, has its origins in common law.
2 *Case law or judicial law.* This refers to the application and interpretation of existing laws by judges. Over time, judgements reached in certain cases have been recorded and have established examples or *precedents* for the treatment of similar subsequent cases. The law on medical negligence, for example, has been laid down largely through judicial opinion.
3 *Statute law.* This is law made by Parliament. The British constitution grants supreme legislative (law-making) power to Parliament. Each year, typically, a hundred bills go through complex procedures in the House of Commons and the House of Lords before becoming acts of Parliament and passing onto the 'statute book'. Some laws are also made by the institutions of the European Union and are incorporated into British statute law.

   Some of the statute law of concern to health and social care workers is referred to later, but it is beyond the scope of this chapter to cover anything but a small sample. Some examples include the Child Support Act 1990, the Children Act 1989, the National Assistance Act 1948, the Chronically Sick and Disabled Persons Act 1970 and the Mental Health Act 1983.

Other important instances of statute law in this context include equal-opportunities legislation and those acts which establish and regulate the health and welfare professions, such as the Local Authority Social Services Act (1970) and the Nurses, Midwives and Health Visitors Acts of 1979 and 1992.

ACTIVITY

The most recent piece of legislation outlining the rights of people with disabilities is the Disability Discrimination Act (1995). Investigate its main provisions and identify how these differ from those of earlier disability-discrimination legislation.

The administrative machinery of the law is divided into two branches, one dealing with *criminal law* and the other with *civil law*.

CRIMINAL LAW

Crimes are offences committed against the state either in the form of an act which the law forbids (such as theft) or in the form of the omission of an act which the law requires. If there is sufficient evidence, the offending individual may be charged by the police with the crime in question and sent for trial. Where the verdict of the jury is 'guilty', the defendant may be sent to prison. (In Scotland only, there is a possible verdict of 'not proven'.)

It may be the case that the defendant will enter a defence plea and argue that although the act or omission is normally wrong, in this case there were special *mitigating* circumstances – in other words, there are special facts about this case which mean that the act or omission which is normally wrong is not so in this case.

The concept of criminal responsibility is important: under common law, for a crime to have been committed there must normally be a guilty mind or *mens rea*, and for this to be inferred there must be evidence of intention, recklessness or negligence. The following extract concerns the case of a registered childminder who was jailed for four years for bringing about the death of a child in her care.

CHILDMINDER WHO KILLED JAILED 4 YEARS

A registered childminder who shook a baby girl to death to stop her crying was jailed for four years yesterday.

Susan Cawthorne, 42, of Helmton Drive, Woodseats, Sheffield, had pleaded not guilty to the murder of eight-month-old Helen Sangar in October 1993 – the second child to die while in her care.

A jury at Sheffield crown court unanimously found her guilty of manslaughter after hearing that the baby had been shaken so violently she was severely brain-damaged.

Mr Justice Holland told Cawthorne he was 'entirely satisfied that in response to her [the baby's] persistent crying you shook her so hard she was immediately rendered blind in the left eye and in a relatively short time her breathing stopped and her heart stopped.'

He accepted Cawthorne did not intend to kill Helen or cause her serious harm, but said 'in some fashion never yet explained, you broke her right arm – and all that occurred when as a childminder you were looking after her safety.' . . .

(From an article in the Guardian, *12 May 1995)*

ACTIVITY

Why did the judge reach a manslaughter rather than a murder verdict in this case?

CIVIL LAW

This involves the rights and duties which individuals have towards each other. In such cases legal action is taken by one private individual against another individual or organisation. Where the verdict is guilty, the outcome is usually the award of monetary *compensation*, e.g. in cases of libel. It is important to note that much law has both a civil and a criminal element (e.g. employment or health and safety law) and that some civil wrongs are also crimes, such as assault and battery and gross negligence (see below). In such cases the wrong is considered so grave that it goes beyond compensation between citizens and amounts to a wrong against the community.

Much of the work of health and social care professionals is covered by civil law, and in particular that part of it known as *torts* (*delicts* in Scotland.) A tort is a civil wrong, and it results in common law action for damages.

The language used in the two branches of law differs: in criminal cases, the person facing charges (the defendant) is *prosecuted* – usually by the state (i.e. the Crown Prosecution Service) – whereas in civil cases one private body or individual *sues* another.

The court system in England and Wales

The court system, staffed by law officers, is at the heart of the legal system:

- At the preliminary level (see Figure 1.2 on p. 21) are *tribunals* which are more informal than other courts and which deal with a large number of disputes concerning things like rent and claims for industrial-injuries compensation. Tribunals are overseen by a chairperson with legal experience who is appointed by the Lord Chancellor.
- *Magistrates' courts:* these are overseen by magistrates or Justices of the Peace (JPs). JPs are not legally qualified (although they attend a compulsory training course), generally work part time and are unpaid. They are assisted by a legally qualified Clerk to the Court. About two million cases a year are dealt with in magistrates courts. Magistrates have the power to sentence an offender for up to six months in cases of minor or *summary* offences, but must pass on more serious offences to higher courts. Care workers may have significant contact with magistrates courts as these deal with family disputes and applications for care orders.
- *Juvenile courts* deal with criminal cases involving young people under 17.
- *Coroners' courts* are presided over by coroners (a solicitor or doctor) and investigate all cases of unexplained death.
- *County courts* hear less serious civil cases and are presided over by legally trained circuit judges.
- *Crown courts* with a judge and jury try all serious crimes. The central criminal court is the Old Bailey.
- *The High Court* has three 'divisions': the Queen's Bench, the Family Division and the Chancery Division. These deal largely with serious civil cases.
- *The Court of Appeal:* this hears appeals against verdicts passed by lower courts and has two divisions: the civil division headed by the Master of the Rolls, and the criminal division headed by the Lord Chief Justice.
- *The House of Lords:* this is the highest court of appeal in Britain (and some other Commonwealth countries) and is presided over by the 'Law Lords'.
- *The European Court and European Court of Human Rights:* cases may also be referred on appeal to these European courts.

Law officers

Whilst magistrates and judges oversee the judicial process, *solicitors*, *barristers* and *probation officers* represent and assist those bringing or defending cases.

Solicitors are general legal advisers accessible to the public who hire their services in a wide range of legal matters. Solicitors may be *advocates* (who officially speak on behalf of clients) in the lower courts but not usually in the higher courts.

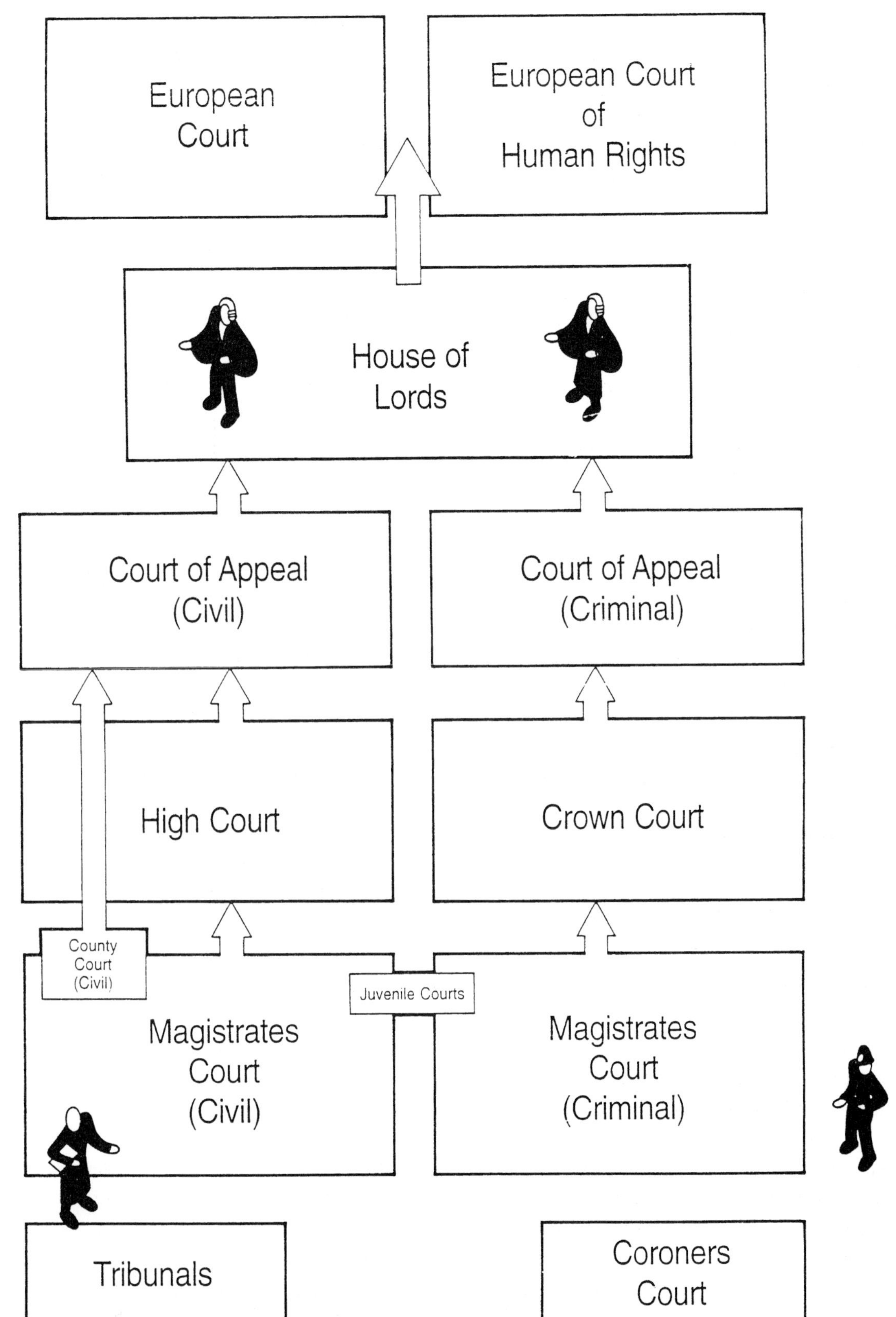

Figure 1.2 The Courts in England and Wales

Barristers have exclusive right of audience (as advocates) in the higher courts and are known as 'counsel' for the prosecution or the defence. Barristers are only accessible via a solicitor. They usually wear wigs. *Judges* must be appointed from experienced barristers.

ACTIVITY

Conduct some research into the socio-economic background of members of the judiciary and construct a profile of a typical judge. Give them a name and write a short biography of them. What conclusions do you reach about the nature and representativeness of British judges?

ACTIVITY

In which courts do you think the following cases would be heard?

- A student at a college of further education has been accused of raping and sexually assaulting a fellow student
- A student has just started a course at university and is found dead in her room. Suicide is suspected
- Three men plan an elaborate bank raid and succeed in stealing several million pounds worth of gold bars
- A woman and her daughter have been repeatedly threatened and harassed by the woman's partner, and she wants to have him excluded from the family home
- A crown court judge gives a defendant found guilty of manslaughter leave to appeal

Probation officers

The probation service is involved at every stage of the criminal justice system. Its key functions are to provide information to the courts by means of pre-sentencing reports, to supervise offenders on court orders (including those 'on probation') in the community and to work with offenders in custody and on release. In this the service is intended to contribute to the:

- protection of the public
- prevention of reoffending
- successful reintegration of the offender into the community

(*Home Office* 1990)

Figure 1.3 below illustrates the position of community sentences in the 'tariff' available to judges passing sentence.

Although the majority of the work of probation officers is in the criminal justice system, they also have a range of statutory court welfare responsibilities. These include the preparation of reports in county court divorce proceedings, conciliation work with divorcing parents, involvement in domestic and family proceedings in the magistrates' courts and wardship proceedings in the High Court. The role of the court welfare service is to help the court to resolve disputes where children are concerned and to ensure that their welfare is paramount.

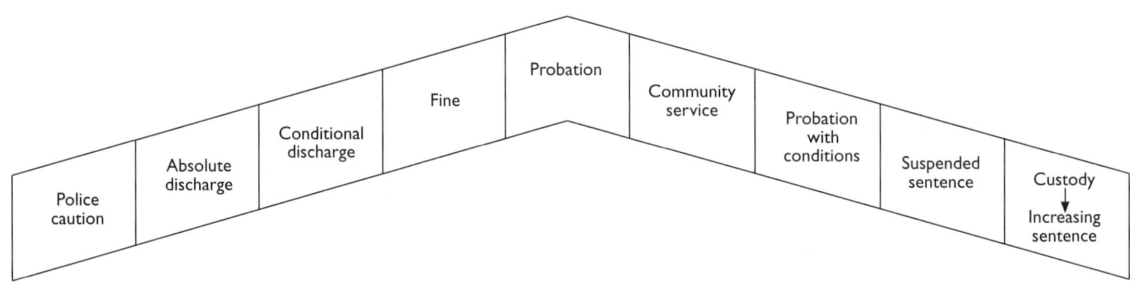

Figure 1.3 The sentencing tariff for offenders

Functions of the legal system

The legal system has a number of broad functions, of which the following are the most important:

PROTECTION

One function of criminal justice legislation is to protect victims and potential victims from further harm by imposing custodial sentences on those found guilty of violent offences against the person. Laws such as the Domestic Violence and Matrimonial Proceedings Act 1976 and the Children Act 1989 can be used to protect children and adults, for example through the granting of court orders or *injunctions* against those who have committed acts of violence or harassment within the home. Similarly, the largely civil laws and regulations concerning the provision of goods and services have a protective function to ensure that users and consumers are not taken advantage of by unscrupulous traders and agencies.

REGULATION

Linked to this is the law's regulatory function, where it seeks to enforce mutual rights, duties and obligations. This is frequently undertaken by means of official circulars and guidelines as well as by specific acts of Parliament. Such regulation may include the monitoring of health and safety standards in schools or factories or the measurement of levels of industrial pollution. Within the field of health and social care, it includes the registration and inspection of residential care facilities under the Registered Homes (Amendment) Acts of 1984 and 1991.

ACTIVITY

1 Investigate the main provisions of the Child Support Act 1990. What rights, duties and obligations does it seek to enforce? Has it been successful in this?

2 Identify three laws, circulars or sets of guidelines which affect professional childcare workers (you could contact the National Childminding Association for advice).

COMPENSATION

The law may also be concerned with securing redress or compensation for the victims of harm. As we have seen, the majority of civil cases aim to achieve monetary compensation for the victim rather than the custodial sentencing of the offender. In criminal cases, on the other hand, compensation may be awarded to the victim by the Criminal Injuries Compensation Board.

ACTIVITY

1 Write to the Home Office for information on the 'tariff' of awards that may be granted to the victims of different types of crime.

2 Collect a range of broadsheet national and local newspapers over the next two or three weeks and identify those court cases where compensation has been awarded to the victim in criminal and civil cases. Do the levels of compensation reflect the severity of the offences?

PUNITIVE

Of course the law also has a punitive or punishment function. This serves to teach the offender that 'crime does not pay', and may also have a deterrent effect on others. There is disagreement amongst professionals in the legal system as to the proper balance between the punitive and rehabilitation functions of custodial sentences, as the following article demonstrates:

MIDWIVES APPALLED AT HANDCUFF RULING

Midwives are 'appalled' that they have been given the responsibility of deciding whether women prisoners can have their handcuffs released during labour.

An instruction issued to governors of women's jails makes it mandatory that females on escort for medical or welfare appointments be handcuffed to a prison officer . . .

Handcuffs will be worn on all maternity visits and it will be up to the doctor or midwife to decide what is the appropriate moment for removal.

Carol Flint, president of the Royal College of Midwives, says she is appalled by the decision . . . She does not regard it as appropriate for midwives to have the responsibility.

Harry Fletcher, assistant general secretary of the National Association of Probation Officers, said the policy was not justified.

'This is a frightening example of the absurdity of ministers' obsession with security and punishment,' he said. 'As a consequence of it, women in labour will be chained and those at child care hearings will wear cuffs . . .

'In practice, cuffing will humiliate, embarrass and stress the women concerned . . .'

In April last year a prisoner, Susan Edwards, gave birth while handcuffed. She also had to feed the child while wearing her handcuffs.

She received a personal apology from the head of the Prison Service, Derek Lewis.

(From an article in the Guardian, *15 July 1995)*

ACTIVITY

1 Why do midwives think the law is too punitive in this case? Do you agree?

2 Write to victim-support organisations and those concerned with the support and rehabilitation of offenders for their views on dealing with crime and possible changes in the criminal justice system. Are there significant differences in their views?

The legal responsibilities of health and social care workers

Health and social care services are provided by a wide range of agencies and organisations, each of which is subject to different laws and regulations in its operation.

ACTIVITY

List six different types of organisation which provide health and social care services.

The main types of provision of health and social care are as follows:

- *Statutory:* this relates to provision established by acts of Parliament, and includes all health and social care provided by public bodies including NHS hospitals and local social-services departments
- *Private:* this refers to services offered by businesses on a profit-making basis. These providers may contract to undertake work on behalf of the public sector, or they may provide services directly to private customers. The Conservative Party has actively encouraged the expansion of the private sector in health and social care (local authorities now provide only 25% of all residential care places for the elderly, as opposed to 55% in 1984 (Social Services Inspectorate 1995))
- *Voluntary:* this refers to services provided by voluntary organisations such as Barnardos or the NSPCC. Many of these are both registered charities and large organisations which receive grants from central and local government to run services on their behalf. Some do make a profit but then reinvest this into their services – such as the sheltered housing provided by the Royal British Legion.

  In some parts of the country, voluntary and *not-for-profit* organisations have stepped in to fill gaps in statutory provision.

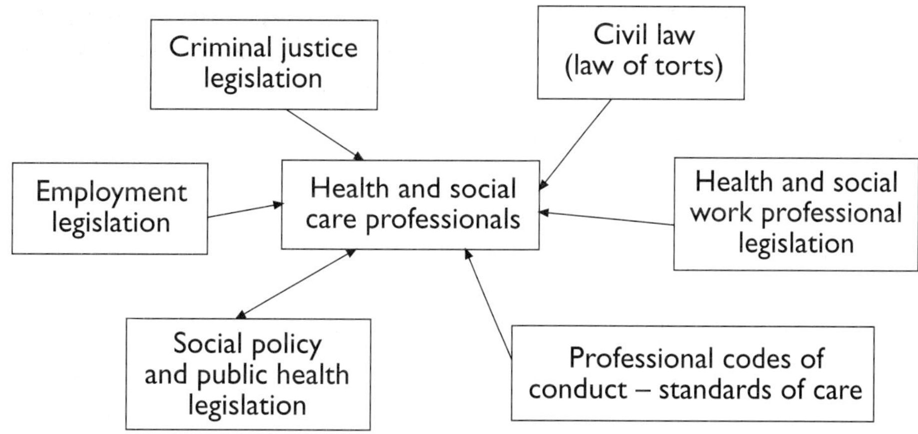

Figure 1.4 The legal framework of health and social care

Each of these types of organisation is governed in its operation by the framework of law as set out in Figure 1.4 above. These laws and regulations all confer legal responsibilities which can be divided into *powers* and *duties*: where a law imposes a duty upon a professional, they are required to carry it out; where the law gives them a power, then it may be exercised at their discretion and in accordance with their professional judgement. Where the professional fails or is negligent in the discharge of these responsibilities, they will be held *accountable* or answerable for the consequences. In some cases this will be under (statutory) *employment* or *contract law*. Recently, concern has been expressed at the fate of 'whistleblowers' who break contracts of employment forbidding them to speak out about poor standards of care in hospitals or nursing homes. Within the NHS, the British Medical Association has expressed concern at the limitations on freedom of speech imposed on doctors who are critical of the new internal market:

INTERNAL MARKET REFORMS 'PUTTING HEALTH AT RISK'

Health standards are slipping due to the 'alien regime' under which the NHS is labouring, Dr Sandy Macara, chairman of the British Medical Association, said yesterday . . .

He condemned the new system introduced by the NHS reforms as 'not so much an internal market as an infernal bazaar' . . .

He asked: 'Where stands equity, when the cash lottery dictates priority to patients with lesser need? Where stands integrity, when doctors are instructed to conceal from fund-holding GPs' patients the reason they had to have treatment deferred was because their doctor's money had run out?' . . .

Dr Macara said the NHS competitive market was a 'grim game of winners and losers', which created pressures that made a mockery of doctors' freedom to speak out and the policy of openness . . .

(From an article in the Daily Telegraph, *4 July 1995)*

ACTIVITY

What ethical and legal principles must care workers consider in deciding whether to speak out against what they see as harmful or damaging practices in their place of work?

Where workers are found guilty of *professional misconduct* (defined as behaviour which is unworthy of the profession), they are liable for discipline or even dismissal. In serious cases such individuals will be struck off their professional register. The most common reasons for removal from the UKCC (United Kingdom Central Council) Register include: 'insensitivity or unkindness to patient's relatives, reckless or unskilful practice, obscene or indecent language in patient areas, concealing untoward incidents, misleading vulnerable patients, neglecting duties, failure to keep essential records, failure to summon emergency aid, falsifying records, failure to protect or promote patients' interests, and failure to act when knowing that a colleague is improperly treating or abusing patients' (Young 1994).

Unfortunately, there will also be cases where health and social care professionals engage in activities which not only constitute gross professional misconduct but also clearly breach criminal law. Two very serious cases include that of Frank Beck, a senior residential social worker who was given five life sentences in 1991 for systematically abusing children in his care, and the more recent case of Nurse Beverley Allitt who was found guilty of murdering four children and attacking nine others in her care in the paediatric ward of a hospital in Lincolnshire.

Although we have not yet reached the situation in the USA where fear of litigation and 'ambulance chasers' dictates much health and social care practice, in Britain members of the public *are* becoming increasingly aware of their rights, and there is a growing trend for patients and clients to take legal action against those who have acted in unprofessional or incompetent ways, as the following article and Figure 1.5 make clear:

Figure 1.5 The public are more willing to take legal action against unprofessional care workers

ABUSE CASES PROMPT SCHEME TO INSURE SOCIAL WORKERS

Social workers are being advised to insure against the growing risk of involvement in an abuse scandal.

Under a scheme launched by the British Association of Social Workers ... members ... will be indemnified ... against claims for negligence, error, omission, libel, slander or breach of confidentiality. The scheme will also offer cover against assault by clients ...

David Jones, general secretary, said ... 'We are working in an increasingly litigious climate. Doctors have had their experience of this and social workers will too' ...

(From an article in the Guardian, *21 September 1992)*

The following sections consider three broad areas of legal responsibility for health and social care workers: *duty of care*, *confidentiality* and *consent*.

Duty of care

In its broadest sense we can all be said to have a duty of care towards other members of our society; it is a part of common law. In a judgement in 1932, Lord Atkin laid down this duty of care as it is owed by ordinary members of the public to each other:

In law a person must take reasonable care to avoid acts or omissions which he can reasonably foresee as being likely to injure his neighbour . . . [defined as] 'a person who is so closely and directly affected by one's act that one ought reasonably to have them in contemplation as being so affected when one is directing one's mind to the acts or omissions being called in question'.

ACTIVITY

List six situations in which you would expect others to exercise a duty of care towards you.

Health and social care workers also have a *statutory* duty of care to their clients and patients, as do their employers, as well as a duty of care to colleagues, relatives and visitors, albeit to a lesser extent.

Similarly, nurses may not refuse to care for patients, nor social workers to assist clients, except in very rare circumstances. The Royal College of Nursing (RCN) and the General Medical Council have both made it clear that failure to care for patients with HIV/Aids constitutes a disciplinary offence (*British Journal of Nursing*, vol. 1, no. 4). For nurses, midwives and health visitors, the professional behaviour expected of them is laid out in the United Kingdom Central Council Code of Professional Conduct. For social workers, the Central Council for Education and Training in Social Work and the British Association of Social Workers publish codes of conduct. The law does not accept that when a nurse or doctor is off duty they no longer have a duty of care, or that such a duty of care extends no further than that of a lay person. Indeed, if a nurse goes to assist someone in the street involved in an accident when they are off duty, they could be sued for negligence if harm results from a failure to provide the *standard of care* expected of a nurse (see below).

NEGLIGENCE

Negligence means carelessness, and is one of the most important torts. Negligence occurs where there is harm resulting from a failure in the duty of care, and can be the consequence of *an act or an omission*. It is through the concept of negligence that the relationship between professional accountability and the duty of care becomes clear.

The legal definition of negligence was laid down in a judgement of 1891: 'Negligence is the omission to do something which a reasonable man, guided upon these considerations which ordinarily regulate the conduct of human affairs, would do, or to do something which a prudent and reasonable man would not do' (*Blyth v. Birmingham Water Works*). In order to prove negligence, there must be evidence that:

1 the defendant owed the plaintiff a legal duty of care;
2 there has been a breach of the standard of care;
3 harm was suffered as a result of negligence (consequential damage occurred).

1 *Duty of care.* We have already seen that 'duty of care' can be widely interpreted, and certainly in the case of a social worker and their clients, or a nurse and their patients, such a duty is owed.
2 *Breach of the standard of care.* Negligence can only be claimed where it can be shown that the individual concerned failed to provide the standard of care that is consistent with the duty of care in that occupation. In the case of nursing, the UKCC's code of practice would provide a guide. The standard of care used as a measure will change over time as guidelines and professional expectations change (for example, guidelines for the nursing of sick children have been revised by the RCN in the wake of the Allitt Inquiry).

For a claim of negligence to be brought by an employer (under the law of contract) or by a professional body, only the first two elements need to be proved. However, for a patient or client to sue for negligence, the third criterion must also be fulfilled:

3 *Proof of consequential damage.* The *burden of proof* lies with the *plaintiff* (the person who brings the complaint) to show that the harm they have suffered is a consequence of the negligent act. The formal legal rule is that the plaintiff must prove negligence on the *balance of probabilities* – that is, that negligence is the *most likely explanation* for the harm caused. In a criminal court, the proof must be of a higher standard: it must indicate guilt *beyond reasonable doubt*. It might be that there are no witnesses to the scalding of a patient in the bath, but if negligence by a nurse is the most likely explanation, the case may be successful.

The following case illustrates these three points concerning proof of negligence:

Gauntlett v. Northampton Health Authority (1985). A woman was admitted to hospital having taken an overdose. Her stomach was pumped and she was transferred to a mental-illness ward where she was diagnosed as depressive. She experienced delusions about Christ, snakes and fire. The registrar gave instructions that she was to continue to be nursed on that ward but that constant supervision was not necessary. Some days later, at the end of a visit, her husband handed the charge nurse a box of matches which his wife had said she intended to use on herself. The charge nurse did not record this in the patient's case notes. A few days later the patient went into the toilets with another box of matches and set fire to her skirt.

The trial judge in the case ruled that both the doctor and the nurse owed a duty of care. In the case of the doctor, the standard of care had not been breached, but in the case of the nurse this standard *had* been breached because any reasonably competent nurse would have recorded the incident with the matches. However, on appeal, the judge overruled the claim of negligence because even if the nurse had recorded the incident with the matches, no changes would have been made to the nursing instructions, and the outcome would have been the same.

ACTIVITY

Read the following case and explain why the doctor was not found to be negligent. Refer to the three proofs necessary for a successful claim to be made.

'TRAGIC MISTAKE' SURGEON IN CLEAR

Mr Justice Gage ruled that Anthony Kenney, a consultant at St Thomas's Hospital, London, was not negligent when he removed 21-year-old Feroze Abbas's entire reproductive system, thinking she had a lethal cancer . . .

The judge held that Mrs Abbas, now 27, probably never suffered from ovarian cancer . . . A tissue sample and pathology report brought from Pakistan were probably from another patient.

Mrs Abbas sued the 51-year-old gynaecologist, who delivered princesses Beatrice and Eugenie, for negligence and accused him of removing her womb without her consent.

The judge said no one could feel anything but the greatest sympathy over the tragedy that had befallen her, but she was a sophisticated and intelligent woman who he believed had consented to the operation.

Mr Kenney told Mrs Abbas . . . that he might be able to limit the operation to removing her right ovary. But, depending on what he found, he would remove the least he could, consistent with saving her life.

He found a mass which he thought meant the cancer had spread, and did a 'total pelvic clearance', removing all her reproductive organs – the standard treatment for ovarian cancer.

In fact the growth was endometriosis – a condition, not requiring a hysterectomy, in which tissue from the lining of the womb grows elsewhere in the reproductive system . . .

It was impossible to say that he had fallen below the ordinary skill of a surgeon operating in this field.

Mrs Abbas was 'the victim of a tragic mistake', but no legal liability for that mistake could be attributed to Mr Kenney.

(From an article in the Guardian, *28 July 1995)*

The plaintiff in a negligence case does not have to show that the negligent act was *wholly* to blame. If, for example, the offender is felt to have at least *contributed* towards the harm suffered, the case will then be one of *contributory negligence*, and any *compensation* awarded will be accordingly reduced.

It is important to note that claims for negligence may be successful in cases not where actions have been omitted but simply where they have not been recorded. In one such case, a staff nurse was officially disciplined for failing to record the outcome of half-hourly post-operative observations. For nurses, midwives and health visitors, the importance of good record keeping is made explicit:

The important activity of making and keeping records is an essential and integral part of care and not a distraction from its provision. There is, however, substantial evidence to indicate that inadequate and inappropriate record keeping concerning the care of patients and clients *neglects* their interests through:

- impairing continuity of care;
- introducing discontinuity of communication between staff;
- creating the risk of medication or other treatment being duplicated or omitted;
- failing to focus attention on early signs of deviation from the norm and;
- failing to place on record significant observations and conclusions.

(UKCC 1993 – italics mine)

Degrees of negligence

The law says that all those who are (even indirectly) responsible for providing care can be found negligent, should harm result. However, there will be degrees of culpability. This means, for example, that although a student nurse may be found to have given inappropriate care, her staff nurse or charge nurse may be found negligent by delegation. Having said that, learner nurses do have a clear responsibility to ask for help: 'acknowledge any limitations in your knowledge and competence and decline any duties or responsibilities unless able to perform them in a safe and skilled manner' (UKCC 1992). Tingle (1992) further points out that primary nurses (who have a greater degree of autonomy in the exercise of their duties) will consequently be required to accept a greater degree of accountability than those who work as part of a team.

Similarly, the health authority or trust may itself be deemed negligent by *vicarious liability*. This means that in law the employer is held accountable for the torts of their employees and can be punished on their behalf. This was made clear in the following case: Roe and Woolly (1954):

Hospital authorities are responsible for the whole of their staff, not only nurses and doctors, but also for anaesthetists and surgeons. It does not matter whether they are permanent or temporary, resident or visiting, whole time or part time. The reason is because . . . they are the agents of the hospital to give the treatment.

Confidentiality

The legal obligation to maintain confidentiality applies to everything that is not public knowledge. A simple test to determine whether you must maintain confidentiality is to ask yourself the following two questions:

1. Do I only know this information because of my professional role?
2. Does my client/patient trust me to keep this information secret?

If the answer to these questions is 'yes', then

you have a duty to maintain confidentiality.

Breaching confidence could lead to legal action by a patient or client only in those cases where it contributes to a negligent breach of duty, but it could also easily provide grounds for official disciplinary action or even dismissal on the part of a professional body or employer. For example, a nurse was found guilty of professional misconduct by the UKCC Professional Conduct Committee for allowing her sister to read patient case notes. Similarly, a doctor was held negligent, in law, for revealing to his patient that her husband thought she was 'paranoid'. The husband had discussed his fears in confidence with the doctor and had expressly not told his wife because he feared it may jeopardise their marriage (Carson and Montgomery, 1989).

BREACH-OF-CONFIDENCE DEFENCES

Sometimes in law, if not always morally, it will be possible, or indeed necessary, to breach the confidence of a patient or client, as in the following situations:

- where the information concerned is in the public domain: as we have said, where information is common knowledge, there is no duty to maintain confidence
- where the patient or client consents: clearly if a practitioner does have to violate a confidence, it is always better to gain the patient's or client's consent first
- where it is in the interest of the subject: it is permissible to breach confidentiality where the interests of the individual are at risk in terms of their health or well-being. But even here, only the minimum information necessary should be disclosed
- where the law requires or permits disclosure. There are legal requirements for the disclosure of certain information such as the following:
  - information which may identify those involved in motor accidents must be passed on to the police;
  - all gunshot wounds must be reported to the police;
  - all notifiable diseases must be reported (the Public Health Act 1984 and Public Health Regulations 1988)
  - court orders to disclose information: the police may seek a court order forcing health or social care workers to disclose confidential information
- where the public interest outweighs the obligation to secrecy: this may include cases where there are serious threats to others (including staff) or where there is a knowledge of child abuse, drug trafficking or other criminal offence
- in the case of the disclosure of HIV/Aids infection to a partner: 'There are grounds for such a disclosure to spouse or sexual partner, only where there is a serious and identifiable risk to a specific individual, who, if not informed, would be exposed to infection' (General Medical Council (1989), *British Journal of Nursing*, vol. 1, no. 4).

Consent

There is a legal requirement to receive consent from a patient or client before attempting any invasive procedure, including surgery. A key defence in the law of tort against negligence is *volenti, non fit injuria*: no legal wrong can be committed against a consenting person. Therefore, if consent is obtained, a tort has not been committed.

FAILURE TO GAIN CONSENT

Where practitioners fail to gain consent for a procedure, or where a patient's or client's wishes are overridden, the individual may sue under the tort of *trespass*. Trespass can be committed against a person, goods or land. A social worker may leave themselves open to the charge of trespass to property perhaps through letting themselves into a client's home with a key which they have been given, whilst nurses are more likely to be concerned with the law of *trespass against the person* which is also known as *assault and battery*.

Assault is an attempt or threat to apply unlawful force to the person of another whereby that other person is put in fear of immediate violence or at least bodily contact. Words alone do not constitute assault, although they may form a part of another illegal act such as that of threatening behaviour. Battery is the actual application of force to the person of another against their will. There are of course many situations in which a nurse or doctor is involved in actions which, if undertaken by anyone else, may be deemed to constitute assault or battery (or both) but in the vast majority of cases they will have adequate defence.

ACTIVITY

You are a social worker, and a client who is not very mobile offers you the key to his flat so that you may let yourself in when you visit. What do you do, and why?

PATIENTS' CONSENT TO TREATMENT

Consent may be *implied* by circumstances. If a patient enters a hospital voluntarily, it may be fair to imply from this that they are willing to undergo the investigations and treatments which medical staff deem appropriate. Consent to treatment may also be *inferred* for example by a patient in the community allowing a district nurse into her home. In such a case where the nurse may need to dress bed sores, there is clearly no further need for formal consent, although the intimacy of contact will necessitate sensitivity on the part of the nurse. In a hospital situation it will be respectful to seek oral permission to undertake an enema or pubic shave, for example, but where the patient rolls over in anticipation of a pre-med injection it is safe to say that consent can be inferred. However, hospitals usually require *express written consent* for procedures or treatments which involve some marked risk to the patient. In such cases, a *consent form* must give details of the operation in question. In a number of cases, patients have sued where a surgeon has undertaken a different or more serious operation than that to which consent was formally given. Where the surgeon suspects that they may need to undertake more radical surgery, this must be made clear when the consent form is signed. The patient retains the right to refuse further treatment or to change their mind at all times

ACTIVITY

Obtain a copy of a hospital consent form. Redesign it so that safeguards are built in to prevent patients giving consent to treatment without a full appreciation of the consequences.

INFORMED CONSENT

The patient must always be given sufficient information to enable them to make a fully informed decision. Such information will usually be given in broad terms, and those risks which are reasonably probable highlighted. A number of factors will determine the amount of information provided, including the extent to which the patient wishes to be informed and the likely effect of such information on them.

CAPACITY TO GIVE CONSENT

Wherever an individual has the ability, or capacity, to understand the information given to them and are deemed to be able to make a rational decision, no one else may give or withhold consent on their behalf. Where there is opposition to treatment from relatives, for example on religious grounds, the courts are unlikely to be sympathetic, and frequently side with clinical advice. In cases where a spouse is opposed to a course of action on the part of their husband or wife, the courts take the view that this can have no bearing on a decision even in cases of the termination of pregnancy or sterilisation.

In other cases, consent may be given, or

withheld, on the individual's behalf by someone else. This is known as *consent by proxy*.

MINORS

In the case of young children, consent must be sought from parents or guardians. However, where parents refuse treatment for their children, this is often overruled, because counterbalancing the parents' or guardians' legal custody and control of their children is their duty of care to their offspring which requires them to provide necessary medical attention. In some cases the health authority will itself obtain a *care and protection order* to enable it to exercise parental authority, or the child can be made a *ward of court*. In other cases parents or guardians have themselves sought wardship. In a 1987 case, Jeannette, a 17-year-old with a learning disability, was made a ward of court because her parents wanted her to be sterilised but they did not have the legal power to give permission for this. Wardship was granted and permission for sterilisation was given by the court (Carson and Montgomery 1989).

In the case of 16- and 17-year-olds, the law seems a rather grey area. Although young people of this age can give consent themselves, where doctors break the confidence of their young patients they appear to incur no legal penalties. However, in a case in 1986 (*Gillick v. West Norfolk and Wisbech Area Health Authority*), it was established that 15-year-old girls may be prescribed contraception by a doctor without their parents being informed. This was a very important judgement in terms of the age at which minors may consent to treatment without the agreement or knowledge of their parents, and in a number of subsequent cases courts have taken into account the maturity of individuals rather than strict chronological age.

ADULTS WITH LEARNING DISABILITIES AND MENTAL ILLNESS

For some adults with severe learning disabilities, consent may be given on their behalf by a guardian or advocate. For adults with mental-health problems, consent by proxy may also be necessary. However, it is important to note that this is not the same as treatment without consent, and because someone has a severe mental-health problem it should not be assumed that they are unable to give consent. In 1994 Mr Justice Thorpe upheld the right of a 68-year-old man with paranoid schizophrenia to refuse to give permission for the amputation of his foot which had developed gangrene. The judge held that the operation could not be performed without the express written consent of the patient. In his ruling the judge suggested a test for capacity to give consent:

- Does the patient comprehend the information given to them?
- Do they believe it?
- Have they weighed up needs and risks before reaching their decision?

If the answer in each case is yes, the patient is deemed capable of giving and withholding consent (Tingle and Childs 1995).

EXCEPTIONS TO THE NEED TO GAIN CONSENT

The Mental Health Act (1983)

This allows for people to be admitted to hospital, or held in hospital, and treated against their will where they are deemed to be suffering from a mental disorder. Different sections of the Act make provisions for the detention of different groups, which is why compulsory admission to mental hospital is known as 'being under section'. In most cases (e.g. under Section 2) a person can be admitted to hospital for assessment for up to 28 days. This can then be extended. The application is made by an approved social worker or nearest relative and supported by two doctors.

Under Section 5(4) of the Act, recognised nurses have the power to detain patients for up to six hours.

Section 7 of the Act also allows for people to be taken under the protection of approved *guardians* in the community. The guardian must be acceptable to the local social-services department. This part of the Act requires the sectioned individual to:

- live at a certain place
- attend for treatment, occupation, education or training
- allow access to a doctor

Under this legislation there is no provision for the compulsory treatment of patients in the community, and no force is authorised. However, the UK government has recently proposed legislation – The Mental Health (Patients in the Community) Bill – which *would* allow for the compulsory treatment of individuals in the community.

NHS BODIES FIGHT MENTAL HEALTH BILL

Health authorities and trusts today deliver a new blow to the credibility of the Government's plans to tighten controls over severely mentally ill people in the community . . .

The Mental Health (Patients in the Community) Bill, would introduce a 'supervised discharge order' for an estimated 3,000 severely mentally ill people discharged from hospital into the community. Designated health workers, expected usually to be community psychiatric nurses, would be given what amounts to a power of arrest of patients in breach of the order . . .

In a joint report sent to the Department of Health, Nahat [the National Association of Health Authorities and Trusts] and the NHS trust federation say the plans are an uncomfortable compromise between compulsory treatment in the community and guaranteeing patients right of access to services . . .

The bill threatens to undermine patients' civil rights and may discourage patients from staying in contact with services, the groups argue . . .

(From an article in the Guardian, *27 June 1995)*

ACTIVITY

What objections to the proposed legislation are made in this article? Do you think they are well-founded?

Public health legislation

The Public Health (Control of Disease) Act 1984 and the Public Health (Infection) Regulations 1988 allow action to be taken without consent, in the interests of public health, where individuals are suffering from *notifiable* diseases. These include tetanus, leprosy, anthrax and measles. Anyone suffering from these illnesses must be reported to the local authority.

The liberty of such individuals is restricted by the criminal offences of either knowingly passing on the disease or exposing others to the risk. People with notifiable diseases are forbidden to use public libraries or public transport. Furthermore, a magistrate can order:

- compulsory testing
- forcible removal to hospital
- detainment in hospital

However, there is no right under statute to treat people against their will (except in the case of mental illness).

HIV is not notifiable (despite calls to make it so – see the *British Journal of Nursing* 1992), but certain provisions of the Public Health Act do apply to Aids so that, with the approval of a magistrate, compulsory testing is possible, as is removal to, and detention in, hospital.

ACTIVITY

Public health legislation violates a number of important ethical principles. Identify these principles and suggest why, in the light of other overriding moral principles, this may be acceptable.

In some states in the USA, pregnant women who are known to be drug addicts face imprisonment and the possible loss of their babies if they refuse to attend detoxification centres. The women's behaviour is treated as deliberate intention to cause harm to, or as gross negligence towards, another person (in this case, the *foetus* is granted personhood).

ACTIVITY

Is this treatment morally justified? Explain your answer and identify any morally significant differences between the treatment of these women and the measures outlined in UK public health legislation.

National Assistance Act (1948)

Section 47 of this Act aims to secure 'the necessary care and attention for people who

(a) are suffering from grave chronic disease, or, being aged, infirm or physically incapacitated, are living in insanitary conditions, and
(b) are unable to devote to themselves, and are not receiving from other persons, proper care and attention'.

In such cases, with the certification of a GP and the agreement of a magistrate, the individual concerned may be removed from their home to hospital, local-authority or private residential accommodation (to the cost of which the individual would have to contribute).

ACTIVITY

Although use of this Act is not uncommon, cases of people compulsorily removed from their homes are not widely publicised. How would you explain this?

REHABILITATION OF OFFENDERS ACT (1974)

The basic function of this Act is to allow people who have been sentenced to imprisonment of not more than two and a half years, or who have received some lesser sentence, to disregard their convictions after a period of time if they have not been reconvicted. Their conviction is then said to be 'spent', and they are under no general obligation to disclose it.

Furthermore, the Act makes it an offence for social workers and others to reveal any information other than that which is required for the conduct of 'official duties'. However, there are some circumstances in which confidentiality can be breached. These include cases of: disclosure to local authorities assessing the suitability of a person to have the care of children and young persons; criminal proceedings; and reports compiled for courts for proceedings involving the adoption, guardianship or wardship of children.

Probation officers have a particular responsibility to prevent any avoidable risk to the life and well-being of children. In this case, those who have responsibility for clients who have abused children are required to disclose to potential employers or others any facts about offences, personality or character which may affect the offender's suitability for a specific job. Probation officers in prisons are also required to notify local social-services departments of the release from custody of those who have offended against children in the family.

Access to information

Closely linked to the issues of consent and confidentiality is the right of access to information which is enshrined in both statutory provisions and official guidelines which stress the importance of openness and access to information for patients and clients. These include:

- The Access to Medical Reports Act (1988)
- The Access to Health Records Act (1990)
- The Patients' Charter

However, there is much evidence to suggest

that, frequently, health and social care professionals fail to provide sufficient information to patients and clients, as the following report indicates:

In one memorable scene from the Doctor series of films of the 1950s and 1960s, Sir Lancelot (James Robertson Justice) draws an extravagant line across a patient's stomach to show his juniors where surgery should commence. 'Now don't worry,' he tells the man, 'this has nothing whatever to do with you.'

An awful fiction? Perhaps not. According to a report today [*What Seems to be the Matter: Communication Between Hospitals and Patients*, HMSO] from the Audit Commission, Sir Lancelot's worst excesses may be only an exaggerated version of the lamentable way some doctors – and nurses – communicate with patients . . .

Andrew Foster, the controller of the commission, says: 'Doctors and managers should experience at first hand what it is like to be a patient in their hospitals. Patients often arrive frightened by their illness. They need full information, in words they can understand. Getting it right is not easy, but getting it better would make a real difference to patients' . . .

One stroke victim told an interviewer: 'You have to fight to be told what's wrong.' A woman who had been diagnosed as having a breast lump said: 'I didn't even know it was malignant. Perhaps they leave it to your imagination.' A man with a prostate condition said: 'They never even told me it was my prostate. I think they expected me to know.'

The commission says good communication with patients can have beneficial effects: research suggests it can reduce anxiety and stress, leading to fewer post-operative complications and quicker recovery, and readier compliance with doctors' instructions and prescribed medication . . .

On clinical communication, the auditors found wide variation among doctors on how they dealt with patients suffering four sample illnesses of breast cancer, enlarged prostate, stroke and rheumatoid arthritis.

Twelve consultant surgeons were assessed on eight criteria on how they dealt with women referred with breast lumps: was the patient dressed on meeting the surgeon (two of the 12); was the patient dressed for discussion of the prognosis (four); was the patient invited to bring a companion (six); did the consultant work with a breast nurse (seven); was the nurse included in discussion of the treatment (three); was there more than one chance to discuss the treatment (six); was there discussion of radiotherapy before a decision on surgery (two); and was written information used (one) . . .

The report says such communication should always be discreet, out of earshot of other patients, and backed up by good-quality written material. It cites with approval the practice of tape-recording the conversation and letting the patient have the tape to go over it again at home, possibly with other family members present, to overcome the problem of the patient being too upset or shocked to take everything in at first hearing. It also urges hospitals routinely to inform patients of voluntary groups they may wish to turn to for support . . .

(From an article in the Guardian, *24 November 1993)*

QUESTIONS

1 Why is good communication so important to patients?

2 What recommendations would you make to improve communication and access to information in cases such as those mentioned here?

ACTIVITY

A general rule of health and social care practice is that the right of access to information must not override the right of others to privacy and confidentiality. How far would you agree with this?

Applying ethical and legal principles to care work

LEGAL AND ETHICAL JUSTIFICATION

Central to the resolution of problems in health and social care is the ability to reach *ethically and legally justifiable* decisions – that is, to be able to identify the relevant legal requirements of the situation and to demonstrate sound ethical reasoning. This means that the principles governing your decision are clearly stated and that you have fully taken into account possible alternative views and courses of action. It is also very important that you demonstrate *consistency*; that is, that in similar cases you apply the same principles and standards of judgement – it is not acceptable to arrive at *different* conclusions in such similar situations, out of prejudice, personal dislike or sloppy thinking.

The following section provides the opportunity to apply and test your knowledge of ethical and legal issues, and to reach justifiable conclusions in typical care-work situations. Frequently this might be difficult, and you will need to strike a balance between competing and perhaps conflicting obligations and duties. You might find it useful to use role play in some of these examples.

CASE STUDIES IN HEALTH CARE

1 Sarah Cohen

Sarah Cohen is 45. She is a teacher, and has two young children. She was admitted to a surgical ward, where you are the charge nurse, to undergo a biopsy which has confirmed that she has breast cancer. However, her prognosis is good because the growth has been detected early. You have built up a good rapport with her, and she seems convinced that with a mastectomy followed by radiotherapy she will have a good chance of survival. She signs an operation consent form. However, on the evening of the following day, as you are leaving after a late shift, you see Sarah getting dressed and she tells you that after talking it over with her partner, she has decided that she does not want to go ahead with the treatment.

Figure 1.6 The politics of nursing

QUESTIONS

1 Can you legally prevent Sarah from leaving the ward?

2 What moral principles are at issue in this case?

3 If you were a consequentialist, what would you do, and why?

2 Brian Mitchel

You are a staff nurse on a psychiatric ward, and have just admitted Brian Mitchel who is 35 and has a long-term history of schizophrenia. On this occasion he has been admitted to the hospital as a voluntary patient. Over the next 24 hours he becomes increasingly aggressive and disturbed. In the past, Brian's episodes of aggression have been only verbal and have always been short-lived. However, on this occasion he grabs a nurse around the throat and threatens to strangle her.

QUESTIONS

1 What action can legally be taken by you at this stage?

2 What action are medical staff likely to take later?

3 What moral principles comes into conflict in this case?

3 Gail White

You are a community psychiatric nurse caring for Gail White who is 25 and has recently been released from psychiatric hospital after six weeks as a patient 'under section'. Her mother who is caring for her has become increasingly worried about Gail's delusional state, and believes that she is no longer taking her medication. She asks you to ensure that Gail takes her medication by supervising this activity yourself.

QUESTIONS

1 Will you accede to this request?

2 What ethical and legal rights does Gail have in this situation?

4 Seema Ahmed

Seema Ahmed has been admitted to hospital, and has signed a consent form for surgery on a malignant tumour which has been found in her colon. As a staff nurse on the ward you are preparing Seema for surgery, and you remark that she seems very composed. She tells you that she knows there is nothing to worry about: the doctor has told her she has a 'blockage'. It is clear that she does not understand the extent of her condition.

QUESTIONS

1 Do you continue preparing Seema for surgery? If not, why not?

2 What legal and ethical factors can be identified in this case?

5 Joseph Mbuti

You are a district nurse caring for Joseph Mbuti who is 76. His twin sister visits him every day, but she is unable to undertake a major caring role. Mr Mbuti believes that he will recover from his illness, but his sister has told you in confidence that Joseph has inoperable liver cancer. One day Joseph asks you directly what you know of his condition.

QUESTION

What action would you take, and what ethical principles would you weigh up in reaching your decision?

6 Simon Stevens

Simon Stevens, aged 30, is admitted to Accident and Emergency after a road accident. As the admitting nurse, you find a card in his wallet which says that for religious reasons he cannot accept a blood transfusion. You know that without a transfusion he will die, so you decide to destroy the card.

QUESTIONS

1 Could you ethically justify your action?

2 What legal action could Mr Stevens take if he recovers?

7 Baby M

You are a paediatric nurse who has taken a special interest in the case of Baby M. She was born three months prematurely with severe congenital abnormalities. On the advice of the paediatrician, Baby M's parents gave permission for her to undergo two major operations. Both have been unsuccessful, and without a third attempt it is certain that the baby will die. The past three months have been very painful and distressing for both the parents and the nursing staff. Baby M's mother now feels that all therapeutic treatment should be withdrawn and nature be left to take its course (palliative care will not be withdrawn). However, the baby's father and the consultant are convinced that a further operation must be attempted.

QUESTIONS

What are the ethical and legal principles at stake in this case? What advice would you give to the parents?

CASE STUDIES IN SOCIAL CARE

1 Elderly woman

The 80-year-old woman is a chronic shoplifter. Her targets are some of London's best known stores and on one occasion she was found with more than £1,000 of goods.

Her shoplifting does not appear to be for personal gain. She is known to give the goods away on the journey home to Hackney, probably in an attempt to win friends. As a result she has been mugged several times.

Police are concerned about her, while security staff in department stores have been given her photograph and told to stop her entering. In one month Hackney social services had two referrals from Marylebone Police after her arrest.

The flat where she lives alone is in a poor state and food was found which was months past its sell-by date. She turns down offers of home care and meals on wheels and refuses access to the district nurse. She talks of suicide and loneliness and is depressed about the death of her husband and sister, but she refuses bereavement counselling.

A case conference is held and she agrees to allow access to health and social services. At a second conference Part III residential care is pursued and a place is found. She agrees but then changes her mind.

A third emergency case conference is held after she is arrested again and the Crown Prosecution Service decides to take action. Conference decides, reluctantly, to seek a Guardianship Order, under which she would be directed to move into residential care, although the application is postponed while alternative action is taken. Once more she agrees voluntarily to go into a residential home but again changes her mind.

She is now being offered Part III accommodation again but if she refuses or fails to stay there, a Guardianship Order will be sought, initially for three months.

ARGUMENTS AGAINST SEEKING A GUARDIANSHIP ORDER

- Her wish to stay in her own home counsels against seeking a Guardianship Order. She is a very independent woman who has declined most forms of help, both physical and financial
- Concern that moral judgements on her shoplifting activities should not influence decisions about her care. Social workers have been at pains to avoid being judgmental despite some pressure from other agencies to do something
- Her rejection of Part III accommodation on two occasions has underlined her desire to remain in her own home, even to the point of barring visitors
- A hope that she may be persuaded to see what was needed voluntarily and co-operate without the need to resort to further action
- Concern a Guardianship Order and Part III accommodation would mean the end of independent living for her

ARGUMENTS IN FAVOUR OF SEEKING A GUARDIANSHIP ORDER

- Among the factors in favour of seeking a Guardianship Order is that the safety and long-term needs of the woman are of paramount importance, particularly in view of her lifestyle
- History of depression, loneliness, self-neglect, threatened suicide and the deterioration in her ability to look after herself were an issue of concern to social workers
- Her feelings of loneliness may be helped by a residential setting with the availability of companionship
- As she has been mugged several times there are increasing fears for her physical safety in Hackney, particularly after dark. She is known to carry money with her
- Concern about the effect on her life of the continued shoplifting and the likelihood the police will pursue a prosecution against her
- Her rejection of home care support and of statutory financial aid
- Some evidence of a decline in mental health had also been recorded with the possibility of early signs of dementia

(From Community Care, *20–26 July 1995)*

BACKGROUND INFORMATION

'Part III accommodation' refers to the Housing Act 1985 Part III which places a duty on local authorities to house certain categories of people.

Guardianship is being sought under the Mental Health Act 1983.

ACTIVITY

1 In your own words, identify the arguments for and against seeking a Guardianship Order.

2 Explain what action you would take, and why.

3 What other acts can be used to remove elderly people from their homes in their own interest?

2 Sunnybank

You have recently accepted a post as a care worker at Sunnybank residential home. Your contract of employment prohibits disclosure to a third party of any information concerning the business. There is a clear-cut internal procedure which you must follow should you wish to raise a grievance.

It soon becomes clear to you that the home is severely short-staffed and that the safety of residents is at risk. You raise the problem with the manager of the care home, but nothing is done about it.

QUESTIONS

What do you do next, and why?

3 Mary and Kevin

Mary is 16 and has just given birth to a premature baby daughter, Sharon. Mary did not know that she was pregnant and does not want to keep her baby. As her social worker, you have talked to Mary and have explained to her that there is support available to her whatever she decides. You ask about the father of the baby, Kevin. At first, Mary says she does not want him to know, but you encourage them to meet and to talk about the baby before making a final decision whether to keep the baby or put her up for adoption. After seeing Kevin, Mary tells you that she has changed her mind: Kevin has told her he would love to be a 'proper' father and he wants the three of them to settle down as a family.

However, it soon becomes apparent that Kevin is well known to the local social-services department: he has a previous conviction for aggravated assault during a burglary, and he has received a caution for possession of drugs (cannabis).

QUESTIONS

1 Do you reveal to Mary what you know about Kevin's past?

2 Can you justify your decision ethically and legally?

4 Suzanne

You are the tutor of Suzanne, who is 17 and has a moderate learning disability. Her parents, and in particular her mother, have found caring for Suzanne very demanding, and they have received very little support. It is likely that Suzanne will live at home for much of the rest of her life. She attended a special school from the age of five which her mother took her to and collected her from every day for 12 years. Suzanne made some female friends at school, but had no social life and has never had a boyfriend. However, she recently started a pre-vocational life-skills course at her local further-education college. She enjoys the freedom of college very much and has now found a boyfriend, Simon.

Suzanne's mother has found out that Suzanne and Simon have started a sexual relationship, and she is very angry and upset. She feels that it is wrong for Suzanne to have sex because she believes that Suzanne is not sexually mature (in fact she believes that Suzanne will never be able to have a 'proper' sexual relationship) and, furthermore, that she has been taken advantage of. She also feels that the college has failed to adequately supervise her daughter by allowing this to happen. At a meeting between Suzanne, her mother and her tutor, Suzanne's mother threatens to withdraw Suzanne from college. For her part, Suzanne says she loves Simon and wants to stay at college.

QUESTIONS

1 What is your response?

2 What suggestions can you make to resolve this conflict whilst recognising and respecting the autonomy and rights of all the people involved?

5 John and June

You work in a residential home for young people with learning disabilities. All of the residents are encouraged to celebrate birthdays, and the staff use these occasions as an opportunity to reinforce life skills such as decision-making, shopping, sharing etc. John will be 17 next week, and is eagerly awaiting his party. However, for the past few weeks he has been very disruptive, and the usual sanctions the staff use have failed to encourage him to cooperate. As on previous occasions, you threaten not to let him have a birthday party, but on the day itself you relent. Some weeks later another resident, June, is equally disruptive and uncooperative at the time of her birthday. On this occasion you decide that you must exercise your authority, so you refuse to give in and her party is cancelled.

QUESTIONS

1 Why is this not a consistent or justifiable decision?

2 What are the likely consequences of your action?

6 Benjamin

Benjamin is a widower of 76. He has recently come to the attention of social services because a neighbour reported that he was looking increasingly dishevelled. You are a social worker and you visit him. He has six cats and his house is very dirty. He cannot manage to wash his clothes very well and he eats mostly from tins. He is rather forgetful, and he tells you that on one occasion he left the cooker on all night.

ACTIVITY

In pairs, each write down an approach to this client: one will stress autonomy, the other paternalism. Which will bring about the best outcome for the client?

7 Joshua

You are a registered nurse who manages a day centre for young people with learning disabilities. You have about 16 members who attend regularly. They benefit from the activities provided, and a number have developed useful work-related skills. One, John, recently left and has just started working for Remploy, a sheltered workshop. However, another member, Joshua, is very disruptive and uncooperative, and you have requested that his parents find an alternative placement for him. They plead with you: they need the respite provided and know of no alternative. You have sympathy for them but are also concerned for the other members of the day centre, a number of whom are very troubled by Joshua's behaviour. Joshua's mother suggests that she sedate him before bringing him to the centre until he gets over his 'difficult period'.

QUESTIONS

1 Whose needs are important in this case? Do those of the majority outweigh the needs of Joshua or those of his family?

2 What will you do, and why?

8 Child protection

You are a social worker involved in child protection. As part of her training, a student social worker must analyse a number of case studies and consider alternative approaches to them. She asks you to suggest two alternative explanations for each of the following:

1 A 12-year-old girl from an ethnic-minority family writes in an essay that she sleeps in the same bed as her father.
2 A 3-year-old clings to the health visitor during a home visit. She wants to be held and is reluctant to return to her step-mother.
3 A 6-week-old baby of middle-class parents, the third child after a gap of six years, has not regained his baby weight. His mother insists he is content and feeds well.
4 A girl aged six arrives in school with a bruise on the side of her face. She says she bumped into a table.

(From an article by the Department of Health in the Guardian, *21 June 1995)*

9 Violet Hayes

As a social worker you have been asked to assess the needs of Violet Hayes, and put together a care package for her. Mrs Hayes is 83 and has been a widow for 20 years. For the past eight years she has been cared for full time by her unmarried daughter, Margaret.

On your first visit you speak to Mrs Hayes alone. She says she is very happy living at home and does not wish even to visit a luncheon club, let alone go into residential accommodation. On leaving, you notice a bruise on Mrs Hayes's neck.

On your next visit, you speak to Margaret and hear a very different story. She says she cannot cope with providing full-time care for her mother any more. She also claims that the only reason her mother refuses to visit a day centre is that she wants to maintain constant control over her (i.e. Margaret). At this point you ask about the bruise on Mrs Hayes's neck, and Margaret breaks down and confesses that she and her mother regularly have physical fights. She tells you that if you do not ensure that her mother attends a day centre at least three times a week, she is frightened of the consequences.

ACTIVITY

Explain what you would do in this case and what ethical and legal principles seem most important to you.

REFERENCES AND RESOURCES

Audit Commission (1989), *The Probation Service: Promoting Value for Money*, London: HMSO.

Bowling, A. (1993), *What People Say About Prioritising Health Care*, London: King's Fund.

British Journal of Nursing (1992), vol. 1, no. 10: editorial.

Carson and Montgomery (1989), *Nursing and the Law*, London: Macmillan Education.

Davey and Popay, J. (eds) (1993), *Dilemmas in Health Care*, Buckingham: Open University Press.

Department of Health (1995), *Key Issues in Personal Social Services: Report of SSI 1994/5*, London: Department of Health.

Dimond, B. (1992), 'Limits and the criminal law in healthcare', *British Journal of Nursing*, vol. 1, no. 10, p. 483.

Foot, P. (1978), *Virtues and Vices*, Berkeley: University of California Press.

General Medical Council (1989), *British Journal of Nursing*, vol. 1, no. 4.

Glover, J. (1977), *Causing Death and Saving Lives*, Middlesex: Penguin.

Home Office (1990), 'Partnership in dealing with offenders in the community', Discussion Paper, April 1990, London: Home Office.

Independent Development Council for People with Mental Handicap (1986), *Pursuing Quality*, London: Independent Development Council for People with Mental Handicap.

Medical Research Council, *MRC News*, Autumn 1994.

Rachels (1986), 'Active and passive euthanasia', in Singer, P. (ed), *Applied Ethics*, Oxford: OUP.

Richards, M. (1988), *Key Issues in Child Sexual Abuse – Some Lessons from Cleveland and Other Inquiries*, National Institute of Social Work Briefing Paper No. 2: National Institute for Social Work.

Singer, P. (1979), *Practical Ethics*, Cambridge: CUP.

– (1986), *Applied Ethics*, Oxford: OUP.

– (1991) *A Companion to Ethics*, Oxford: Basil Blackwell.

Thomas, T. and Wall, G. (1992), 'Towards an ethic of caring', in Elders (ed) *The Journal of Care and Practice*, vol. 1, no. 3, pp. 49–64.

Thomson, H. et al. (1995), *Health and Social Care for Advanced GNVQ*, 2nd edn, London: Hodder & Stoughton.

Tingle, J. (1992), 'Primary nursing and the law', in *British Journal of Nursing*, vol. 1, no. 5, pp. 248–51.

Tingle, J. and Childs, A. (eds) (1995), *Nursing Law and Ethics*, Oxford: Blackwell.

United Kingdom Central Council (UKCC) (1989), *Exercising Accountability*, supplement to Code of Conduct, London: UKCC.

United Kingdom Central Council (UKCC) (1992), *Code of Professional Conduct*, London: UKCC.

United Kingdom Central Council (UKCC) (1993), *Standards for Records and Record Keeping*, London: UKCC.

Vernon, S. (1993), *Social Work and the Law*, London and Edinburgh: Butterworths.

Warnock, M. (1987), 'Ethics, decision making and social policy', in *Community Care*, 5 November 1987.

Young, A. (1994), *Law and Professional Conduct in Nursing*, London: Scutari Press.

USEFUL ADDRESSES

British Association of Social Workers
16 Kent Street
Birmingham B5 6RD

Central Council for Education and Training in Social Work
Derbyshire House
St Chads Street
London WC1H 8AE

Department of Health
Richmond House
79 Whitehall
London SW1A 2NS

Home Office
50 Queen Anne's Gate
London SW1H 9AT

LIFE (anti-euthanasia and anti-abortion)
15 Edge Street
London W8 7PN

NACRO (National Association for the Care and Resettlement of Offenders)
169 Clapham Road
London SW9 0PU

National Childminding Association
8 Masons Hill
Bromley
Kent BR2 9EY

Royal College of Nursing
20 Cavendish Square
London W1M 0AB

United Kingdom Central Council (nursing and midwifery)
23 Portland Place
London W1N 3AF

Victim Support National Association
Cranmer House
39 Brixton Road
London SW9 6DZ

Voluntary Euthanasia
13 Prince of Wales Terrace
London W8 5PG

2

VALUES AND PRINCIPLES IN THE CARE SETTING

HUMAN VALUES

The *values* that we, as humans, hold are less fixed and more liable to change than either our *attitudes* or our *beliefs*. Frankl (1963) has described three types of such value:

- *creative* values – which we discover through what we do, and particularly through helping others
- *experiential* values – which we discover through appreciating people, events and artistic and natural beauty
- *attitudinal* values – which we discover through our reactions to circumstances beyond our control, such as our own and other people's suffering.

Society, background, upbringing and training all shape our values. Frankl asserts that we do not create our values but *discover* them; and that values do not *push* us but *pull* us.

The caring ethos

Care is based on and given in a *relationship*. In a caring – and professional – relationship, it is expected that the client's or patient's interests must come first. This poses dilemmas both for the social worker – for example, when a client is desperate to keep the family together but the father is abusing the children – and for the nurse – for example, when a patient attempts suicide and asks to be left to die.

Dignity and choice

The national Charter standards (see below) include the 'respect for privacy, dignity and religious and cultural beliefs', and suggest that all health authorities publicise their own local standards.

CHARTER STANDARDS

The *Charter* set a number of national Charter Standards and suggested that health authorities, FHSAs and GPs should also publicise their own local standards. Some of the standards concern themselves with the way people should be treated and the standards of behaviour they should expect from NHS staff, while others are more quantitative measures.

The national Charter Standards are:

1 *Respect for privacy, dignity and religious and cultural beliefs.* Patients' dietary requirements should be met, and private rooms should be available for confidential discussions with relatives.
2 *Arrangements to ensure that everyone, including people with special needs, can use services.* This includes ensuring that buildings are accessible to people in wheelchairs.
3 *Information to relatives and friends.* Health authorities should ensure that, if you wish it, friends and relatives are informed about the progress of your treatment.
4 *Waiting times for the ambulance service:* 14 minutes if you live in an urban area, 19 minutes in a rural area.
5 *Waiting time for initial assessment in accident and*

emergency departments: you should be seen immediately and your need for treatment assessed.

6 *Waiting time in out-patient clinics:* you should be given a specific appointment time and be seen within 30 minutes of that time.
7 *Cancellation of operations:* your operation should not be cancelled on the day you are due to arrive in hospital, though this could happen due to emergencies or staff sickness. If your operation has to be postponed twice, you will be admitted to hospital within one month of the date of the second cancelled operation.
8 *A named qualified nurse, midwife or health visitor to be responsible for each patient.*
9 *Discharge of patients from hospital.* Before you are discharged, a decision should be made about any continuing health or social care you may need, and if necessary, any arrangements for this should be made.

(Source: Today's Health Service)

Empowerment and social justice

Patient advocacy is a growing movement in which users of health and social services provide each other with mutual support. An *advocate* is someone independent from these services who befriends an individual user of services on a one-to-one basis and represents their interests to professionals. *Empowerment* incorporates the principle of advocacy which enables the service-user to exercise some power over the care they receive. Empowerment and social justice are most appropriately applied in the case of vulnerable or disadvantaged groups, e.g. children, or people with disabilities. At the individual level, some people are better able to represent their own interests to health-care professionals, and those who pay for private health care, in particular, feel that they can influence the doctor for whose services they pay directly.

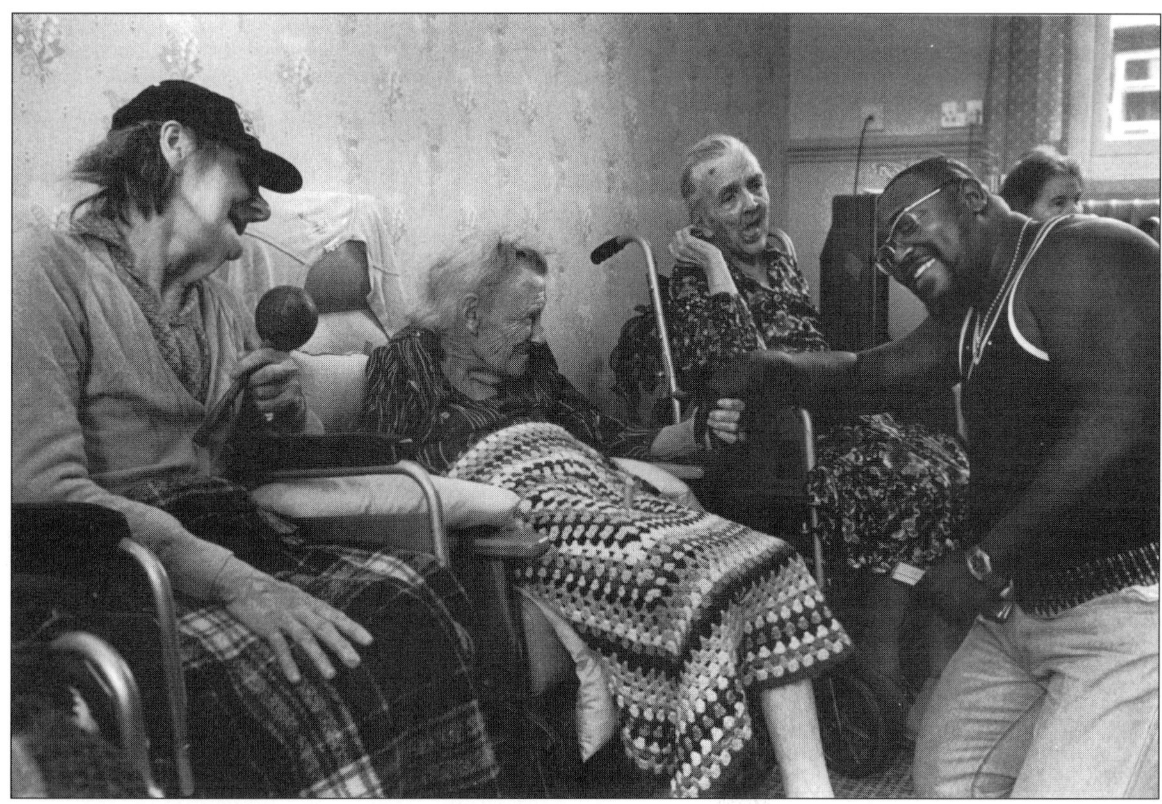

Figure 2.1 We all have the right to be treated with respect and dignity

The NVQ value base

The National Vocational Qualification (NVQ) in Care identifies, in the *NVQ Value Base Unit*, those principles of good practice which health and social care workers must apply to all aspects of their work. Also called the 'O' Unit, this Unit is entitled 'Promote equality for all individuals' and is divided into five elements of competence:

- Element A: Promote anti-discriminatory practice
- Element B: Maintain the confidentiality of information
- Element C: Promote and support individual rights and choice within service delivery
- Element D: Acknowledge individuals' personal beliefs and identity
- Element E: Support individuals through effective communication

The various scenarios that occur during the rest of this chapter will enable you to explore the values and principles embedded in the NVQ value base which underpins quality care. A structured assignment at the end of the chapter will direct students to explore the application of those values in the care setting.

SCENARIO 1

Winston is a 24-year-old man who has recently been diagnosed as being HIV positive. He and a friend, Paul, have been involved in a serious car accident, and the staff at the busy Accident and Emergency Department are dealing with the aftermath. Both men are left alone in separate cubicles, each bleeding from wounds to the face and arms, and are waiting for the harassed house officer to suture the wounds. When the officer does arrive, he performs the necessary tasks in an atmosphere of total silence, not even bothering to ask if the local anaesthetic is having an effect. Winston asks after his friend, Paul, and the doctor snaps at him, saying, 'If you people didn't insist on partying all night and then driving around town, we'd all get along better.'

QUESTIONS

1 What do you understand by 'HIV positive'? What is its relevance in this context?

2 Describe the discriminatory practice shown to the two patients. Is there any justification for discrimination of this kind?

The following passage is taken from an essay by Lois Keith called 'This week I've been rushed off my wheels':

Rachel was three and Miriam just two weeks past her first birthday when I was run over by a speeding driver in Australia. My separation from them, my inability to be their mother, was more painful than knowing I would never walk again. People who do not live with a disability find this impossible to understand. Now I try to be a strong enough mother to them, and mostly I succeed. They understand more than other children about fairness and justice and why disabled people have to be fighters. They don't like the way people stare at us when we're out together and have an acute awareness of when people are being patronising. When someone passes the three of us going about our business in the supermarket or the shopping centre and smiles in a sickening way muttering 'How sweet' or asks me (or them) if I'd mind telling them how I came to be in a wheelchair, we imagine replying, 'It's a disease that strikes people who say stupid things.' We don't, of course.

Source: Keith, L. (1994) *Mustn't Grumble*, The Women's Press Ltd.

QUESTIONS

1 Is the patronising behaviour of outsiders a form of discrimination?

2 Examining your own attitudes to disability, how would *you* like to be treated if you had a disability?

CONFIDENTIALITY OF INFORMATION

Interpersonal communication often involves the giving of information in confidence. How much of such information should be shared is open to question. The following extract is taken from R. S. Downie and K. C. Calman's excellent book *Healthy Respect*:

Level of information: It is possible to identify a series of levels of information, which might be used to decide on whether or not the information could be shared. There are four levels. Look at each one carefully and ask whether this information could be divulged within the team.

- *Identification:* Name, address, sex, marital status, and primary disease
- *Medical information:* Disease, extent of disease, treatment investigations, past medical information, drug information
- *Social information:* Housing, work, family, social relationships
- *Psychological information:* Anxiety, stress, sexual problems, emotional state

At present this information is stored, presented and shared in a variety of ways:

- Documents, reports, case-sheets, nursing Kardex, etc.
- Tutorials, or formal doctor–doctor, nurse–nurse contact
- Ward meetings, formal or informal, where problems are shared and discussed
- Ward rounds, with discussion between the staff
- Letters giving information are exchanged between staff
- Investigation forms are completed and sent throughout the hospital, and into the community

In the process of sharing this information two assumptions are made:

1. The patient has agreed to this sharing.
2. The information remains confidential within the team. A typical team on a medical or surgical ward would include doctors, nurses, social workers, physiotherapists, dieticians, pharmacists, and others. Related to this team are secretaries, receptionists, porters and ward maids. These individuals are vital to the working of the team.

As an exercise read the following clinical profile and try to answer the questions at the end. The profile has been arbitrarily divided into the four levels of information given above.

1. Mrs Irene McGregor is a 55-year-old married woman who lives on a housing estate in the suburbs of a large city. She has been admitted for a hysterectomy related to fibroids*.
2. A routine chest radiograph (X-ray) shows evidence of previous tuberculosis. Other investigations are normal. In the past she has had no serious illness, but 10 years ago was investigated for possible epilepsy.
3. She has three children, all of whom are well, but one has recently been suspected of drug-taking. She has told this only to the social worker. Her husband is a postman and she works part-time in a shop. There is an elderly mother-in-law who lives nearby and is visited daily by the family.
4. She is naturally anxious about the operation, and the fact that her eldest son may be involved with drugs has made her particularly anxious about the admission. She is otherwise well adjusted although, because of her symptoms, normal sexual relationships with her husband have been difficult. She is quite concerned about this.

- This information, except for that associated with her son, has been obtained from her case-sheet. Who should have access to it?
- How much of each of the four levels of information should be shared with members of the professional staff?
- How much should be shared with other members of the team, porters, receptionists, etc.?
- Do all members of staff need to know all the information?

* Hysterectomy: surgical removal of the uterus or womb. Fibroids: benign (not cancerous) tumours of the uterus.

- During the weekly ward meeting, a member of the nursing staff feels that the patient is more anxious than she should be. How much information about the son should be divulged and openly discussed?

While answering these questions have you formed any views on the rules for maintaining confidentiality?

It is sometimes useful, when deciding on who should be given confidential information, to separate people into the following groups:

1 those who must know;
2 those who should know;
3 those who could know;
4 those who shouldn't know.

Look again at Mrs McGregor and the issues and questions which have been raised. Divide the professional groups, the supporting staff and others into the categories listed above.

Confidentiality, outside the health care team: So far it has been assumed that information about an individual *might* be shared between members of the team. There are circumstances, however, when information about a particular patient is requested by other groups. Consider Mrs McGregor again. Information is requested by the following. Would you divulge it?

- The husband: He asks for information about the medical problems
- A close friend: A neighbour (female) asks to see the ward sister and requests information about treatment
- The social services: They are concerned about possible problems at home while the patient is recovering. They wish to know details of the family background
- The police: Questions are being asked about possible drug problems in the area and they suspect her son
- The press: They have found out from the police that her son is a possible addict. They phone you for information
- Your colleagues: You meet a colleague at a social event. He (or she) is very interested in family problems associated with drug-taking. He asks if you know anyone who might help in this important research project.

These points raise important issues in confidentiality, and you should now be clearer about when, and to whom, you would divulge information.

Source: Downie, R.S., Calman, K.C., (1994) *Healthy Respect: Ethics in health care*, by permission of Oxford University Press.

ACTIVITY

Read the case study carefully, and answer the questions about confidentiality which arise within it.

RIGHTS, FREEDOM OF CHOICE AND EMPOWERMENT

All service users in care settings have the same rights as any other individual or 'consumer'. In a caring relationship, it is expected that the client's interests should always come first. The rights of patients receiving medical care have been set out in the Patients' Charter. Every individual needs to be able to exercise freedom of choice, but being a recipient of care often curtails such freedom, chiefly by excluding the patient or client from the decision-making process. *Advocacy* (as already mentioned) is one means of *empowering* people. Advocacy has variously been defined as 'pleading the cause of another' or 'a means of transferring power back to the patient, to enable him to control his own affairs'.

SCENARIO 2

Simone is a 15-year-old girl who weighs just four and a half stone. For the last two years she has suffered from *anorexia nervosa*, and her parents are at their wit's end trying to cope with Simone's illness. Simone attends school regularly, but finds it difficult to concentrate in lessons because of an overwhelming fatigue. Apart from being very fussy about what she eats, Simone also takes the family dog out for a 6-mile run every morning before school. Simone has twice been admitted to a special unit for people with eating disorders, where her weight is monitored, she is encouraged to eat regularly and she receives specialist counselling. Each time, Simone has reluctantly gained weight in order to be discharged home, only to revert to a 'near-starvation' diet and steady weight loss at home. Simone is a cheerful girl who is aware that she has a problem but finds it very difficult to follow the advice of the specialists to maintain a healthy weight. Her parents are now worried that Nicola, Simone's 12-year-old sister, will become anorexic as well.

QUESTIONS

1 Has anyone other than Simone the right to control how she uses – or indeed *abuses* – her own body? As long as there is no real threat to life, has anyone else the right to intervene?

2 Caring for Simone in the Special Unit may pose a dilemma for nurses. Could any professional care worker act as an *advocate* for Simone, when to do so may cause a delay in recovery?

3 Social rights, that is, the rights that we all expect to have in a social setting, are:

- dignity
- privacy
- the right to be alone
- the right to choose diet, dress and activity
- the right to choose whom we associate with
- the right to have a say in the organisation of the care setting

Consider each right in turn. Do you think that Simone's rights are being respected?

ACKNOWLEDGING INDIVIDUALS' PERSONAL BELIEFS AND IDENTITY

The differences between individuals should be recognised and treated in a positive way, so that services can be provided which cater for these differences. Respect for others' needs and beliefs should be fundamental to any caring activity, and much respect is bound up with the concepts of *rights* and *empowerment*. Finding out about a client's preferences and beliefs will help in forming care plans and will promote a greater understanding and spirit of cooperation.

SCENARIO 3

Doreen Parker and her husband, Tom, are both in their sixties and live in a small house in the suburbs of a large town. Doreen has had multiple sclerosis for 10 years and is now confined to a wheelchair. In addition to the effects of multiple sclerosis (described on pp. 80–82), Doreen also suffers recurrent respiratory infections as she had tuberculosis as a child. Both Tom and Doreen are committed Christian Scientists, and this has led to problems concerning Doreen's medical care. Tom has arthritis of the spine and is no longer able to attend to Doreen's needs: the hoist and wheelchair are too difficult for him to manage.

The district nurse calls twice a day to get Doreen in and out of bed, and to supervise her catheter care. One day, the nurse visits and finds that Doreen has a severe chest infection as well as a urinary infection; her temperature is raised and she is having difficulty breathing. Doreen and Tom never call the doctor as their religion states that only God can heal the sick. The nurse feels that without antibiotic treatment, Doreen will succumb to the combined infections, and she unsuccessfully pleads with Tom and Doreen to let her call the doctor and to accept his prescriptions. Doreen becomes more ill, and after four days she dies.

QUESTIONS

1 Do you think that the nurse was right to try to persuade Doreen and Tom to accept medical treatment?

2 Would it have been better for everyone if Doreen were cared for by someone who shared her faith?

Activity

Find out about the following religious beliefs and how they may influence the way care is delivered in terms of diet, dress, hygiene etc.

- Christian Science
- Islam (the Muslim faith)
- Judaism (the Jewish faith)
- Sikhism (the Sikh faith)
- Hinduism
- Buddhism
- Jehovah's Witnesses

SUPPORTING INDIVIDUALS THROUGH EFFECTIVE COMMUNICATION

Effective communication is vital to the caring relationship, and care workers should learn to adapt their method of communication to suit the needs of the patient or client. This does not mean that all care workers have to learn Braille, British Sign Language, Makaton or lots of foreign languages, but they should be able to employ strategies such as non-verbal communication to overcome barriers to communication (see Thomson et al. 1995, Chapter 2, pp. 71–4).

SCENARIO 4

Matthew is a 6-year-old child who appears to have difficulty in communicating with other children. It has been suggested to his parents that he may be *autistic*. Matthew is a solitary boy who will happily spend lesson time staring at the patterns on his pencil case and twiddling his hair in his fingers. He does not appear to enjoy the rough and tumble that his classmates love, and rarely speaks – except to his parents. His teacher and his family are all very concerned, and share the opinion that Matthew appears to be 'locked' in his own secret world and that nobody has the key to reach the boy within.

Questions

First, research the condition known as autism.

1 What special needs does Matthew have?

2 How would you try to communicate with Matthew?

3 Find out about the different therapies that may help a person with a communication disability.

Assignment

This assignment is in five parts, each part relating to the different elements of the NVQ Value Base Unit (Unit O). Students should try to complete the tasks in their work placement.

Task 1

1 Using appropriate reference books, make a *glossary* of terms which will help you to understand this section of the assignment:

- discrimination
- abuse
- ageism
- racism
- stereotyping
- exploitation
- sexism
- heterosexism
- prejudice
- institutionalisation

2 Find out about the specific codes and policies which relate to anti-

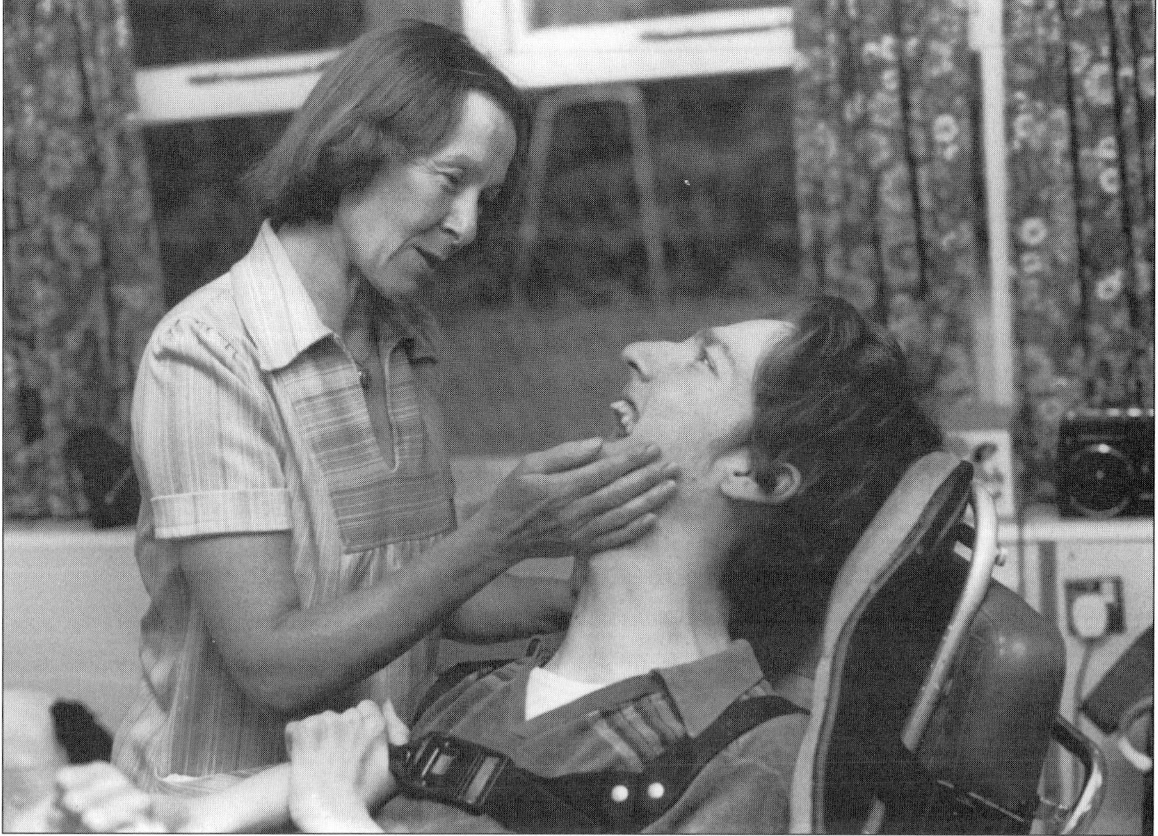

Figure 2.2 Communication can take many forms: actions speak louder than words

discriminatory practice in the work setting.

Task 2

1 Research the issue of confidentiality in the workplace. Consider:

- the storage of information – computer systems, filing cabinets etc.
- accessibility of information – do patients and clients have a right to see everything that is written about them?

2 Ask to see the *mission statement* of the care setting; does it give an accurate impression of the *ethos* of the organisation?

Task 3

1 Make a list of the basic rights that you would like to be recognised as important for yourself (it may include the right to privacy or the right to leave your bedroom in a mess).

2 Most care settings now have a *charter* or *statement of rights*. Ask to look at this statement, and reflect on the effects such documents have on the quality of care delivery.

Task 4

1 Find out how people of different faiths are cared for in your care setting. Are festivals and other special days recognised and valued? Does the daily menu reflect the fact that the United Kingdom is a multicultural community?

2 Find out about the religious centres in your local community: If possible, arrange for a speaker to come into your college to talk about his or her faith.

Task 5

Look at Maslow's hierarchy of needs (in Thomson et al. 1995, Chapter 4, pp. 205–16) and then select two clients. For each client, list their individual needs and describe how each need is met in the care setting. If there is a need you feel is not adequately met, include that need and give possible reasons for its omission.

DEVELOPING STRATEGIES FOR COMMUNICATION

The key to effective communication with patients or clients in care organisations is the consideration of *individual needs*. Care workers need to be flexible in their choice of communication method and to be aware of the need to ask for help if they perceive any barriers to communication (see section on barriers to effective communication in Thomson et al. 1995, Chapter 2, pp. 82–5).

Study the following short case studies:

1 Charles Baker, aged 72, was admitted to hospital having suffered a stoke (i.e. a *cerebral vascular accident* or *CVA*). He has been unable to speak, walk or feed and dress himself. His family are concerned that one week after admission, Charles appears to be tearful, frustrated and depressed. His wife, Helen, spends most of each day with him, and he receives help from a speech therapist, a physiotherapist and an occupational therapist. Charles had been enjoying his retirement, and was a keen gardener and walker.
2 Fatima Coelho is a 17-year-old Portuguese girl who was admitted to hospital after an epileptic seizure. She had been on a two-week holiday visiting her sister, who is married to an Englishman, when the attack occurred. She has never been abroad before and does not speak English. This is her first serious illness and her first experience of hospital life.
3 May Warren is a 70-year-old woman who has severe rheumatoid arthritis and deafness. Her husband used to care for her at home, but now that he has died, May has been admitted to a residential home for the elderly. May is able to walk with a special zimmer frame and can usually manage to feed and dress herself. The staff at the home were told that May and her husband always communicated by a private system of sign language, and that May has never worn a hearing aid.

ACTIVITY

1 Identify the individual needs for each person and consider the barriers to communication.

2 List the strategies which could be used to improve communication.

3 What outside agencies could you refer to for assistance?

4 Write a short report on *strategies for communication within care settings*.

COPING WITH AGGRESSION AND ABUSE IN CARE SETTINGS

Although most of the people you will meet in the work placement are grateful for your efforts, there are occasions when people can be disruptive or aggressive. Such behaviour may take the form of *verbal assault* or *physical assault*. As stated in Chapter 1, all health and social workers have an explicit moral as well as legal duty to protect vulnerable patients from harm and always to act in their best interests. The following article by Elaine Aspinwall-Roberts entitled 'Old age: the right to be alone' illustrates a severe case of self-abuse or neglect which poses a dilemma for the social worker:

I'm the social worker on the duty desk who gets the call about Miss Otley, one very cold Friday afternoon in December. Found on the floor by her home help. GP requesting a Section 47. House very cold, stinking of urine, Miss Otley clearly not caring for herself very well, wrapped in dirty blankets. Like the GP I would be very concerned about leaving her in this situation, possibly with a broken hip, certainly at risk of hypothermia, and alone. The chances of getting a Section 47 are exceedingly slight (perhaps 200 such orders are made each year according to Age Concern in *The Law and Vulnerable People*); in all probability nothing can be done for Miss Otley unless she gives her consent. It is irresponsible to suggest that old people like Miss Otley will be forcibly removed from their homes as a matter of course .... A Section 47 is a 'last resort' court order which is only granted if the circumstances are truly appalling – for example, if there are years of accumulated faeces, food crawling with maggots, urine soaked bedding and clothing.... Perhaps what is at fault is a system which sends two (very powerful) doctors and an Environmental Health Officer round to put the frighteners on an old lady. This shouldn't have to happen – social services should be involved with this lady, along with the GP, district nurses, health visitors, housing – this is community care. Moving into residential care should never have to be a 'defeat', and can, if handled properly, be a relief from fear and isolation .... On Friday afternoon I was called out to the flat of an elderly lady who had not been seen for some time and from whose flat a dreadful smell was coming. When the police broke in, there were piles of mice-infested newspapers and buckets of faeces; there was no food, blankets or heating. The lady lay, emaciated and saturated with urine, dead on her bed. If a Section 47 could have been used to prevent her sad and lonely death, would it have been wrong?

(Extract taken from the Guardian, *15 February 1995)*

ACTIVITY

1 Neglect is one form of abuse. In this sad case, how could such extreme neglect be prevented? If, as John Stuart Mill claims, 'the only reasons for removal should be to prevent harm to others', should Miss Otley be left to live in the way she may have chosen?

2 Find out about the procedures for 'Sectioning' within the Mental Health Act.

AGGRESSION IN CARE SETTINGS

Before a situation develops in which a client or patient becomes disruptive or aggressive, there are often distinct warning signs. Identifying the stressors in a care setting which may trigger such behaviour is an important skill. For example, some clients may react aggressively to any change to their normal routine, or there may be obvious physical warning signals such as signs and symptoms of anxiety. The person may begin to shake uncontrollably, or may show altered breathing or speech patterns. Prevention is better than cure, so it is vital to learn how people react to certain situations.

Sometimes, on the other hand, there appears to be no reason for a client's changed behaviour, and you will need to know how to handle such a situation. The most important tactics are:

- Make a quick assessment of the situation
- Respond as a care professional, not just as a person
- Try to predict what could happen next
- Never meet the aggression with aggressive behaviour yourself
- If you think that you may be in danger yourself, summon help immediately
- Try to reduce the tension by reacting with calmness – this often results in the client 'matching' your behaviour
- Try to limit the difference in status by getting your eyes on the same level as theirs
- Only use physical restraint as a last resort – and only when *control* is necessary

NB: Only attempt the last tactic if you have been trained in the techniques of physical restraint; you may need to consider isolating the client whilst you decide what to do next. When the situation has calmed down, always talk it over with your supervisor and try to learn from the unpleasant experience.

ASSESSMENT OPPORTUNITY

1 In your work placement, find out about your care setting's policy in dealing with aggression. In particular, find out about:

- the reporting of incidents
- specific techniques which may be used

2 Set up a *role-play scenario*. One person acts the part of a 3-year-old child who will not let any other child play with the dolls in the home corner at the day nursery; and another person acts the part of the care worker – when you try to persuade the child to share the toys, they react by kicking and punching you whilst screaming 'I hate you!' Appoint an observer whose task is to record the strategies used by the care worker to diffuse the situation. In the wider group, discuss the effectiveness of the strategies used.

REFERENCES AND RESOURCES

Downie, R. S. and Calman, K. C. (1994), *Healthy Respect: Ethics in Health Care*, 2nd edn, Oxford Medical Publications.

Moon, G. and Gillespie, R. (1995), *Society and Health*, London: Routledge.

Thomson et al. (1995), *Health and Social Care for Advanced GNVQ*, 2nd edn, London: Hodder & Stoughton.

Frankl, V. (1963), *Man's Search for Meaning*, New York: Pocket Books.

Keith, Lois (1994), *Mustn't Grumble*, London: The Women's Press.

3

PROMOTING INDIVIDUAL INDEPENDENCE AND AUTONOMY

INTRODUCTION: WHAT DO PEOPLE NEED?

The term 'special needs' evokes an image in many minds of elaborate equipment and technology. Paradoxically, an individual is regarded as having *special needs* when they require help to satisfy one or more of the most *basic* human needs.

Every human being has certain basic needs. These have been defined (Maslow 1970) as:

- sufficient appropriate food and drink
- to eliminate waste products
- to breathe properly
- to have the body at a comfortable temperature
- sleep and rest
- to keep clean and maintain health
- communication and interaction with others
- to wear suitable clothing
- to be free from discomfort and pain
- to feel safe

Maslow's hierarchy has been modified by Richard A. Kalish (Weller 1989), who proposed an additional level, the *need for stimulation*, which he placed between the levels of physiological needs and the need for safety and security. This new level includes the *need to explore and manipulate the environment*, which is particularly important to the growth and development of the individual. Kalish also puts the needs for *sex*, *activity* and *novelty* on this level.

DEFINING THE TERMS

Obviously there are wide variations in the ways of fulfilling these basic needs, and the term 'special needs' refers to far more than those people with well-defined physical or mental disabilities.

Disability

The term 'disability' is one which persists because of our society's need to label anyone

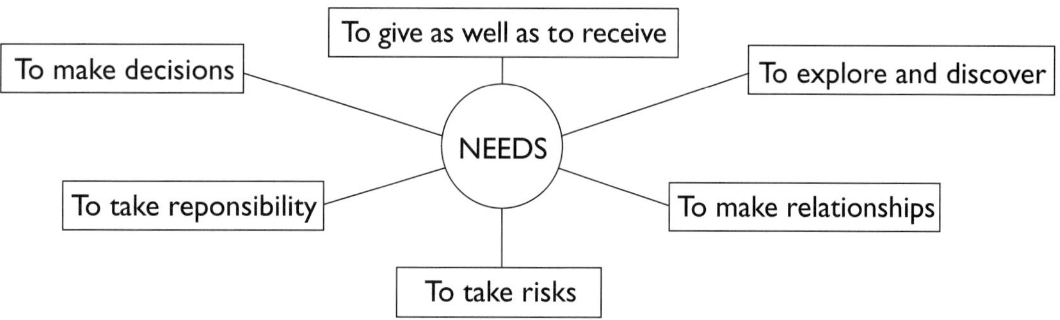

Figure 3.1 Client needs
Source: Moore, S. (1993) *Social Welfare Alive*, Stanley Thornes (Publishers) Ltd.

who differs from the normal (in this case, normal = healthy). Throughout history, disabled people have been marginalised by society. One example is the way in which 'cripples' were excluded from participating in the creation of social wealth. Because industrialised society required able-bodied workers to operate machinery etc., those classed as 'cripples' or 'mental defectives' were reduced to begging or to relying on charitable hand-outs.

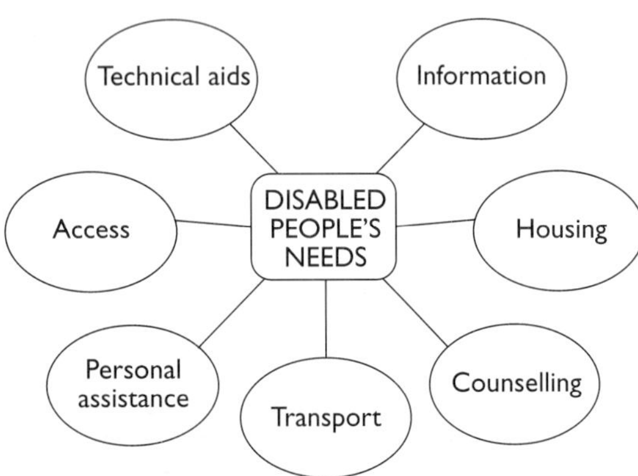

Figure 3.2 Disabled people's needs

In the late 1950s and early 1960s, there was a growing concern to provide more services for disabled people. Before legislation could be formulated, a definition of terms had to be reached. Many people are now trying to move away from the term 'disability', and use descriptions such as 'physically challenged' instead. Such phrases emphasise the positive side and stress that although people may need help in meeting their basic needs, the challenges they face *can* be met.

Handicap

Many people who have a disability reject the term 'handicap' as it implies a patronising attitude and dependence on charity. (The term originates from the notion of 'hand in the cap', i.e. begging for money or charity.) However, charities such as Mencap continue to prefer the use of the words 'mentally handicapped' as they feel that the public thereby has a clearer understanding of those they are trying to help through their work. (The charity for people with cerebral palsy has recently (1994) changed its name from The Spastics Society to SCOPE, placing more emphasis on *ability* rather than on *disability*.)

Advocacy

The movement of 'child advocacy' began in the USA in the 1960s. In the UK, the Children Act 1989 makes social-services departments responsible for providing for children with special needs: 'A child is disabled if he is blind, deaf, or dumb or suffers from mental disorder of any kind or is substantially and permanently handicapped by illness, injury or congenital deformity or other such disability as may be described.' The concept of advocacy is also enshrined in the Act, and it recognises that this category of children are the least likely group to be able to speak up for themselves, that is, to perceive their own needs and to know how to achieve them. Therefore, they need an advocate. Usually, the advocate is an adult care worker who acts as a spokesperson for the child 'in need'. An adult with a severe learning disability may also require advocacy.

Empowerment

This concept is closely linked to that of advocacy. In the case of children with special needs, the adult should undertake activities with the child which will *empower* the child to make their own wishes known by helping with communication, giving the child choice and decision-making skills.

The British Council of Organization of Disabled People (BCODP) was formed in the 1980s to develop *self-empowerment* among groups of disabled people. In this context, self-empowerment is seen as greater involvement by disabled people in policy-making.

Autonomy and independence

The general movement by people with disabilities towards greater integration into mainstream society and greater control over their own futures has become embodied in the Independent Living Movement. There are now approximately 200 Centres for Integrated Living (CILs) in the USA and seven in the UK. The ways in which CILs promote independence are as follows:

- they are organisations *of*, not *for*, disabled people
- disability is made more visible
- disabled people have more control in service provision
- more emphasis is placed on personal growth and less on any dependent role

The main criticism of official definitions of disability is that they fail to take account of the views of disabled people and see them instead as passive subjects. Most experts in this field now recognise the need for disabled people to become involved in research, and particularly in the design process. Finkelstein (1981) asserted that if the physical and social world were adapted for wheelchair users, their disabilities would disappear and able-bodied people would become disabled.

Disability is neither a medical condition nor a 'personal tragedy'. It is *society* which constructs barriers that perpetuate the notion of disability – barriers to education, leisure, employment and housing. Only when we fully understand the needs of those who are disabled can we arrive at a humane and practical method of ensuring that those needs are met.

A disability is a disability, but whether it is handicapping or not is socially determined. Factors affecting this are:

- where you live
- how you live (your lifestyle)
- your level of income
- the job you do or would like to do
- the attitudes of both yourself and those around you

The following three activities explore the possibility of independence within relationships in which special needs are met and physical assistance offered. The first looks at issues of *access* and *exclusion*; the second uses an example of *overprotection* and challenges students to diagnose it and creatively to improve on it; and the third gives students a brief experience of being *dependent*.

ACTIVITY

Exclusion

Over a set period of time, when you see a men's toilet and a women's toilet:

- Note whether there is also a disabled toilet
- If there is, is the disabled toilet unlocked and functioning?
- If someone is needed to unlock it, ask why. (It may not be advisable actually to ask for the toilet to be unlocked, particularly if the asker doesn't need the disabled toilet.)

Students need to prepare for this activity in class time. A blank pro forma is useful, with locations of toilet facilities (to be filled in by the students) down the left boxes across the top to tick or cross for whether there was a disabled toilet and whether it was unlocked and functioning, and space to record answers for why it was locked (if this is asked).

Ideally, each student carries out the investigation in their own time, to report back during a specified lesson. The alternative is to carry out the investigation in class time, with students working in pairs. A preliminary reconnaissance by the teacher of the area is needed to ensure that enough data will be forthcoming.

Now consider the following extract:

One student [at Gallaudet University for deaf students in the United States] . . . went to the

Outreach Office; they had announced there would be an opportunity to practise interviewing for jobs. [The student signed up for an interview] . . . The next day a woman from the Outreach Office called and told him she had set up the interview, had found an interpreter, had set up the time, had arranged for a car to take him . . . and she couldn't understand why he got mad at her.

(Seeing Voices)

ACTIVITY

A case of overprotection

1 Read the extract above from *Seeing Voices*.

2 Discuss why the Gallaudet student became angry.

3 Suggest how the Outreach Office could have arranged things better, starting from the point where they had a list of names of students who wanted a practice interview.

(The interpreter was needed so that the student, using sign language, could communicate with the interviewer, using English.)

ACTIVITY

Issues in physical assistance
Equipment: One pot of yoghurt (or similar) and one spoon each for half the members of the group.

Procedure: Each member of the group is given the number 1 and 2. All number 1s are asked to sit on their hands and not speak until the exercise is over. All number 2s are asked to feed a pot of yoghurt to the number 1s.

Discussion afterwards: All members of the group are invited to talk about how they felt during the exercise. Feelings of embarrassment, awkwardness and even shame may be voiced – by both 1s and 2s. Ask the 2s (if it hasn't emerged anyway) if they found out whether their partner *wanted* the yoghurt or about how they reacted to signs that the yoghurt wasn't wanted.

Variation: The students could be told beforehand that the purpose is for them to get some feeling of what it is like to be physically dependent, or to perform an intimate task for someone else. Afterwards, the group can be given another go at feeding each other with attention and respect for the wishes of the recipient of the food, followed by a further debriefing session.

MODELS OF SPECIAL NEEDS

The development of models arose from the need to give a structure or framework to the provision of services for people with disabilities. *Formal models* are those which aim to determine such provision in its broadest sense, i.e.:

- which organisations will provide services
- how the provision of services is regulated and funded
- which professionals in health, education and social care are involved
- how groups of people with special needs can best be served

The World Health Organization (WHO) model

The WHO published a threefold classification of disability in 1980 which has been used in surveys carried out by the Office of Population Censuses and Surveys (OPCS) to determine the prevalence of disability among adults. The WHO model definition is:

- *Impairment:* lacking all or part of a limb, or having a defective limb, organ or mechanism of the body (i.e. a part of the

body does not work properly or is missing)
- *Disability*: the loss or reduction of functional ability (i.e. you check what people *cannot* do when compared with the majority of other people)
- *Handicap*: the disadvantage or restriction of activity caused by disability (i.e. what an individual can and cannot do in a particular situation and in relationships with other people)

The medical model

This model has been criticised as having a negative focus: it does not highlight the abilities and requirements that people with disabilities have in common with everyone else. On the other hand, its usefulness is apparent where an individual has recently sustained a permanent impairment (as in the case of Mark – see p. 84 below). In conditions such as this, medical intervention and *rehabilitation* are necessary to establish new skills in body management. However, the limitations of the medical model are obvious when we turn to examine the service provision for disabled people. By focusing on the *dis*ability rather than the ability of the individual, a climate of *dependency* is fostered where many disabled people are cared for in institutions; as long as there is no medical cure, disabled people are inherently 'socially dead' and permanently dependent upon others for their care in the community or in an institution.

The traditional medical model starts by looking at the specific physical impairment and its preceding causes, where these are known. It recognises that physical impairment has two consequences:

- *functional limitation*, i.e. how the condition affects mobility, communication and bodily functions
- *activity restriction*, i.e. what specific activities are difficult or impossible

It also recognises *social handicap*, which may result from changes both in self-perception and in the expectations of others (often through *stereotyping* or *stigma*). Social handicap may in its turn affect and exacerbate the underlying physical impairment (see Figure 3.4, p. 60).

The social construction model

This model emphasises the need to change society in order to remove real barriers to

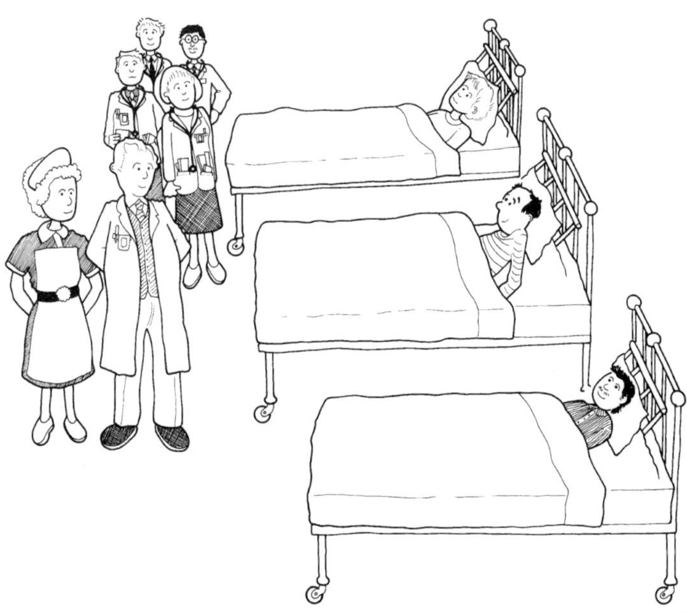

'Now we have a stroke in Bed 1, an MS in Bed 2 and a Parkinson's in Bed 3 – yes?'

Figure 3.3 An extreme example of the medical model in practice

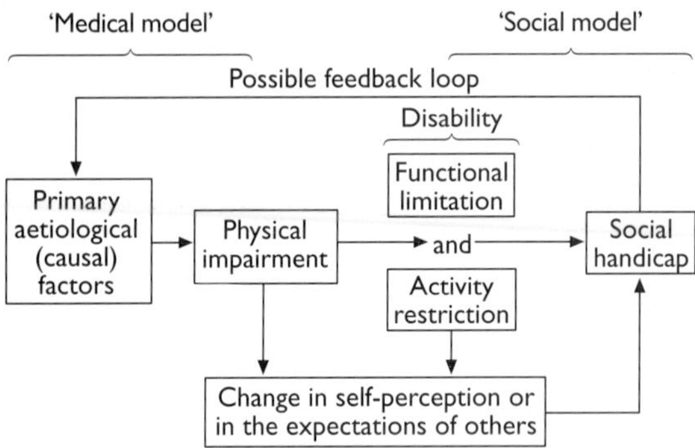

Figure 3.4 A model of impairment, disability and handicap
Source: After WHO 1980.

equality of opportunity. The extent of medical interventions should be guided by an analysis of the social and personal barriers to be overcome rather than by a consideration of any functional limitations on the part of the individual. The model has the following features:

- It sees disability as having a *social dimension*, i.e. the problem of disability is one that is created by the institutions, organisations and processes that make up the whole of society
- It focuses on *attitudes*, i.e. it implies that if the attitudes of the able-bodied change, then the problems of disability will be resolved
- It redefines the WHO's definition (which uses the words 'impairment' and 'disability') by saying that disability is not the lack of function, e.g. the inability to walk, but is the *social response* to that lack of function, e.g. lack of ramps for wheelchairs, fire regulations which ban wheelchair users, etc.

The following changes are suggested:

- The Department of the Environment should be the main agency for organising disability-related services in the community. This would enhance the role of disciplines such as engineering and architecture in the lives of disabled people
- Such services should no longer be service-led but provided as a resource with clear access rights for disabled people
- CILs (Centres for Integrated Living; see p. 57 above) which are run by disabled people should provide guidance on all services used by disabled people, including medical, educational, housing and transport services
- Those responsible for providing services for disabled people (the service providers) should place less emphasis on a functional assessment of disability and more emphasis on designing appropriate intervention (service) models. This shift of emphasis would lead to a greater identification with the needs of disabled people and a subsequent removal of barriers
- Civil rights legislation should be enacted to provide a framework for guiding the development of community-based support systems for disabled people living in their own homes, and to ensure both equal opportunities in employment and equal access to education and medical services, housing, leisure, the environment and information

See Fig 3.5 on p. 61 for a summary of formal models of disability.

The social deviancy model of disability

This model depends on the process of *labelling*. An adult who is over 6 feet 8 inches or under 4 feet 6 inches tall may be described as *physically deviant* from the normative height measurement. However, they are not described as *socially deviant* unless their behaviour is equally 'abnormal'. An outstanding musician or scientific genius is described as deviant but is also highly regarded. A person with multiple disabilities, on the other hand, is also deviant but is not regarded as a valuable member of society.

There are two concepts of deviance: *primary* and *secondary*.

PRIMARY DEVIANCE

This concept relates to the labelling of a state of behaviour as deviant. It separates and labels

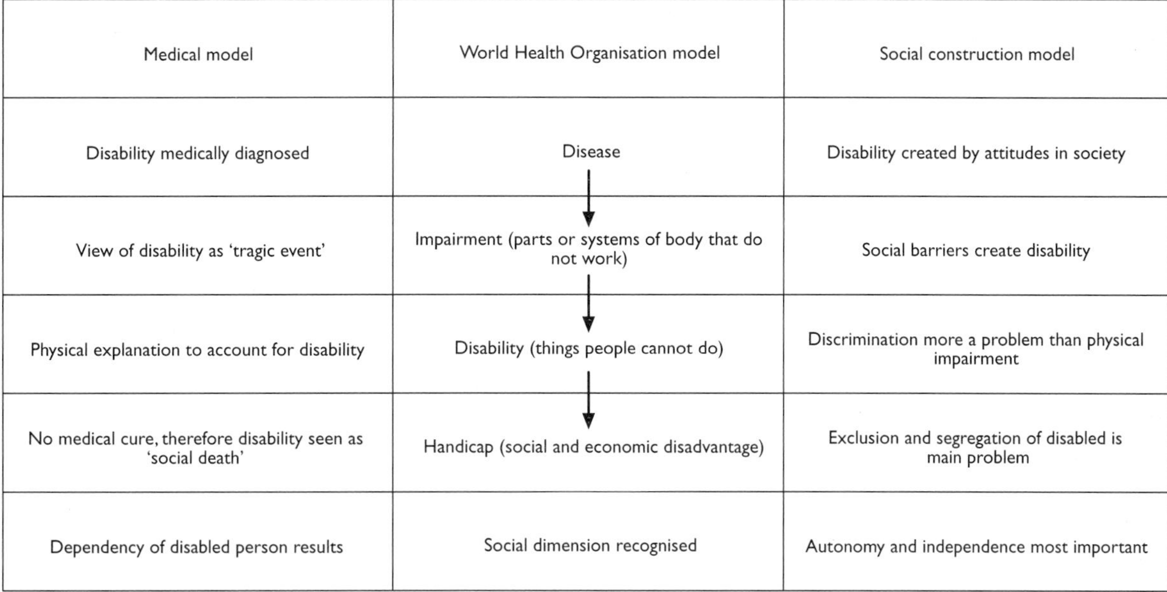

Medical model	World Health Organisation model	Social construction model
Disability medically diagnosed	Disease ↓	Disability created by attitudes in society
View of disability as 'tragic event'	Impairment (parts or systems of body that do not work) ↓	Social barriers create disability
Physical explanation to account for disability	Disability (things people cannot do) ↓	Discrimination more a problem than physical impairment
No medical cure, therefore disability seen as 'social death'	Handicap (social and economic disadvantage)	Exclusion and segregation of disabled is main problem
Dependency of disabled person results	Social dimension recognised	Autonomy and independence most important

Figure 3.5 Formal models of disability – a summary

behaviour according to what is socially acceptable and what is socially unacceptable. One example here is that of *glossolalia*, or 'speaking in unknown tongues'. This is a common feature of religious practices all over the world which usually takes place within a church and at a specified time. To those who believe in glossolalia, it is thought to arise from a supernatural power entering into the individual and controlling the organs of speech. *In context*, this behaviour is socially acceptable and therefore *not* socially deviant. However, if a student in your class were to stand up, close their eyes and start to utter incomprehensible words, their behaviour would then be unacceptable and *would* be classed as socially deviant.

SECONDARY DEVIANCE

This concept relates to the *effect* that the labelling has on the individual's behaviour. Being labelled or stereotyped tends to encourage conformity with the label, thus creating a 'self-fulfilling prophecy'. For example, patients in hospitals who are always referred to by staff as 'difficult and demanding' are more likely to evoke, from the staff who care for them, those kinds of reactions which *perpetuate* the 'difficult' behaviour. Similarly, if a teacher is told that certain children are very intelligent even if they are only of medium ability, those 'labelled' children will achieve better results than children of supposed similar ability.

IMPLICATIONS FOR SERVICE PROVISION

Once labelled, the individual may change their behaviour to conform to the public *stereotype* that fits the label. For example, a man fully recovered from a heart attack may respond to the public image of a 'coronary cripple' by refusing to return to work or to leave the house. The response of health and social care services has been to segregate 'social deviants' into large institutions where they are encouraged to fulfil the role assigned to them. This inevitably leads to *institutionalisation*, where it becomes increasingly difficult for the individuals to function normally outside the home or hospital. The implications are greater for people with learning disabilities and mental illnesses than they are for those with physical disabilities.

The loss of autonomy and independence on the part of people with learning disabilities is often seen to be a necessary consequence of society's need to be protected from those who cannot function adequately in the wider community (care in the community is discussed in Chapter 7).

Personal models of special needs

These models have been developed mainly by those in the nursing profession. They all have the following features:

- they focus on the *individual*
- an *assessment* of the needs of the individual is fundamental to each model
- *health promotion* is an important part of the model

THE INDEPENDENT OR SELF-CARE MODEL

Based on work about self-care nursing by Dorothea Orem, this model advocates allowing people to hold onto the control they would normally have over their own lives as they experience the health care and treatment that they need.

Orem suggests that health depends on a person's ability to be *self-caring*. In order to be self-caring, people need:

- information
- appropriate support
- assistance and help
- to be willing, able and prepared to participate in self-care

Orem describes a number of individual needs which have to be met in order to maintain health. These *universal self-care requisites* are:

- the maintenance of air intake
- the maintenance of food and water intake
- the maintenance of waste elimination
- the balance between activity and rest
- the balance between solitude and social activity
- the prevention of hazards to oneself
- 'being normal'

In addition, there are *developmental self-care requisites* concerned with the specific needs relating to a person's stage of growth, development and life experiences. A third category of self-care requisites relate to the effect of disease, trauma, injury and illness. These are called *health deviation self-care requisites*.

It is important to recognise the difference between self-care and a kind of 'do-it-yourself care' which may, in reality, mean the shifting of responsibility onto others in an inappropriate way.

SELF-HELP GROUPS: AN AUTONOMOUS MODEL

Some diseases and illnesses pose particular problems for care. Health professionals and lay people can provide treatment and help, but this may not always be of the right kind. Self-help groups could be seen as existing to remedy the deficiencies in the National Health Service, although they also often represent an attempt by people with a disability to 'demedicalise' their complaint and to gain *autonomy*, i.e. the power or right of total self-determination.

Features of this model are:

- support and advice are obtained from others with similar conditions
- specialised knowledge is acquired about the particular disease or condition
- funds are raised to enable sponsorship of research into the causes and possible treatment of the condition

Some self-help groups are very successful and number a membership of many thousands. Sometimes the self-help group may be taken over by doctors and used as an extension of the health service, whilst other groups choose to remain wholly independent of medicine, keeping their autonomy but losing any benefits that medicine may confer.

SKILLS FOR DAILY LIVING: A SUPPORTED MODEL

In the 1970s Nancy Roper devised a model for nursing based on 'The activities of daily living'. Drawing on studies in the fields of psychology and sociology, she identified 12

Independent model	Supported model	Autonomous model
Describes self-care requisites	Describes activities of daily living	Self-determination sought through membership of self-help group
People need: –information	External factors recognised : –psychological and emotional	Support and advice (both needs–specific)
–appropriate support	–sociocultural	Specialised knowledge acquired about specific condition
–assistance and help	–environmental	Research often direct result of sponsorship by self-help group
–to be willing and prepared to practise self-care	–political/economic	Often wholly independent of medicine

Figure 3.6 The personal model of special needs – a summary

activities essential to life and, more importantly, to the *quality* of life. Dying is seen as the final activity of living, and each activity can be related to two continua, the first relating to lifespan (conception–death) and the second relating to the level of independence (dependence–independence). These aspects provide a useful way of considering how each activity of daily living is influenced by the age and maturity of the person and their level of dependence or independence.

The activities of daily living

1 *Maintaining a safe environment:*

- comfort, freedom from pain
- avoiding injury and infection, monitoring change

2 *Communicating:*

- verbally and non-verbally
- forming relationships
- expressing emotions, needs, fears, anxieties
- dealing with emotions, positive and negative
- maintaining an awareness of the environment
- using smell, touch, taste, hearing, seeing and sensitivity

3 *Breathing:*

- meeting body oxygen needs
- maintaining a clear airway and lung expansion

4 *Eating and drinking:*

- meeting nutritional needs
- maintaining a healthy diet, appropriate to the individual
- food practicalities: getting food to mouth, chewing, swallowing, appropriate presentation of food
- taking in adequate and suitable fluids

5 *Body functions:*

- passing urine and faeces
- maintaining normal and regular functioning and control

6 *Personal cleansing and dressing:*

- skin, hair, nails, mouth, teeth, eyes, ears
- selecting appropriate clothing
- dressing and undressing

7 *Maintaining normal body temperature:*

- physical temperature
- adjusting clothing and covers
- economic and environmental influences

8 *Mobility:*

- exercising for health
- maintaining muscle tone, circulation
- counteracting the effects of immobility, relieving pressure to skin, changing position, aids to mobility

9 *Working and playing:*

- enjoyment of recreation and pastimes
- sense of achievement, independence;
- partnership in care, rehabilitation

10 *Sexuality:*

- expressing sexuality, fulfilling needs
- reactions to intimate procedures
- reproduction

11 *Resting and sleeping:*

- enjoying a normal sleep pattern
- taking rest as desired
- a restful environment, without stress, noise

12 *Learning:*

- discovering, satisfying curiosity
- gaining knowledge and skills
- awareness of the self as an individual
- learning how to care for the self and maintain health
- accepting realistic and appropriate goals

13 *Religion:*

- according to faith and culture
- freedom not to worship or believe
- movement towards personal spiritual goals, particularly in illness

14 *Dying:*

- as an inevitability
- peacefully, without stress, pain, anxiety
- needs met, needs of importance to others met

This model recognises the importance of the influence of external factors:

- *Physical factors:* the person's particular illness or condition
- *Psychological and emotional factors:* the person's intellectual ability and anxiety or depression will lead to particular needs and priorities; e.g. severe anxiety may adversely affect all the activities of living, and its alleviation will therefore assume a priority
- *Sociocultural factors:* whether or not the person is part of a family, the type of family and the relationships within the family will all influence needs. Similarly, the individual's wider community and the social class to which they belong are very influential
- *Environmental factors:* e.g. a person living in a cold, damp house with an outside toilet will have different needs concerning 'controlling body temperature and eliminating waste' from someone who is more comfortably housed
- *Political/economic factors:* poverty or belonging to a disadvantaged group leads to less choice in day-to-day living

By considering all these factors, we are acknowledging that a person's needs are likely to change according to different circumstances, and that any assessment of needs must involve this understanding of the wider context in which we all live.

Models of residential care

THE WAREHOUSING MODEL

The main purpose of this form of residential care is to prolong physical life. Staff are employed to provide physical care, such as feeding, washing and toileting clients, in a routine manner. The term 'warehousing' likens client care to the storage of furniture in a warehouse; clients are encouraged to be *dependent* and *depersonalised*. Any assertion of independence by clients is discouraged because it would disrupt the primary routine task of physical care. Some elderly persons' homes still exhibit this kind of care: chairs arranged in rows with understimulated occupants.

THE HORTICULTURAL MODEL

The main purpose of this form of care is the opposite to that of warehousing: the client is positively encouraged to become *independent*. The main task is to develop the individual's potential. This is normally attempted through organising social activities and providing a 'home-like' environment. Clients who are mentally confused or who have learning disabilities are encouraged to interact with others and to become more independent.

THE NORMALISATION MODEL

This model was proposed by Wolfensberger in 1972 (see Bond and Bond 1994), and as its name implies, it emphasises the need to integrate people into the wider society – to provide as normal a life as possible, often in small 'sheltered' group homes where support is provided by a professional care worker. The practice of putting elderly people and people with disabilities into institutions led to their being undervalued and stereotyped. It also perpetuated the notion that people with disabilities have less right to be valued for themselves than do others.

THE SOCIAL ROLE VALORISATION MODEL

Wolfensberger later refined and renamed the normalisation model as that of *social role valorisation*. Key features of this model are that:

- people with learning disabilities should not be hidden away but be part of the wider community
- individuals should be encouraged to develop their skills and so increase their confidence at functioning in 'normal' situations
- people with learning disabilities should be encouraged to understand their situation and to make their own decisions and choices

Table 3.1 Models of Residential Care – A Summary

Model of Care	Main Features	Effects on clients or patients
Warehousing model	Physical care seen as paramount. Care is given according to a set routine, which may ignore the social and emotional needs of the recipient	Clients or patients become dependent and depersonalised
Horticultural model	Every effort is made to provide an environment as close to a 'real home' as possible. Developing the client's full potential is paramount	Clients or patients enjoy a range of social activities and are encouraged to become more independent
Normalisation model	Life for the 'resident' should be as near normal as possible; ideally, people are integrated into society by providing small units or homes with professional support	Clients or patients experience higher self-esteem and feel themselves to be part of the wider environment
Social role valorisation model	Similar to normalisation model, but with more emphasis on the development of skills for living and the need for a radical change in attitudes to those with learning disabilities	Clients or patients enjoy maximum possible independence and increased confidence in their own abilities

- individuals should participate fully in society and have a wide network of relationships
- society must value and respect people with learning disabilities rather than viewing them as second-class citizens

This model has been influential in shaping the current policy of care in the community, but most experts in the field would agree that attitudes and stereotyping take a long time to change.

DISABILITY AND DISCRIMINATION

Having a physical disability means living in society as part of a *minority group* whose particular needs are not adequately recognised or taken into account, and whose different appearance often leads to its being treated differently and less equally. Of course, not all disabilities are readily recognisable as such; for example, deafness, epilepsy or diabetes are not immediately obvious.

The following are all attitudes commonly encountered by disabled people from able-bodied people:

- *Stereotype:* a term used when certain characteristics of any given group are applied to all the individuals within that group. The logo denoting access for disabled people is a sign showing a person in a wheelchair, yet less than 5% of the 6 million people with disabilities in the UK use wheelchairs
- *Dependency:* the assumption of dependency on the part of people who have a disability can take the form of trying to be helpful without being asked and thus invading the privacy of the disabled person's life, as Enid described in the following incident:

Another time, I tried to go and see Leonardo da Vinci cartoons at The Royal Academy. We drove into London, found a parking place and all that palaver. There was a huge queue, and this terrible man ran out, grabbed my wheelchair and said 'Mind out for the wheelchair!' I would have been quite prepared to queue. He shoved us right up to the front.

We go in, and the head person in charge said 'Oh, wheelchairs were yesterday.' And I wasn't politically aware enough to fight him. He wouldn't let me in to see them. And I've never gone back there. I really should have written a letter of protest. *Now*, I would . . .

(Swain, Finkelstein, French and Oliver 1993)

- *Hostility:* this may take the form of loud comments being made about the disabled person, or aggression
- *Exclusion:* physical or intellectual differences make disabled people less than human in the eyes of non-disabled people; they can be excluded from normal human activity because they are 'not normally human'
- *Invasion of privacy:* the attitudes of others to those with a disability which is highly visible is often one of well-meant over-chumminess, or worse, expressions of revulsion. In these ways, privacy is invaded and the person's body is made public property
- *Patronage:* e.g. the humiliation of people: talking to the disabled person's able-bodied companions as if the disabled person would not be able to understand what is being said (see Figure 3.7).

ACTIVITY

This activity involves an investigation of discrimination against the disabled: its forms and effects, and possible ways of preventing it. In particular you will need to find out about:

- the different forms which discrimination may take
- the ways in which people are affected by the experience of discrimination

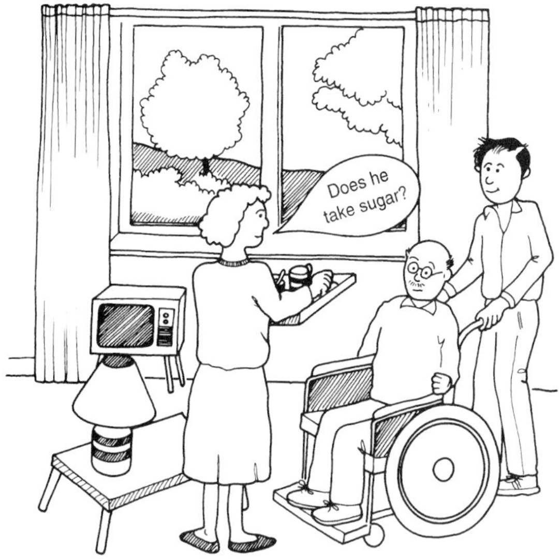

Figure 3.7 The patronising attitude towards disability

Stage 1

(a) As a whole group, and with the help of your teacher, research and discuss ideas for designing, carrying out and analysing a survey into people's attitudes towards and experiences of discrimination and disability. You will be expected to work constructively within the group, participating in discussion and suggesting ideas.

Stage 2

(a) In small groups, write down ideas for questions to ask as part of this survey. These questions will then be collated into a pilot survey.

(b) As a whole group, share the task of piloting the survey and redesigning questions where necessary. Produce a final version of this survey.

Stage 3

(a) As a whole group, share the task of administering the survey to the sample decided upon.

(b) Play an active part in designing and using an observation sheet to collect the data generated by the survey. Working within the whole group, collate and present the results of the survey as a wall display, using different modes of representation such as tables, graphs and scales.

Stage 4

(a) Complete, individually, a written report (along guidelines set by your teacher or using the guidelines set out below) which

- analyses and interprets the results of the class survey
- suggests ways in which discrimination against people with disabilities may be prevented.

Stage 5

(a) Interview in depth (on tape or on video) three separate individuals of different ages concerning their views about experiences of (or both) discrimination relating to

- gender
- age
- race

or a combination of two or more of these factors.

(b) Write a summary of these interviews (including the questions you asked). Compare the views and experiences you found out about.

(c) Prepare a short (3–5 minutes) video presentation of this summary, briefly describing the interviews and what you learned from them. This video will be shown to the rest of the group.

Stage 6

Individually, complete an evaluation sheet to say how the investigation went, how each member of the group (including yourself) contributed to the tasks and what you learned.

Guidelines for a written report on the survey investigating people's attitudes towards and experiences of discrimination and disability

1 *Why did you carry out this survey? What were you looking for?* To answer these questions, look at the questions you asked in the survey. What did you want to know?

2 *How did you carry out this survey? What methods did you use?* To answer these questions, explain exactly how you did the survey. How did we decide on the questions? What was the pilot survey for? How many people did you ask, and why? Did you ask people to fill in the questionnaires, or did you do it for them? Did you have different types of questions? If so, why?

3 *What did the results of the survey show?* To answer this, explain each of them using the display of graphs and tables or your copies of these, or both. Write a summary of the results of each question in the survey. Say what the results show and what they might imply about disabilities and discrimination. Try to explain this and account for each of the results.

4 *If you had a chance to do a survey like this again, how would you improve it?* To answer this, say what you think you could have done to improve this survey. Could you have improved the methods you used or the questions you asked? If so, how? What could have been done better or differently? Could you have made more use of the results in any way? Did you actually find any useful or interesting information? Try to think of at least three ways in which the survey could have been improved, and explain each one carefully.

5 *Does the survey give you ideas about how discrimination against people with disabilities might be prevented?* Explain these ideas.

Why carry out a survey into disability and discrimination?

We can answer this question by looking at the survey carried out by the Royal Institute for the Blind in 1991. This was the first survey of people with visual handicaps. They interviewed 600 people and found that:

- nearly 1 million people could register as blind or partially sighted – a far higher number than government estimates
- four out of five blind people of working age are unemployed
- nearly half of the visually impaired live on their own; 26% of these say that they are *never* visited by friends or neighbours
- many of the people interviewed reported that they faced both direct and indirect discrimination when applying for work
- most blind people live on an income of less than £70 a week

ACTIVITY

Study the summary above of the RNIB's survey findings. Discuss why these survey results might be useful and important.

CAUSES OF DISABILITY

There are three main ways in which a person can become disabled:

- *congenital*, when a faulty gene leads to a disabling condition
- *developmental*, when the foetus is growing in the womb
- *through illness or accident*, affecting individuals who are born with no disability

Hereditary and congenital factors

Many of the disorders listed below can now be diagnosed prenatally, thus enabling

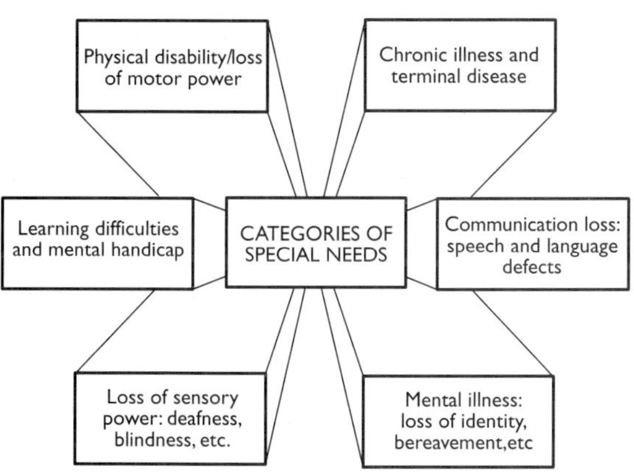

Figure 3.8 Categories of special needs

prospective parents to decide on a course of action.

Growth and development of the embryo and foetus are controlled by genes. Abnormal genes cause abnormal growth and development.

DOMINANT GENE DEFECTS

A parent with a *dominant gene defect* has a 50% chance of passing the defect on to each of their children. Examples of dominant gene defects are:

- *tuberous sclerosis* (a disorder affecting the skin and nervous system)
- *achondroplasia* (once called dwarfism)
- *Huntington's chorea* (a disorder of the central nervous system)

RECESSIVE GENE DEFECTS

These defects are only inherited if *two* recessive genes meet. Therefore if both parents carry a single *recessive gene defect*, there is a one in four chance that each of their children will be affected. Examples of defects transmitted this way are:

- *cystic fibrosis* (detailed below)
- *sickle-cell anaemia* (a blood disorder)
- *phenylketonuria* (a defective-enzyme disorder)
- *thalassaemia* (a blood disorder)
- *Tay-Sachs disease* (a disorder of the nervous system)
- *Friedreich's ataxia* (a disorder of the spinal cord)

X-LINKED RECESSIVE GENE DEFECTS

In these conditions, the defective gene is on the X-chromosome and usually leads to outward abnormality in males only. Women can be carriers of the defect, and half their sons may be affected.

Examples are:

- *haemophilia* (prevents normal blood clotting)

Dominant gene defects	Recessive gene defects	X-linked gene defects
tuberous sclerosis achondroplasia Huntington's chorea neurofibromatosis Marfan's syndrome	cystic fibrosis Friedreich's ataxia phenylketonuria sickle-cell anaemia Tay–Sachs disease thalassaemia	haemophilia Christmas disease 'fragile X' syndrome muscular dystrophy – Duchenne type colour blindness most types
Unaffected parent ○○ / Affected parent ○△	Unaffected parent (carrier) ○△ / Unaffected parent (carrier) ○△	Carrier mother (X)● / Unaffected father (Y)(X)
Unaffected child ○○ – I in 2 chance Affected child ○△ – I in 2 chance	Unaffected child ○○ – I in 4 chance Unaffected child (carrier) ○△ – I in 4 chance Unaffected child (carrier) ○△ – I in 4 chance affected child △△ – I in 4 chance	Unaffected boy (X)(Y) – I in 4 chance Affected boy ●(Y) – I in 4 chance Unaffected girl (X)(X) – I in 4 chance Unaffected girl (carrier) ●(X) – I in 4 chance
Key: △ = defective gene; ○ = normal gene	● = normal x chromosome	(X) = defective x chromosome; (Y) = y chromosome

Figure 3.9 A summary of genetic defects and their pattern of inheritance

- *Christmas disease* (mild form of haemophilia)
- *'Fragile X' syndrome* (causes mental subnormality)
- *muscular dystrophy* (Duchenne type) (wasting of muscle fibres)

ACTIVITY

1 In pairs, each choose a different one of the genetic and chromosomal disorders listed above and research it in preparation for a talk which you will present to the rest of your class. Use the following guidelines to help you structure the talk:

- what your chosen disorder is
- causes and incidence (using charts)
- how it is diagnosed/genetic screening availability
- effects
- treatment and care needs

2 The presentation may be recorded on video, assessed on a verbal presentation or graded as a written assignment (or both), and then placed in a fact file to be used as a class resource.

NB: The teacher/lecturer could allow three to four weeks for preparation of the talk so that students have time to write off for relevant information to specialist groups (see the Useful Addresses section at the end of this chapter).

CHROMOSOMAL DEFECTS

These vary considerably in the severity of their effect on the individual. About one in every 200 babies born alive has a chromosomal abnormality, i.e. the structure or number of chromosomes varies from normal. Among foetuses that have been

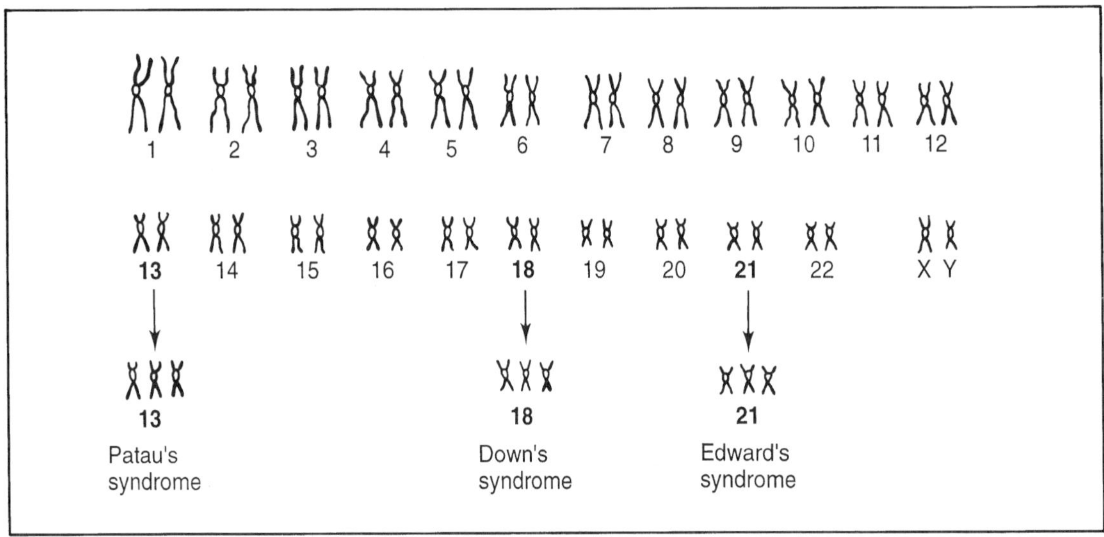

Figure 3.10 Types of trisomy. In all trisomies, a child has three, instead of the usual two, chromosomes of a particular number. Down's syndrome is by far the most common trisomy

spontaneously aborted, about one in two has such an abnormality. This suggests that most chromosomal abnormalities are incompatible with life, and that those seen in babies born alive are generally the less serious ones.

Examples of defects transmitted this way are:

- *Down's syndrome* (trisomy 21): this results in short stature as well as mental handicap and an increased susceptibility to infection
- *Klinefelter's syndrome* (47xxy): boys are very tall with hypogonadism
- *Turner's syndrome* (45xo): girls have ovarian dysgenesis, webbed neck and broad chest; they may also have cardiac malfunctions
- *Cri du chat syndrome:* a very rare condition in which a portion of one particular chromosome is missing in each of the affected individual's cells

Genetic counselling is available for anyone with a child or other member of the family with a chromosomal abnormality, and chromosome analysis is offered in early pregnancy.

THE DISABLED CHILD AND THE FAMILY

When a mother gives birth to a baby who has a handicap, she may experience feelings of guilt – 'It must be because of something I did wrong during pregnancy' – or even of rejection, albeit temporary. Research shows that the mothers of blind babies withdrew from them because they did not make eye contact and were therefore unresponsive. Such an experience can seriously interfere with the normal bonding process.

Bonding is the formation of special and very deep attachments, and occurs as a result of the intensity of the relationship between the baby and the primary carer. The main attachment is generally with the mother and father, but it is possible for other bonds to be formed, e.g. with a nanny, nursery worker or grandparent. A lack of bonding in the early years may lead to a child feeling emotionally insecure.

The following article was written by a mother whose third child has Down's syndrome. It describes her and her husband's feelings immediately after the birth.

A MOTHER CELEBRATES THE BIRTHDAY OF A VERY SPECIAL BABY

My third child was born just before Christmas, a beautiful baby boy with squashy fingers and crinkly ears. I was overjoyed – and relieved. I was 37 and the triple test had given me a slightly worrying result. Carried out in pregnancy, it uses a sample of blood to estimate your chances of having a baby with Down's syndrome. Women scoring 1/250 or less are considered high risk and offered an amniocentesis. I scored 1/260, so had no further tests.

I tried to pick the baby up but the umbilical cord was very short. He was reluctant to feed but after much persuasion took the breast. He lay in my arms, a curiously serene little bundle with a dusting of fine hair. I couldn't wait to get him home but the doctor said they would carry out some routine tests because of his initial refusal to feed . . .

The paediatrician arrived just as we decided to call the baby Euan. He let the baby slip through his fingers, stroking the back of his head with a practised hand. Sitting on the bed, he glanced at John, then back at me. 'Here comes the tricky bit,' he said calmly. 'I think your baby's got Down's syndrome.' He went over the telltale signs – the short umbilical cord, stubby fingers, low-set ears, poor muscle tone. We listened numbly, unable to comprehend that the nightmare had come true: there was something wrong with the baby.

As John leant over the cot and kissed the sleeping child, I realised I was crying, great sheets of tears moving slowly down my face. Inside I felt cold, hard, cruel. The paediatrician kept on talking, as if his words were a charm to keep our suffering at bay.

'. . . There's nothing *wrong* with this baby, he's just different. He's not suffering, you are. He'll be in touch with things we aren't.' He made it sound as if anyone in their right mind would have Down's syndrome.

'What about intelligence?' I asked sharply. 'Only intelligent people worry about intelligence.'

He correctly predicted the emotions we would feel: grief for the child we thought we would have, sorrow for the disastrous human being we thought he would be . . .

John went home to see the children and I was left alone with the baby who didn't belong to me but Mr and Mrs Down's syndrome. He didn't bear our features but theirs, his personality rose from their union, not mine and John's.

They offered to take him to the nursery but I refused, terrified that in his absence I would reject him. I had to keep him close, make him mine once more. Waking in the dead of night, I stared into his sleeping face. He almost frightened me, this tiny, alien being wearing a mask which separated him from the rest of humanity. He was branded, set apart and now so was I. Stroking his head, I felt an agony of guilt, pity and fear. I had done this to him, I had blighted the flower before it had a chance to bloom. What terrible blackness inside me had afflicted my own child?

Later on they struggled to take blood from a vein in his head and I felt upset in a remote kind of way, the needle made him cry out. He was given a heart scan and I watched curious about my own reactions. Did I want him to be healthy? Would it be better if he slipped away now? . . . The scan was normal. I took Euan home, just in time for the parties.

Twelve months later, it's nearly Christmas again . . . Euan plays near the foot of the Christmas tree; he has slanted eyes, sticky-out ears and a tongue that pops from his mouth like the label of a collar which refuses to lie flat. He might not go to primary school, let alone university, but every time he smiles – which he does all the time – my heart turns over.

. . . Euan has taught me so many things: that the ability to communicate is more important than IQ and may have nothing to do with it, and that creating love in others is so simple, a child can do it. Try as I might, I can't feel tragic about a baby who shakes with silent laughter as his sister wraps tinsel round his head. Most of all, Euan has made me realise just how much we underestimate our capacity for loving.

Every woman who gives birth to a handicapped child does so in a climate of rejection and fear. Yet even as I struggled to come to terms with Euan's birth, I continued to bond with my baby.

In the end, loving him was as easy and – I cannot emphasise this word enough – as natural as falling off a log. Loving Euan, I find I like myself better too . . . When next you see the parents of a handicapped child, don't automatically feel sorry for them, because you have absolutely no idea what they are feeling.

(Pat Evans in the Guardian, *16 December 1992)*

Activity

Read the above extract and answer the following questions:

1 Do you think that the paediatrician showed understanding when he told the parents that their new-born baby had Down's syndrome? Give reasons for your answer.

2 Why does the author say that 'every woman who gives birth to a handicapped child does so in a climate of rejection and fear'?

3 Research the condition Down's syndrome, including the following points:

- the cause
- the incidence in the UK and worldwide
- the characteristics of a child with Down's syndrome
- the prognosis and help available

Developmental factors

The first three months (the first *trimester*) of a pregnancy are when the foetus is particularly sensitive. The lifestyle of the pregnant woman

Figure 3.11 Doing what comes naturally – a mother and a baby with Down's Syndrome

affects the health of the baby in her womb. Important factors are:

- a healthy diet
- the avoidance of alcohol and other drugs
- not smoking
- regular, appropriate exercise

Rubella ('German measles') is especially harmful to the developing foetus as it can cause deafness, blindness and mental retardation. All girls in the UK are now immunised against rubella before they reach childbearing age, and this measure has drastically reduced the incidence of rubella-damaged babies.

Thalidomide was a drug widely prescribed during the 1960s to alleviate morning sickness in pregnant women. Unfortunately, it was found to cause limb deformities in many of the babies born to women who had used the drug, and was withdrawn in 1961.

Toxoplasmosis is an infection caused by the protozoan *Toxoplasma gondii*. It may be contracted by the pregnant woman eating undercooked meat (usually pork) from infected animals, or by poor hygiene after handling cats or their faeces. In about one-third of cases, toxoplasmosis is transmitted to the child and may cause blindness, hydrocephalus or mental retardation. Infection in late pregnancy usually has no ill-effects.

Irradiation: If a woman is X-rayed in early pregnancy, or if she receives radiotherapy for the treatment of cancer, the embryo may suffer abnormalities. Radiation damage may also result from atomic radiation or radioactive fallout (following a nuclear explosion or leak from a nuclear reactor). There is also an increased risk of the child developing leukaemia in later life after exposure to radiation.

ACTIVITY

1 Find out all you can about

(a) *amniocentesis*
(b) the *AFP Blood Test*
(c) *Chorionic Villus Sampling*
(d) *Ultrasound*

For each, answer the following questions:

- What is it?
- What conditions can be detected?
- What are the risks?

The Association of Spina Bifida and Hydrocephalus produces an information sheet on antenatal screening.

2 Spina bifida is a congenital defect in which part of one or more vertebrae fails to develop completely, leaving a portion of the spinal cord exposed.

- Describe the three forms of spina bifida
- What is hydrocephalus and how is it treated?

Cerebral palsy

This is the general term for disorders of movement and posture resulting from damage to a child's developing brain in the later months of pregnancy, during birth, in the neonatal period, or in early childhood. It affects two to three children in every 1,000 – in the UK, about 1,500 babies are born with or develop the condition each year – and it can affect both boys and girls, and people from all races and social backgrounds.

Its most common cause is cerebral hypoxia (poor oxygen supply to the brain) during pregnancy or around the time of birth, and its effects may include, in varying degrees of severity:

- slow, awkward or jerky movements
- stiffness
- weakness
- muscle spasms
- floppiness
- unwanted (involuntary) movements

The start of one movement often results in other unwanted movements. Some children develop certain patterns of movement.

SENSORY IMPAIRMENT

This is the general name given to the group of disabilities which involve disorders of the senses: sight, hearing, touch, taste or smell.

Blindness and partial sight

The picture of total darkness conjured up by the word 'blindness' is inaccurate: only about 18% of blind people in the UK are affected to this degree; the other 82% all have some remaining sight. In the UK, there are just over one million blind and partially sighted people, of whom 40% are blind and 60% partially sighted.

CAUSES OF VISUAL IMPAIRMENT

The main causes of visual impairment are:

- anomalies of the eyes from birth, such as *cataracts* (cloudiness of the lens)
- *nystagmus* (involuntary jerkiness of the eyes)
- *optic atrophy* (damage to the optic nerve)
- *retinopathy of prematurity* (the abnormal development of retinas in premature babies)
- hereditary factors such as *Retinoblastoma* (a tumour of the retina which is often inherited)
- *rubella* (German measles) in pregnancy
- *glaucoma* (excessive pressure in the eyeball which causes degeneration of nerve fibres at the front end of the optic nerve)
- *diabetes mellitus* and *hypertension* (which can cause bleeding into the cavity of the eyeball)

Childhood glaucoma and diabetic retinopathy are quite rare in children, but are common causes of visual impairment in adults.

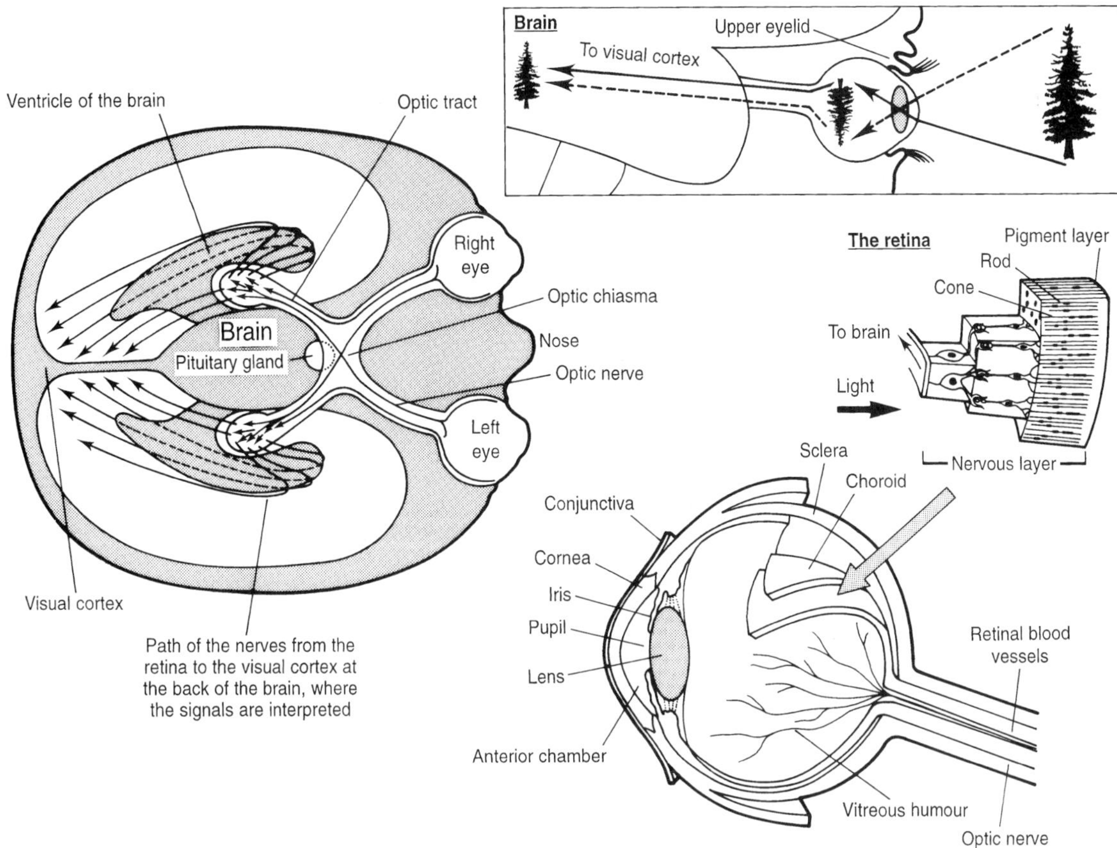

Figure 3.12 The eye and how it works

TREATMENT

Some conditions which cause visual impairment are treatable, particularly if detected at an early stage. For example:

- Glaucoma can be halted by medical or surgical means
- Cataracts may be removed by removal of the lens

Laser therapy is also now being used to correct various visual defects.

EDUCATION AND TRAINING

More than 55% of visually impaired children in school attend mainstream schools along with sighted children, where most will receive a *Statement of Special Educational Needs* which details the support and special equipment they need. These facilities are provided by the school, with advice and support from the Local Education Authority Visual Impairment Service, and from other sources of information, advice and training such as The Royal National Institute for the Blind (RNIB). Many move on to further-education colleges and universities, using special grants to enable them to pay for readers and to buy special tape recorders to help them in their studies.

Specialist counselling and vocational training are available for those of working age, and may be accessed through local authorities, the RNIB and colleges of further education.

ACTIVITY

1 *An exercise in empathy*
The following exercise cannot give a real experience of blindness, but may help to promote understanding.

- In pairs, one student ties a blindfold (e.g. a scarf) around the eyes and the other student escorts them around the school or college
- On return, the sighted one offers the 'blind' person a drink and a sandwich
- The two students then swap roles

After the exercise, evaluate the activity: how did it feel to be so reliant on someone else? How did it feel, on the other hand, to be *responsible* for someone else? Draw up a list of practical points to help future students offering refreshment and guidance to someone who is blind.

2 Find out about the aids available for those with visual impairment, including the Braille alphabet.

Deafness and partial hearing

Deafness is often called the 'hidden disability'. As with blindness, *total* deafness is rare and is usually *congenital* (i.e. present from birth). *Partial deafness* is generally the result of an ear disease, injury or degeneration associated with the *ageing process*.

There are two types of deafness:

- *conductive* – when there is faulty transmission of sound from the outer ear to the inner ear
- *sensorineural* – when sounds that *do* reach the inner ear fail to be transmitted to the brain

CAUSES OF CONDUCTIVE DEAFNESS

- Earwax – some people experience a build-up of *cerumen*, a waxy discharge, which can form a plug in the eardrum
- *Otosclerosis* – the stapes loses its normal mobility (see Figure 3.13)
- *Otitis media* – infection of the middle ear (common in children)

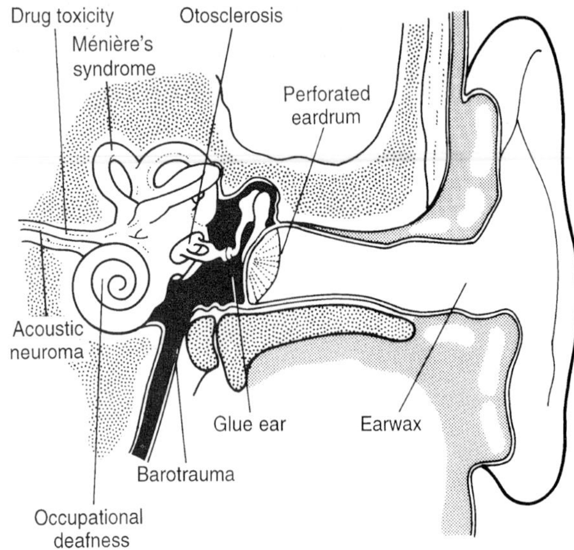

Figure 3.13 Some possible causes of deafness, showing the part of the ear affected

- *Glue ear* – a childhood complaint where there is a build-up of sticky fluid in the middle ear

CAUSES OF SENSORINEURAL DEAFNESS

- *Heredity* – there may be an inherited fault in a chromosome
- *Birth injury*
- *Rubella* – there may be damage to the developing foetus if the mother is infected with the rubella (German measles) virus during pregnancy
- *Severe jaundice* – in the new-born baby with severe jaundice, there may be damage to the inner ear
- *Damage to the cochlea or labyrinth (or both)* – e.g. resulting from injury, viral infection or prolonged exposure to loud noise
- *Meniere's disease* – a rare disorder in which deafness, vertigo and *tinnitus* result from the accumulation of fluid within the labyrinth in the inner ear

DIAGNOSIS

Hearing tests are performed as part of a routine assessment of child development. Early detection of any hearing defect is vital in order that the best possible help be offered at the time when development is at its fastest.

ACTIVITY

Arrange to visit the local child health clinic or invite a health visitor to college. Find out the following information:

(a) How and when are hearing tests carried out?
(b) If the child 'fails' a test, how is a follow-up test carried out, and by whom?
(c) How many operations for glue ear (*myringotomy and insertion of grommets*) are carried out in your district health authority each year?

TREATMENT

For conductive hearing loss:

- syringing of the ear in the case of earwax
- surgical correction of the defect
- a hearing aid

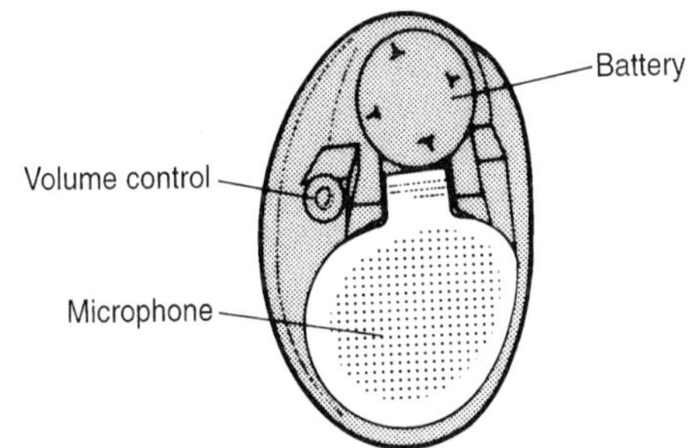

Figure 3.14 A hearing aid

For sensorineural hearing loss:

- a hearing aid
- special training:
  (a) language acquisition
  (b) auditory training
  (c) speech therapy
  (d) perceptual motor training

See Figure 3.15 on p. 78 for the standard manual spelling alphabet.

PROBLEMS ASSOCIATED WITH HEARING IMPAIRMENTS

- *Communication* – if possible, children should learn to express themselves through a recognisable speech pattern (language acquisition). *Isolation* may result from the deaf child's inability to hear the familiar voices and household noises that the hearing child takes for granted
- *Lack of auditory stimulation* may lead to delayed developmental growth
- *Potential for injury* – related to the failure to detect warning sounds
- *Anxiety and coping difficulties* – related to reduced social interaction
- *Parental anxiety* – related to having a child with impaired hearing

ACTIVITY

Care Plan
A 6-year-old child, Laura, is admitted to hospital for a *tonsillectomy* (surgical removal of the tonsils). She has a severe hearing impairment of the sensorineural type. Draw up a list of questions you should ask the parents to enable a specific *Care Plan* to be formulated. Some guidelines to follow:

- Work out how to ensure continuity of care from home to hospital so as to minimise frustration and fear for Laura
- Use the Activities of Living model (p. 63) to ensure that all her needs will be met

ILLNESS AND ACCIDENT

Illness and accident are the main causes of disability for those born with no *inherent* problems. In developing countries, dietary deficiencies such as *rickets* and *pellagra* can lead to disability, and common childhood illnesses such as measles may result in permanent damage to the child. *Poliomyelitis* (an infectious disease causing muscle wasting and paralysis) is still endemic in many areas of the world today, but has been eradicated in the UK by widespread immunisation.

Accidents in the home, on the roads and at work are also still a major cause of disability.

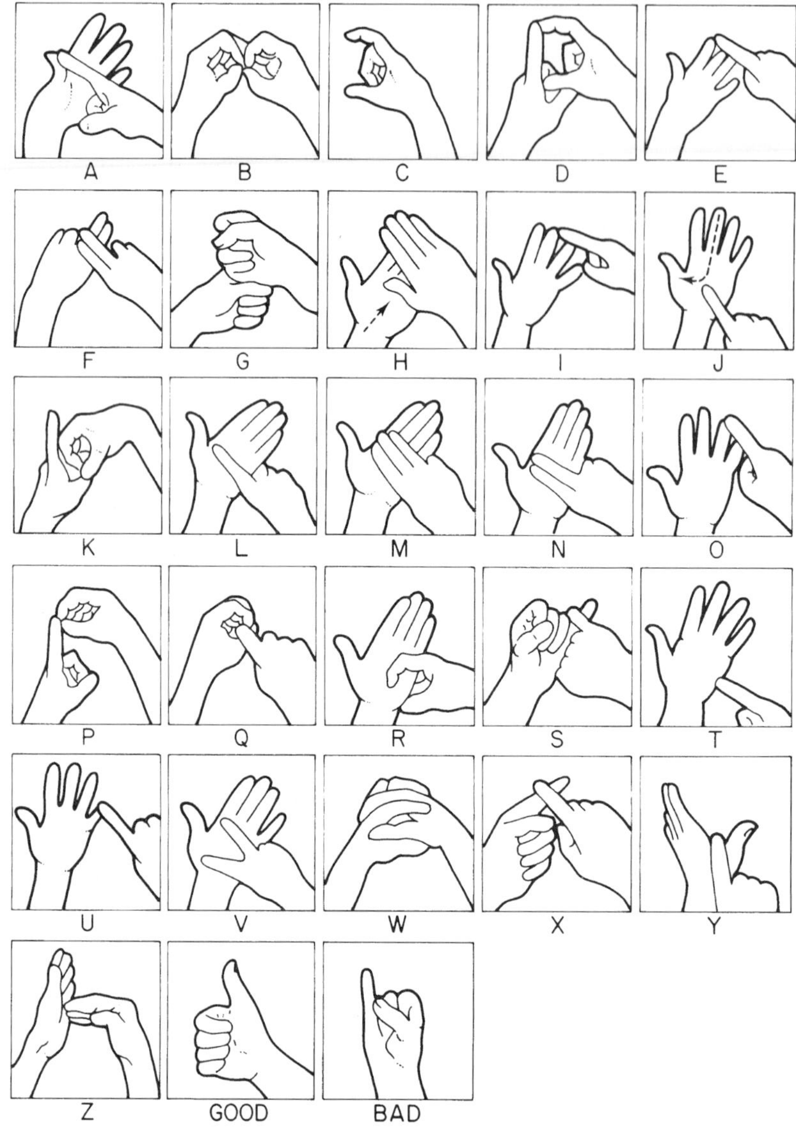

Figure 3.15 The standard manual spelling alphabet ('finger spelling')
Source: Stopford, V. (1987) *Understanding Disability*, Edward Arnold.

Other disabling conditions

There are many diseases and disorders which occur after birth, with varying effects on the individual. These include:

- Alzheimer's disease
- Parkinson's disease
- poliomyelitis
- rickets
- asthma
- coeliac disease
- diabetes
- emphysema
- motor neurone disease (MND)
- myasthenia gravis
- osteoarthritis
- psoriasis
- rheumatoid arthritis
- stroke (cerebrovascular accident)
- autism
- cystic fibrosis
- eczema
- epilepsy
- muscular dystrophy
- incontinence
- Paget's disease

- tinnitus
- brittle bone disease
- ankylosing spondylitis
- dyslexia
- spinal cord injury

ACTIVITY

Your lecturer can number the conditions listed above and allocate them randomly to you for individual project work.

1 Find out all you can about the condition selected:

- what it is
- causes, or theories on causes
- its effects on the individual
- where to go for advice and help

2 Prepare a booklet on the condition suitable for the newly diagnosed person or their family (or both). Presentation is important and will benefit from the use of illustrations.

Resources

- lay medical books, e.g. the British Medical Association's *Complete Family Health*
- encyclopaedias
- a reference library
- information from support groups and associations (see 'Useful Addresses' at the end of the chapter)

CASE STUDY: PETER

Peter Hayward is 65 years old and lives with his wife, Doreen, in a Victorian terraced house that belongs to the water authority, where Peter worked until two years ago as a machine operator. He had joined the Water Board, as it was then known, as a 15-year-old apprentice, and fully expected to retire at the age of 65. Two years ago, however, Peter collapsed suddenly while working on his allotment. He was rushed to hospital, and it was found that he had suffered a stroke. He now has a left hemiplegia (paralysis of the left side of the body) and dysarthria (difficulty in articulating speech).

Doreen had always worked as a shop assistant in the local supermarket, but has had to give up her job in order to look after Peter. The Haywards have no children but are popular members of their community and still take an interest in the local church. Doreen is not able to help Peter meet all his needs, but wants to do as much as she can and is very grateful for all the help she receives. Recently, Doreen herself has not been feeling well: her back aches and she has put on quite a lot of weight since giving up work.

Peter can manage to get around the house by using a tripod walking aid. His speech is greatly improved but he still becomes frustrated at his inability to say what he means to say. He has always been independent, and he is now worried for Doreen's health as she looks so tired all the time. Peter's main hobby is gardening, and he misses the companionship of his allotment friends – he feels 'cooped up' since they decided to move his bed downstairs.

Peter's package of care includes visits from a district nurse and a home care assistant, and his needs were originally assessed by an occupational therapist. Both Peter and Doreen feel they need a holiday as the past two years have been stressful, but they don't know whether going on holiday might in itself be *more* stressful.

ACTIVITY

Read the above case study on Peter.

1 What are the main problems for Peter? And for Doreen?

2 How could the quality of their lives be improved?

3 Think of ways in which voluntary organisations could help.

4 Research strokes or cerebrovascular accidents:

- What actually happens in the brain during a stroke?
- What is the frequency of strokes? Are men or women more likely to suffer a stroke, and at what age is it likely to occur?
- Can strokes be prevented, and do some lifestyles or activities predispose certain people to suffer strokes?

5 Prepare a fact sheet that outlines the help available from private and voluntary organisations.

Multiple sclerosis

Multiple sclerosis (MS), sometimes referred to as *disseminated sclerosis*, is a disease which affects the brain and the spinal cord, which are together known as the *central nervous system* (CNS) (see Thomson et al. 1995, Chapter 3, pp. 140 & 150). The damage to the CNS in this condition occurs in many widely scattered places (multiple = many), and the damaged area is filled with hard material or scars (sclerosis = scars); see Figure 3.16.

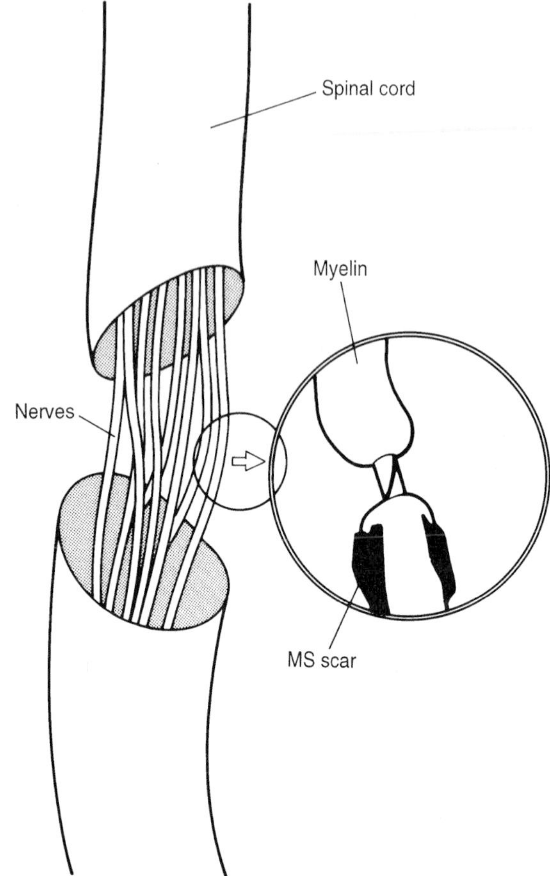

Figure 3.16 A diagram of the spinal cord, showing the scarring effect of multiple sclerosis on the nerves

INCIDENCE

MS is the most common *acquired* disease of the nervous system in young adults. It is a disease largely found in temperate countries where approximately one in every 1,000 people is affected. Women are more likely to acquire MS than men – the ratio of female:male is 3:2.

FEATURES

The course and severity of multiple sclerosis vary considerably from person to person, but it is generally slowly progressive. There may be alternating periods of *remissions* (when symptoms are mild or absent) and *relapses* (when symptoms are present and often severe in effect). Areas affected are:

- *Vision:* this may become blurred; there may be double vision or *nystagmus* (involuntary movement of the eyes from side to side)
- *Movement:* damage to the spinal cord may lead to tingling, numbness or a feeling of constriction in any part of the body. The extremities (arms and legs) may feel heavy and become weak. *Spasticity* (increased rigidity) and paralysis sometimes develop
- *Coordination:* if the nerve fibres in the brain stem are affected, there may be loss of balance, loss of coordination and double vision
- *Sensation:* when the nerve fibres which carry the impulses for sensation are involved, there may be areas of numbness or a feeling of pins-and-needles in the skin
- *Continence:* if the spinal cord is severely damaged, urinary incontinence develops due to loss of sphincter control in the bladder
- *Emotions:* mood changes are common; there

may be depression or euphoria (a state of confident well-being, or both)

Many people with MS find that the emotional and psychological problems that go with having the disease are a worse handicap than the disease itself, and more difficult to handle than the physical defects.

DIAGNOSIS

There is no single diagnostic test for multiple sclerosis. A neurologist may perform a *lumbar puncture* (removal of a sample of fluid from the spinal canal for laboratory analysis), a *CT scan* (computer-aided X-rays) or *MRI* (magnetic resonance imaging) to exclude other disorders and to arrive at the correct diagnosis.

CAUSES

The cause of multiple sclerosis is unknown, but there are many theories, including:

- *Auto-immune disorder:* the body's defence system starts to treat the *myelin* sheath (which protects the nerve fibres) as foreign tissue, and so destroys it
- *A genetic factor:* relatives of affected people are eight times more likely than others to contract the disease
- *Environmental factors:* MS is five times more common in temperate zones (e.g. Europe and the USA) than in the tropics
- *Viral:* an unknown virus may be contracted by a susceptible person and later give rise to MS

TREATMENT

There is no known cure or treatment for MS, but Judy Graham in her excellent book *Multiple Sclerosis* suggests the following approach to managing the illness:

- Eat a healthy, low-fat diet
- Supplement the diet with essential fatty acids (evening primrose oil) plus vitamins and minerals
- Take daily exercise or physiotherapy
- Maintain a positive attitude to life
- Keep the brain active and stimulated
- Get enough rest
- Avoid fatigue
- Lead a stress-free life
- Have satisfying relationships with other people
- Try *hyperbaric oxygen treatment*, a method of increasing the amount of oxygen in the tissues by placing the patient in a special chamber where oxygen is pumped at up to three times normal atmospheric pressure

CASE STUDY: SHEILA

Sheila Grant is 42. She was diagnosed with multiple sclerosis when she was 30, and has been confined to a wheelchair for the last 10 years. Sheila is philosophical about her illness, but does admit to having weeks when she feels very low in spirits and dreads the future; these feelings usually coincide with some physical setback or new discomfort.

Sheila lives in a semi-detached three-bedroomed house in the suburbs of a large town. She is married to Peter, an electrical engineer for a small retail and repair business. They have two children, Matthew (aged 17) and Claire (aged 15). The family has made many alterations to their house to enable Sheila to live as independent a life as possible. Sheila has recently decided to use an indwelling catheter to ease the problem of urinary incontinence; the community nurse calls regularly to supervise the management of this and to give practical help and advice on other matters. Peter has recently suffered from a recurrent back injury, so the occupational therapist has arranged for a manually operated hoist to be fitted (see Figure 3.17); this means that Sheila can be transferred from bed to chair or shower unit by Claire or Matthew before they leave for school and college.

On good days, Sheila is able to wash herself and dress herself in easy-to-manage clothes, but sometimes fatigue takes over and it is all she can do to muster a smile for Pamela, her home care assistant. Pamela visits daily to provide routine care, e.g. assisting Sheila with washing and toileting. She also prepares an

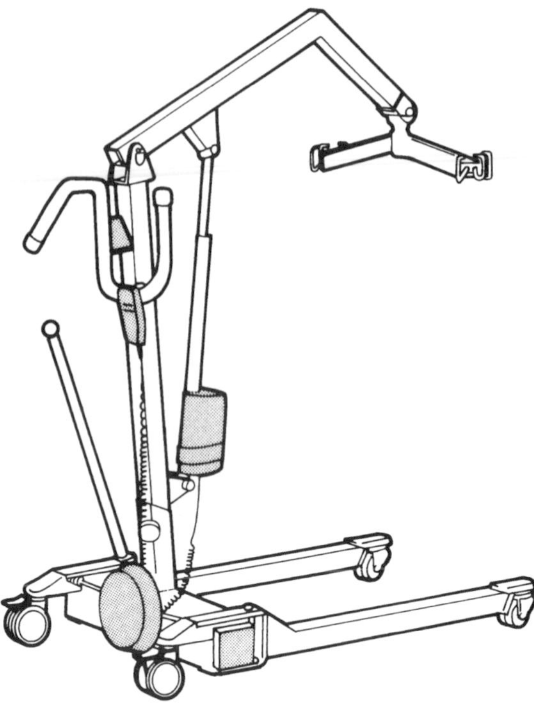

Figure 3.17 A manually operated hoist
Source: Nursing Times, 11 May 1994

evening meal for the family and organises the family shopping.

Sheila is an active member of her local MS society, which organises social events and offers support via a local telephone helpline. She is also very interested in local history and visiting stately homes. One of her main worries is the effect that her condition has on the family; she is aware that Matthew will leave home soon and that she may have to lean more heavily on Claire for daily support. She also worries that she is unattractive to her husband, although he is as caring as ever. Her friends seem busier now – most of the women she knows have full-time jobs – and sometimes the days seem endless, with only the television and radio for company.

ACTIVITY

Read the above case study on Sheila carefully.

1 Draw up a list of specific needs using the 'activities of daily living' model (see p. 63).

2 Design a 'package of care' (see p. 88) for Sheila:

- First, decide who is to be the *case manager*. It could be Peter, Sheila's husband; a district nurse; a physiotherapist; or a home care organiser
- Find out what specialised equipment will be necessary; where it may be obtained; and how much it will cost
- List the services which you feel should be provided; state to which category they belong (statutory, voluntary, private or informal
- Write a letter (word-processed if possible) to the Multiple Sclerosis Society asking about the help it can offer and, in particular, the availability of *respite care* for Sheila
- Write up your proposed package of care, including any adaptations to the home you feel may benefit Sheila

LEARNING DISABILITIES

Learning disabilities range from mild to severe in the same way as do physical and sensory disabilities. Terminology has changed in this area: the terms *mental handicap* and *mental or educational subnormality* have now been replaced by *learning difficulty*, *severe learning difficulty* and *learning disability*. Specific conditions which cause learning disability are:

- *Autism* – a rare developmental disorder which impairs the child's understanding of their environment. It affects about four to five children in every 10,000, although many *more* children may exhibit certain autistic features
- *Birth injury* – any damage to a baby's brain before, during or shortly after the birth can result in a learning disability. One of the commonest causes of brain damage is *anoxia*

or *cerebral hypoxia* (lack of oxygen to the brain cells)

- *Down's syndrome* (see pp. 71–74 above) is a condition which results in short stature as well as learning disabilities and an increased susceptibility to infection
- *Hydrocephalus* is a condition resulting from excessive fluid in the cranium. Today, the condition can be controlled, but people who suffered its effects before treatment was available may show various learning difficulties, ranging from mild to severe.

There are many other unusual syndromes which cause learning disability. Many of these are inherited.

ACTIVITY

Find out about your *local* statutory provision for:

(a) children with learning disabilities;
(b) adults with learning disabilities.

Write a report detailing the provision and the roles of the key personnel involved in the care, education and training of people with learning disabilities.

CHRONIC ILLNESS AND TERMINAL DISEASE

Under the broad definition of 'special needs', people suffering from a chronic illness (e.g. ulcerative colitis, Crohn's disease, chronic bronchitis, emphysema) may require specialist services on a regular basis in the same way that a person with a physical disability requires assistance. The difference is mainly in the specific needs which arise from the condition.

The majority of people suffering from chronic illnesses are able to manage without help from another person and do not have any significant mobility problems. As the diseases are normally confined to adults, even those with persistent symptoms are usually able to look after themselves.

ACTIVITY

Choose one of the following chronic illnesses to research:

- ulcerative colitis
- Crohn's disease
- rheumatoid arthritis
- ischaemic heart disease
- leukaemia

1 Prepare a short presentation to the rest of your class or group, to include the following points:

  - a brief description of the condition; who suffers from it?
  - what special needs does the person with the illness have?
  - who are the carers in the community, and what equipment and services may be needed?
  - are there any voluntary organisations which deal specifically with that illness?

2 Evaluate each other's presentations, having agreed on the criteria beforehand with your teacher/tutor.

Assessment

An assessment of the individual with special needs is not a once-only event but a *continuous process*. Information gained about the person is added to over a period of time so that a clearer picture is formed of the person's needs.

ACTIVITY

1 Read the following case study about Mark. Identify Mark's need using the 'activities of daily living' model (see p. 63 above). How are Mark's daily

needs met at the moment? What needs, if any, do you think are not being adequately met?

2 List the delivery of care under two headings, 'statutory' and 'voluntary'. What in general do you think contributes most to Mark's quality of life?

CASE STUDY: MARK

Mark, a former secondary school teacher, is 47. He was diagnosed as having cancer of the spine at the age of 28. He had several operations to remove the tumour, but it has left him paralysed in both hands and legs. His breathing, normal skin sensation, bowel and bladder functions are also affected.

Mark's day begins between 8 and 9 am when the district nurse arrives at his one-bedroom ground-floor flat. He lets her in by means of an automatic computerised control system (see Figure 3.18(a)) that was installed by social services to help Mark operate various appliances around the house. Thus, he can answer the telephone and front door, or switch on his TV, heater and lights, simply by pressing a touch pad next to his pillow. Before the nurse has arrived, Mark has already used the system to open the curtains and turn on the radio.

Once she has gained entry, the nurse helps Mark with his personal needs. He is unable to empty his bladder without assistance, and so each morning it is emptied by inserting a catheter. The nurse then applies a penile self-adhesive sheath and drainage bag to collect the urine that he will pass during the course of the day. The same regular attention is given to emptying his bowels, although this is only done twice a week and at the time when Mark showers in his specially adapted bathroom.

Getting washed and dressed is another daily activity with which Mark requires the nurse's help. Because of his paralysis and an inability to sense heat or pressure over most of his body, she must check for signs of pressure sores and adjust his shoes and clothing so that they keep him warm, don't cause unnecessary harm to the skin and don't restrict his movement. She also helps him to put on leg callipers and a reinforced bodybrace that improve his balance and sitting position. Once this has been done, the nurse makes a final check of the urinary drainage system before leaving Mark to busy himself with other routine tasks.

These usually begin with the preparation of a light breakfast. His kitchen has lowered work surfaces and is fitted with appliances that he can operate from his wheelchair. However, a wish not to have too many gadgets and to do as much for himself as he can means that Mark only makes very simple

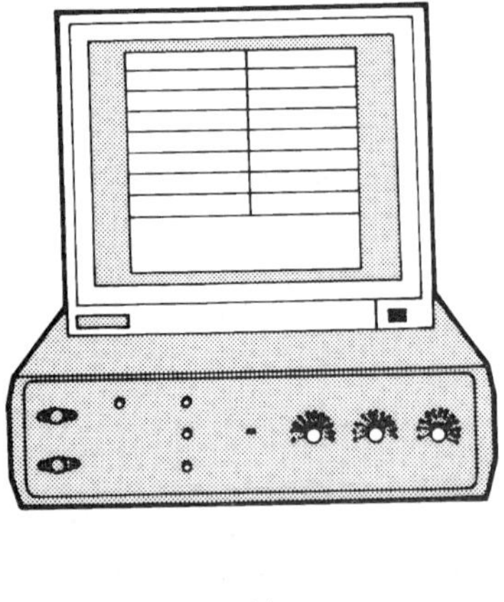
(a)

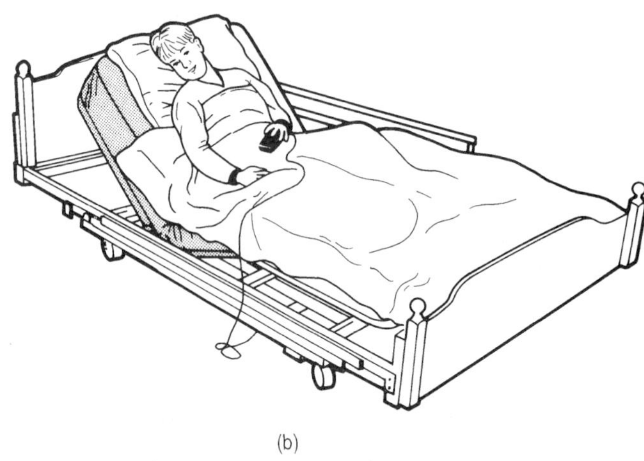
(b)

Figure 3.18 (a) The PSU6 environmental control system; (b) user's control pad in operation
Source: (a) Possum Controls Limited; (b) *Nursing Times*, 11 May 1994

convenience meals which don't always provide him with a full, nutritionally balanced diet.

Mark's wish to be self-reliant also extends to his doing all his own shopping, and here he is enormously dependent upon having his own means of transport. Although he receives some state benefits, Mark decided that his freedom to come and go as he pleased was very important, and so he used his savings to buy an outdoor electric wheelchair and specially adapted car. The vehicle's automatic ramp and hand steering controls enable him to drive from the wheelchair and to have the type of flexibility and independence that he feels local public or voluntary transport services cannot offer him.

Having his own transport has also helped Mark develop and maintain a busy schedule of other activities. Each week, he spends time managing a helpline for disabled people and attending the regular meetings of several local committees and advisory groups. He also uses his car to attend a two-year college course, and now conducts weekly counselling sessions for people who, like himself, have a spinal-cord injury. These activities have given Mark outside interests as well as focusing his time and energies on things he considers worthwhile.

Mark's social life also offers a change from the domestic routine. He likes eating out, watching rugby and going to the theatre. However, poor wheelchair access and the limitations of the 'back-to-bed' evening nursing service mean that he has to plan ahead and confine his outings to places which have facilities for disabled people. He is also aware that his own inhibitions, as well as other people's prejudices and assumptions about disability, can be a barrier to making new friends and forming long-term relationships.

Being independent and in control are important to Mark, and he has taken a great deal of time and effort to negotiate and secure a *package of care* that reflects his needs. He recognises that his general physical and emotional well-being, ability to communicate and level of income have helped him to achieve this, although he is also aware that the overall quality of his life is influenced by social and institutional 'barriers' that restrict *all* disabled people, and over which he has only limited personal control.

A HISTORICAL PERSPECTIVE ON SPECIAL-NEEDS PROVISION

It was not until the middle of the nineteenth century that a distinction was made between those with a mental handicap and those suffering from mental illness. The Idiots Act (1886) allowed local authorities to erect special asylums for the mentally handicapped. Those who were physically or mentally handicapped and were unable to be cared for in their own homes were placed in workhouses, psychiatric hospitals and asylums. The terms 'idiot' and 'imbecile' were recognised and acceptable ones until well into the twentieth century.

Twentieth-century legislation: the main measures

THE DISABLED PERSONS (EMPLOYMENT) ACT 1944

This Act required employers of certain-sized companies to employ a 'quota' of disabled employees. For companies employing more than 20 people, the quota was 3%. The Act also required the Secretary of State for Employment to:

- reserve certain kinds of work for those with a disability
- provide sheltered employment to severely disabled people
- provide vocational training (this is now usually provided by the local authorities' personal social services departments, or through the Department of Employment's rehabilitation centres)

THE NATIONAL ASSISTANCE ACT 1948

This Act compelled local authorities to provide suitable accommodation for all those people who had need of shelter because of age or infirmity.

THE CHRONICALLY SICK AND DISABLED PERSONS ACT 1970

This Act was prompted by a government survey which found that

- at least 3 million adults were disabled to some degree
- 200,000 families had a severely disabled member but did not have access to an inside lavatory
- one in five of the severely disabled lived alone without the help of the welfare services

The Act imposed two extra duties on the newly reorganised local authorities:

- to compile a register of the disabled in their area
- to publicise their services

Unfortunately, the services listed under Section 2 of the Act only needed to be provided where it was 'practical and reasonable' to do so; many authorities found it was not and consequently did not provide them. The services included:

- adaptations to property to enable people to be mobile in the home, or at least to be able to undertake a range of normal household activities
- help in the home
- recreational and certain educational facilities: this covers a wide range of services, e.g. holidays, day centres, etc.
- ensuring all buildings open to the public were provided with means of access and toilet facilities suitable for disabled people
- representation of disabled people on government advisory bodies and local authority committees
- provision of meals

THE DISABLED PERSONS (SERVICES, CONSULTATION AND REPRESENTATION) ACT 1986

This Act was designed to give people with disabilities a greater say in the decisions taken regarding them. Those with disabilities have the right to:

- assessment
- information
- consultation
- representation
- advocacy: i.e. an advocate (e.g. a social worker) should be present at any meeting where their needs are being assessed

THE DISABLED PERSONS' BILL 1994

In June 1994, the Disabled Persons' Bill, which would have delivered human rights to people with disabilities, was blocked by no fewer than 80 government-prepared amendments. Protesters at the blocking of the Bill demonstrated in London by obstructing traffic. The feeling was that change is long overdue; people with disabilities want civil rights, not charity.

THE MENTAL DEFICIENCY ACT 1913

This Act reflected the prevailing strong moral outlook of the time which classed any socially deviant act, such as becoming pregnant outside marriage, as immoral and as a threat to the fabric of society. Little distinction was made between those who were mentally ill and those with learning disabilities. Many young pregnant girls who lacked family support were sent to an asylum well away from their home town.

THE MENTAL HEALTH ACT 1959

This Act ensured that incarceration because of mental handicap or illness was either voluntary or based on a considered medical diagnosis. The Act also advocated an expansion of community care services, but there was still some confusion between mental illness and mental handicap.

THE MENTAL HEALTH ACT 1983

This Act defined mental disorder as a general category subdivided into 'mental illness, arrested or incomplete development of the mind, psychopathic disorder, and any other disorder or disability of mind'. It also laid down rules (referred to as 'Sections') which applied conditions to the compulsory admission of patients against their will. The role of the social worker was central to the compulsory admission of patients, and there was an increased recognition of the legal and social rights of the individual.

THE EUGENICS MOVEMENT

Eugenics is the doctrine and study of improving a population by controlled breeding for desirable inherited characteristics. Advocates of eugenics seek either to promote the procreation of supposedly superior human beings or to prevent the procreation of supposedly inferior human beings. This was a philosophy which flourished under Hitler and Nazism in Germany, when the German people were encouraged to think of theirs as the superior race, and to eliminate non-Aryans, principally the Jewish people. In spite of the revulsion most people feel towards the eugenics movement as it applied during the 1940s in Europe, eugenic principles still underlie practices all over the world, for example:

- the selective sterilisation of young adults with severe learning disabilities
- the denial of the right of people with disabilities to have children
- the offer of amniocentesis and the option of termination of pregnancy (abortion) if the results show a chromosomal abnormality

THE NATIONAL HEALTH SERVICE AND COMMUNITY CARE ACT 1990

This Act was passed in 1990 and is now fully implemented. A key concept in the new legislation is 'care in the community': the provision of support services to people who need help to live as independently as they can in the setting of their own choice; this could be in their own homes, in a residential home or in local-authority sheltered housing.

The Act has six identified 'key objectives':

1 to promote domiciliary, day and respite services to enable people to live in their own homes wherever feasible and sensible;
2 to ensure that service providers make practical support for carers a high priority;
3 to make the proper assessment of need and good care management the cornerstones of high-quality care;
4 to promote the development of a flourishing independent sector alongside good-quality public services;
5 to clarify the responsibilities of agencies and so make them more accountable;
6 to secure better value for taxpayers' money by introducing a new funding structure for social care.

Under this new Act, the NHS no longer carries the main responsibility for service provision; instead, local authorities now have the major function of providing social care for the elderly, for those with physical disabilities and for people with learning difficulties. These changes have implications for the roles of social worker and community nurse. A key feature in implementing the Act is that of *care management*: the central elements of this are

- assessment
- the implementation, monitoring and reviewing of a care plan

A PACKAGE OF CARE

The local authority social services department has the responsibility of assessing the needs of the disabled person or family under the NHS and Community Care Act 1990. Once an assessment has been carried out, a person or team is appointed to act as care manager. The care manager has the duty of coordinating and managing the package of care (see Figure 3.18). Services may be arranged from any available source:

- *informal*: neighbours, friends and relatives
- *statutory*: the NHS, social services, housing, education and other departments
- *voluntary*: e.g. charities, Meals on Wheels, housing associations
- *private*: e.g. chiropodist, taxi services and private residential and nursing homes

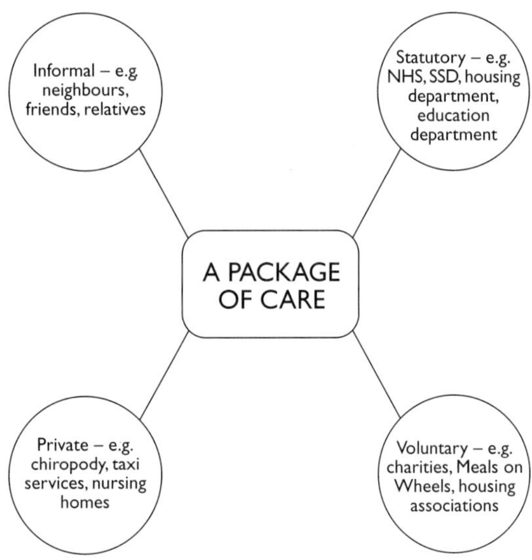

Figure 3.19 A package of care

The *care manager* should be the primary point of contact for both clients and their carers, and the package of care must be based on

- an individual's abilities
- the help already available from family and friends
- the suitability of their living accommodation

Assessment may involve an occupational therapist, who will advise on any structural modifications necessary, and a physiotherapist may advise on the purchase of specialist equipment (see also the Activity and case study on p. 84 above).

- *Equipment* may be supplied by social services or the NHS
- *Services* are arranged from the most appropriate provider
- *Respite care* should be included in the package of care. This is when a carer is given a rest from their responsibilities for a short period of time. The respite may be achieved through the client's moving out temporarily to a hospital, home or holiday care setting, or by another carer moving in to take over the usual carer's duties

THE VOLUNTARY SECTOR

Voluntary organisations (or non-statutory organisations) are non-profit-making bodies operating for the public good. They range from small local support groups (for instance, for blind people) with no paid staff to large international agencies with paid professionals (sometimes known as *Non-Governmental Organisations* or NGOs) such as the Save the Children Fund and the World Wide Fund for Nature.

There are approximately 350,000 different voluntary organisations in the UK today; about 40% of these are registered as *charities*. In order to be registered as a charity, the organisation must prove that it meets at least one of certain conditions. It must

- benefit the community in some way, or
- advance religion or education, or
- relieve poverty

or a combination of these. Key features of voluntary organisations are:

- They are not part of the statutory provision of the country
- They may, however, be closely associated with statutory bodies, and may receive funding from the state
- It is the organisation which is voluntary, not the people working for it
- They must not engage in any direct political activity – although many do exert political pressure

- If registered as a charity, the organisation gains tax relief and rate relief and is able to receive money in the form of covenants at beneficial rates
- They can respond quickly to new needs that arise. (The growth in Aids organisations, such as the Terence Higgins Trust for example, occurred long before the government began to respond to the increases in such cases)

Many voluntary organisations do, however, make a charge for their services, and even a neighbour may be given an allowance to call in a few times a day to check on somebody.

The Association of Crossroads Care Attendant Schemes

This is a voluntary organisation which can provide 'care attendants' to help in the home if the normal care situation collapses or if *respite care* (see above) is needed. The attendants are not professionals, but they are fully trained by the organisation.

The Winged Fellowship Trust

Winged Fellowship runs five UK holiday centres for severely physically disabled people, enabling carers to take a break from their duties. The centres are run by a combination of trained staff and volunteers, and 24-hour care is provided. Each centre is fully equipped for the use of disabled people and also has a shop, bar and garden. Guests are taken out each day to a place of interest, and evening entertainment is provided, either at the centre or elsewhere.

ACTIVITY

Choose a voluntary organisation which represents disabled people. Research the following information:

- What is its *rationale*, i.e. why was it formed?
- How does it *fund* its work?
- What *services* does it provide for disabled people? Are these services unavailable from the statutory care sector?
- Does the organisation *employ* people, and are any of them disabled?

Find out if there is a local branch or office in your area and contact people who work for it. Has it set up any projects locally? (NB: Remember to enclose an s.a.e. when you write to any voluntary organisation.)

SPECIAL NEEDS AND EDUCATION

Education is obviously a lifelong process, but in formal terms, it involves schooling between the ages of four or five years and either 16 or 18, with the option thereafter of attending a college or university or undertaking a training scheme with an employer.

Until the 1950s, in the UK, children born with an obvious disabling condition, such as Down's syndrome or cerebral palsy, would have been cared for within the family for the first few years of life before being admitted to a large mental-handicap hospital where they may have spent the rest of their lives.

Twentieth-century legislation: the main measures

As we have seen with the provision of care for adults classified as having a disability, various attempts to define special needs in the educational sphere have been made.

THE EDUCATION ACT 1921

This act defined five categories of handicap:

- blindness
- deafness
- physical defectiveness
- mental defectiveness
- epilepsy

Not all children recognised as suffering from one of these disabilities were offered special educational facilities, but many were placed in residential homes for the blind or deaf and dumb.

THE EDUCATION ACT 1944

This Act defined 11 categories of handicap:

- blind
- partially sighted
- deaf
- partially deaf
- physically handicapped
- delicate
- diabetic
- epileptic
- maladjusted
- educationally subnormal
- speech defective

All local education authorities (LEAs) were legally bound to provide education for children with such disabilities, although this was provided not necessarily within schools but often as an add-on facility within the large institutions mentioned above. As these institutions or hospitals were nearly always situated on the outskirts of large towns, it was not easy for parents or family to visit children there, and often valuable family ties were broken.

THE EDUCATION ACT 1970

This Act further expanded the previous provision to include those children with *severe* mental handicaps. Such children had hitherto been pronounced 'ineducable'.

THE EDUCATION ACT 1981

Mary Warnock chaired a committee in 1974 which published the *Warnock Report* (1978). The committee's brief was to 'review the educational provision in England, Scotland and Wales for children and young people handicapped by disabilities of body or mind'. The report provided the basis for the 1981 Act. Key points were:

- Where possible, children should be integrated into mainstream schools
- Special educational needs were defined as mild, moderate or severe
- The assessment of a child's specific needs should be a continuing process
- Reference should be made to a child's *abilities* as well as to its disabilities
- The term 'specific learning difficulties' was introduced for those children who may have difficulty in just one area of the school curriculum (as a result of, for example, dyslexia)

THE CHILDREN ACT 1989

This states that every local authority should provide services designed to:

- minimise the effect on disabled children within the area of their disabilities
- give such children the opportunity to lead lives which are as normal as possible

The statementing process

The process of the assessment of the specific needs of individual children is known as 'statementing'. This is usually a process of negotiation between the education authority and the parents. Its aims are to identify the areas of need and define the treatment/educational requirements for such needs. The *Statement of Special Educational Needs* is a legal document which must describe precisely the child's individual needs.

The Code of Practice introduced in 1994 gives guidance on the procedures involved. Every school now has to appoint a member of staff who takes responsibility for special educational needs. There are five steps towards statementing (which is only expected to be relevant for 2% of children):

- *Step 1: cause for concern*. The family worker or class teacher, through the observations made in the established record-keeping system, might become concerned. This concern should be shared with the SENCO (Special Educational Needs Co-ordinator) and preferably also with the parents.
- *Step 2: observation and monitoring*. The child is

observed and monitored more closely, and an Individual Education Plan is developed with the SENCO and the parents: for example, making sure that a child with a serious stutter has plenty of time to talk and chat without being rushed
- *Step 3: outside help.* The school asks for outside help, for example from an educational psychologist; a new Individual Educational Plan is drawn up
- *Step 4: procedures for statutory assessment begin.* This must take place within 26 weeks
- *Step 5: a statement is drawn up*

Features of such a statement are:

- The statementing process may be instigated by the local education authority at any time in a child's school life (i.e. between the ages of 4 and 18 years)
- If statementing is required before the age of 4, it is undertaken by the health authority. Pre-school nursery opportunities are usually provided as a result
- A statement *must* be updated regularly – generally once a year
- Extra resources required by children with special needs who attend mainstream schools should be clearly described so that funding is available. This may entail the provision of a peripatetic speech therapist or other specialist
- Special facilities needed by children with physical disabilities, e.g. physiotherapy or hydrotherapy, also need to be clearly documented in the statement

Integration

It would not be possible to achieve full integration of all children with special needs into mainstream schools; some disabilities involve intensive one-to-one care and a specific programme tailored to meet particular needs. Working towards the achievement of integration wherever possible will, however, break down barriers and ensure that children learn from an early age that some people may need help at certain times and that there is no stigma attached to those with special needs.

In the UK, integration is understood to take place at three levels: locational, social and functional:

- *Locational* integration is simply the placement of a child with special educational needs in a unit or class for disabled children in a mainstream school, or in a special school that shares the same site as an ordinary school
- *Social* integration occurs when the children in the unit/class mix with mainstream children for a range of non-academic activities
- *Functional* integration occurs when children with special educational needs follow courses, or elements of courses, with their peer group with any necessary support they require. Specialist training is needed to teach special groups, such as those with vision or hearing impairment. Some schools employ peripatetic teachers to work with one child with special needs within mainstream schools

Inclusion

MAINSTREAM SCHOOLS

Mainstream schools will need to consider the specific needs of disabled children in order to promote independence and foster learning. These needs are:

1 *Access*

- Specialised equipment such as ramps and lifts for wheelchairs should provide access for *all* the children in the school
- Toilet facilities should be large enough to accommodate wheelchairs
- Computer equipment must have touch-sensitive controls
- Play equipment should be adjustable, e.g. water troughs that can be set on stands at varying levels
- Learning materials should be available in audio, large print or Braille format for visually impaired children

- Communication aids should be available such as British Sign Language, which has to be properly taught – as does any language if a child is to be supported through its use in school

2 *Information*
Staff will need information about specific disorders and disabilities in order to plan learning goals which are realistic for the individual child's needs. Such information is available from the various voluntary organisations and self-help groups, e.g. The National Autistic Society, The National Deaf Children's Society, The Royal Institute for the Blind and SCOPE.

3 *Training*
All staff in schools offering inclusive education must be trained in disability awareness and equal opportunities. Some specialist teachers may be required to work with an individual child; e.g. a partially sighted child may work on a one-to-one basis with a teacher who adapts the learning materials being used during lessons.

4 *Role models*
Children with special needs need positive role models. Schools and nurseries can help to improve children's self-image by:

- involving disabled adults at all levels of care and education
- carefully selecting books and activities that promote the self-image of disabled children – in the same way that using multi-cultural resources promotes the self-image of minority ethnic groups.

Table 3.2 Children looked after by local authorities[1]: by type of accommodation

England, Wales & Northern Ireland Percentages

	1981	1993
With foster parents	39	61
In local authority homes	28	13
Placement with parent regulations[2]	19	11
Voluntary homes and hostels	4	2
Schools for children with special educational needs[3]	3	1
Other accommodation	7	14
All children in care (=100%) (thousands)	99	56
All children in care per 1,000 population aged under 18	7.6	4.6

[1] *At 31 March. All data for Northern Ireland and data for 1981 for England and Wales relate to children in care.*
[2] *All data for Northern Ireland and data for 1981 for England and Wales relate to children under the charge and control of a parent, guardian, relative or friend.*
[3] *England and Wales only.*

Source: Social Trends 26. 1996 Central Statistical Office. Crown copyright 1995. Reproduced by the permission of the Controller of HMSO and the Central Statistical Office.

CHILDREN IN RESIDENTIAL CARE

The Children Act 1989 emphasises that the best place for children to be brought up is within their own families, and the table (see Table 3.2) shows that the vast majority of disabled children *are* living at home. Some residential special schools offer weekly or termly boarding facilities; children may be in residential care for medical reasons or because the family cannot manage the care involved. All homes must be registered and inspected by social-services departments to safeguard the interests of this particularly vulnerable group.

FOSTER PLACEMENTS

The Foster Placement (Children) Regulations 1991 apply safeguards to any child in foster care. Some voluntary organisations provide specialist training programmes for carers fostering disabled children, and their active involvement in the child's education is encouraged.

RESPITE CARE

This should ideally be renamed 'natural-break' or 'short-stay' care as 'respite' implies that the carers need relief from an unwanted burden. The aim of such care is to provide support and encouragement to enable the parents/carers to continue caring for their child within the family.

There are four types of respite care:

- care in a foster placement
- residential care, in a home or sometimes in a hospital unit
- holiday schemes e.g. diabetic camps etc.
- care within the child's own home

The latter is often the best provision of care if the right substitute carer can be found. Provision is patchy and is only worthwhile if the child derives as much benefit from the break as do the carers.

ACTIVITY

1 Think of ways in which carers of *able-bodied* children get respite from full-time care. Why can the same avenues not be opened to *all* carers?

2 List the possible problems for parents of disabled children in obtaining respite care, and then list solutions to these problems.

The availability of educational services

UNESCO (the United Nations Educational, Scientific and Cultural Organisation) has estimated that 85% of the world's disabled population reside in nations where few or no special education facilities exist. Where developing countries *do* provide special education, it is usually only for children with severe impairments. Cost–benefit analyses by UNESCO have shown that, overall, 80–90% of people with learning difficulties *are* employable if appropriate education and training programmes are completed.

SERVICES FOR PEOPLE WITH DISABILITIES

A large number of services are provided for those with disabilities, but there is considerable overlap and fragmentation within this provision. Where these services are well developed, they may include:

- practical assistance at home
- day centres offering activities and companionship
- special education
- support for employment in sheltered and ordinary workplaces
- temporary and permanent residential care
- suitable transport, e.g. through a subsidised taxi service

People with disabilities have themselves in recent years fought to increase both their *autonomy*, i.e. their ability to live according to their own rules, and their *independence*, i.e. their ability to perform key functions such as working, dressing and eating without assistance from others.

In some affluent countries, notably in Scandinavia, Canada and the USA, measures to increase autonomy and independence have been taken, for instance by adapting housing and by paying allowances directly to disabled people to spend on services as they wish, rather than leaving decisions to professionals. This goes a long way to increasing self-empowerment. In the USA, the Clinton administration has established a special Washington unit dedicated to disability with a staff of 414 and a budget of $5.3 billion (£3.5 billion). The head of the unit is herself wheelchair-bound and believes that disabled people now enjoy considerable political leverage on Congress Hill.

In the UK, the legal status of disabled people is still by comparison primitive.

In developing countries, where almost 80% of the world's disabled people live, but where only 10% of the resources allocated to disability are spent, services are limited. Here, as in most of the industrialised world, families bear the main responsibility for their disabled members.

Medical services

In the UK, medical treatment is free under the NHS, and for people with specific disabilities, specialist services are provided, including

- physiotherapists
- community nurses
- occupational therapists
- speech therapists
- remedial gymnasts
- dietitians.

Rehabilitation services

Occupational therapists work in hospitals (general or mental), for social-services departments (in the community) or for voluntary organisations that cater for the severely disabled. The overriding aim of occupational therapy is to help the person to be as independent as possible. The therapists will assess limitations on physical abilities and organise appropriate aids, such as chair-lifts etc. They are also trained to help people maximise the physical abilities they have.

A new scheme called Easy Street has been developed in the USA and Canada. Rehabilitation departments in American hospitals are being transformed into small-scale, highly crafted replicas of their local high street. Shops, banks, post offices, cafés and cinemas are being used to enable disabled people to relearn everyday skills in realistic, yet controlled settings. The pioneers of the concept believe that Easy Street supplements rather than replaces the use of exercise equipment and allows patients to build up their strength and confidence in an enjoyable and therapeutic environment.

In the UK, the trend has been away from using simulated environments and towards sheltered environments, but the American scheme will be examined with interest.

Sport and leisure

Central government assistance for sport and recreation for all, including that for disabled people, is channelled through national and regional sports councils. Both the government and the councils are concerned to promote wider opportunities for active recreation for disabled as well as able-bodied people, and to encourage integration with the more able-bodied wherever appropriate. The government provides the councils with an annual grant to help achieve these aims and objectives.

The sports councils work closely with the British Sports Association for the Disabled. Sports-council funding is available for administration and development work, and for the training and participation of national teams abroad.

The Wildlife and Countryside Act 1981 requires that grants given by the Nature Conservancy Council for buildings open to the public take account of the access needs of disabled people.

The Outward Bound Trust is the largest outdoor personal-development organisation in the world, with 38 centres in 25 countries worldwide. It was originally set up about 50 years ago to promote self-confidence and a will to live in young merchant seamen sailing the gruelling Atlantic convoys during the Second World War. It is the leader in developing courses for people with a wide range of disabilities including

- cerebral palsy
- paraplegia
- amputation
- deafness
- blindness
- mental handicap
- diabetes
- cystic fibrosis

The Outward Bound Trust also runs courses for carers and works closely with other organisations, e.g. the British Deaf Sports Council, to ensure appropriate programmes are devised.

Transport

One of the main problems facing someone with a physical disability is transport. The following schemes are in operation:

- The Disablement Services Authority provides artificial limbs for amputees
- The Department of Health provides wheelchairs for those who need them
- The 'mobility' part of the disability living allowance enables some of those with disabilities to put additional state benefit towards the purchase of a car
- The 'Motability' scheme is a charity run jointly by the government and car manufacturers. Its aim is to provide discounts for those with disabilities on the leasing or credit purchase of cars
- To assist disabled people who drive a vehicle or travel as a passenger, the Chronically Sick and Disabled Persons Act 1970 introduced the 'Orange Badge Scheme'. Local authorities issue orange badges to allow parking concessions for disabled people. About 5% of cars carry these badges
- Many towns now have a 'Dial-a-Ride' bus service specifically for people with mobility problems
- British Rail will make arrangements for people with special requirements if given advance notice
- Most airline and passenger shipping companies have special facilities available for people with disabilities
- Some taxi firms specialise in transport for disabled people and hold contracts with local authorities and health authorities to offer the service
- The Transport Act 1968 gives all county and district councils powers to provide concessionary bus fares for disabled people,

Figure 3.20 Water-skiing is just one of the many activities organised by the Guide Dogs for the Blind Association Holidays, for partially sighted people

although there is wide variation in the concessions offered

- Disabled people are permitted to use invalid carriages on the footway providing the vehicle complies with prescribed requirements relating to maximum speed, weight, braking systems, etc.

Employment and training

The public employment and training services, including those intended for disabled people, are provided by the Manpower Services Commission in the UK, and by the Department of Economic Development in Northern Ireland. Certain jobs are reserved for people with disabilities, and employers are required, under the terms of The Disabled Persons (Employment) Act 1944 to employ a small number of disabled people. Disablement resettlement officers (DROs) are employed by the Department of Employment and use medical evidence in order to register people as disabled for employment-legislation purposes.

Figure 3.21 The logo for equal-opportunities employers

In 1991 a new symbol began to appear in job advertisements denoting equal-opportunities employers (see Figure 3.21). Organisations using this symbol must abide by the Code of Good Practice on the Employment of Disabled People. They are expected to provide all the help they can by:

- training
- providing special equipment
- the recruitment and retention of disabled employees

The Department of Employment offers Jobcentres, as well as specialist facilities through a Disablement Advisory Service and DROs.

Remploy is a national organisation which provides sheltered employment for disabled people.

Housing

Physically disabled people should enjoy the same standard of comfort, choice and independence in housing as able-bodied people. Existing houses and flats are rarely built to meet the special requirements of a disabled person. Under the Local Government and Housing Act 1989, anyone wishing to adapt their house or flat to make it a more suitable home for a disabled person can apply for a Disabled Facilities Grant. The grant is:

- mandatory, provided certain conditions are met
- intended to provide access to and around the property
- available only after a detailed survey of the property has been carried out to assess the cost and extent of the works required
- available only to those who are eligible for housing benefit

People who are vulnerable because of mental or physical disabilities come within the priority category of homeless people for whom local authorities must secure accommodation under the Housing (Homeless Persons) Act 1977.

ACTIVITY

Conduct a survey of your local town and find out the following information:

- How easy is it to visit the local theatre or cinema if one is wheelchair-bound?

- How many pubs and cafés have facilities for the disabled, e.g. ramps, lifts, toilet facilities?
- What car-parking spaces exist for drivers with a disability?
- Do the cars using them have orange badges?
- Could people with mobility problems use local buses?
- Does the sports centre or swimming pool cater for people with disabilities?

The survey could be carried out by *simulation* (i.e. with one student in a wheelchair) or by means of a *questionnaire*. If feasible, the trip could be recorded on video and evaluated by the rest of the class.

Technical aids

Aids may be provided to enable disabled people to live in the community and to participate in various activities. Central government agencies directly provide:

- artificial limbs
- wheelchairs
- aids for war pensioners
- environmental control systems (see Figure 3.18) and typewriter systems
- aids to enable disabled people to obtain or retain suitable employment

Local authority social services departments have a duty to provide the necessary aids to assist disabled people with everyday tasks such as washing, dressing and cooking (see Figure 3.22).

Local education authorities may provide necessary equipment and aids required by disabled schoolchildren and students for use in schools and colleges.

WHO CARES FOR PEOPLE WITH DISABILITIES?

In the UK today, approximately six million people are caring for sick, disabled or elderly persons on a regular basis, i.e. assisting in some of their essential daily functions. These are the *informal carers* who, rightly or wrongly, occupy an important role in community care. Only a small proportion of people with a physical disability need help with daily living skills, and the vast majority of them are looked after by relatives or friends. They may be a wife whose husband has a physical disability, a daughter looking after her frail elderly mother or parents caring for a child with a mental handicap.

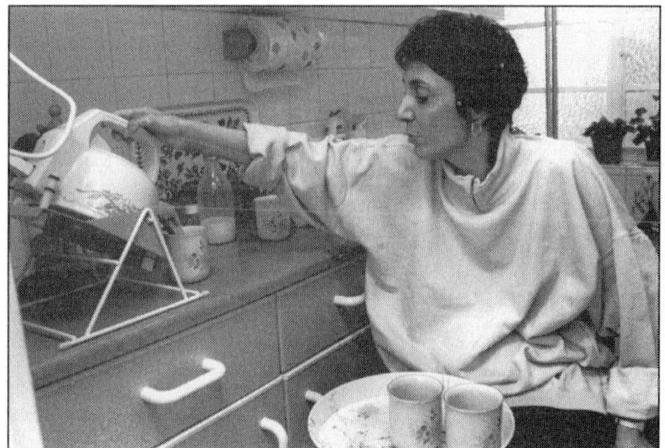

Figure 3.22 There are a number of physical aids available to assist people with the activities of daily living

A recent study by the King's Fund Centre (*Carer's Needs: A Ten-point Plan for Carers*) (see Skelt 1993) suggested the following needs:

1. *Status:* recognition of the carers' own contribution to society and of their own needs as individuals is required.
2. *Services:* these should be tailored to their individual circumstances and should be planned in response to the needs of the individual.
3. *Cultural diversity:* every effort should be made to provide services which recognise that people from different backgrounds may well have different requirements. The obvious example is dietary differences, but there are other

Figure 3.23 An advertisement for the Samaritans

issues, e.g. touch by members of the opposite sex.

4 *Leisure:* carers must have opportunities for a break, both to relax and to have some 'personal space'.

5 *Practical help:* domestic help, adaptations to the home, incontinence services and help with transport may provide invaluable help to the carer.

6 *Support:* carers often want someone to talk to, with whom they can share their problems and frustrations. These emotional needs should be met before and during the caring task and after it is over.

7 *Information:* specific needs of the person being cared for must be detailed, and knowledge of the available benefits and services is vital.

8 *Finance:* an income is required which covers the costs of caring and which allows the carer to take employment or to share the care with other people.

9 *Planning:* carers should have opportunities to explore alternatives to family care, for both the immediate and long-term future.

10 *Consultation:* services should be designed through consultation with carers at all levels of policy planning.

BENEFITS AND DISABILITY

Some of the benefits available from the Department of Social Security (DSS) are described below.

Attendance allowance

This benefit is paid to those people who become disabled at or after the age of 65 and who can prove that they need to be looked after. There are two rates which apply:

- a *lower rate:* paid to those who need attendance during the day (or night) only
- a *higher rate:* paid for those who need help both day and night

The attendance allowance is tax-free and is paid on top of other benefits. (You have to have needed help for at least six months to become eligible for the benefit.)

Disability living allowance

This is a tax-free benefit introduced in April 1992. It is split into two parts:

- *care*, for people under 65 (but over 16) and needing help with personal care (e.g. washing, dressing or using the toilet) or cooking a meal, or both
- *mobility*, for people over 5 (and up to 65) if they have difficulty in getting around

Within the two components, there are different pay scales. This factor, coupled with the obvious difficulties of assessing eligibility, make this a very complicated system to administer.

Invalidity benefit

This is also a tax-free benefit, and is split into three components:

- *Invalidity pension* replaces sickness benefit after the first 28 weeks of incapacity for work. It is based on having sufficient National Insurance stamps
- *Invalidity allowance* is paid on top of invalidity pension if the disability or illness began before the age of 55 for women and 60 for men
- *Additional pension* is an earnings-related amount, introduced in 1978. You can work and earn a limited amount (£39 in 1992) and still be eligible for benefit

Severe disablement allowance

This can be claimed by those who have not paid enough National Insurance contributions to be eligible for invalidity benefit. SDA is payable to those under retirement age. However, if you become disabled after your 20th birthday, you can only get a maximum of 80% of the SDA.

If the person with the disability is under 19 and in 'mainstream' education they may claim SDA, but not if they are in some form of special education.

Disability working allowance

This is a tax-free benefit paid to those whose disability puts them 'at a disadvantage in getting a job' and who are in a low-paid job for at least 16 hours a week.

Eligibility depends on getting disability living allowance or on having an invalid three-wheeler from the DSS. Savings of £3,000 and more affect the levels of payment.

Invalid care allowance

This is available for carers rather than for the person with the disability. Carers who spend more than 35 hours each week looking after someone who receives attendance allowance can claim invalid care allowance. The carer cannot earn more than £30 a week from other sources.

Income support

Income support is payable to anyone whose income falls below set levels. It can only be claimed by those without work or those working for fewer than 16 hours per week. People of working age with disabilities are normally eligible as they are more likely to be unemployed than those without disabilities, and, if employed, are likely to be in low-paid employment.

Industrial injuries disablement benefit

For people ill as a result of industrial diseases known to be linked to certain kinds of employment (e.g. asbestosis, silicosis), this benefit is paid on top of invalidity benefit. You need to be 14% disabled to qualify; doctors are appointed by the DSS to assess the claimant's degree of disability. Two other allowances are related to this benefit: constant attendance allowance and exceptionally severe disablement allowance.

ACTIVITY

There are many exclusions and regulations concerning *age* in the rules for eligibility for benefit if you are disabled.

1 Draw up a table or chart to summarise which age groups can claim which benefits.

2 Go to your local post office and obtain a copy of the current guide to benefits for the disabled and a claim form for the disability living allowance. Fill in the claim form on Mark's behalf (see the case study on pp. 84–85 above) and answer the following questions:

- Was the form easy to understand and complete?

- What other benefits would Mark be entitled to?
- Was any allowance made for people who do not speak English?
- Can Braille or audio applications be made?

REFERENCES AND RESOURCES

Armstrong, D. (1989), *An Outline of Sociology as Applied to Medicine*, 3rd edn, Kent: Wright.

Bee, H. (1987), *The Developing Child*, New York: Harper & Row.

Bond, J. and Bond, S. (1994), *Sociology and Health Care*, Edinburgh: Churchill Livingstone.

Dickinson, H. and Erben, M. (1993), *Just Like Us? A Threat? Or What? Short Exercises as an Introduction to Issues of Disability*, Social Science Teacher, 1993.

Evans, P. (1992), 'A mother celebrates the birthday of a very special baby', *The Guardian*, 16 December.

Graham, J. (1982), *Multiple Sclerosis*, Northants: Thorsons Publishers.

Hayes, N. and Orrell, S. (1993), *Maslow in Psychology: an Introduction*, London: Longman Group.

Keith, L. (ed) (1994), *Mustn't Grumble: Writings by Disabled Women*. London: Women's Press.

Landsdowne, R. (1980), *More than Sympathy*, London: Tavistock.

Lonsdale, S. (1992), *Women and Disability*, Basingstoke: Macmillan.

Moore, S. (1993), *Social Welfare Alive*, Cheltenham: Stanley Thornes.

O'Hagan, M. and Smith, M. (1993), *Special Issues in Child Care*, London: Bailliere Tindall.

Orem, D. E. (1980), *Nursing: Concepts of Practice*, 2nd edn, New York: McGraw-Hill.

Roper, N. (1985), *The Elements of Nursing*, 2nd edn, Edinburgh: Churchill Livingstone.

Skelt, A. (1993), *Caring for People with Disabilities*, London: Pitman.

Swain, J., Finkelstein, V., French, S. and Oliver, M. (1993), *Disabling Barriers, Enabling Environments*, London: Sage.

Thomson et al. (1995), *Health and Social Care for Advanced GNVQ*, 2nd edition, London: Hodder & Stoughton.

Weller, B. (1989) Ed: *Basillières Encyclopaedie*, Department of Nursery and Health Care.

WHO (1980), International Classification of Impairments, Disabilities and Handicaps, Geneva: WHO.

WHO (1990), *Is the Law Fair to the Disabled?*, European Series No. 29, WHO Regional Publications.

Will, BBC Television, *Everyman*, 10 April 1994.

USEFUL ADDRESSES

Alzheimer's Disease Society
Gordon House
10 Greencoat Place
London SW1P 1PH
Tel.: 0171 306 0606

Association for Spina Bifida and Hydrocephalus (ASBAH)
42 Park Road
Peterborough PE1 2UQ
Tel.: 01733 555988

Association to Combat Huntington's Chorea
34A Station Road
Hinckley
Leics LE10 1AP
Tel.: 01455 615558

British Council of Organizations of Disabled People (BCODP)
St Mary's Church
Greenlaw Street
London SE18 5AR
Tel.: 0181 316 4184

British Diabetic Association
10 Queen Anne Street
London W1M 0BD
Tel.: 0171 323 1531

British Epilepsy Association
Anstey House

40 Hanover Square
Leeds LS3 1BE
Tel.: 01532 439393

British Medical Association
BMA House
Tavistock Square
London WC1H 9JP

British Polio Fellowship
Bell Close
West End Road
Ruislip
Middx HA4 6LP
Tel.: 01895 675515

British Sports Association for the Disabled
34 Osnaburgh Street
London NW1 3ND
Tel.: 0171 383 7277

Chest, Heart & Stroke Association
Tavistock House North
Tavistock Square
London WC1H 9JE
Tel.: 0171 387 3012

Contact a Family
16 Strutton Ground
London SW1P 2HP
Tel.: 0171 222 2695
(for information on conditions affecting children)

Cystic Fibrosis Research Trust
5 Blyth Road
Bromley
Kent BR1 3RS
Tel.: 0181 461 7211

Disability Alliance
25 Denmark Street
London WC2H 8NJ
Tel.: 0171 240 0806

Disabled Living Foundation
380–384 Harrow Road
London W9 2HU
Tel.: 0171 289 6111

Disabled Persons Information Centre
Wimpey House
382–384 Newport Road
Cardiff CF3 7UA
Tel.: 01222 488184

Disablement Information and Advice Lines (DIAL UK)
Tel.: 01302 310123

Down's Children's Association
Quinbourne Community Centre
Ridgacre Road
Birmingham B32 2TW
Tel.: 0121 427 1374

ENABLE (formerly Scottish Society for Mentally Handicapped)
6th Floor
7 Buchanan Street
Glasgow G1 3HL
Tel.: 0141 226 4541

Friedreich's Ataxia Group
Copse Edge
Thursley Road
Elstead
Godalming
Surrey GU8 6DJ
Tel.: 01252 702864

Haemophilia Society
123 Westminster Bridge Road
London SE1 7HR
Tel.: 0171 928 2020

Head Injuries Association
200 Mansfield Road
Nottingham NG1 3HX
Tel.: 01602 622382

John Groome Association for Disabled People
10 Gloucester Drive
London N4 2LP
Tel.: 0181 802 7272

Marie Curie Cancer Care
28 Belgrave Square
London SW1X 8QG
Tel.: 0171 235 3325

Motor Neurone Disease Association
PO Box 246
Northampton NN1 2PR
Tel.: 01604 250505

Multiple Sclerosis Society
25 Effie Road
London SW6 1EE
Tel.: 0171 736 6267

Muscular Dystrophy Group
Nattrass House
35 Macauley Road
London SW4 0PQ
Tel.: 0171 720 8055

Mencap
Mencap National Centre
123 Golden Lane
London EC1Y 0RT
Tel.: 0171 454 0454

National Autistic Society
276 Willesden Lane
London NW2 5RB
Tel.: 0181 451 1114

Parkinson's Disease Society
36 Portland Place
London W1N 3DG
Tel.: 0171 323 1174

PHAB (Physically Handicapped and Able-Bodied)
Padholme Road East
Peterborough PE1 5UL
Tel.: 01733 54117

RADAR (Royal Association for Disability and Rehabilitation)
25 Mortimer Street
London W1N 8AB
Tel.: 0171 637 5400

Royal National Institute for Deaf People
105 Gower Street
London WC1E 6AH
Tel.: 0171 387 8033

Royal National Institute for the Blind
224 Great Portland Street
London W1N 6AA
Tel.: 0171 388 1266

Scottish Council on Disability
Princess House
5 Shandwick Place
Edinburgh EH2 4RG
Tel.: 0131 229 8632

SCOPE
12 Park Crescent
London W1N 4EQ
Tel.: 0171 636 5020

Telephones for the Blind Fund
Mynthurst
Leigh
Reigate
Surrey RH2 8RJ
Tel.: 01293 862546

Tenovus Cancer Information Centre
142 Whitchurch Road
Cardiff CF4 3NA
Tel.: 01222 691998

Terrence Higgins Trust
52–54 Gray's Inn Road
London WC1X 8JU
Helpline (3–10 pm daily): 0171 242 1010
Legal line (Weds 7–10 pm): 0171 405 2381
(information and advice on all matters concerning HIV and AIDS)

Wales Council for the Deaf
Maritime Offices
Woodland Terrace
Maes y Coed
Pontypridd
Mid Glamorgan CF37 1DZ
Tel.: 01443 485687

Wales Council for the Disabled
Llys Ifor
Crescent Road
Caerphilly
Mid Glamorgan CF83 1XL
Tel.: 01222 887325

Winged Fellowship Trust
Angel House
20–32 Pentonville Road
London N1 9XD
Tel.: 0171 833 2594

4

PSYCHOLOGY IN THE CONTEXT OF HEALTH AND SOCIAL CARE

WAYS OF EXPLAINING HUMAN BEHAVIOUR

The analysis of human behaviour may be approached from a variety of perspectives. Each offers a different explanation of why individuals behave in a certain way. The five perspectives outlined below could be used individually to study one human behaviour, for example, aggression, and each would make a contribution to our conception of the total person.

The behavioural approach

(Main theorists: Watson, Skinner and Thorndike)
This approach studies individuals by looking at their outward behaviour rather than their internal workings. J. Watson, the 'father of behaviourism', proposed that introspection is not measurable, and that if psychology were to be a science, its data must be observable and measurable. This approach is sometimes referred to as *stimulus-response* psychology, and it ignores any mental processes that occur between the stimulus and the response. Human behaviour is shaped by external environmental forces, through the processes of *reinforcement* and *punishment*.

Perhaps the simplest form of learning is 'associative learning' which occurs through the process of *conditioning*: *classical* and *operant* (for an explanation of these terms, see Thomson et al. 1995).

EXPLAINING AGGRESSION

This approach has promoted studies which show that children are more likely to express aggressive responses, such as hitting another child, when such responses are rewarded (by the other child withdrawing) than when the aggressive response is punished (the child hits back).

ACTIVITY

1 Research classical conditioning by describing Pavlov's famous work concerning his dogs.

2 Investigate the following terms:
- *reinforcement*
- *punishment*
- *negative reinforcement*

The social learning approach

(Main theorist: Bandura)
The social learning approach is the descendant of the behavioural approach. For social learning theorists, behaviour is the result of a continuous interaction between a person and their environment. Behaviour develops through learning: operant conditioning, classical conditioning and observational learning, the latter involving *imitation* and *identification*.

A child will not simply observe someone and then copy them, since some people will be more important to a child than others. Consequently, certain people's behaviour is more likely to be copied: the child will *model* aspects of its behaviour on these 'important' people (*role models*). Reinforcement isn't necessary for observational learning, although it *is* important that the *correct* behaviour be reinforced if performance is to improve.

Children will thus observe and copy aspects of the behaviour of different people. Children will also be rewarded or punished for different sorts of behaviour; and according to this theory, different learning experiences acquired during the course of growing up account for individual differences in behaviour.

EXPLAINING AGGRESSION

Various studies have shown that children tend to imitate aggressive role models shown on television or videos, or at home or in school, especially if the child perceives the 'model' as similar to themselves.

The cognitive approach

(*Main theorists: Piaget, Kohlberg and Brunner*)
This approach argues that the mind actively processes the stimuli it receives and rearranges them into new forms and categories; in other words, we are not just passive receptors of information. *Cognition* refers to the mental processes of perception, memory, reasoning and problem-solving by which the individual acquires knowledge and makes plans for the future. *Cognitive psychology* is the scientific study of cognition. Its aim is to develop, through experimentation, theories that explain how mental processes function and are organised. The key analogy for cognitive psychology is that of the modern high-speed computer, an information-processing system that selects information, encodes it, stores it and retrieves it when necessary.

EXPLAINING AGGRESSION

The importance of knowledge here is clear: if someone insults you verbally, you are more likely to return the aggression if the person is an acquaintance than if they are a young child or mentally ill person.

The psychoanalytic approach

(*Main theorists: Freud, Jung and Erikson*)
This approach was developed by Sigmund Freud at about the same time that behaviourism was evolving in the USA. Freud's basic assumption was that most of our behaviour stems from processes that are unconscious, that is fears, beliefs and desires of which the individual is unaware but which nevertheless influence their behaviour. Freud believed that *all* actions have a cause, but that cause is often an unconscious motive rather than the rational reason we may give for our behaviour. Instincts forbidden expression in early childhood move into the unconscious, where they remain to affect dreams or slips of the tongue ('Freudian slips'), or manifest themselves as, for example, emotional problems.

EXPLAINING AGGRESSION

This approach views aggression as an instinct which needs to be discharged (*sublimation*), through sport or debating for example, to prevent a dangerous build-up.

ACTIVITY

Freud reworked and developed his theory of aggression later in his life. Research the full psychoanalytic theory of aggression in order to answer the following questions:

- According to this theory, which defence mechanisms are used in the discharge of aggression?
- How can this theory be used to explain sudden extreme violence from an individual who is normally quiet and inhibited?
- How could this theory, involving the death wish *Thanatos*, explain suicide?

The phenomenological (humanistic) approach

(Main theorists: Maslow and Rogers)

In contrast to the psychoanalytic approach, this approach suggests that we are not controlled by unconscious motivation but are instead free to control our own destiny. This is the issue of free will versus determinism. A primary motivational force in the individual is towards growth and self-actualisation. This approach was the approach of Maslow and Rogers (see the explanation of Maslow's 'hierarchy of needs', in Thomson et al. 1995, pp. 205–6). Whereas the psychoanalytic approach focuses upon the past experience, this theory suggests that present experience is just as important. Its proponents accept, however, that it is less scientific than the other approaches.

Figure 4.1 Abraham H. Maslow (1908–70)

EXPLAINING AGGRESSION

This approach distinguishes between (a) natural and positive aggression, which may motivate people, for example, to join pressure groups and work for a more just society, and (b) pathological aggression which is inward-looking and destructive.

METHODS USED IN RESEARCHING HUMAN BEHAVIOUR

The main methods used in researching human behaviour include:

1 experiments
2 observations
3 questionnaires and interviews (surveys).

These methods are described in much detail in Thomson et al. 1995.

Experiments

An experiment is a study of cause and effect, that is, it looks at the causal relationship between two different things. This is explored by deliberately producing a change in one variable (the *independent variable – IV*) and measuring what effect this has on the other variable (the *dependent variable – DV*). It differs from non-experimental methods in that it involves the deliberate manipulation of one variable while trying to keep all other variables (e.g. heat, noise, etc.) constant.

ADVANTAGES

- They determine a causal link
- They can be well-controlled and replicated

DISADVANTAGES

- They are artificial and therefore may not generalise to real life (i.e. they may lack ecological validity)
- Some subjects, e.g. children, may react poorly under experimental conditions
- They can be affected by, for example, an experimental bias, demand characteristics or a sample bias

NATURAL EXPERIMENTS

In some situations it may be unethical to carry out investigations by controlled experiments; for example, newborns couldn't be taken away from their mothers to study maternal deprivation. So the researcher would have to use situations where the conditions may very naturally occur, e.g. in the case of an orphanage. One such study would be Freud and Dann's study of six children who spent their early lives in a concentration camp during the Second World War.

Observation

In *naturalistic observation*, the psychologist remains as inconspicuous as possible while observing behaviour. This method is much used in studying the behaviour of children, who are used to having adults around and soon relax and behave naturally. Adults, however, do not act naturally once they realise they are being observed, and this could make any observation of their behaviour meaningless.

Observations should be replicable on another occasion by another researcher. Therefore, inter-observer reliability must be established: that is, an agreement on what precisely is to be observed, with the prior preparation of recording charts.

ADVANTAGES

- It gives a more realistic picture of spontaneous behaviour
- It has a high ecological validity

DISADVANTAGES

- One cannot infer cause and effect
- It is difficult to replicate
- A lack of controls: one cannot exclude the effect of other variables.

ACTIVITY

Equipment that may be used in naturalistic observation includes the video camera and the one-way mirror.

1 Discuss the advantages and disadvantages of using
   (a) a video camera
   (b) a one-way mirror

with

   (a) children and
   (b) adults.

2 Identify situations where these methods could usefully be used with the two client groups.

3 Define:
   (a) what behaviour you would seek to observe;
   (b) how you would organise the observation study.

EXAMPLES OF IMPORTANT NATURALISTIC-OBSERVATION STUDIES

The Robertson film

James Robertson's film 'A two-year-old goes to hospital' was made in 1952. The subject was a two-year-old girl, awaiting surgery for an umbilical hernia, who had never previously been out of her mother's care. She was filmed for two 40-minute periods, at the same time each day, for the eight days of her hospitalisation. The film charted her distress, and challenged the view that a quiet child is 'settled'. The advantage of the video film was that it could be shown over and over again to sceptical medical experts, and it eventually served to change the treatment of children in hospital.

ACTIVITY

Carry out research into routines in children's wards in the early 1950s with regard to visiting hours and contact with parents. What is the policy concerning these matters in children's wards in the 1990s?

The 'strange situation'

In 1978 Mary Ainsworth and her colleagues devised a method for studying *attachments*, called the 'strange situation', which is regarded as highly reliable, and which has been used in many studies in which attachment is the main dependent variable. The 'strange situation' comprises a sequence of eight episodes in which the parent (mother or father, or both) and a stranger come and go from a room in which a child is playing (most studies have involved one-year-old children). Each episode lasts about three minutes.

The method used is that of *controlled observation*. One or more trained observers record the child's attachment behaviour in the following situations:

- in the parent's presence
- when the parent leaves
- when the parent returns

and notes

- how the child responds to the stranger
- how the child's play is affected

The major findings from studies using the 'strange situation' have led to the identification of three types of attachment:

1. *Anxious-avoidant:* When the parent leaves, the child shows little distress. Play is little affected by the parent's absence or presence. The child tends not to seek contact with the parent. When the parent returns, typically the child ignores or only casually greets them, approaching only tentatively, and may turn away. The child is distressed by being alone rather than by being left by the parent: it shows no distress with the stranger (play is little affected), and is as easily comforted by the stranger as by the parent.
2. *Securely attached:* The child plays happily with toys in the parent's presence. It maintains contact with the parent but does not stay particularly close. It resists being put down and is distressed during the parent's absence, when play is reduced. When the parent returns, the child quickly goes to them. It calms down rapidly in the parent's arms and is then able to play happily again. It reacts happily to strangers in the parent's presence. The child is distressed not just by being alone but also by the parent's absence. The stranger can provide some comfort, but not as much as the parent.
3. *Anxious-resistant:* This type of attachment is angrier or more passive than the other two types. When the child is with the parent, it cries more and explores less. It seeks the parent, but at the same time resists contact with the parent and shows anger. When the parent returns, the child may quickly go to them, but once picked up may struggle to get down. It does not return readily to play, glancing frequently at the parent. The child actively resists the approaches of strangers, even in the parent's presence.

Ainsworth et al. concluded that sensitive parents have secure babies who can explore strange environments, using the parent as a safe base. Babies of insensitive parents are so insecure that they either become very angry when the parent leaves or seem almost indifferent to their absence, and so do *not* use them as a safe base.

In *participant observation*, the observer *takes part* in the group they are observing. This approach, used in conjunction with hidden cameras, has been effectively applied in television documentaries. Two recently screened such documentaries used participant observation:

1. An investigator pretended to be schizophrenic and homeless on the streets, and thereby tested out the services for city down-and-outs.
2. An elderly investigator pretended to be looking for a place in a private old people's home, thereby uncovering the poor standard of care provided in many such homes.

Such investigations raise the ethical problem of *deception*, which in these cases may perhaps be overruled in the interests of exposing bad practices and furthering social justice.

Surveys

This is a term which covers: questionnaires, attitude scales, opinion polls and interviews.

These methods are useful for obtaining information from adults and from older clients (and, in some situations, from children also). Their presentation can be in written or spoken form and can range from unstructured to highly structured.

The advantages and disadvantages of these methods are discussed in detail in Chapter 8 of Thomson et al. 1995, pp. 409–21. Questionnaires and interviews are useful in the caring context, for example in showing how greatly individuals may differ in their reactions to the same event or idea, such as the prospect of going into residential care for an elderly person.

APPLICATIONS OF PSYCHOLOGICAL RESEARCH WITHIN HEALTH CARE SETTINGS

Psychological research has been applied to many areas within the health and social care field.

The behavioural approach

For instance, learning theory (with regard to operant conditioning and social modelling) offers a simplistic explanation of health-related behaviour. For example, with lung cancer, punishment – in terms of negative reinforcement – is often delayed, and consequently this may explain why some people fail to take advice.

On the basis of research, the behavioural approach has also developed many treatment methods. It is important to note that advocates of behaviourism assume that looking at the cause of the illness is unnecessary as they believe that only behaviours that are presently observable are important; unlike Freud they do not look into the patient's past history. They also believe that psychological problems are the result of maladaptive behaviour patterns which have developed through inappropriate learning and which need either relearning or unlearning.

Walker (1984) distinguished between two types of treatment. *Behaviour therapy* involves treatment methods based upon classical conditioning. Using this technique, maladaptive behaviours are extinguished and appropriate ones are substituted. Techniques using *behaviour modification*, however, are based on operant conditioning and will either increase the frequency of appropriate responses or decrease the inappropriate responses, or even develop appropriate behaviour where it didn't previously exist.

CASE STUDY: SELF-MUTILATION TREATED BY OPERANT CONDITIONING

A boy suffering from Lesch-Nylan syndrome, a rare genetic disorder which involves neurological disorders, psychomotor retardation and often self-mutilation, began showing self-injurious behaviour at about age three. He was eventually confined to a wheelchair, his arms were constrained by splints and he wore a helmet and shoulder pads. At night, he slept in a jacket and safety straps to stop him biting. He held his breath, removed his finger and toe nails, spat, displayed projectile vomiting and head-banging, screamed and used foul language. Despite the restraints, he could still inflict wounds on various parts of his body, and while doing so, would often shout 'I hate myself'. His abnormal behaviour seemed to be associated with periods of anxiety and agitation, and was sometimes provoked by the removal of his restraining devices, about which he felt very ambivalent (he didn't want them on but nor did he want them off!).

Treatment was aimed at: (i) allowing him to tolerate being without his restraints; and (ii) extinguishing the self-injurious behaviour. Initially, the removal of even a peripheral part of the protective equipment could only be achieved by using nitrous oxide as a relaxant. It was also observed that treating his self-inflicted wounds served to reinforce the self-injurious behaviour, so that was done under anaesthetic to avoid any association between self-injury and reward.

The boy was then put in a room on his own

(containing a one-way mirror), and his self-injurious behaviour stopped, suggesting it was motivated by the need for attention. Consequently, attention was used as a reinforcer, being withheld during self-mutilation and given at other times instead.

Over the course of 15 one-hour sessions, the withdrawal of attention during self-injury led to the reduction and ultimate extinction of biting behaviour. The process was repeated for the other abnormal behaviours.

Eighteen months later, the improvement had clearly been maintained. The boy had no restraints, could feed himself, was learning to walk with crutches, was attending a special class in a normal school and was interacting and communicating with other children.

(Gross 1992)

EXAMPLES OF BEHAVIOUR THERAPY

Aversion therapy

Alcoholics are given a drug (e.g. antabuse) which when paired with alcohol will cause severe nausea and vomiting and both these symptoms will become a conditioned response to alcohol.

In one study it was found that 50% of alcoholics following this therapy abstained for one year (at least), and that aversion therapy is better than no treatment (Meyer and Chesser 1970).

Systematic desensitisation (SD)

This is often used to treat *phobias*, which are irrational fears. This technique replaces the state of anxiety associated with a state of *relaxation*:

1 Deep muscle relaxation is learnt by the patient.
2 A hierarchy of increasingly threatening situations is constructed by the patient.
3 Whilst relaxed, the patient is asked to imagine each scene.

Rachman and Wilson, and McGlynn et al. have found that SD is more effective with minor phobias (animal phobias) than it is with more serious phobias such as agoraphobia.

Flooding

The patient is exposed to their fear with *no* relaxation, so for example a patient suffering from arachnophobia would have to hold a large spider and let it crawl over them.

This technique has been used with agoraphobics and has been found to be very successful. Studies have found an improvement which continued for up to nine years after the treatment. One famous study was by Wolpe whose patient had a fear of cars. She was forced into the back of a car and was continuously driven around for four hours. Although hysterical during the treatment, by the end of the journey her fear had disappeared.

ACTIVITY

1 Discuss how aversion therapy can be applied to (i) nail biting (ii) smoking.

2 Draw up a hierarchy listing what you would least fear to what you would most fear with a particular thing, e.g. a snake.

3 Discuss how you could study the techniques of SD and flooding to see which is the most effective technique for treating fear.

TECHNIQUES USING BEHAVIOUR MODIFICATION

Social skills training using operant conditioning

1 Lovaas et al., using shaping and positive reinforcement, trained autistic children in language skills. This involved three stages:
   - Whenever the autistic child made eye contact the therapist paired food with verbal approval
   - This type of reinforcement was then extended to whenever the child made any kind of speech sound

- The therapist would then use selective reinforcement: the child would only receive reinforcement if they uttered speech sounds without prompting or successfully imitated complete actions, sounds, syllables, words and, lastly, a combination of words

2 Azrin et al. successfully toilet-trained children with enuresis (bed-wetting) by taking each child hourly to the toilet and giving positive reinforcement only when it was successfully used – any accident was not praised.

3 One technique used to train hyperactive children is called 'time out' – often, when their uncontrollable behaviour receives attention (i.e. is positively reinforced) this serves to *perpetuate* that very behaviour. This vicious cycle needs to be broken, and in order to do this the children should only be positively reinforced for good behaviour, whilst inappropriate behaviour, on the other hand, is treated with temporary isolation – until they are calmed down.

4 A training package for disruptive pupils has been developed by Goddard and Cross. This includes training in skills such as listening, apologising, dealing with teasing and bullying.

5 This type of therapy has also been used to try to control pain. To reverse the association between pain and the aversive stimulus, operant conditioning and the setting of goals is used, e.g. to help a child overcome a fear of injections. However, this works best when pain behaviours are ignored, otherwise attention will only reinforce and strengthen them.

ACTIVITY

1 Discuss the limitations of the behavioural therapies generally.

2 A student called Paola is disruptive in class as she gets up from her chair and goes to chat with her friends in the class. The teacher tells Paola off but finds her behaviour gets worse, not better. What advice could you give the teacher with respect to behaviour modification using operant conditioning?

Cognitive theory applied to health and social fields

How people attribute control over their health will influence their coping strategies. For example, an *internal attribution* would occur when a patient feels they can control their illness, whilst an *external* one would occur when the patient feels there is nothing they can do – as the cause of their illness is fated. Attribution therapy aims to teach a person how to take control and thereby overcome their illness.

Research concerning the symptoms of premenstrual tension (PMT) found that women who read an article attributing PMT to 'negative societal myths' reported a decline in symptoms. This was in contrast to those who read an article focusing upon the *biological* effects of PMT.

Langer et al. (1975) studied coping strategies concerned with cognitive control for those having surgery. When the patients trained in self-control were compared with a group of controls, they were found to be less anxious. Langer's cognitive methods have been used to try to control pain, which is done by changing the way the person's *understanding* of pain works – in terms of cognitions (beliefs, expectations).

Research on patients with severe burns found that they spontaneously decided to reduce medication when their sense of control had been increased. Girodo and Wood found that by training the patients to make positive statements (e.g. 'I can cope'), and by enhancing their personal control even more by giving them explanations as to why this method works, they did seem able to make the patients suffer from less pain.

The psychotherapy approach

This form of therapy is based upon Freud's theory. However, there are many adaptations, such as the *humanist* approach developed by Rogers.

Freud's theory assumes that neuroses are the result of repressed or unfulfilled desires. It may be that any disturbance in personality development is the result of a fixation at one of the *psychosexual stages*. It could also be that the *ego* needs strengthening as it fears being overwhelmed by the *id* (all the primitive instincts and energies in the unconscious mind), and consequently defence mechanisms, e.g. the repression of anxiety-provoking memories, are employed.

One of Freud's case studies involved a 5-year-old boy called 'Little Hans':

Hans had a phobia of being bitten by a horse and was especially afraid of white horses with black around the mouth and wearing blinkers; he tried to avoid horses at all costs. [Freud's interpretation: fear of being bitten represented Hans's fear of castration.]

Hans was particularly frightened when he once saw a horse collapse in the street. [Freud's interpretation: seeing the horse collapse reminded him, unconsciously, of his death wish against his father, which made him feel guilty and afraid.]

Is there any reason to believe that Hans saw the horses as symbolizing his father?

1 Hans once said to his father as he got up from the table: 'Daddy, don't *trot* away from me'.
2 On another occasion, Hans said: 'Daddy, you are lovely, you're so white'. This suggests he may have thought his father resembled a white horse (as opposed to a dark one).
3 Hans's father had a moustache ('the black on the horses' mouth').
4 His father wore glasses, which resembled blinkers as worn by horses.
5 Hans had played 'horses' with his father, with Hans usually riding on his father's back.

Hans claimed that his fear stemmed from the time he saw a horse collapse in the street: 'When the horse in the bus fell down it gave me such a fright really; that was when I got the nonsense (i.e. the phobia)'. This was confirmed by Hans's mother. But his father, and Freud, paid little attention to this plausible explanation of the phobia.

Freud believed Hans was a 'little Oedipus', loving to be in bed with his mother and going to the bathroom with her, and regarding his father as a rival and wanting him out of the way.

(Gross 1992)

Activity

1 Discuss the limitations of case studies generally.

2 Discuss and research the other alternative explanations as to why Little Hans was frightened of horses – your other interpretations should incorporate the ideas of Fromm (1970) and Bowlby (1973).

To see this case as evidence for the 'Oedipus complex' (the desire of the male child to possess his mother sexually and remove his father) is problematic for various reasons. For instance, Freud had apparently settled for one explanation of Hans's phobia and consequently interpreted all the data accordingly. It is also important to note that Freud only met Hans on one or two occasions, as Hans's psychoanalysis was mainly conducted by his father who followed Freud's ideas, and with regard to this, even Freud recognised that there was a problem of objectivity.

Such case studies as Freud's are usually seen to be the least scientific of research methods used by psychologists as they are open to distortion; for instance, Freud made his case notes several hours after his treatment sessions. In 1977 Fisher and Greenberg suggested that one problem concerning case studies is that the researcher can select or emphasise material which supports particular interpretations. Freud defended his methods by saying: '. . . a psychoanalysis is not an impartial scientific investigation, but a therapeutic measure. Its essence is not to prove anything but merely to alter something' (Freud 1909).

Figure 4.2 Sigmund Freud (1856–1939)

The aims of Freudian therapy include making the unconscious conscious and providing the client with self-knowledge and understanding so that their conflicts can be resolved. These aims are achieved through various techniques, such as the *transference*. In classical psychoanalysis, the analyst should remain totally 'anonymous'. This entails not revealing any information about themselves, which includes not making any value-judgements concerning the client's problem. During the session the client is unable to see the analyst, as the latter sits behind the client. This anonymity should encourage a process of transference which involves the client's projection and displacement of repressed feelings onto the analyst.

The analyst must then be able to interpret the transference in order for the client to understand what it means and be able to relate to it. Simultaneously, the client's ego needs to be strengthened in order for the client to be able to cope with any anxiety caused by making repressed wishes/memories conscious. This is achieved through a 'working alliance' between the analyst and the client.

Two other major Freudian techniques include *free association* – which involves the therapist introducing a topic and the client talking about anything that comes into their mind – and *dream interpretation* – which also reveals the unconscious mind, especially through repressed 'wishes'.

ACTIVITY

1 Discuss some of the practical limitations of classical psychoanalysis.

2 Research the humanist (Rogers) approach to psychotherapy. Compare and contrast this with Freud's classical psychoanalysis.

THEORIES OF PERSONALITY

Various theories of personality, such as the humanist, type, trait and psychoanalytic theories, have been covered in Thomson et al. 1995, pp. 205–12. This section will add to that range by focusing upon *learning* theory, *cognitive* theory and *narrow-range* theories.

Learning theory

This theory sees personality as being the product of learning, and regards human behaviour as involving a set of *learned associations*. Watson argues that the mind of a child was a *tabula rasa* at birth, that is, a clean slate which will be enscribed upon by life's experiences. It is in fact these experiences that, according to Watson, are what make up our personality.

Watson's quote illustrates this point of view:

Give me a dozen healthy infants . . . and my own specialised world to bring them up in, and I'll guarantee to take any one at random and train him to become any type of specialist I might select – doctor, lawyer . . . and yes, even beggarman and thief, regardless of his talents, penchants, tendencies, abilities, vocations, and race of his ancestors.

(Watson 1924)

Figure 4.3 John B. Watson (1878–1958)

Watson is not, however, advocating here that he can make anybody anything in *society as it is*. Instead, he is arguing that he would need his *own specified world* to enable him to do this.

ACTIVITY

1 How far do you agree with Watson's claim?

2 What sort of specified world would he need?

3 Why could it be suggested that not everyone can become *anything* in today's society?

B. F. Skinner (1972) proposed that learning happened as a result of the Law of Effect – that is, actions with satisfying consequences are those more likely to be repeated. Consequently, he argues that human beings inevitably behave in ways that are rewarding or that allow them to escape from unpleasant consequences. Skinner takes the extreme view that the concepts of freedom and human dignity do not exist, as he believes that everyone is unconsciously controlled by the learned behaviours that make up an individual's personality. People can be differentiated from each other because they act differently, and this is the result of their experiencing subtly different *reinforcement contingencies*.

Neither Watsons's nor Skinner's theories allowed for the existence of a *mind*, as they both believed in 'black box' theories which focused upon the input of stimuli and the output of behavioural responses to those stimuli (*stimulus–response – SR*). Consequently, both theories can be seen as involving *reductionist* views of personality.

SOCIAL LEARNING THEORY

Bandura thought that *social learning* was a prerequisite for personality development. This process includes not only classical and operant conditioning but also imitation and identification. Imitation involves copying behaviour from a role model, and Bandura saw this as the first step of personality development. The second step is when the child takes certain individuals to be their role models with whom they then identify. By doing this they can generalise their learning to new behaviour. This is because the child can imagine the role model in that new situation and then behave in the appropriate way. With imitation, the child can only replicate existing behaviours. Through identification, however, the child can produce novel behaviour.

Consequently, Bandura sees personality as being a result of the individual's experiences, and as developing through the processes discussed above which were not included in the strictly behaviourist models.

Cognitive theory

KELLY'S PERSONAL CONSTRUCT THEORY

Kelly was a clinical psychologist whose first principle was 'If you don't know what's wrong with the patient – ask him – he may tell you,' (Kelly 1955) implying that the patient knows what's wrong with them. Kelly likens people to scientists forever making and testing hypotheses about their observations about everyday life and the people they meet. One of Kelly's main assumptions concerns *constructive alternativism*. He suggests that people have their subjective views about how the world and people work. We react to our own personal understandings of what the world is like. These guide us in our own behaviour, and are known as *personal constructs*.

Figure 4.4 George A. Kelly (1905–66)

Personal constructs can be seen as statements with two opposing ends (what are known as *bipolar statements*), e.g. 'happy – sad'. A set of constructs is unique to that individual: in fact, for other people the same word may have *different* associations. Kelly proposes that on average seven or eight *major constructs* are used when trying to comprehend other individuals, but that we do also have *minor* ones, *general* ones and *specific* ones.

Kelly therefore argues that what is unique about personality is the fact that everyone has their own theories with which they try to make sense of their experiences. Consequently, they all behave differently, and it is this that makes us all unique individuals.

ACTIVITY

To discover your own main personal constructs, write down the names of eight important people in your life and label them A, B, C, . . . H. Consider these individuals in combinations of three at a time, and for each combination, ascertain one way in which any two of the three have something in common which is *not* shared by the third. Write out each result as follows: 'A and B are ______, but C is ______.'

The next step is to arrange your constructs in grid form (a *repertory grid*):

	Mother	Father	Sister	Brother →
Caring ✓ Not caring ✗	✓			
Generous ✓ Not generous ✗	✓			
Authoritarian ✗ Not authoritarian ↓	✓ ✓			

Place a tick or a cross if the person (known as an *element*) has that construct.

Narrow band theories

Narrow band theories of personality focus on one part of a person's personality rather than trying to describe the whole personality. One narrow band theory concerns Adorno's authoritarian personality. This is discussed in more detail in the next section on attitudes and prejudice.

TYPE A AND TYPE B BEHAVIOUR

Friedman and Rosenman investigated why some people are prone to coronary heart disease while others who work equally hard are not. They focused in particular on those who were managers in highly stressful careers and they found that those with a tendency to coronary heart disease appeared to have certain personality characteristics in common. These people they called the *Type A* personality.

This type of personality has three aspects to it:

1 *Competitive achievement orientation:* this involves hard driving behaviour towards goals that are attained with a sense of anti-climax and self-criticism.
2 *Time urgency:* Type A individuals are often impatient and rushed, arranging too many commitments in their diaries and frequently trying to do too many things at once. It has been said that Friedman and Rosenman first noticed this type of behaviour when they realised the seats in their waiting room were only worn on the front: the coronary patients never seemed to sit back in their chairs as they were in too much of a hurry to get back to work.
3 *High level of anger or hostility, or both:* Type A individuals can be easily aroused with regard to these emotions. However, they may not always *demonstrate* them.

In comparison, *Type B* personalities experienced these three aspects of behaviour less, and as a result were less stressed than Type A individuals although they were just as productive.

In 1974, Friedman and Rosenman published the results of their 12-year longitudinal study of over 3,500 healthy middle-aged men. When their findings had been adjusted for smoking, lifestyle etc., it was found that those with Type A behaviour were twice as likely to develop heart disease and more than twice as likely to have a second heart attack as those with Type B behaviour.

Other researchers have found that different aspects of Type A behaviour correlate with different types of coronary disease. For example, those who were intolerant and impatient had a tendency for angina, while those who were hurried and rushed had a susceptibility for heart failure.

Glass suggests that a fundamental difference between Type A and Type B people concerns the way they respond to being helpless. One study consisted of subjects who were either Type A or Type B being asked to complete puzzles, not all of which, however, were solvable. When this became apparent, Glass found the Type A subjects became far more stressed and even attempted to regain control with regard to their situation. When, however, they found they could not achieve this, they totally gave in, not even trying to attempt similar but solvable puzzles. In contrast, Type B individuals approached the problem-solving exercise more calmly, and even tried novel strategies to try to solve further problems.

As a result, it can be assumed that what distinguishes Type A from Type B individuals is the cognitive-emotional aspect of the personality. In other words, the difference is due partly to their cognitive make-up and partly to the underlying emotional-orientation to pressures. Another suggestion which is physiological in nature is that the sympathetic nervous system of Type A personalities is very reactive, so that their blood pressure would increase greatly under stress.

However, three problems with Type A behaviour have made research problematic. These concern how to measure it, what to measure and what relationship there is between what you measure and the risk of developing heart disease.

Type A behaviour can be measured by questionnaire or, more effectively, by a short, structured and fairly stressful interview designed to indicate latent coronary-prone behaviour. Friedman and Rosenman's original description of Type A behaviour includes:

Table 4.1 Type A/Type B personality questionnaire, with scoring scale

Each of the 13 items listed below has 2 extremes (e.g. easygoing – hard driving), one at each end of a continuous scale. Circle the number which you feel most closely represents your own behaviour.

a	Never late	5 4 3 2 1 0 1 2 3 4 5	Casual about appointments, easygoing
b	Not competitive	5 4 3 2 1 0 1 2 3 4 5	Very competitive
c	Anticipates what others are going to say (nods, interrupts, finishes for them)	5 4 3 2 1 0 1 2 3 4 5	Good listener
d	Always rushed	5 4 3 2 1 0 1 2 3 4 5	Never feels rushed (even under pressure)
e	Can wait patiently	5 4 3 2 1 0 1 2 3 4 5	Impatient when waiting
f	Goes all out	5 4 3 2 1 0 1 2 3 4 5	Casual
g	Takes things one at a time	5 4 3 2 1 0 1 2 3 4 5	Tries to do many things at once, thinks about what they are about to do next
h	Emphatic in speech (may pound desk)	5 4 3 2 1 0 1 2 3 4 5	Slow, deliberate talker
i	Wants good job recognised by others	5 4 3 2 1 0 1 2 3 4 5	Cares about satisfying themselves no matter what others may think
j	Fast (eating, walking etc.)	5 4 3 2 1 0 1 2 3 4 5	Slow doing things
k	Easy going	5 4 3 2 1 0 1 2 3 4 5	Hard driving
l	Hides feelings	5 4 3 2 1 0 1 2 3 4 5	Expresses feelings
m	Many outside interests	5 4 3 2 1 0 1 2 3 4 5	Few outside interests

Each item scores on an 11-point scale, but some of the scales vary. The following scales score from 1 on the left to 11 on the right: b, e, g, k, l, m

The following score from 11 on the left to 1 on the right: a, c, d, f, h, i, j

So, for instance, if you are only very occasionally late, and have therefore completed item a) as shown below, your score for the first scale would be 10.

A	Never late	5 4 3 2 1 0 1 2 3 4 5	Casual about appointments, easygoing

Your final score is the sum total of all the scales.

Source: Banyard, P. and Hayes, N. (1994), *Psychology – Theory and Application*, Chapman & Hall.

'any person who is aggressively involved in a chronic incessant struggle to achieve more and more in less and less time'.

The most significant trait of the Type A man is his habitual sense of time-urgency or 'hurry sickness'. The characteristic of constantly feeling rushed is measured by asking questions about whether the subjects eat fast, walk fast and try to get things done as quickly as possible.

PSYCHOLOGICAL CLUES TO CORONARIES

Eight questions from the 'structured interview'. The first four measure the subject's level of drive and impatience, the second four tap his or her latent hostility. The last is also a measure of Anger-In.

- Would you describe yourself as a hard-driving, ambitious type of person in accomplishing the things you want, getting things done as quickly as possible, or would you describe yourself as a reasonably relaxed and easy-going person?
- Do you think you drive harder to accomplish things than most of your associates?
- Do you eat quickly? Do you walk quickly? After you finish eating do you like to sit around the table and chat or do you like to get up and get going?
- Do you always feel anxious to get going and finish whatever you have to do?
- If you are driving a car and there is another car in your lane going far too slowly for you, what do you do about it? Would you mutter and complain to yourself? Would anyone riding with you know that you were annoyed?
- What irritates you most about your job or the people you work with?
- Do you think you have as much faith in doctors as your parents probably did?
- When you get angry or upset, do the people around you know it? How do you show it?

(New Scientist, *13 March 1986)*

However, it is not just *what* is said regarding their answers but also the *sound* of what they are saying that is important. Type A personalities often demonstrate rapid, loud and explosive speech patterns where sentences often go unfinished, and they will often interrupt the questioner. Non-verbal communication such as fidgeting, grimacing and pointing are also assessed.

Yet, not all of the characteristics revealed by the structured interview will predispose such an individual into having a heart attack. Recently, research has identified which particular characteristics can indicate coronary-prone behaviour. These include emotional intensity, the amount of emphasis put into speech and the degree of self-involvement.

Trying to modify Type A behaviour through therapy has been fairly successful thanks to behaviour therapy and stress-management techniques, including relaxation and delegation of responsibility. These techniques were used in a five-year intervention programme for 1,035 post-heart-attack patients which demonstrated that further heart attacks, fatal and non-fatal, were reduced to half the number of those found in a control group.

Ragland and Brand followed up one study which had first identified Type A and B personalities and then later confirmed that Type A behaviour was effective in predicting who was susceptible to heart disease. Ragland et al. found in the follow-up that the *mortality rate also* could be related to Type A and B behaviour. One unexpected result was that in a group of 231 men who had survived their first heart attack (for 24 hours or more), Type B subjects died at a quicker rate than the Type A subjects. It could be assumed from this that the response to a coronary event is different depending on whether the person is Type A or B. It may be that Type A individuals may not be at such an increased risk after such an event as they may finally heed the warning and change their high-risk behaviour.

Apparently, Friedman and Rosenman's original study was conducted on *men* simply because they have more heart attacks. Consequently, differences between Type A men and women may be assumed. Indeed,

Table 4.2 Features of Type A behaviour in American women

- The incidence of Type A behaviour in the USA is comparable for men and women when socioeconomic factors are controlled
- Type A behaviour in women is positively correlated with socioeconomic status (SES), occupation, education and incidence of coronary heart disease
- Type A women tend to show greater autonomic arousal to laboratory stressors as well as greater time urgency and speed, more goal directedness, a preference to work alone under stress conditions and more competitiveness/aggressiveness than Type B women
- Type A positively correlates with various estimates of anger, hostility and masculine sex role orientation
- Depression and anxiety in Type As depends on the woman's sex role orientation and locus of control

Source: Banyard, P. and Hayes, N. (1994), *Psychology – Theory and Application*, Chapman & Hall.

Baker et al. found five different types of Type A behaviour to be prevalent in women in particular (see Table 4.2).

Hayenes and Feinleib investigated the health of women over a wide occupational range. Their findings illustrated that there seemed to be very little difference concerning the incidence of heart disease in those who had executive/managerial posts compared to those who occupied other positions. These results indicated that women who take on more male-populated ('high stress') careers do not necessarily put themselves at a greater risk of coronary heart disease.

ACTIVITY

Do you think that women who take on more male-populated executive posts have to take on male characteristics to succeed, or not?

THE TYPE C PERSONALITY AND CANCER

There seems to be evidence to suggest that there is a certain type of personality that has a susceptibility to cancer. The kinds of people involved here include those who are unassertive, unaggressive, compliant and passive, and those who suppress emotions – especially anger – are apathetic and are hopeless and depressed. Dattore et al. conducted a study which illustrated that if people are tested whilst they are still healthy, this type of personality predicts the development of cancer over the next 10 years. Personality, it seems, can also predict the *speed* at which the cancer develops, whether patients survive or not, but it seems to have little influence, on the other hand, once the illness is well-advanced.

ATTITUDES

A fundamental question here is what is an attitude? There are numerous definitions, including Bem's: 'attitudes are likes and dislikes.'

Attitude formation

There are three main ways in which attitudes are formed, the first being through *instrumental conditioning*. This process can be explained through the above-mentioned terms *reinforcement* and *punishment*. A child, for example, would be rewarded for holding appropriate views and punished for having inappropriate views. The second process involves *modelling* or *observational learning*. For example, children are influenced by 'hero figures' in the media that deter them from taking up or carrying on smoking. The final process by which attitudes can be formed concerns *direct experience with the issue in question*. Consequently, from research on attitude formation, health professionals should conclude that:

1 It will be harder to change a person's attitude when it's already formed, so they

should be looking to influence attitudes on health sooner rather than later.

2 The social learning theory has highlighted the importance of the media in drawing attention to health education by using media personalities that children can respect.

Attitudes and behaviour

Fishbein and Ajzen propose a structural approach to attitudes which looks at attitudes in conjunction with beliefs, values, intentions and behaviour. This approach illustrates the three components of an attitude: the *affective* component refers to how a person *feels* about the attitude object; the *behavioural* component refers to how the person *responds* to the attitude object; the *cognitive* component is what a person *believes* about the attitude object. The assumption concerning these three components is that they are highly correlated.

However, one intrinsic problem relating to attitude measurement is that there is not necessarily a correlation between how a person *feels* and how they *act* towards a certain object. LaPière illustrated this difficulty. He travelled around the USA with a Chinese couple at a time when there was a strong prejudice against the Chinese. They encountered only one case of prejudice even though they had visited over 200 hotels and restaurants. When he returned home he wrote to all of the establishments they had visited asking whether or not they would take Chinese guests, and 92% of those that replied to the letter indicated that they wouldn't. This study demonstrates that people often don't act in a way which is consistent with their attitudes.

Owens and Naylor found that for a dying person, trying to conduct life in a normal fashion was made even more difficult by the attitudes of their friends and relatives towards them. They illustrated that Western society had produced *negative* attitudes towards the dying. For the terminally ill, these attitudes make the situation worse as they tend either to produce avoidance behaviour or to make people act as if the dying person had somehow become *someone else entirely*.

St. Lawrence et al. randomly sampled psychologists and asked them to read a passage concerning a male college student who was either heterosexual or homosexual, and who had contracted either Aids or leukaemia. On completion, the psychologists then filled in numerous attitude scales. The findings illustrated extreme negative attitudes towards the Aids patient which were not, however, applied to the leukaemia patient. The Aids patient was held more responsible for his illness and more dangerous to other people; and in contrast to the leukaemia patient, the psychologists appeared less willing to see the Aids patient professionally, or to work in the same office, or to continue a past friendship or to allow children to visit him. This study clearly illustrates how people's attitudes towards particular types of illness can influence how they act towards those who have those illnesses.

It is important, however, to note two problems with the St. Lawrence study. First, the aim of the study was not well disguised and could consequently be easily guessed; and second, only 37% of the sample responded to the survey, which had been a postal one.

Research has been carried out into how institutions can develop and determine the attitudes and behaviour of the people who work in them. For instance, Miller et al. investigated residential homes that catered for people with irreversible and severe physical handicaps. They pointed out two different types of environmental climate. First, there was a 'warehousing' philosophy in which the clients were dependent upon the provision of good physical care, and second there was a 'horticultural' approach where the focus was more upon the residents' *psychological* well-being as determined by the institution (see Chapter 3). These two environmental climates seemed to produce very different kinds of behaviour on the part of the care staff (though individual staff attitudes *were* in fact consistent with the general climate of the institution), and individual personality variables, moreover, served to influence the attitudes of the staff: for example, staff who had more authoritarian personalities seemed to demonstrate more custodial attitudes.

The Health Belief Model

This model (Rosenstock 1966, modified by Becker et al. 1975) aims to predict when a person will engage in health behaviour – i.e. comply with advice. A person's behaviour can be predicted from three groups of sociocognitive factors:

1 the perceived threat of disease;
2 perceived benefits of treatment;
3 personal variables, e.g. age, sex and class.

This model has aided research into predicting who will make use of free health examinations, yearly medical check-ups and screening programmes. Research in this area proposes that health beliefs are an important factor in the decision as to whether or not to adopt health behaviours. A review of studies by Haynes et al. found a link between compliance and perceived vulnerability, and between the severity of the illness and the costs/benefits involved.

Cognitive dissonance

Festinger (1957) put forward the idea that if we realise that two or more of our attitudes contradict each other, it will make us feel tense and uncomfortable. Consequently, we will need to change one of the attitudes so that the dissonance disappears. Festinger illustrates his theory with an example concerning smoking. For a person who smokes cigarettes, the fact 'I smoke cigarettes' and the knowledge that smoking causes lung cancer should produce a state of dissonance. In the light of this, consonance (consistency) could be achieved in one of two ways:

1 the person stops smoking;
2 the person could ignore or refute the evidence linking smoking with lung cancer.

Recent research seems to support Festinger's example with regard to smoking. McMasters et al. studied the knowledge and beliefs of smokers, non-smokers and ex-smokers. They found that, although all of the groups had a similar amount of factual knowledge concerning the effects of smoking, the smokers estimated their general probability of contracting lung cancer as being greater than that for the people in the other two groups, but that when they were asked to estimate their own personal risk, they rated it as lower than it would be for the 'average smoker'. They were also more likely to support rationalisations and justifications for smoking than were either of the other two groups. The researchers proposed that it was the dissonance produced by knowing that they were engaged in risky behaviour that produced the different beliefs. Many continue to smoke even though they are aware of the harmful effects of smoking, and this suggests that people may have different tolerance levels for dissonance.

Dissonance can also occur when a decision has been made between two equally attractive options. When one option has been decided upon there is a certain degree of dissonance over the alternative option that has been lost. Most people, at one time or another, will have had to make a decision as to which party to go to. When the decision has been made, the option chosen is then bolstered whilst the advantages of the non-chosen alternative are played down and its disadvantages played up.

It can be difficult to comprehend why some do not heed the advice of a health professional especially when presented with evidence that their particular lifestyle is adversely affecting their health. For example, instead of giving up smoking, a smoker may instead decrease their dissonance by *increasing their liking for smoking*. Consequently, dissonance, in this way, may be working against the health professional. However, individuals are more likely to change their attitudes to fall in line with those of someone they like and respect, and health professionals can profit from this fact in their interaction with patients.

Research on attitude change has been very useful in combating the prevention and spread of diseases such as Aids. First, the target population has to be identified. Those that perform inappropriate sexual practices or use hard drugs will be at high risk, and they need to be viewed in the light of why they participate in these activities. It is usually seen as more effective to 'modify' behaviour rather than to try to change it completely. Consequently, instead of trying to prevent people from having many sexual partners, it may be more effective to try to encourage them to modify their sexual behaviour by promoting the use of condoms. In the case of drug abuse, providing 'clean needles' would be necessary in preventing disease.

When trying to persuade someone to change their attitudes, aspects of the method of communication used need to be considered. For example, if methods use fear as a technique to try to prevent disease, this will only be successful if:

1. people become frightened:
2. they perceive themselves to be at risk if they continue their present behaviour;
3. they think they will be safe if they follow the advice given.

Since many believe that having monogamous relationships and using condoms will result in high levels of safety, it can be assumed that the last condition *is* working, but that maybe 1 and 2 are not. It could be that the 'messages', e.g. 'Aids – don't die of ignorance' initially frightened people but have stopped doing so as they do not see the evidence of Aids around them. In fact, people may not see themselves at risk unless they actually meet an Aids patient and come to realise the similarity between them. Therefore, an important role concerning prevention is to try to counter processes such as dissonance and illustrate to those who feel they are not at risk that many of those now affected once thought the same.

ACTIVITY

Try to design a health-campaign advert (poster, video) for a specific target group. It could be about an area of your choice, e.g. smoking, drugs, immunisation etc.

There have been various attempts to encourage health-conscious behaviour through mass media appeals, though it is difficult to judge how effective such appeals are, for they are not like product advertising where the effect can be measured in sales. Taylor studied the Stanford heart-disease-prevention programme, which involved three towns matched for size and socioeconomic status but with different amounts of health information, and found that media campaigns alone produced only very small changes in behaviour. They really need to be accompanied by *personal intervention* before people will change their behaviour.

PREJUDICE

Secord and Backman defined prejudice as an 'attitude that predisposes a person to think, feel, perceive and act in favourable or unfavourable ways towards a group or its individual members'. Prejudice is an extreme attitude, and consequently consists of all the three previously mentioned components of an attitude: cognitive, affective and behavioural. Discrimination stereotypes and the self-fulfilling prophecy (all of which can be strongly related to prejudice) have been covered in Thomson et al. 1995, pp. 27–41.

The origins of prejudice

THE AUTHORITARIAN PERSONALITY

Adorno et al. related prejudice to a group of personality traits which together form the authoritarian personality predisposed to be hostile towards ethnic, racial and other minority groups. The personality

Table 4.3 Traits of the authoritarian personality

Conventionalism Highly authoritarian people tend to be extremely conventional in their approaches to things, and very suspicious of anyone who is different from the majority
Authoritarian submissiveness Highly authoritarian people tend to be extremely deferential to those who are in authority, and expect others to be deferential as well
Authoritarian aggression Such people are extremely hostile to anyone who challenges authority, or suggests that it is inadequate in any respect
Anti-intraception Highly authoritarian people tend to adopt a very tough-minded and punitive approach to any form of social misdemeanour: they usually regard leniency as weak and socially corrupting
Superstition and stereotype Such people tend to believe that events are 'fated', inevitable or externally controlled, and can't be controlled by individuals, except through luck
Power and 'toughness' Authoritarian personalities tend to behave in a dominating and sometimes bullying manner towards other people
Destructiveness and cynicism Highly authoritarian personalities tend to show high levels of hostility and aggression towards other people and towards ideas with which they disagree
Projectivity Authoritarian personalities show a powerful tendency to project their own unconscious impulses on to others
Sex Authoritarian personalities tend to show an exaggerated concern with sexual misbehaviour, regarding it with extreme hostility

Source: Hayes, N. (1994), *Foundation of Psychology – an Introductory Text*, Routledge.

characteristics involved here include obedience to authority, hostility to people of perceived inferior status, inflexibility, intolerance and a belief in conventional values. It has been suggested that the authoritarian person develops these traits in part due to punitive child-rearing practices which create a pattern of submissive obedience to authority and a rejection of groups other than their own. However, there are problems with this theory. For example, it cannot explain the widespread uniformity of prejudice in certain societies.

The impact of social norms – prejudice as conformity

Reich and Adcock suggest that the need to conform and not to stand out as different may result in milder prejudices, whilst active discrimination against, and ill treatment of, minorities can be viewed as reflecting a deeper-rooted prejudice which is maintained and legitimised by conformity. Minard found that the white and black coal-miners in West Virginia in the USA were integrated below ground but appeared to follow almost total segregation above ground. Thus, it could be that just as we learn other types of attitudes, so we learn to be prejudiced.

The theory of intergroup competition

This theory suggests that prejudice will arise out of competition between different groups for unequally distributed goods or resources. This theory was very well illustrated by Sherif et al.'s (1961) famous Robber's Cave experiment.

ACTIVITY

Research Sherif's 'Robber's Cave' study and describe its three stages.

Minimal groups

Tajfel et al. suggested that if another group is perceived merely to be in existence, this in itself can produce discrimination. Even when two groups are assigned purely at random, just to know of the other group's existence is a sufficient condition for the development of pro-in-group and anti-out-group attitudes – this is referred to as the *minimal group* hypothesis. Tajfel argues further that prior to any discrimination, people must be categorised as either belonging or not belonging to the group, and that this very act of categorisation can produce conflict and discrimination.

Social identification

Tajfel further suggests that *social categorisation* is the first stage in the development of prejudice. Once people are aligned in a group, a sense of social identification is created, and the similarities of those within the group, on the one hand, and the differences between various groups, on the other hand, are both exaggerated. A group identity is then formed which becomes part of *our* social and personal identity. In-group and out-group members can then be clearly distinguished through dress or language. The group is then compared with other groups, and its relative status is determined. Through such social comparison, there is a tendency for members of a group to take more notice of the beliefs and values expressed by members of their own group and to disregard those of people from different groups. Tajfel and Turner suggest that people seek to belong to groups that will have a positive effect on their self-esteem. If, however, a group results in low-esteem, the member will either try to leave the group or look for ways to enhance the group's status by comparing the group with one of a lower status rather than one of a higher status.

Skevington found some evidence for Tajfel's theory in a nursing context. Sixty-four first- and second-year nursing students completed a questionnaire designed to measure status differences and desired social mobility. The *registered* nurses, it was found, had more positive subjective characteristics and a high positive social identity, while the lower-status, enrolled nurses were found to have 'a preponderance of attributed disadvantages' and a less positive social identity. Furthermore, 50% of these enrolled nurses wanted change. In contrast to Tajfel's claim that groups will enhance perceived differences through social comparisons, Skevington found (1981) that the nurses in both groups tended to *decrease* the perceived differences between themselves. She suggests two reasons for her findings:

1 The nurses worked closely together, and this would decrease the kind of stereotyped impressions obtained from groups in other studies.
2 The enrolled nurses were trying to become more similar to the registered-nurse group as means of achieving a similar *social identity* to that of the registered nurses.

This study would suggest certain measures that can be taken to reduce prejudice.

Reducing prejudice

INCREASED CONTACT

The first stage in any technique for reducing prejudice concerns the individual's being *aware* that they are prejudiced. As was seen in Skevington's study, one reason for the lack of prejudice between the nursing groups was the high levels of *intergroup contact*. Deutch and Collins, working in New York, compared a mixed-race housing estate with one which was segregated. The findings suggested that prejudice can be reduced with increased contact, as they found that housewives in the former estate were less racially prejudiced than those in the latter.

COOPERATION

In Texas in the USA, the education authorities asked Aronson et al. to examine ways of decreasing prejudice in schools, and as a result they devised the *jigsaw method*. A class was divided – irrespective of ethnic origin – into groups that were assigned a project. Each member of a group had a piece of the 'puzzle' to research and then teach to the other group's members for an end-of task test. The study found enhanced self-esteem, improved academic performance, an increasing liking of peers and improved ethnic perceptions, but the overall change, however, was insignificant.

Other techniques for reducing prejudice include education and social modelling.

ACTIVITY

1 Think of as many stereotypes as you can and list them.

2 Work through ways that you think could break these negative stereotypes down.

THE SELF

According to Murphy, 'the self is the individual as known to the individual.' More recently, Burns defines it as the 'set of attitudes a person holds towards himself'. Traditionally, the self-concept is seen as a general term covering three main components:

- the self-image
- self-esteem
- the ideal self

These aspects of the self have been covered in Thomson et al. (1995), pp. 200–205.

Theories of the self-concept

As long ago as 1890, William James advocated that the self-concept develops from *social comparisons*. In particular, we compare ourselves to the 'significant others', and then through these comparisons we develop an idea of what we ourselves are like. Cooley extended this idea further when he suggested that feedback from others was vitally important in the development of the self-concept. He suggested that the self is reflected in the reactions of others (which reflect what others think of us), and that feelings such as embarrassment are influenced by the way we think others perceive us.

Figure 4.5 William James (1842–1910)

Mead (1934) focused upon the importance of *social interaction* in the development of the self-concept. Indeed, the self-concept he thought developed as a direct result of *social experience*. 'Social experience' is meant in the broadest sense in that it includes not just social interaction but also social norms, personal values and cultural patterns. Once these aspects are internalised we can use them as standards for appraising our own behaviour, whether other people are present or not. Goffman (1959), on the other hand, suggests that the self-concept is a reflection of the *social roles* played by the individual. He proposes that all individuals will develop a number of aspects to their personality reflecting the different social roles they play.

> **ACTIVITY**
>
> Social roles create a set of expectations concerning behaviour. Write down how many roles you perform within a week. Do any of these roles conflict with each other?

CARL ROGERS' THEORY OF THE SELF

This theory became popular in the 1950s and 1960s, and is described in detail in Thomson et al. 1995, pp. 205–7.

Figure 4.6 Carl Rogers (1902–87)

Rogers believed that we are born with a tendency to 'self-actualise'. This means that we try to be as healthy as possible, not just physically, however, but also in terms of mental and even spiritual fulfilment. The process of self-actualisation involves us trying to become closer to our *ideal self*, and in this way the self has a goal which involves a constant process of growth towards self-actualisation.

Congruence, that is, consistency between the self-image and the ideal self, enables people to realise their potential and move towards self-actualisation. On the other hand, *incongruence*, that is, inconsistency between the self-image and the ideal self, leads to dissatisfaction, neuroticism and, eventually, maladjustment. Congruence results from having received *unconditional positive regard*: that is, the individual feels specially valued by one or two people, even when their feelings, attitude and behaviour are less than ideal. Rogers believed that, in order to be able to self-actualise, people need to feel 'safe' and to be valued as a person. A self-actualised person does not have to act in a way that does not suit them because they are *valued for who they are.* Incongruence, on the other hand, results from *conditional positive regard*, as when children receive the message that they are only loved if they behave in certain ways and therefore have to deny some parts of themselves. Such children grow up striving for approval from others and ignoring their own self-actualisation in the process. Such people tend to have unrealistically high standards for their own behaviour. Rogers found that many of his patients had suffered conditional positive regard, and he sought to redress the imbalance in their lives with the therapeutic idea of *encounter groups* (see Thomson et al. 1995, p. 206).

The effect of care settings on the self-concept

It is important to remember that when people require any of the care services due to a particular need, whether it is an illness, disability or not being able to cope with a life event, good quality care will make the clients feel valued instead of feeling at risk or vulnerable. The staff have the power to influence the quality of the client's life, and in turn this will affect their self-concept. Good practice will ensure that clients are empowered for this to happen – i.e. that the power is *shared* between clients and staff. There are, however, examples of when this doesn't happen – examples of when care is disempowering.

One study of a London borough's provision of residential care for elders reported:

- Elders being woken up between 5.45 and 6.30 in the morning without choice
- Lack of choice about when to go to bed
- Lack of opportunity to get drinks and snacks when wanted
- Lack of choice and consultation about meals
- No choice over bringing in personal possessions, no personal furniture, telephone, TV or radio
- No procedures for washing, mending and marking personal belongings or clothing
- Lack of attention to clothing which was often allowed to become dirty

(S. Tomlin 1989, p. 11)

ACTIVITY

1 Explain why the type of care described in the above extract is disempowering.

2 What sort of care would you hope for if you or a relative entered a residential home? In your responses, can you recognise what is empowering about the quality of care you would expect?

To feel out of control of the situation and not respected is to feel disempowered, and unfortunately this can easily happen in care situations even when the carer has the best of intentions. For instance, the physically or mentally disabled are often treated like children when carers assume power and when the clients have their right to choice removed. It is all too easy to slip into the 'Does he take sugar' situation where not only is the client talked about in front of them, but in addition everything is done for them – even their sugar being stirred.

To be able to give good-quality care will require adequate economic resourcing such as appropriate staff levels and facilities. If, however, this isn't possible and disempowerment occurs, how the client reacts will depend on the situation. It may be that after being initially angry, the client will emotionally withdraw from the situation that they feel is overpowering them.

HURRIED DOCTORS 'LEAVE PATIENTS IN DARK'

Patients' rights are being trampled underfoot because doctors have neither the time nor the inclination to explain medical and surgical treatments to them, the consumer magazine *Which?* claims today.

As a result, many do not understand their rights, says *Which? Way to Health*. It wants the Department of Health to make it clear on consent forms that patients have the absolute right to know about proposed treatment, the alternatives and the risks of operations. The department is revising guidelines on the subject.

The magazine says that medical students rarely get systematic training in medical ethics and underestimate how much patients want to know. 'Doctors need consent for every kind of touching – even only taking your blood pressure.'

It asks for a commitment from doctors and the courts to the doctrine of informed consent, and fact sheets on different operations and procedures. A *Which?* spokesman said last night: "Some doctors argue that detailed information is time-consuming, could frighten patients unnecessarily and that there's no guarantee that patients will understand what they are told.

"Surgeons in Dundee did a survey of 100 patients following their operations and 27 did not even know which organ had been operated on. However, people aren't as interested in technical details as in implications – what an operation will mean for them personally. They also need to be told about other available options." . . .

(The Guardian, *12 June 1989)*

LEARNED HELPLESSNESS

Those that are disempowered may in turn feel helpless, which can consequently cause depression (Seligman). The concept of *learned helplessness* can be seen as a passive condition in which people and animals refuse to take any action that could improve their situation, even when they know what action *could* be taken. In other words they *learn to give up*. This may be due to finding that any course of action they took in the past was useless, so even when their situation *can* be changed, they fail to realise this.

There are many examples of learned helplessness in numerous settings. For instance, in an educational environment, Dweck observed that boys seem to attribute their academic failures to a lack of ability. Dweck proposes that boys come to believe that poor academic performance comes from lack of ability over which they have little control, and that they consequently come to see themselves as less likely to succeed.

In a very different context, Walus-Wigle et al. (1979) applied learned helplessness to 'battered woman syndrome'. They suggested that there are three stages to a cycle in a violent marriage:

1 a period of tension building which is characterised by minor assaults;
2 a major violent attack or series of attacks;
3 a period of remorse and loving between cycles of violence.

It has been suggested that female victims go through a range of psychological feelings, starting with feelings of helplessness, guilt and lowered self-esteem, which leads to a pattern of learned helplessness. They often become passive and submissive, and feel that the violence is inevitable. However, lowered self-esteem is also an important aspect of *depression* – which the learned helplessness model fails to account for on its own. This model was thus redefined in attributional terms, and Abramson et al. (1978) suggested that how people make an attribution for this lack of control over what happens to them has important consequences for their depressive state in general and their self-esteem in particular.

Weiner's model for success and failure was also considered appropriate to be applied to depression. This model has three attributional dimensions:

1 *Internal–external:* whether the behaviour is attributed to the person or the environment.
2 *Stable–unstable:* whether the perceived cause of the behaviour is a constant or changing feature of the person or environment.
3 *global–specific:* whether the perceived cause is specific to that behaviour or occurs in many different aspects of a person's life.

Abraham and Martin (1981) suggest that someone who was very depressed after failing to get a job at an interview would make an internal, stable and global attribution as follows:

1 Internal attribution: 'It's my fault.' Results in lowering of self esteem.
2 Stable attribution: 'That's the way it will always be.' Results in a lack of motivation to change.
3 Global attribution: 'That's the way I am at every interview.' Results in lack of motivation to change.

The depressive person makes attributions in such a way that negative things are perceived to be their own fault while good things only result from other people's efforts.

A questionnaire was devised by Seligman et al. (1979) for assessing a person's attributional style: see Table 4.4. This involves 12 different hypothetical situations, and for each situation the person has to say what the major causes would be. Then, on 7-point scales, a question relating to each of the three dimensions – internal–external, stable–unstable and global–specific – has to be answered. The person has also to indicate, again on a 7-point scale, how important each of the 12 situations would be for them. This is included because an attributional style is

Table 4.4 Attribution Style questionnaire from Seligman et al. 1979

Hypothetical situations

(a) *Positive Achievement Items*

(i) You become very rich
(ii) You apply for a job (college place) that you badly want and get it
(iii) You get a raise

(b) *Negative Achievement Items*

(iv) You have been looking for a job unsuccessfully for some time
(v) You give an important talk in front of a group and the audience reacts negatively
(vi) You can't get all the work done that others expect of you

(c) *Positive Interpersonal Items*

(vii) You meet a friend who compliments you on your appearance
(viii) Your spouse (boyfriend/girlfriend) has been treating you more lovingly
(ix) You do a project which is highly praised

(d) *Negative Interpersonal Items*

(x) A friend comes to you with a problem and you don't try to help him
(xi) You meet a friend who acts hostilely toward you
(xii) You go out on a date and it goes badly

Questions asked about each item

(i) Write down *one* major cause ....

(ii) Is the cause of your friend's compliment due to something about you or something about the other person or circumstances? (Circle one number)

Totally due to the other person or circumstance	1 2 3 4 5 6 7	Totally due to me

(iii) In the future when you are with your friends, will this cause again be present? (Circle one number)

Will never again be present	1 2 3 4 5 6 7	Will always be present

(iv) Is the cause something that just affects interacting with friends or does it also influence other areas of your life? (Circle one number)

Influences just this particular situation	1 2 3 4 5 6 7	Influences all situations in my life

(v) How important would this situation be if it happened to you? (Circle one number)

Not at all important	1 2 3 4 5 6 7	Extremely important

Source: Pennington, B. F. (1986), *Essential Social Psychology.*

only significant for what people consider to be important in their lives. Once the attributional style of a depressed person is known, therapies which are oriented towards changing how the person makes attributions concerning their behaviour can be offered. For instance, Abramson and Martin suggest four ways in which depressives need to change their thoughts about the world in general:

1 How the person perceives control over the outcomes of their behaviour must be reversed, i.e. so that they can take control of the situation.
2 The patients must set themselves realistic goals in life.
3 The importance of unattainable but often desirable goals must be decreased.
4 The patient must believe that the degree of control they have is equal to that of others.

THE LOCUS OF CONTROL

The two themes of control and internal–external attributions are claimed to constitute a single personality dimension, and this was suggested by Rotter (1966) to be the *locus of control*. An *external* locus of control is when an individual doesn't feel in control of the situation, whereas a person with an *internal* locus of control *would* perceive themselves as having personal control over the situations they find themselves in. Rotter proposed that the locus of control can directly influence psychological well-being. For instance, people who, due to an external locus of control, suffer much stress will, he argues, suffer ill health and psychological problems.

The locus of control is concerned with whether we feel empowered or not – which, as previously mentioned, is an important issue for human beings. For example, it is often found that when the elderly move to a nursing home, they show a decline in activity and health. Langer et al. investigated this decline by manipulating the amount of responsibility allowed to residents on two floors in a nursing home. They indexed happiness and activity, and found that the health and degree of control of the sickest people in these areas immediately improved. This difference was still illustrated even 18 months later: those with more control were healthier, and fewer had died.

Table 4.5 Examples of items from Rotter's locus of control scale

The I-E Scale asks you to choose one of two alternatives from items such as the following.

1a) In the case of the well-prepared student there is rarely, if ever, such a thing as an unfair test.
1b) Examination questions are often so unrelated to course work that studying is really useless.

2a) The average citizen can have an influence on government decisions.
2b) This world is run by the few people in power and there is not much the little guy can do about it.

3a) Most people do not realise the extent to which their lives are controlled by accidental happenings.
3b) There is no such thing as 'luck'.

4a) What happens to me is my own doing.
4b) Sometimes I feel that I do not have enough control over the direction my life is taking.

People with an *internal* locus of control tend to choose 1a), 2a), 3b), 4a); and people with an *external* locus of control tend to choose the alternatives.

Key reference: Rotter, J. B. (1966), 'Generalised expectancies for internal vs. external control of reinforcement', *Psychological Monographs*, 80 (1).
Source: Banyard, P. and Hayes, N. (1994), *Psychology – Theory and Application*, Chapman & Hall.

Bradley et al. studied the locus of control in diabetics. Patients were offered a choice of:

1 continuing with conventional treatment;
2 experiencing an intensified programme of conventional therapy;
3 adopting a newly developed technique which involved delivering insulin by an infusion pump.

They found that the group of those who chose the latter treatment perceived themselves as having less personal control over their condition than the other two groups. Within this first group they further found that those who had a stronger internal locus of control had the most effective blood-glucose control one year later. Consequently, they concluded that the development of better half-monitoring systems resulting in an improved long-term health of the patient could occur if the patients' *beliefs and ideas* were taken account of.

SELF-EFFICACY

Beliefs concerning self-efficacy are the opposite of those associated with learned helplessness, and cognitive therapy for depressives often focuses on encouraging clients to develop positive self-efficacy beliefs. Bandura (1989) suggested that one of the most fundamental features in self-perception comprises that which we believe we are capable of achieving. Self-efficacy beliefs are perceptions about our own perceived competencies – what we believe we can do well or at least adequately. These beliefs will influence *how* we interact in a given environment and with other people. Major et al. studied how women cope with having abortions. They found that the women who felt that they were receiving a high level of social support from family and friends also had higher self-efficacy for coping, which was also related to better psychological adjustment.

SELF-DISCLOSURE

This refers to the ways in which people let details of themselves be known to others. Remember that in a care setting there is the self-disclosure of both the health professional and the patient to consider. Disclosing aspects of yourself can help engender a sense of empathy between individuals.

Jourard suggests that self-disclosure is an important social skill, but that it can be difficult to achieve the right balance.

Inappropriate self-disclosure

This may result from any of the following:

1 *Burdening the patient:* it may be that the client has their own problems and doesn't necessarily want to hear those of others.
2 *Seeming weak and instable:* clients often want to perceive the health professionals as strong and 'together', and it may be that too many self-disclosures allow the profession to appear weak.
3 *Domination:* too much self-disclosure can make patients feel dominated (the 'You think you've got a problem' syndrome).
4 *Doing it for yourself:* this is where health professionals self-disclose to meet their own needs – for example, to obtain approval or affection at the expense of the patient.

ACTIVITY

This task is designed to illustrate the difficulties in discriminating between those who are telling the truth and those who are lying. Ask three members of the group to tell the rest of the group what they did last weekend. Two are to tell the truth whilst one is to lie – this is to be decided without the rest of the group knowing who the liar is and who the truth-tellers are. After they have given their talk, the rest of the group can ask questions to try to establish which one is lying. The group then vote on who they think was lying, and finally the one telling the lies can be revealed.

Points to note

1 Ask the person who lied how they did it. Did they use substitution, i.e. did they talk about what they actually did on some other day, or did they use invention, i.e. invent a different set of circumstances? Which was easier, and why?
2 Did the body language differ between those telling the truth and those who did not?

Blocks to self-disclosure

It may be that clients fear that the interaction may become too intense too quickly in the relationship, and consequently they may be resistant to self-disclosure. Another block is that the client may find it difficult to trust anyone at all. And a third block to self-disclosure concerns the fact that the client may have to face details they would rather remain hidden.

It may be that some clients are generally reluctant to talk about their real problems and need to be encouraged gently. In contrast, however, there may be some who wish to engage in self-disclosure in depth and are only too willing to talk about themselves, and therefore need to be diplomatically discouraged.

Guidelines for appropriate self-disclosure

Nehon-Jones suggests a few points to remember concerning appropriate self-disclosure (all situations will differ, however, so only general guidelines can be proposed):

1 Be direct: speak about yourself clearly and honestly.
2 Be sensitive: try to be aware when self-disclosures are helpful and when they are a burden.
3 Be relevant: keep to the patient's concerns and needs.
4 Be non-possessive: ensure the client isn't encouraged to meet your needs.
5 Be reasonably brief: not everyone will want to be involved in long, in-depth self-examinations.
6 Do not do it too often: doing it too often will raise doubts about your professionalism.

Johari Window

Luft and Ingham (1955) developed the notion of *overt* and *covert communication* in their Johari Window. This window represents the four parts of the self:

1 The *open self* – consists of details that we and others know about ourselves.
2 The *blind self* – is unknown to us but known to others.
3 The *hidden self* – is known to us but not revealed to others.
4 The *unknown self* – the details are unknown to ourselves and others. This may include unconscious motives/desires that may influence us without our knowing.

The effect of self-disclosure is to increase the size of the open self, and by doing this the client as well as the health professional may have more insight into the make-up of their personality.

ACTIVITY

Fill in the Johari Window for yourself.

Things I know about myself
Things I don't know about myself

OPEN SELF	BLIND SELF
HIDDEN SELF	UNKNOWN SELF

ATTACHMENT AND SEPARATION

Bowlby (1969, 1973, 1980) refers to attachment as 'an affected bond' between the child and the adult. In *'Mothering'* (1977) Schaffer suggests that there are three stages involved in the development of attachment:

1 The child is attracted to human beings rather than to the inanimate features of the environment.
2 The infant begins to distinguish between different humans, so the parents can be recognised in contrast to strangers.
3 The baby is capable of forming a lasting, emotionally meaningful bond with specific individuals whose company it will actively seek.

Two behaviours can be observed when the bond has been formed:

1 *separation anxiety*: the ability to miss the mother when she is away.

2 *stranger fear*: unfamiliar individuals will cause distress and crying.

Klaus and Kennell illustrated that it was very important for mothers to have early contact with their babies. They felt that the first 6–12 hours after birth constituted a 'critical period' for the mother's development of an attachment to her child. They also felt that it was essential to provide immediate (skin to skin) contact, and that failure to do so would result in weak attachments. As a consequence, hospital practices changed, and parents are now encouraged to hold their babies immediately after delivery.

Grossman et al. found evidence to suggest that those mothers who handled their babies immediately after birth seem to demonstrate more tenderness towards them in the first few weeks of life than those who did not have the opportunity to interact with their babies until later. O'Connor et al. found that early contact may even reduce the risk of later parenting problems among mothers who may otherwise be at a high risk for abuse. Yet, Grossman et al. argue that for the vast majority of parents, the long-term effects of being separated from their babies for a few hours after birth are *not* critical.

This research has particular implications for premature children: they are particularly 'at risk' since they are separated from their parents for the initial weeks or months and are then unresponsive after they return home from hospital. Many parents will try hard to stimulate and become involved with their children, yet due to the child's lack of interaction, inevitably the parents will eventually withdraw. Brackbill et al. found that in their review of nearly 60 studies, when mothers had received high levels of medication when giving birth to babies who infrequently smiled and who were inattentive and irritable, those babies were also difficult to feed and comfort. They assumed that this may be associated with problems in bonding. These babies continued to demonstrate problems in mental and physical development for at least one year after birth.

Figure 4.7 Father and child, and their own special relationship

Monotropy

Bowlby, in 1957, proposed that infants form a very special relationship with their mother, and that this occurs within the first six months of life. He argues that this relationship is different from any other relationship formed with anybody else, and he calls it *monotropy*. However, others such as Schaffer and Emerson argue that it is possible for an infant to have multiple attachments, and that in fact, even if there were only a single attachment it needn't be to the mother-figure as fathers, siblings, grandfathers etc. can also be involved.

Maternal deprivation

Bowlby argues that if the mother–child bond is broken for any reason, the child will suffer adversely. In his study of 44 juvenile thieves, he found that 17% of them had suffered from such *maternal deprivation*. His results have, however, been strongly criticised.

ACTIVITY

1 How far do you agree or disagree with Mead's statement 'Fathers are a biological necessity but a social accident'?

2 What different roles do mothers/fathers play concerning parenting?

ACTIVITY

Brainstorm as many reasons as possible for juvenile delinquency.

In addition, Bowlby suggested that if a child failed for one reason or another to form a bond with their mother, they could suffer from a condition known as 'affectionless psychopathy'. They then find it difficult to form any relationship with anybody, they are cold and they lack a social conscience. Rutter has suggested that this area should be investigated by distinguishing short-term separations, e.g. in the case of 'working mothers' and hospitalisation, from long-term separation such as in the case of divorce, death and institutionalisation.

HOSPITALISATION

Douglas found that there was a significant association between the number and duration of hospital admissions for children during pre-school years, on the one hand, and 'troublesomeness', 'poor reading', 'delinquency' and 'unstable job history' in their late adolescence on the other hand. However, this doesn't necessarily suggest a causal relationship between hospitalisation and psychiatric disorder as the hospital admissions may have been due to many factors, including poor home conditions.

Like that of Douglas, Quinton and Rutter's survey illustrated an association between repeated hospital admissions under the age of five and later problems in adolescence. However, the same problem relates to this study as that which related to Douglas' research.

CHILD CARE

Bowlby argues that the children of working mothers miss the care, love and attention that they need, and that as a result they will be psychologically damaged. Bowlby sees the first five years as being crucial to a child's emotional, social and intellectual development. This is known as the *continuity hypothesis*: an adversely affected infancy will adversely affect childhood which in turn will adversely affect adulthood.

Research within this area includes that of Belsky who found, as against Bowlby, that many 1-year-olds of working mothers *were* securely attached. And in two British studies, Mayall and Petrie and Bryant et al. concluded that within the childminder's home, the infant was secure. Furthermore, Andrews et al. found that children who were disadvantaged could benefit from being in day care: rather than the separation affecting the child, it could be the quality of the care and facilities outside the home instead. From the mother's perspective, Brown and Harris found that being at home all the time with two or more children could be one cause of depression in women.

ACTIVITY

1 Discuss whether women with children under five should or should not go to work – full- or part-time.

2 Do you think men should stay at home and be a 'house husband', caring for the children, whilst the mother goes to work?

When studying short-term separation, Bowlby identified three stages/sequences (the *separation response*) that a child goes through: *protest*, *distress* and *detachment*. The Robertsons suggested a slightly different separation response: *despair*, *distress* and *detachment*. How the child passes through these stages will be influenced by their past experience and the particular situation they are in.

With maternal deprivation, the effects are usually short-term and can be referred to as *distress*. However, with *maternal privation*, which refers to the *absence* of a maternal bond, the effects are usually long-term and can be seen as entailing *developmental retardation*.

Maternal privation

It can be the case that no attachments are made when a child is in institutional care. Bowlby (1951) advocates that even a bad home is better than an institutional upbringing – that is, if the maternal bond remains unbroken. Two studies that seem to support Bowlby are those of Goldfarb and Spitz et al. The latter studied poor orphanages in South America and found that the infants suffered from *anaclitic depression*, cried a lot and lost weight. However, these children appeared to be suffering from *social isolation* as well as from just maternal privation.

Death and divorce

With regard to Bowlby's hypothesis, there should be little or no difference between separation as a result of divorce and separation as a result of death, since he suggests that behavioural problems are a consequence of bond disruption between the child and its mother.

Rutter found no association between a parent's death and behavioural problems, but did suggest one between divorce and *deviant personality*. This only occurred, however, if there was much stress and disharmony surrounding the divorce, and for Rutter it was this that was responsible for adversely affecting the child psychologically. Rutter found a correlation between personality disorders and separation from both parents, but this only applied in homes where there was much marital discord. It appears that for boys whose parents have divorced or separated, the delinquency rates are significantly higher, whilst for those who have lost a parent through death, the delinquency rate was *only slightly higher*.

Hetherington suggests that age and experience will influence the child's response, and that a disruptive home may be more unsettling than a divorce. She found from her studies that depending on the situation, some children remain insecure, others recover and some can even be positively advantaged by developing coping strategies.

A child can feel particularly unsettled following the death of a parent, and there may be many reasons for this:

1 It may be that the death followed a long and harrowing illness.
2 The surviving parent's grief may be more distressing than the death of the other parent.
3 The death of a parent may result in economic difficulties.

Bereavement

Loss and bereavement have been covered in Thomson et al. 1995, pp. 222–4.

It has been suggested by Kubler-Ross that there are five stages involved in the psychological adjustment to death:

1 Denial ('It's a mistaken diagnosis');
2 Anger ('Why me?');
3 Bargaining (making a deal with God for more time);
4 Depression;
5 Acceptance.

Although these stages are widely believed (and as a result are seen as the 'natural' way to approach death), Wortman and Silver argue that there is little evidence to uphold them. In fact, there seem to be many misconceptions concerning how people respond to death. For instance, it's normally assumed that for those who are grieving, there will be an absence of positive emotions – or at least a reduction in them. Yet when Wortman and Silver studied the emotional responses of parents after the sudden death of an infant (SIDS), they found that generally parents did still experience positive emotions.

Another assumption concerning bereavement is that it's important to 'work through grief' and to arrive at an emotional and cognitive resolution. Yet, Wortman and Silver found very little evidence to support this idea, and in fact found the exact opposite in their study which showed that those parents who had done the most 'working through' of their grief illustrated the most distress both at the time and 18 months after the loss.

Late adoption

Adoption agencies usually work on the principle that children should be adopted during the first five years of life if they are to compensate and overcome their early deprivation. This assumption has stemmed from the work of researchers such as Bowlby who focus on the importance of early experience. Consequently, adoption agencies are generally resistant to placing older children for adoption as they believe that it will be too late for the child to form a genuine attachment to the adoptive parents. However, research seems to dispute this belief. For instance, Kadushin investigated 91 families who had adopted children who were older than five and found that in 89 cases the adoptions had been successful to the extent that the children and families were still together six years after their initial placement. Roe found similar results when looking at other studies of late-adopted children. In a study of 36 adults who were adopted after the age of five due to repeated abuse, Roe found that these adults had no trouble in forming friendships or close relationships. In fact, there were no differences between them and a control group of adults who had had their childhood disrupted due to the death or serious illness of a parent. Studies like these pose a direct challenge to the assumption of the importance of early attachment in the first five years of life. They illustrate that children are in fact far more resilient than theories such as Bowlby's would suggest, and that they *can* overcome early maternal deprivation, but only if the child's later situation is one that provides the emotional and social contact for this to happen, so that the child can develop a more positive self-image and the growth and development of new attachments can then be encouraged.

Children suffering extreme privation

Bowlby argues that mothering is practically a waste of time if it is delayed for two and a half to three years – indeed, for the majority of children, if it is delayed for 12 months. That is, he suggests that there is a critical period for attachments to develop, and that if they don't happen within this time, they never will. There are, however, quite a few case studies where children have been rescued from severe privation and isolation. These include: Anna (Davis), the Czechoslovakian twins (Koluchova) (see the following extract), Genie (Curtis) and a Japanese brother and sister (Fujinaga et al.). All the children demonstrated some recovery in terms of physical maturation, socialisation and cognitive and linguistic development, yet they were unable to recover their full potential. The very fact that they recovered to the extent that they did, however, contradicts Bowlby's idea of a critical period and furthers the notion that it may be a *sensitive period* instead.

THE CASE OF THE CZECH TWINS (KOLUCHOVA 1972, 1976)

Koluchova (1972) reported the case of two identical twin boys in Czechoslovakia, who were cruelly treated by their stepmother and found in 1967 at about seven years of age. They had grown up in a small, unheated closet, had often been locked in the cellar and were often harshly beaten. After their discovery, they spent time in a children's home and a school for the mentally retarded, before being fostered in 1969. At first they were terrified of many aspects of their new environment and communicated largely by gestures; they had little spontaneous speech. They made steady progress, both socially and intellectually.

A follow-up in 1976 reported that, at 14 (seven years after discovery), the twins showed no psychopathological symptoms or unusual behaviour. In a personal communication to Clarke (reported in Skuse 1984), Koluchova reported that by 20 they had completed quite a demanding apprenticeship (in the maintenance of office machinery), were above average intelligence, still had very good relationships with their foster mother and her relatives and their adopted sisters, and they had developed normal heterosexual relationships, both recently experiencing their first love affairs.

(Gross 1995)

According to Waddington, 'the human organism appears to have been programmed by the course of evolution to produce normal development outcomes under all but the most adverse of circumstances.'

Conclusion with regard to Bowlby

So it can be seen that there is much empirical evidence against Bowlby and consequently his theory has been questioned recently. However, certain practical implications *have* emerged as a direct result of his work, and these can be found in Thomson et al. 1995, p. 195.

SURROGACY – THE PROBLEMS

There have been 100 to 125 surrogate births in Britain since 1980. Most of them have been unofficial and clandestine arrangements – and surrogacy remains controversial around the world . . .

It was after the baby Cotton case, Britain's first commercial surrogate; that the Government was forced to legislate on the subject.

Kim Cotton, 32, became a surrogate mum through an American agency. Paid £6,500 she never saw the parents.

The baby was made a ward of court and kept in hospital for seven days, until the judge ruled that the child could go with the American couple.

It was from this controversy that the 1985 Surrogacy Arrangement Act was born. It bans commercial surrogacy agents and advertising; and also states that any surrogacy contract is unenforceable – if the woman changes her mind about handing over the baby, there is nothing the couple can do about it . . .

In Britain the Surrogacy Act has left many grey areas and while the Government has not banned surrogacy, the British Medical Association advises doctors not to get involved.

Gena Dodd, 41, runs Triangle, the only surrogacy agency in Britain. It is non commercial, but her information service, called Cots, does accept donations.

Gena is also the mother of a surrogate son. She explains: "My husband Michael and I had been childless for 17 years. I then had a hysterectomy and my ovaries were removed. Surrogacy was my only chance."

(*Woman's Own*)

NHS READY TO PAY £10,000 FOR SURROGATE PREGNANCY

The National Health Service is negotiating to pay for a surrogate mother to have a baby for a childless couple at a cost likely to exceed £10,000.

A district health authority is in talks with the Assisted Conception Unit at King's College Hospital, London, to make the arrangement for a woman who has lost her uterus. It is believed to be the first NHS surrogacy. Many health authorities refuse to pay even for in-vitro fertilisation.

The news came as the British Medical Association, which used to advise doctors to have nothing to do with surrogacy, issued ethical guidelines which acknowledged the growing public acceptance of the practice. Dr Fleur Fisher, head of the BMA's ethics committee, said: 'This is still a technique that can be very helpful to some couples.' John Parsons, head of the King's College unit, said it was right for the NHS to pay for surrogacy as a last-resort treatment. The district health authority, from the South of England, would need to pay for psychological assessments, the collection of eggs, the in-vitro fertilisation, monitoring, counselling and insurance for the surrogate mother.

The NHS would be expected to pay the surrogate's expenses, usually between £7,000 and £10,000.

(The Times, 13 February 1996)

GROUPS

Groups have been covered in Thomson et al. 1995, pp. 99–105. We all belong to various groups – family, friends and work groups, besides many other groups. Such groups are either formal, such as staff associations or residents committees, or informal, such as a network of friends. It should be noted that often informal groups are of far more importance to individual clients than formal committees as they have more direct interaction with them on a day-to-day basis.

Social groupings and their effect on health

The importance of social support groups can be illustrated by the Alameda County study which followed 7,000 adults over ten years. The researchers, Berkman and Syme found that those with fewer social networks were more likely to have died by the time of the ten-year follow-up than those who had many. The social networks that had been investigated included: marriage, contact with friends and relatives, church membership and participation in other groups. It should be noted, however, that the people who had died could possibly have had an undiagnosed illness at the beginning of the study, as this study was based upon the subjects' self-reports. Consequently, House et al. repeated this study, following 3,000 people in Michigan, but this time they took into account the participants' medical records. These findings supported Berkman et al.'s study, as they found ten years later that those who had few social relationships were more likely to have died than the people who had many, even after age, health and other risk factors had been taken into account.

It may be that social support somehow affects the immune system. Indeed, studies seem to indicate this; for instance, lonely people who have few friends have poorer immune function than people who are not lonely. Students in a network of friends have better immune function before, during and after exam periods than students who don't have enough social support, and spouses of cancer patients, although under much stress themselves, do not show a drop in immune support (Baron et al.). In fact, Kulik and Mahler suggest that social support even *speeds* recovery from illness.

Achterberg and Lawks demonstrated that having a poor or no network of friends can even be influential in terminal illness. Although the illness may have originated due to physical reasons, patients who had little or no social support showed poorer prognoses, were apt to die sooner than people who had a good group of supportive friends and family, and, interestingly, seemed to experience less pain.

Sometimes as a result of a health problem the patient may find that their lifestyle has to change. This can have many social consequences, especially for the relationships of the patient. For instance, those who suffered kidney failure and need haemodialysis for two or three times a week would experience the social problems listed in Table 4.6. Long found that almost half of the renal patients who were questioned concerning how they were adapting to their new lifestyle found some emotional difficulties in coming to terms with this. Often, what a patient is given is physical care, but Long stresses that psychological care is frequently needed to help patients make the necessary adjustments in their social relationships.

When friends help you cope

The effect of friends on your health depends on what the friends are doing for you and how much stress you are under. Rook studied more than 2,000 adults and found that:

- for those with an average amount of stress, social support had no influence on health
- for those who had above-average levels of stress, social support did help reduce their physical and emotional symptoms
- for those who had below-average levels of stress, social support was actually harmful

Rook suggests that friends can offer advice and reassurance when going through a stressful time, but that talking to friends too much about trivial irritants may simple perpetuate and strengthen stress levels rather than help them to manage it. It can be that being a member of a group, for instance a group of friends, can be stressful in itself, as they may make too many conflicting demands on us and may be the cause of quarrels. In fact, Dunkel-Scheffet found that cancer patients are often upset by the well-intentioned but unhelpful comments from family/friends that 'all will be fine', and often feel better talking to another group of people – particularly other cancer patients.

The stressful aspects of friendship concern the:

- *contagion effect* – when a depressed friend makes you feel depressed
- *burdens of care* – when you yourself become exhausted because too many require your energy

It was found, in a study of 34 individuals who were caring for a relative with Alzheimer's disease, that their immune system was adversely affected (Kiecolt-Glaser et al.).

It seems that there are several factors that will dictate whether or not support helps (Dakof and Taylor, Lehmann et al.):

1 *Amount of support*: having too much help can create dependency and consequently lower self-esteem. For example, Revenson et al. found that those, with cancer, who have people doing many things for them tend to have a decreased sense of mastery and self-esteem than those who have no one to rely on.
2 *Timing of support*: after a loss, whether

Table 4.6 Social consequences of haemodialysis

1 Family problems
2 Marital problems
3 Financial burdens
4 Severe role disruption in work and social spheres: e.g. unemployment
5 Patients exercise excessive control over family
6 Children of patients: 30% show high levels of anxiety and depression
7 Partner stress increases with time on dialysis

Source: Long, 1989.

through death or divorce, a person would need lots of understanding.

3 *Type of support:* the friend's support must be what the person needs (Dakof and Taylor). People who have stressful situations at work feel supported if they can talk their problems over with work colleagues as opposed to family who may lack the experience to effectively understand the situation.
4 *Density of support:* dense networks can help a person's sense of stability and identity, and Shumaker and Hull suggest that women, more than men, seem to benefit from living in dense networks.

Characteristics of small groups

Small groups may be defined as 'involving at least three persons who communicate with one another to coordinate their activities in the pursuit of common goals. The structure of a group typically consists of role differentiation, leadership, a set of norms and rules of membership' (Tedeschi and Lindskold). Pennington (1986) suggests that this definition makes three points:

1 Group members communicate and interact – in *group processes*.
2 Groups come together to perform certain tasks or achieve goals – the *task performance*.
3 Groups are *structured* – which means that individuals occupy certain roles and conform to the group's norms.

Consequently, this type of approach would look at the systems of relationships existing within a group rather than at the individual group members.

Thus, it can be seen that a small group proper differs from a group of people who just happen to be together in a doctor's waiting room because:

- the members would have interacted/communicated over a length of time
- individuals believe that the group exists
- there is a general expectation that the group members will conform to group norms
- the group members take on roles and have a sense of shared goals

Normally, as groups get larger the satisfaction of the group members will vary, as will their participation within the group. Consequently, there is a need for effective leadership (McGrath).

The carer (in whatever capacity), the nurse, the social worker and the psychologist will work together as part of a team in order to meet the needs of the client. A team within a care setting thus comprises a group of people who work together to meet the aims of the establishment; for example, a residential home for the elderly provides care for, and meets the needs of, those who are in their later years. However, a team can be seen as more than a group, for it is clear about its aims – i.e. about why it is formed in the first place.

Group norms

Social behaviour is generally governed by our expectations as to what is appropriate or inappropriate behaviour. These expectations are known as *social norms*. When we act appropriately according to whatever social role we happen to be playing, we are conforming to social norms. The reason we conform is that we want to be accepted by others and to belong to social groups (see Maslow's hierarchy of needs in Thomson et al. 1995, pp. 205–6).

One study which illustrates how group norms can determine how people behave at work was Roethlisberger et al.'s investigation of the Hawthorne works of the Western Electric Company in Chicago. The study had been looking into various ways to increase the output at work, which had generally met with success. However, the group that worked in the 'Bank Wiring Observation Room' had worked together for a very long time and consequently had firmly established norms. So despite all the various techniques used by the researchers to increase the group's output, they resisted these attempts and kept to a steady output.

The norms can be summarised as in Table 4.7.

Table 4.7 Group norms

1 A member of the group should work at the same rate as other members of the group. Working too hard or too little would put pressure on other members of the group, either to keep up or to make up the slack, and so this was unacceptable.
2 A member of the group should never say anything to a superior in the work hierarchy which might have the result of getting a colleague into trouble.
3 People in positions of authority, such as the group foreman or others, should not act officiously.

Source: Banyard, P. and Hayes, N. (1994), *Psychology – Theory and Application*, Chapman & Hall.

Social identity

When people feel they belong to a group, they can then assimilate that particular group membership into their self-concept. Consequently, during social interaction the individual can act as a representative of that group. Social identification will obviously occur at work, and as it will help make up our self-concept it has an important part to play with regard to self-esteem. Zani illustrated how social identification took on an important role when trying to understand psychiatric nurses' responses to the changes that were happening in the psychiatric services. Zani found that when faced with the decentralisation of psychiatric services, the nurses used various techniques to try to keep a sense of group distinctiveness, despite all the changes. By doing this, they could help maintain their self-esteem and professional values.

Because people can belong to more than one group, they can categorise themselves in different ways accordingly, whether in a positive or in a negative light and this gives them the opportunity to focus, perhaps, upon a particular positive social status. Rehm et al. found that female senior citizens who lived in residential homes were able to be more open-minded with regard to the stereotypes of 'old and young women' if they participated in gymnastics. The researchers suggested that by belonging to the gymnastics group, which had a positive social status, they were able to compensate for the point of view that went with their also belonging to another, *low-status* group.

Group structure and influence

McGrath suggests that the properties of a group structure are 'the relatively stable patterns of relationships that exist among members of the group'. To be aware of a group structure will give some insight into the dynamics of the group, and hence into how change takes place, either on an individual level – when it relates to changes in attitudes and to non-conformity to a groups' expectations/norms – or at a group level – when it relates to a change in relationships – e.g. a change in the leadership or morale of the group.

Group cohesiveness

Group cohesiveness relates to the extent to which individual group members are attracted to each other and to the group as a whole. The cohesiveness of the group can be measured by how often the members use the term 'we'. When it is high, group performance is usually good. Highly cohesive groups can exert strong influences upon the individual members to behave in accordance with the norms and expectations of the group. For a fuller discussion of this factor, see Chapter 5.

The *affective* structure of a group can be measured by a technique known as *sociometry* (Moreno 1953) (see also Chapter 5) which illustrates pictorially the interaction between members of a group.

ACTIVITY

First, you will need to attend some type of meeting, then draw a circle for each group

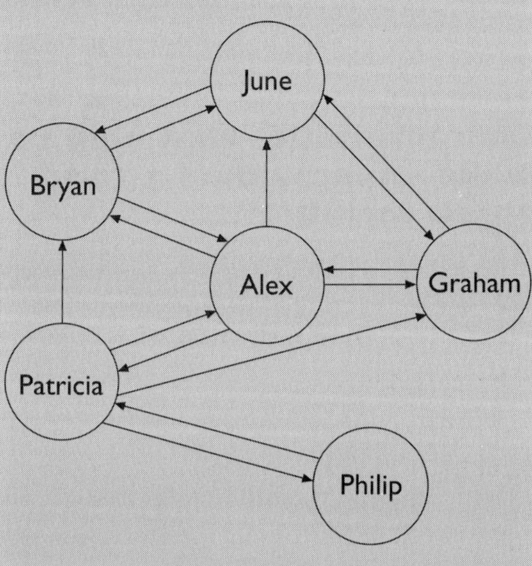

Figure 4.8 A sociogram

member. Put each person's name in a circle and draw an arrow from the circle to people they speak to on each occasion they make a contribution. If the person addresses their comments to the whole group rather than to just one individual, then draw the arrow to the centre of the group.

Analyse your *sociogram* (Figure 4.8 gives one example) and see who made the most contributions, and to whom, and if anyone did not contribute but just sat quietly and listened.

Sociograms can be used with any 'natural' group (at school, college, work etc.), and as well as recording interaction at a meeting they can also be used to chart popularity within the group. In this case, each member of the group is asked to name another who would be their most preferred partner for a task or friend, and to say who is popular, unpopular or isolated, and if there are any leaders that can be identified. One practical example would be to complete a sociogram for a class which has integrated those students with special needs into it. This can then tell you how successful the integration policy has been with regard to certain situations, e.g. friendships.

Roles

How a person behaves will be determined by the role they are expected to perform and by the status that person has in relation to others. Pennington defines the term *role* as: 'the behaviours expected of a person occupying a certain position in a group'. Roles are normative in that we expect people to behave in *accordance* with their role. It can be that if a person occupies more than one role over different groups and if the behaviours demanded from that person at one and the same time are different, then there will be a *role conflict*. This can be resolved by the person enacting only that role which has greater attraction/importance to them.

The communication structure

Bavelas demonstrated the development of *communication networks* via subjects placed in their own booths which had openings in the walls to pass messages to other group members. Leavitt used this technique to illustrate that a centralised network that was focused around a leader (such as the 'wheel' network in Figure 5.8) was faster and led to fewer errors in problem-solving tasks. On the other hand, *individual satisfaction* was highest in a decentralised, leaderless network. Shaw found that for complex tasks the 'all-channel net' was the best to ensure a free exchange of information.

Communication networks (see Chapter 5, pp. 175–177, for a fuller discussion) can be seen in terms of *status* rather than in terms of centralisation. Back et al. planted a rumour in a factory at five different status levels and waited to see who reported it to whom. They found the majority of reports were upwards in the status hierarchy, with few rumours either being reported to those of the same status or going downwards to those with low status.

Kelly (1951) found that status can affect the content of communication in two ways:

1 Low-status people make more comments irrelevant to the group task.
2 Less criticism of a role is made if it is occupied by a high- rather than a low-status person.

For group formation, leadership styles, different levels of participation in groups and promoting communication with groups, see Thomson et al. 1995, Chapter 2, pp. 101–5.

The power structure

Power can be seen as the capacity to produce intended effects in others. From this it can be seen that the concept of power is obviously closely related to that of leadership. Collins and Raven (1960) have suggested six types of power which can explain why certain individuals have a greater influence over others (for a fuller discussion, see Chapter 5):

1 *Reward power:* tangible or social rewards such as money or group membership are promised.
2 *Coercive power:* threats, warnings, punishment – too much, however, can have the reverse effect.
3 *Legitimate power:* e.g. by the employer or parent, and through the *role* rather than the personality of the occupant.
4 *Referent power:* this is accrued through being liked/respected. The *charismatic* leader has great referent power (which may be more important than their legitimate power).
5 *Expert power:* the power a person has by being in possession of particular knowledge – e.g. doctors, teachers etc.
6 *Informational power:* when a person has access to important sources of information, e.g. through the media.

ACTIVITY

Groupwork
Brainstorm all the characteristics that make an individual (i) a good group member, and (ii) a bad group member.

Characteristics that help to make an individual a good group member

- Someone who can effectively communicate with others but also, very importantly, needs to be willing to listen to other people's opinions
- Someone who is adaptable and flexible and can take on responsibility
- Someone who is reliable and honest and will work hard
- Someone who can work independently using initiative but can also cooperate well with others
- Someone who realistically knows their limitations and will ask for advice and support when necessary

Decision-making

Many decisions are made by the individual patient, although decisions are also frequently made by a team of health professionals. As to whether a decision made by a group is better than one made by an individual, this is dependent on how the word 'better' is interpreted and used. The following extract gives one example of a study in group and individual decision-making:

You are a member of a space crew originally scheduled to rendezvous with a mother ship on the lighted surface of the moon. Due to mechanical difficulties, however, your ship was forced to land at a spot some 200 miles from the rendezvous point. During the crash landing much of the equipment aboard was damaged and since survival depends on reaching the mother ship the most critical items available must be chosen for the 200 mile trip. Below are listed the 15 items left intact and undamaged after landing. Your task is to rank order them in terms of their importance in allowing your crew to reach the rendezvous point. Place the number 1 by the most important item, the number 2 by the second most important item, and so on. Place the number 15 by the least important item.

Individual Ranking
Box of matches...........................
Food concentrate.........................
50 feet of nylon ropes ....
Parachute silk ....
Portable heating unit ....
Two .45 calibre pistols ....
1 case dehydrated milk.....................
2 hundred-pound tanks of oxygen............
Stellar map (of the moon's constellation) ......
Life raft ....
Magnetic compass.........................
5 gallons of water.........................
Signal flares ....
First Aid kit containing injection needles.......
Solar powered FM receiver-transmitter........

Subjects were given 10 minutes to do the ranking task, then put in groups of four to six and instructed to reach a group consensus on the rankings of each of the 15 items. Group consensus is where each member of the group agrees upon the ranking decision for each item. Half the groups then proceeded with this task, the other half were given the following guidelines for reaching consensus:

1. Avoid arguing for your own individual judgements. Approach the task on the basis of logic.
2. Avoid changing your mind only in order to reach agreement and avoid conflict. Support only solutions with which you are at least able to agree partially.
3. Avoid conflict-reducing techniques such as majority vote, averaging, or trading, in reaching your decisions.
4. View differences of opinion as helpful rather than a hindrance in decision-making.

Groups in both conditions were allowed 45 minutes to reach consensus on each of the items. Individual and group rankings for each item were then compared with the rankings given by experts* (in this case NASA). For both individuals and groups a *total difference* score is worked out by calculating the deviation of each item ranked from the rank given that item by the NASA experts, these are then added together. The higher the score the greater the disagreement with NASA rankings and hence the poorer quality of decision making.

Hall and Watson found groups to perform better than individuals, although, as previously, the best individual usually produced an overall higher quality decision than the group.

*the NASA rankings were as follows: Box of matches – 15; food concentrate – 4; 50 feet of nylon rope – 6; parachute silk – 8; portable heating unit – 13; two .45 calibre pistols – 11; 1 case of dehydrated milk – 12; 2 hundred-pound tanks of oxygen – 1; stellar map – 3; life raft – 9; magnetic compass – 14; 5 gallons of water – 2; signal flares – 10; first aid kit – 7; solar powered FM receiver-transmitter – 5.

(Pennington 1986)

'RISKY SHIFT PHENOMENON' AND GROUP POLARISATION

Stoner was the first to propose that when people are in a group they are willing to make far riskier decisions than they would when they are acting as individuals. This became known as the 'risky shift phenomenon'. Wallach et al. put forward the *diffusion of responsibility* explanation for this process. This suggests that the group members feel less individually responsible for the end result and so consequently feel able to make an increased risk decision. However, this hypothesis was challenged by Moscovici and Zavalloni when they demonstrated that groups can make cautious decisions as well as risky ones, so that it was not a risky shift that was happening but *group polarisation* – that is, after a group discussion, the groups' views shifted towards one extreme or the other. For example, they found that if the group were cautious when first discussing the problem, the shift would be towards *caution*; and vice versa for a *risky* shift.

Lamm and Myers, accordingly, suggested two theories as to how this might happen:

1 *Information*. During the discussion, the group members may receive more information which will help to clarify the issue.
2 *Social comparison*. During the discussion, people will discover whether risk or caution is more socially desirable within the group, and will make their decision accordingly. Or it could be that members who had perceived themselves to be either risky or cautious have found, when comparing themselves to others, that they are not as extreme in that personality characteristic as they thought. As a result they then adopt a more extreme approach to maintain their self-concept.

Group think

The term 'group think' was identified by Janis (1972) and refers to 'how a group may be influenced by in group pressure to conform and express solidarity rather than to objectively evaluate a decision' (Flanagan 1994). Janis investigated a number of decisions which had been made by high-ranking officials. In the cases he studied, the decision-making had been poor, and the consequences had been terrible. Some examples include:

- President Kennedy's decision to support exiles trying to invade Cuba – known as the 'Bay of Pigs' incident, it was a disaster both militarily and diplomatically
- President Johnson's decision to step up the Vietnam War in the mid 1960s – this, again, was a military and diplomatic disaster
- The decision to market the drug Thalidomide, which as a result led to many babies being born with deformities

After recognising similarities in how the decisions had been made, Janis identified eight points all relating to group think – these are listed in Table 4.8. Janis felt that these decisions occurred because the groups involved were so insular that they had made decisions on an unrealistic view of the situation, and because they weren't flexible enough to entertain anybody else's *more realistic* view. The groups were particularly cohesive, and this may have been due to a need to placate a particularly strong leader, which in itself discourages dissension. It has been found that any minority group putting forward a contrary view *can* be valuable from the point of view of the whole group if that view is taken into account in the decision-making process. For this minority influence to be effective, Zimbardo et al. proposed three qualities that should be emphasised:

1 The minority should be assertive and confident.
2 It must not appear to be rigid in its outlook.

Table 4.8 The eight symptoms of groupthink

1 *Illusion of invulnerability.* The highly cohesive decision-making group members see themselves as powerful and invincible.
2 *Illusion of morality.* Members believe in the moral correctness of the group and its decision. Members view themselves as the 'good guys' and the opposition as bad or even evil.
3 *Shared negative stereotypes.* Members have common beliefs that minimise the risks involved in a decision or belittle any opposing views.
4 *Collective rationalisations.* Members explain away any negative information that goes against the decision of the group.
5 *Self-censorship.* Members suppress their own doubts or criticisms about the decision.
6 *Illusion of unanimity.* Members believe, mistakenly, that there is a general consensus for the decision because there are no alternative views being expressed.
7 *Direct conformity pressure.* When an opposing view is expressed, pressure is exerted to get the dissenter to agree to the decision.
8 *Mindguards.* Some members protect or insulate the group from any opposing views or negative information.

Source: Banyard, P. and Hayes, N. (1994), *Psychology – Theory and Application*, Chapman & Hall.

3 It should be skilled at social influence.

Social facilitation

Triplett (1987) made one of the first discoveries concerning social behaviour. He found that when one individual works with another, their performance can be enhanced due to their *mutual presence*. Triplett found that cyclists performed better when in a race than in practice, and suggested that it is the *presence of others* that enhances performance.

The element of competition increases arousal and motivation, but there are also other factors:

- A state of *evaluation apprehension* may occur
- The individual will want to present a favourable image to themselves and others, and this will again increase motivation and effort

In most situations, social facilitation will make people work harder at the task set. However, it can have the reverse effect in other situations. For example, when working with other people, the individual puts *less* effort into the task instead of more. Latane et al. refer to this as *social loafing*. This tends to happen when the person's contribution is anonymous and is integrated with that of the others in the group.

Conformity

Crutchfield defines conformity as 'yielding to group pressures'. Note that the definition points out that conformity is typically thought of in terms of group pressure rather than in terms of individuals.

SHERIF

Sherif used the *autokinetic effect* (a spot of light, seen in total darkness, that appears to move). The subjects saw this visual illusion individually and were required to estimate how far and in which direction it moved. An average was calculated for each subject and grouped with other subject's averages which were as different as possible. It was found that the judgements of the group tended to converge despite the fact that the individual members hadn't been asked to give group estimates. When the subjects were once again tested individually, it was found that the group estimates tended to persist.

Brown argues that in Western culture, to be in general accordance with others satisfies an important psychological need, particularly when the situation is an ambiguous one.

ASCH (1951, 1952, 1956)

This is perhaps one of the most famous studies in this area.

In his study, Asch told his subjects that they were all participating in a perception exercise. They were asked to judge the correct length of a given line by saying which of the three sample lines it was identical to (see Figures 4.9 and 4.10). The comparison was repeated, and each time the subjects answered

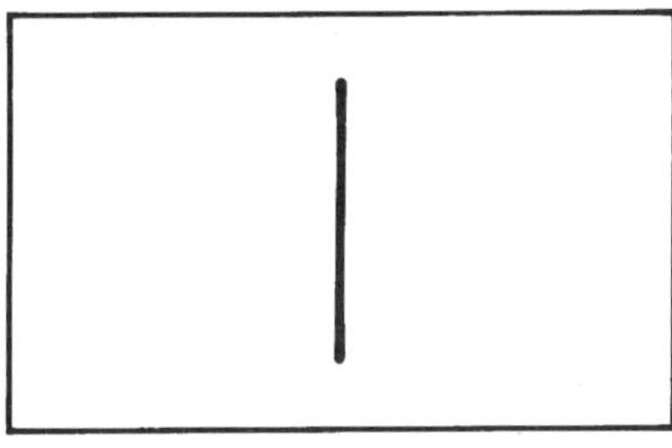

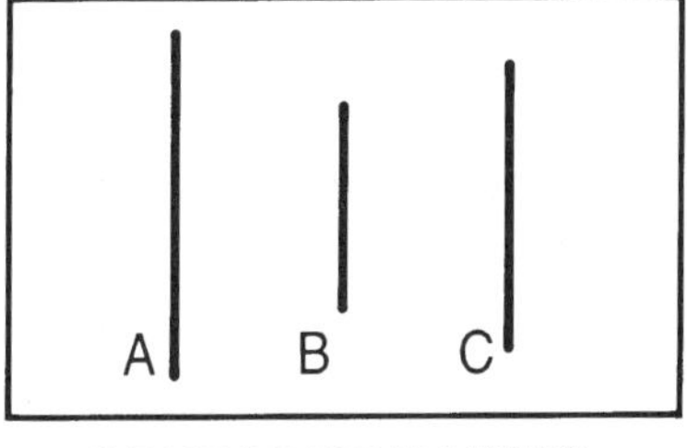

Figure 4.9 Stimulus cards used in Asch's experiments

Figure 4.10 Asch's famous experiment where a minority of one faces a unanimous majority

out loud. Unknown to the subjects, who were always the penultimate group member, the rest of the group was made up of 'stooges' who gave prearranged and obviously wrong answers. The subjects clearly found it anxiety-provoking when they found themselves disagreeing with the majority, and many of them at one time or another during the study gave answers which they knew to be wrong but which conformed with the majority judgements. The results were that:

- 75% of the subjects conformed at least once but not all the time
- 5% conformed all the time
- 20% never conformed
- 37% was the average rate of conformity

Asch commented that 'people submit uncritically and painlessly to external manipulation by suggestion'.

Later variations showed that:

- Three subjects was all that was needed to create a conformity effect
- If there was another stooge that dissented, this cut the conformity rates by 25% – even when the dissenter's choice disagreed with that of the subject
- If the rest of the group members were perceived as being experts, the conformity level increased
- The conformity level decreased if the group members were not face-to-face.

Perrin and Spence replicated Asch's experiment, and they found that although the subjects experienced clear anxiety, they did not conform as they did in Asch's study. They suggested that consequently Asch's experiment might be a 'child of its time' rather than a general effect. Yet, Doms and Avermaet queried this finding, arguing that the Asch effect has been demonstrated in more recent replications of Asch's work, e.g. Vine.

CRUTCHFIELD (1954)

Crutchfield's study involved subjects being seated in a cubicle which had various switches to indicate their choices and lights to show what other subjects had chosen – though in fact no other subjects existed! (This piece of equipment is more commonly referred to as the *Crutchfield apparatus*.) He tested his subjects with a set of obvious problems and attitudinal statements – e.g. that the life expectancy of American males is only about 25 years – and found that the responses were affected by the majority but to a slightly lesser degree than in Asch's study. Further results showed that individuals were more prepared to conform with difficult items and that when the subjects were tested by themselves, the level of conformity decreased considerably.

Kelman identified three main types of conformity, all of which work in different ways:

1. *Compliance:* this is the most superficial and can be explained by people conforming to avoid rejection or to be rewarded with social acceptance. This type of conformity will, however, only last as long as the situation does.
2. *Identification:* this is where individuals conform to a social role and act out the expected behaviour. For example, a nurse will be happy, pleasant and caring with their patients. The behaviour will come from the person identifying with the role of a nurse.
3. *Internalisation:* this is where an individual may accept another's opinion and then conform to their demands because they agree with the principles involved. This type of conformity lasts much longer than the actual situation because the person has adopted it into their own internal value system.

It can be seen that just as there are different types of conformity, so people conform for various different reasons. Another important point is that although conformity is often seen as a negative thing, this is not necessarily the case. Conformity can lead to behaviour which can be predictable, and this in turn can simplify social interactions. To learn to conform to roles etc. can be seen as an essential part of the socialisation process.

REFERENCES AND RESOURCES

Banyard, P. and Hayes, N. (1994), *Psychology – Theory and Application*, London: Chapman & Hall.

Gross, R. D. (1992), *Psychology – The Science of Mind and Behaviour*, London: Hodder & Stoughton.

Hayes, N. (1994), *Foundations of Psychology – an Introductory Text*, London: Routledge.

Hayes, N. and Orrell, S. (1993), *Psychology – an Introduction*, Harlow: Longman.

Pennington, B. F. (1986), *Essential Social Psychology*, Sevenoaks: Edward Arnold.

5

WORKING IN CARE ORGANISATIONS

Most health and social care in the UK is provided by, and within, a framework planned and controlled by the state, the services involved being funded by government. However, other care organisations do exist, for example:

- neighbourhood voluntary care groups
- Crossroads care schemes
- hospices and respite homes set up by charitable (voluntary) organisations
- private hospitals and residential homes
- support groups, e.g. one set up by and for parents of children with disabilities

Health care generally relates to actions designed to cure sickness or to manage the symptoms of ill health or disability. *Social care* relates to the non-medical interventions directed to ensure that a person is able to lead a full social life. A *care work group* is one that provides health or social care to a client group, i.e. the sick or socially disadvantaged. Caring for others involves entering into a relationship with one or more people – a mother cares for her children, or a son looks after his disabled mother. Working in care organisations involves a formal, usually paid form of caring. The individual qualities necessary to be an effective carer are the same in any caring relationship, formal or informal.

THE STRUCTURE OF CARE ORGANISATIONS

The way in which a health or social care organisation is structured will depend upon many factors:

- the *size* of the organisation
- whether it is statutory, private, voluntary or 'not-for-profit'
- the degree of *specialisation* within the organisation
- the need for collaboration with other organisations

Statutory organisations

Statutory organisations, such as the NHS and the social care services, appear to be highly *bureaucratic* in structure; that is, they have the following key features:

- They involve a pyramidal structure representing a *hierarchy* of authority; people control the activities of those at the level beneath them, from the highest level downwards
- The conduct of staff members is governed by a set of written rules
- Full-time, salaried staff are appointed to a specific position in the hierarchy
- The work role of staff is clearly separated from their life outside work
- Members of the organisation do not *own* the material resources which they use at work

Private organisations

There has been a recent growth in *private care organisations*, such as residential nursing homes for the elderly and hospitals which have opted out from the National Health Service and acquired *trust status*. Such private organisations are established purely to make a profit. The management of private organisations tends to be hierarchical, with the *manager* or *director* of the organisation holding maximum power. The individual roles of the care workers may differ from those of their counterparts in the statutory sector as there is a less well-defined structure of specialisation. For example, a nurse working in a large hospital will not be expected to take on the role of a cleaner when food is spilt by a patient, but *may* be expected to clean up spills in a private residential home.

Care provided within the private sector must comply with the minimum standards laid down by the National Health Service and Community Care Act 1990.

Voluntary organisations

Voluntary care organisations are set up by volunteers to provide a service which is not included within statutory services. Features of such organisations are:

- They may operate at a local or national level
- They are registered with the Charities Commission
- Any funds raised are used to improve the service provided
- They are often known as *'not-for-profit' organisations*

Not-for-profit organisations

Not-for-profit organisations differ, however, from voluntary organisations in that:

- The boards that run them consist of *salaried members*
- They do not involve the giving of *voluntary effort* either in time or money
- Many are staffed by ex-local-authority personnel and provide services under contract to social-services departments

The term *not-for-profit* originated in the USA, where it is used instead of 'voluntary sector'. The structure of not-for-profit organisations varies widely all over the UK but it is a growth area within care organisations, and the services provided overlap with those of statutory, private and voluntary organisations. Most such organisations are *not-for-profit trusts* which have been established to run residential care homes for the elderly.

ACTIVITY

Providing health and community care services for elderly people

1 Identify the services needed to provide adequate health and community care services for elderly people.

2 Present the information in the form of an *organisation chart* (see p. 176) to illustrate the range of service providers that might be involved.

ROLES

A *role* is a total and self-contained pattern of behaviour typical of a person who occupies a social position. Some roles remain with us from birth, e.g. gender roles, whilst other roles are acquired during the course of our lives, e.g. those of parent, social worker, footballer, etc. People occupy multiple roles throughout their lives (see Figure 5.1).

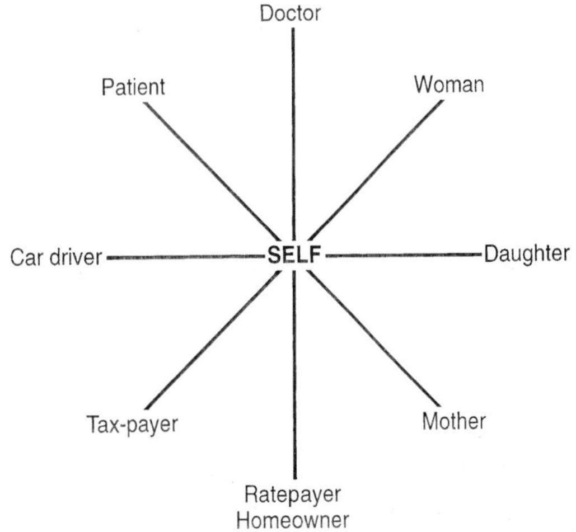

Figure 5.1 Multiple roles
Source: Bond and Bond 1986.

A person's *role set* (see Figure 5.2) comprises all the other people with whom they interact in the context of a *particular role* – not in the context of their *multiple roles*. A charge nurse or ward sister will have a very large role set consisting of many role relationships, some of which relationships will be less important than others.

A good way of looking at a job or *occupational role* is to see it as a *role web*. You are the spider at the centre of the web, and there are lines connecting you to everyone else with whom you have contact in that job. Some lines will be short and thick because the people are important to you and you have a lot to do with them. Some lines will be long and thin because the people are less significant and the contact less frequent. Then there will be the occasional line which is short but thin because contact is infrequent but is with someone much higher up in the organisation.

Roles in organisations

Everyone behaves differently with different people. Each role in an organisation will imply certain rights and obligations, methods of communication, authority, etc. How the individual acts in an organisational role will depend on their role perceptions, i.e. their feelings about what makes up 'correct' behaviour in a particular role.

Role expectations

People assume that they will behave in a certain way in a particular situation, and they also hold similar expectations regarding the behaviour of others. Colleagues who have worked together for several years usually enjoy efficient working relationships because they are able to anticipate exactly how the other will react to a given situation; each is then able to adapt their own behaviour in appropriate ways.

Role conflict

Role conflict occurs when the demands of one role are incompatible with the demands of another. There are two types of conflict:

- *inter-role conflict*, when two simultaneously held roles conflict – e.g. the working mother who is at work on the day of her son's performance in the school play will experience conflict between her role as mother and her role as worker
- *intra-role conflict*, when there is more than one expectation for an occupational role and no immediately obvious way of coping with the ensuing conflict – e.g. a nurse may

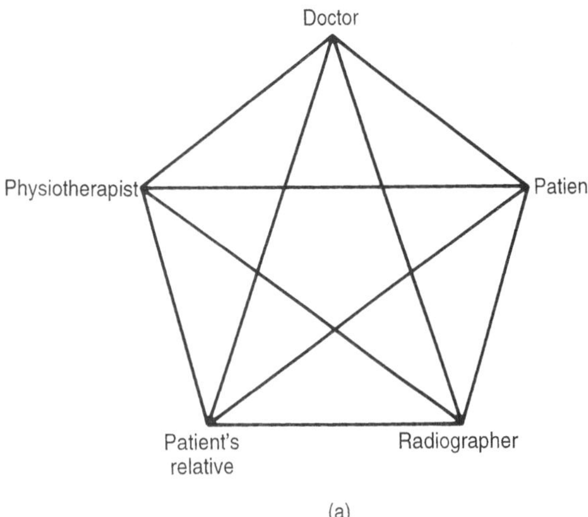

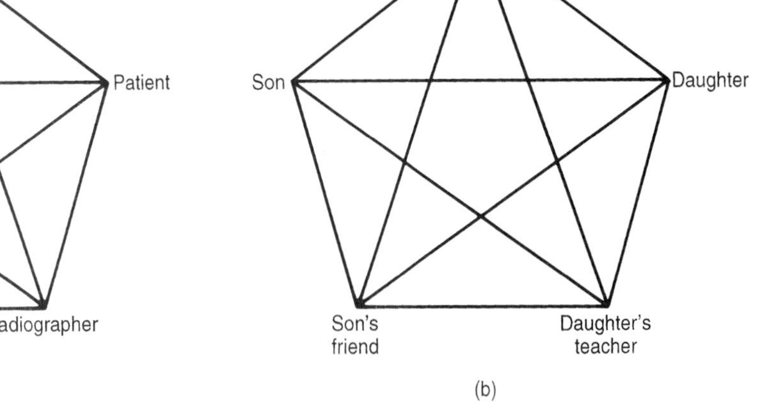

Figure 5.2 Simplified role sets
Source: Bond and Bond 1986.

be expected to participate in abortion procedures or the delivery of ECT (electroconvulsive therapy) to a mentally ill person

Role compliance

In 1963 S. Milgram conducted some experiments which demonstrate how powerfully roles can influence our actions, often leading us to act counter to our privately held views or vested interests. In these experiments, paid adult subjects heard that, as part of a study on punishment and learning, they as 'teachers' would be asked to deliver an electric shock to a 'learner' (actually an associate of the person conducting the experiment) every time they committed a memory error. The experimental setting was very realistic, complete with a buzzing, blinking 'shock machine'. Only the experimenter and the 'learners' knew that no shocks were actually delivered. The point of the study was to find out at what point the 'teacher' would refuse to comply with the conditions of their role as obedient research participant.

Nearly all the 'teachers' began to show signs of reluctance as they were asked to increase the intensity of the shock and the 'learner' cried out in pain. If the 'teacher' refused to administer the shock, the experimenter urged them on by saying such things as 'Please continue' or 'You must go on'. Only if the 'teacher' persisted in their protests despite the experimenter's demands were they excused from the study.

The 'teachers' who continued with the experiment even when the 'learners' were screaming with pain showed signs of stress and emotional disturbance: some broke out into nervous laughter, others dug their fingernails into their palms or bit their lips. Yet, in spite of the obvious distress, over 60% of the subjects administered the *maximum* shock voltage (450 volts) to the 'learner'. In fact, even when the 'teacher' was required to hold the 'learner's' hand to the shock plate by force, this figure only dropped to 30%: *role compliance* was generally not disrupted.

Milgram's results have been replicated in several different countries. The data from these studies imply that a good number of us could be persuaded into committing a variety of harmful or even immoral actions if the *role pressure* were severe enough.

ACTIVITY

1 Draw a role set for yourself (see Figure 5.2).
- How many roles do you occupy?
- Do you ever experience any inter-role or intra-role conflict?

2 If possible, obtain a copy of the film of Milgram's experimental study, or else re-read the extract. Discuss the following issues:
- Why is peer pressure so strong?
- Do you think you would be more likely to carry out orders issued by someone wearing a white coat than by someone dressed casually?
- What implications does the issue of role compliance have for those working in care organisations?

Individual qualities of an effective carer

Caring as a quality is largely invisible, difficult to quantify and more noticeable when absent than when present. The main individual characteristics of an effective carer are:

- *Listening:* attentive listening is a vital part of the caring relationship. Sometimes a person's real needs are communicated more by what is left unsaid than by what is actually spoken. Facial expressions, posture and other forms of body language all give clues to a person's feelings. A good carer will be aware of these forms of *non-verbal communication*. Communicating well with the patient or client will not only make them feel wanted and valued but also help to relieve pain and distress

- *Comforting:* this has a physical and an emotional meaning. Physical comfort may be provided by touch; a nurse may plump up a patient's pillows or a social worker may provide a reassuring safe environment for a distressed child. Touching, listening and talking can all provide emotional comfort as well
- *Empathy:* this should not be confused with *sympathy*. Some people find it easy to appreciate how someone else is feeling by imagining themselves in that person's position. Others may find it easier if they can simulate the situation, e.g. by being fed by someone else (see Chapter 3).
- *Sensitivity:* this is the ability to be aware of and responsive to the feelings and needs of another person. Being sensitive to others' needs requires the carer to anticipate their feelings, e.g. the stages of grief experienced by someone recently bereaved, or the worry of being admitted to hospital
- *Patience:* a good carer will be patient and tolerant of other people's methods of dealing with problems even when they feel that their own way is better
- *Respect:* a carer should have an awareness of a person's personal rights, dignity and privacy, and must show this at all times. Every person is different, and so the carer's approach will need to be tailored to each individual. For example, some patients in hospital find it very difficult and embarrassing to have their intimate personal needs attended to by a stranger
- *Interpersonal skills:* a caring relationship is a two-way process. One does not have to *like* the person one is caring for, but warmth and friendliness help to create a positive atmosphere and to break down barriers. *Acceptance* is important: the carer should always look beyond the disability or disruptive behaviour to recognise and accept the *person*
- *Self-awareness:* a carer can be more effective if they are able to perceive what effect their behaviour has on other people. Being part of a team enables us both to discover how others perceive us and to modify our behaviour in the caring relationship accordingly
- *Coping with stress:* caring for others effectively in a full-time capacity requires energy, and it is important to be aware of the possibility of *professional burn-out*. In order to help others we must first help ourselves: the carer who never relaxes or develops any outside interests is more likely to suffer 'burn-out' than the carer who finds his or her own time and space

ACTIVITY

1 Think about the qualities outlined above.
   - Do you feel you already possess these qualities?
   - Do you think academic knowledge is important for someone working in care organisations?

2 Evaluate your own interpersonal skills. Can you *empathise*, i.e. put yourself in someone else's situation?

WORK GROUPS IN CARE ORGANISATIONS

Aspects of groups

A group (see also the discussion on groups in Chapter 4) is a collection of two or more people who possess a common purpose.

- *Formal groups* are deliberately created by management in organisations for particular planned purposes; it is the management that selects the group members, the leaders and the methods of working
- *Informal groups* are formed by people who feel they share a common interest.

Members organise themselves into groups and develop both a sense of affinity with each other and a common cause

Group cohesion

This has to do with the extent to which group members are prepared to cooperate and to share common goals. Cohesion encourages compliance with group norms and causes groups to be more stable in their functioning.

Certain factors contribute to the creation of group cohesion:

- *Frequency and closeness of interactions:* the more often people meet and the closer the contacts, the more they will perceive themselves as belonging to a distinct group
- *Exclusivity of membership:* if membership of the group is selective, members feel a sense of achievement in having been chosen
- *The nature of the external environment:* the environment in which a group operates may offer protection from a hostile external environment, e.g. Neighbourhood Watch groups
- *Good interpersonal communication:* if communication is easy, then a collective sense of purpose will readily emerge. The less contact with outsiders, the greater the internal cohesiveness
- *A shared task:* if the members are all engaged on similar work, then they will more readily perceive themselves as a group
- *Homogeneity of membership:* where members are alike in terms of background, education, age or ethnic or social origin etc., they will share common attitudes
- *Rewards and penalties:* a group that can offer rewards or bonuses or even punish its own members can exert great pressure on individuals to conform. Group cohesiveness tends to be very strong in these cases

High cohesiveness or cohesion in a group can result in high morale and productivity; but there is also always the risk that with such a powerful interest group, all of whose members are working towards common goals, there may be a conflict with the aims of management. Other disadvantages of a highly cohesive group are:

- *Dependency* on the group, where management can have little effect on any individual's behaviour because the group is so tight-knit and seemingly self-governing
- *Alienation:* unless management harnesses the qualities of the cohesive group by means of much social interaction, mutual support and interpersonal cooperation, the objectives of management can become alienated from the group norms

Intergroup conflict

This is the conflict that occurs *between* groups. As with stress, not all conflict is inherently bad: it can be a good thing when it causes the group members to explore new ideas and to test their position and beliefs. How conflict is resolved (see Table 5.1) will affect group behaviour. Organisations should try to prevent damaging conflicts arising and have methods for resolving them if prevention fails.

CAUSES

The many causes of intergroup conflict include:

- differing opinions about the *aims* of the organisation
- the failure of senior *management* to coordinate the groups' activities
- conflicting *goals* and frames of reference
- attempts by one group to *dominate* others
- competition for limited *resources*

PREVENTION

To prevent intergroup conflict, the organisation could try the following methods:

- *move* individuals from one group to another regularly
- keep all groups *informed* of the organisation's wider aims and objectives
- set up *project teams* that cut across departmental *boundaries*: e.g. a team within a

Table 5.1 Ways of resolving conflict

Style	Characteristic behaviour	User justification
Avoidance	Ignore issues. Non-confrontational. Denies issues are a problem.	Differences too minor or too great to resolve. Attempts may harm relationships or create even greater problems.
Accommodating	Non-assertive behaviour. Cooperative even at the expense of personal goals.	Not worth risking damage to relationships or general lack of harmony.
Win/lose	Confrontational, assertive and aggressive. Must win at any cost.	Must prove superiority. Survival of the fittest. Most morally or professionally correct.
Compromising	Important that all parties achieve basic goals and maintain good relationships. Aggressive but cooperative.	More than one answer to the problem. No-one person or idea is perfect. You must give in order to get.
Problem-solving	Needs of both parties are legitimate and important. High respect for mutual support. Assertive and co-operative.	Open discussion of issues will lead to a mutually beneficial solution – no-one makes a major concession.

hospital could be looking at the problem of infection control; each department involved would be represented on the project team and would have its own clearly defined role

RESOLUTION

Conflicts between people or groups of equal rank may be resolved through *arbitration* at the next highest level of authority within the organisation. In other types of conflict, the following methods might be used to resolve disputes:

- *Joint negotiating committees:* these committees meet at predetermined intervals to discuss problems that have arisen since the last meeting. If an issue is raised at the committee, then there is an implied willingness to compromise and to avoid a stalemate
- *Redeployment:* this means transferring certain individuals to other departments, which is not always possible or advisable
- A *clarification* of the roles and responsibilities of those in dispute

ACTIVITY

Look at Table 5.1 on ways of resolving conflict.

- Which style is characterised by assertive behaviour and yet represents the maximum in cooperation?
- Which style is totally assertive and uncooperative?
- Which style takes the middle ground on assertiveness and cooperation?
- Which style is the most uncooperative and least assertive?
- Which style is totally cooperative but unassertive?

Methods of analysing groups

INTERACTIONAL ANALYSIS

In 1969, Herbert Blumer devised this method of studying the meanings that underpin human action. There are three key elements of interactional analysis:

1 Individuals act towards things – other people, objects, institutions, situations etc. – on the basis of *meanings*. Few, if any, human actions are meaningless, but it is not always easy to discern *what* the actions mean to the individual.

Example: the key to understanding why some people may react badly to a stay in hospital is to try to see the situation from their point of view.

2 Meanings derive from past experiences and methods of social interaction; they are not preordained. Objects and events do not have fixed meanings: they are *made to mean* certain things by the interactions people have with one another.

Example: take a doctor's refusal to write a prescription. Person A may interpret this as reasonable in the light of current overprescribing; person B may interpret it as a sign of indifference; and person C may see it as a sign of incompetence.

3 Meanings *shift and change* in the light of new experience. Thus, people's relationships and attitudes to events, to situations and to each other may also be modified.

Example: 50 years ago, it was considered fashionable and sophisticated to smoke cigarettes, whereas in the last years of the twentieth century, smoking is generally frowned on as anti-social and harmful to health.

Interactional analysts see the social world as assembled from the encounters people have with one another. Research methods favoured by interactionist sociologists include semi-structured and open-ended interviews, and participant observations.

Interactionist ideas have been used to analyse a wide range of health issues. One study by Julius Roth in 1972 demonstrated the idea central to interactionist thought – that the meaning of human encounters is constructed by observers and participants through *interpretation*. Roth observed the behaviour of staff towards patients being admitted to the accident and emergency departments of six hospitals in the USA. His observations enabled him to distinguish between those patients who were regarded as 'deserving' the full attention of the staff and those who were felt to be more 'undeserving'. Roth writes:

> Take for example, patients who are labelled as drunks. They are more consistently treated as undeserving than any other category of patient. They are frequently handled as if they were baggage when brought in by the police; those with lacerations are usually treated roughly by physicians; they are usually treated only for drunkenness and obvious surgical repair without being examined for other pathology; no-one believes their stories; their statements are ridiculed; they are treated in an abusive or jocular manner; they are ignored for long periods of time . . . Emergency ward personnel frequently comment on how they hate to take care of drunks.
>
> *(Aggleton 1990)*

The amount of alcohol consumed by these patients was unimportant; it was the *interpretation* of an individual's actions as drunkenness which resulted in the stereotypical treatment.

ACTIVITY

1 Working in groups of three or four, choose one of the following health issues and devise a study using the interactional analysis approach. Read through your notes on research methods and select the ones that are best suited to discovering the meanings which lie behind the actions described:

- under-age drinking
- overweight middle-aged businessmen
- dietary disorders among teenage girls – e.g. *anorexia nervosa* or *bulimia*
- people with tooth decay who refuse to go to the dentist

Keep the study small: collect data from a maximum of four people.

2 When you have finished the study, evaluate it and discuss any problems that may need to be resolved.

3 Present your findings to the rest of the class.

SOCIOMETRY

Sociometry (see also Chapter 4, pp. 140–42) is a means of presenting simply and graphically the entire structure of relations existing at a given time among members of a given group. A group's cohesion may be measured by the use of a *sociogram* or *sociometric test*. A sociogram (see Figure 4.8 for an example) is a diagram showing who communicates with whom; it is usually used in conjunction with an *analysis grid*, which records the contributions each group member makes. The major lines of communication, or the *pattern of attraction and repulsion* in its full scope, are made understandable at a glance, and the resulting sociogram may be described as *a measure of social distance*. J. L. Moreno depicted groups as being constituted by strands of like and dislike which he called *teles*.

The technique has been applied in informal groups, school classes, prisons and other organisations. It has also proved useful when introducing new skills and knowledge, such as immunisation techniques, to a group, for example in a small village in a developing country, where it is important to find out the channels of power, gossip and communication at work.

Group formation

(On the stages of group development, see Thomson et al. 1995, pp. 100–101.)

There are two major types of group formation in health and social care settings:

1 *Multidisciplinary groups*. For example, a general practitioner (GP), a health visitor (HV), a community psychiatric nurse (CPN), the daughter of the patient and a social worker will meet to discuss the future care of an elderly man who suffers from Alzheimer's disease (a form of senile dementia) and who is at present cared for by his daughter.
2 *Groups of people in similar circumstances*. People who share a common problem will often form a group in order to provide mutual support. They can then work through their problems in cooperation with others. Examples are: groups for the wives of men serving prison sentences; groups for the parents of drug abusers; Alcoholics Anonymous, an international self-help group.

ACTIVITY

1 Set up a role-play situation to act out the meeting of the multidisciplinary group outlined above. Decide who should lead the discussion and what information you require beforehand.

2 Appoint a *scribe*, who should record what information the group needs and who should be asked to contribute.

3 What options are open to you as a care work group?

4 Discuss the advantages and disadvantages of residential care from the viewpoint both of the elderly man and of his daughter.

Leadership styles

Leadership is the ability to influence the thoughts and behaviour of others. A leader's position may be formal and result from designated organisational authority, e.g. that of a ward manager, or informal, e.g. depending on the individual's personal ability to exercise power.

There is a continuum of possible leadership styles extending from complete *autocracy* at one extreme to total *democracy* at the other.

AUTHORITARIAN STYLES

(See Chapter 4, pp. 121–122, for a discussion of the 'authoritarian personality'.) This style may be *dictatorial* or *paternalistic*. The *dictatorial* approach has the following features:

- The leader tells the subordinate exactly what to do, without comment or discussion
- There are rewards for good performance and penalties or threats of sanctions for underperformance
- There is strict control and a highly formal network of interpersonal relations between the leader and group members

The paternalistic style is similar, but with the following features too:

- There is close supervision, but the leader attempts to win the respect and loyalty of subordinates
- Special favours are awarded to those who obey the leader
- Some disagreement is tolerated, though never approved

Advantages of the authoritarian style

- Everyone knows precisely what is expected of them: tasks, situations and relationships are clearly defined
- Time management is usually good since the management sets the standards and coordinates the work
- Decisions are arrived at speedily as there is no consultation
- Employees receive direct and immediate help towards achieving their goals

Disadvantages of the authoritarian style

- It stifles workers' initiative
- It does not make maximum use of the employees' knowledge, skills and experiences
- Staff cannot reach their true potential
- If the group leader is absent, e.g. ill or on holiday, important work may not be completed

Autocratic or authoritarian styles of leadership are not often seen in care organisations since, by virtue of their size, these tend to involve a bureaucratic system.

THE DEMOCRATIC STYLE

At its extreme, this style is the *laissez-faire* approach where a group does not have a leader at all (though it may have a care worker who acts as a facilitator).

The democratic style involves:

- much communication and consultation between the leader and the group, recognising that everyone has a contribution to make
- the active participation of group members in the leader's decisions; if unanimity is impossible, then a vote is taken

Advantages of the democratic style

- The job satisfaction of group members is greater, as their responsibilities are widened and their work is made more interesting and varied
- The morale of group members is good as they have a key role in planning and decision-taking
- Specialist knowledge and skills are recognised and used towards achieving goals
- Targets are more likely to be achieved because they have been formulated by group consensus

Disadvantages of the democratic style

- Some group members may not want to become involved in the decision-making process
- Time management may be more problematic because of the extra time necessary for full consultation on the part of the group
- The lack of a positive direction may prevent goals from being attained
- Employees may feel resentful because they are only involved in minor day-to-day issues and do not have any real say in the major issues
- Subordinates may require closer supervision that this style allows

Types of power

All large organisations have a recognisable power structure, and *social power* may be defined as the influence that one person has over another. French and Raven (1968) have identified several types of power by describing the ways in which 'person A could cause person B to do something which was contrary to B's desire'.

COERCIVE POWER

The holder of this type of power is in a position to control the environment by withholding or threatening to withhold resources considered necessary for the maintenance of a satisfactory environment.

Example: A nurse may punish an elderly patient for being incontinent by being too busy to attend to her.

REWARD POWER

This is based on one person's perception that someone else is able to grant valued rewards in return for the former's obedience or completion of certain tasks, or both.

Example: GPs can reward district nurses and health visitors by the amount of space provided for them in the surgery. A ward sister can reward a student nurse for extra help by giving a good report.

EXPERT POWER

This is based on the belief that someone else has special knowledge and ability in a particular situation, e.g. through the possession of recognised qualifications. Research shows that this form of power is the most acceptable since we all have the potential to become experts, even if only in small ways. Expert power is normally restricted to the specific subject area of the influencer's expertise.

Example: The advice of a medical doctor will generally be followed when related to physical ailments, but not necessarily in relation to other matters, e.g. politics or financial investment.

REFERENT POWER

This kind of power relates to the prestige of individuals: people who possess high prestige or charisma are endowed with referent power. Peers as well as occupational superiors can exert referent power.

Example: The higher status accorded to doctors means that they have higher referent power than social workers or nurses.

LEGITIMATE POWER

This power stems from the moral authority of a particular position in an organisation which gives the power-holder control over invisible assets – particularly information, right of access and the right to organise.

Example: Doctors control information on diagnosis and prognosis, so that other professionals as well as patients depend on the doctor for that information.

ACTIVITY

Read through the sections above on group formation, power and leadership.

On work-experience placement, try to analyse the group in which you are working:

1 Draw a sociogram, using a key to show the frequency and importance of each contact.

2 Is there an obvious leader and leadership style?

3 Find out about the functions of the group, i.e. how often members meet, how decisions are taken etc.

4 How much a part of the group did you feel? Did you notice the different types of power?

The role of teams within care organisations

Most people who work in care organisations are members of at least one team. Features of teams are:

- They work together to meet common aims or goals.

  Examples: to provide health care in the community may be the broad goal of the Primary Health Care Team (PHCT); to meet the social and emotional needs of people with learning disabilities may be the goal of a local voluntary organisation.

  The aims of a team are often set out in a *mission statement*.
- Each member of the team has a well-defined and important role. Team members recognise their *interdependence*, and that team goals are best accomplished through mutual support.

  Example: a team in an operating theatre may comprise the following members: a consultant surgeon, a surgical house officer, a theatre charge nurse, an operating department assistant (ODA) and an anaesthetist. All team members have clearly defined roles and support the common aim, that is, to perform a surgical operation on the patient
- Team members are clear about *leadership*. Most teams have leaders, although the leadership may change according to the membership of the team. The final decisions must rest with the team leader in cases where a team decision cannot be reached: positive results, not conformity, is the goal
- Team members work in a climate of trust, and are encouraged to express ideas and disagreements – that is, they can openly challenge another team member without fear of retribution
- Teams can measure their own performance. In care settings, performance indicators or an *audit tool* may be used in order to monitor and improve the quality of care (see pp. 165–168 on quality assurance etc.).

One important individual has been left out of our discussion of the team: the patient or client. In practice, the patient and their relatives are often key team members, together with the district nursing staff: decisions are taken after discussion between all team members, and care is often then shared between nurses and relatives.

ACTIVITY

Do you think that patients should always be part of the team, and therefore part of the decision-making process, or are there specific circumstances when they should be excluded? Discuss.

Contributing to team meetings

Team meetings are usually held regularly, and are conducted according to an agreed *agenda*. Ideally, a written agenda should be given to all team members and should include a space for anyone to add their own item for discussion. Certain factors may detract from the value of team meetings:

- distractions – constant interruptions, either from telephone calls or visitors
- irrelevant topics – some meetings become a forum for gossip or other topics irrelevant to the task in hand

- a dominating member – one person may be aggressive and outspoken, with the effect of blocking other people's contributions

Assertiveness makes this communication at team meetings more effective. This should not be confused with loudness or aggressive behaviour: assertiveness may be defined in this context as standing up for your own basic rights and beliefs without isolating those of others, and as making your behaviour 'match' your feelings. (See Chapter 2 on interpersonal interaction in Thomson et al. 1995.)

Stress and conflict in the workplace

There are a number of reasons why conflicts arise in the workplace. The nature of the caring relationship imposes particular stresses which can lead to conflict between team members. There may be:

- low morale – if individuals feel unsupported and undervalued in their role
- confusions over *individual roles* in the hierarchy of the organisation
- responsibility and accountability for providing care for people who are ill or disadvantaged
- a lack of communication with superiors and colleagues
- ambiguity over which tasks should take priority during the working day
- an excessive workload (both quantitatively – i.e. having too much work to do – and qualitatively – i.e. finding work too difficult)
- feelings of personal inadequacy and insecurity – often following destructive criticism of one's work

ACTIVITY

In work placement, carry out the following tasks:

1 Investigate the role of teams within the care setting; explain their structure and their function.

2 Read through the section on skill mix below and Table 5.2 on p. 161. Describe the benefits of skill mix in relation to teamwork in your placement.

3 List the advantages and the disadvantages of teams within the care setting. Which type of leader is best suited to teamwork?

Skill mix

The introduction of skill mix in community nursing and health visiting is a response to the need to rationalise costs by employing cheaper staff with specific skills. The Patient's Charter (Department of Health 1992) emphasises a 'service provision' approach and a move away from the generic health care worker who views patients and clients as 'my patients' or 'my families'. See Table 5.2, p. 161.

HOW CARE ORGANISATIONS FUNCTION

The culture of an organisation

An organisation is 'the rational coordination of the activities of a number of people for the achievement of some common, explicit purpose or goal, through a division of labour and through a hierarchy of authority and responsibility' (Schein 1969). There are three main types of organisation:

- *mutual benefit associations*, e.g. political parties, trade unions, men's clubs and women's groups
- *public service organisations*, e.g. schools, hospitals, colleges and old people's homes
- *business organisations*, e.g. banks, industries, supermarket chains

Many hospitals in the UK have now become NHS trusts and are managed as business

Table 5.2 The advantages and disadvantages of skill mix in nursing

Advantages	Disadvantages
• It can create new opportunities for practitioners, e.g. learn management skills • it can lead to more opportunity for the practitioner or team leader to focus on wider issues, e.g. health promotion • it may lead to greater job satisfaction for team members • patients and clients may benefit from the collective experience shared by the team	• nurses may be viewed as too expensive a resource • support workers are replacing trained nurses, de-skilling nurses and eroding the professional role • the supervision of untrained staff is more difficult to carry out effectively in the community than in a hospital ward • it can lead to job dissatisfaction if the practitioner feels 'de-skilled' • it may make the concept of the 'named nurse' (enshrined in the Patient's Charter) more difficult to implement

organisations within a framework of *purchasers* and *providers*.

An organisation's culture develops gradually, and employees may not be aware that it even exists. It is made up of:

- its members' shared perceptions of issues
- a customary way of doing things
- styles of behaviour
- attitudes towards work and motivation
- the nature of the organisation or enterprise

TYPES OF ORGANISATIONAL CULTURE

Charles Handy (1985) described four types of organisational culture: power, role, task and person (see Figure 5.3).

1 The *power culture*, frequently found in small enterprises, depends on a central power source with rays of power and influence spreading out from that central figure, like a web with a spider in the middle. All the important decisions are taken by very few people, and the web needs to remain small as it can break if it seeks to link too many activities. It can only grow by spawning other spiders with webs of their own.

Examples: new business situations, deals and brokerage transactions, the artistic and theatrical worlds, politics.

2 The *role culture* can be pictured as a Greek temple. It is highly bureaucratic. The role organisation rests its strength in its pillars, which are its functions or specialities. It operates through formal roles and procedures, and there are clearly defined rules for settling disputes. As it is so rigidly structured, it can offer security, but it cannot adapt quickly to allow for change.

Examples: administrative organisations, e.g. the vehicle licensing centre or the Inland Revenue.

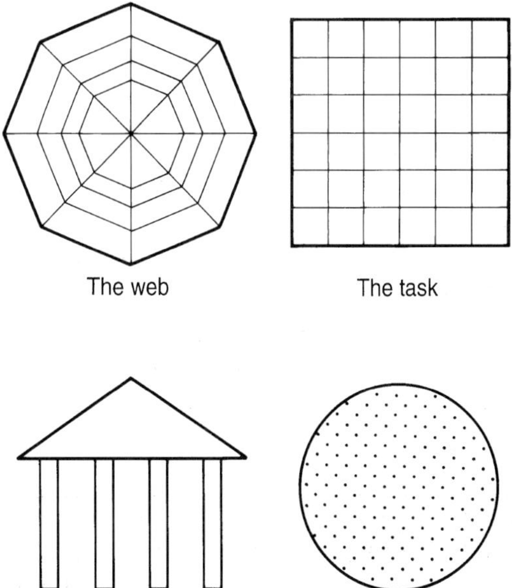

Figure 5.3 The web – power culture
The Greek temple – role culture
The net – task culture
Stars – person culture

3 The *task culture* can be pictured as a *net* or *matrix* organisation, with some of the strands of the net thicker and stronger than others and much of the power lying at the *interstices* or *knots*. The task culture is job- or project-oriented. There is no single dominant leader: *all* group members work towards completion of the collective task. A task culture is ideal for an environment of change as it encourages a problem-solving approach. Job satisfaction is high, and there is much group cohesion.

   Examples: advertising agency, consultancy, product development groups, surgical teams.

4 A *person culture* puts the individual first and makes the organisation the resource for the individual's talents. It can be pictured as a loosely grouped cluster of stars. The terms 'organisation' and 'manager' are avoided, replaced by talk of 'partners', 'bursars', etc.

   Examples: doctors who, for their own convenience, group themselves in a practice; barristers in chambers; architects in partnerships; etc.

According to Handy, no one type of culture is better than any of the others.

A culture arises from:

- historical circumstances
- the existing environment
- technology
- the human needs of people within the organisation

FACTORS INFLUENCING ORGANISATIONAL CULTURE

Six key factors influence the culture and structure of an organisation:

1 *History and ownership:* How old the company is and whether it is owned centrally will affect the type of culture. Most family firms are power cultures. New organisations are often a combination of power (aggressive and independent) and task (flexible and sensitive) cultures.

2 *Size:* the larger the organisation, the more it tends to be a role culture. Members of a large organisation usually perceive it as offering more potential; it is thought to be more efficient but more authoritarian in style.

3 *Technology:* routine, programmable operations are more suitable to a role culture, as are tasks with a high degree of interdependence. The one-off job or unit production is more suited to power or task cultures. In general, the tendency towards increasing automation results in the development of a role culture.

4 *Goals and objectives:* goals not only influence cultures, they are influenced by them. The objectives of hospitals, schools and local government are often a mixture of service to community and maintenance of standards, within the limits of constrained resources. *Growth* goals are more appropriate to a power or task culture. Quality-of-product goals are more easily regulated in a role organisation.

5 *The environment:* this includes:
   - the economic environment
   - the market
   - the competitive scene
   - the geographical and societal environment

   Different nationalities prefer different organisational cultures. A task culture is more suited to coping with changes in the market or product. A role culture is more suited to businesses with standardised markets and products with a long life-cycle.

   A threat or danger in the environment, e.g. mergers, takeovers or nationalisation, are best served by power cultures; this is because merger battles and crises are often decided by personalities.

6 *The people:* the role culture suits individuals who need security and like clearly prescribed roles. The power or task culture is appropriate to the individual who needs to establish an identity at work.

CULTURAL LAG

The restructuring of the caring services, in

particular the National Health Service, has necessitated a corresponding change in underlying cultures. Whereas an organisation's needs and activities will regularly change, its underlying culture might remain constant, i.e. the employees may still hold out-of-date attitudes which better suit the previous organisational culture. This is termed 'cultural lag'.

Management styles

All organisations have to be managed, although styles of management vary considerably. The management of nearly every organisation, however, must:

- plan
- establish goals
- control operations
- appraise its employees

In 1976, Maccoby made a socio-psychoanalytic study of 250 corporate managers in American organisations. He described four character types which can be found in different combinations (see Handy 1985).

1 THE JUNGLE FIGHTER

The jungle fighter needs power. He sees life as a battle for survival in which winners destroy losers. He is protective towards his 'family' and ruthless towards competitors. His domineering attitude upsets independent insubordinates, and his obsession with the need for defence can create enemies.

2 THE COMPANY MAN

This person is concerned with the human side of the company and committed to maintaining corporate integrity. He can turn into a senseless careerist, obsessed with organisational politics, but at his best he can sustain an atmosphere of discipline and service. He is too conservative to lead an innovative organisation.

3 THE GAMESMAN

The gamesman likes to take calculated risks and is fascinated by techniques, new methods and problems. He thrives on competition and can inspire his group. He is a team player who looks for glory rather than riches. At extremes he can live in a fantasy world, finding games and competitions where none need exist.

4 THE CRAFTSMAN

The craftsman is an individualist interested in making something. Self-contained and exacting, he can become uncooperative at times. He is a good master to apprentices but a poor member of a team. He leads by ordering subordinates to act upon *his* decisions.

ACTIVITY

Read through the section on *organisational culture types* and then consider which *management type* would fit best into each culture style. Give reasons for your choice.

THE CHARACTERISTICS OF EFFECTIVE MANAGERS

In 1986, Pedlar et al. described the following characteristics of effective managers:

- *A command of basic facts:* the level of awareness that managers have about their organisational plans, roles, relationships and networks
- *Relevant professional understanding:* the technical or professional knowledge which managers have about the goods or services being produced, the targeted markets and the management principles
- *Continuing sensitivity to events:* insights into 'hard' information (e.g. statistics) and 'soft' information (e.g. political sensitivities within the organisation)
- *Analytical, problem-solving, decision-/judgement-making skills:* the ability to respond rationally in clear-cut circumstances requiring decisions to be made, and the ability to make sensible judgements in uncertain and ambiguous situations

- *Social skills and abilities*: interpersonal skills, e.g. communication, negotiating and persuading
- *Emotional resilience*: the ability to cope successfully with stress when working to tight deadlines and when dealing with interpersonal conflict
- *The proactive approach*: an inclination to respond purposefully to events; the ability to decide on, and achieve, goals on one's own initiative
- *Creativity*: the ability to arrive at new ways of dealing with new situations, and to recognise and use the same ability in others
- *Mental agility*: the ability to grasp complex problems quickly, and the capacity to switch from one problem to another fairly easily
- *Balanced learning habits and skills*: the ability to think conceptually as well as in concrete terms
- *Self-knowledge*: the knowledge that one has about oneself – one's values, goals, feelings, strengths and weaknesses

Quality and quality assurance

The measurement of the quality of services is now becoming more widespread than ever before. Maxwell (1984) has devised a set of criteria which can help to indicate the standard of performance in a health care agency:

1. *Effectiveness*: the degree to which objectives are achieved.
2. *Efficiency*: the ratio of benefits to costs.
3. *Equity*: equal treatment for equal needs.
4. *Appropriateness*: relevance to need.
5. *Acceptability*: to individuals, groups and society at large.
6. *Accessibility*: in terms, for example, of time and location.

Users of health and social care services will be more likely to define a good-quality service as 'that which gives me what I want'.

In the NHS, which is highly labour-intensive, it is the most junior members of staff who interact most frequently with the recipients (or 'consumers') of health care; thus, it is primarily these groups of staff that the service must address to implement quality systems.

Monitoring standards in health and social care

The restructuring of the health and social care services has introduced a strong element of the *enterprise culture* into public service organisations. The *service user*, previously called 'the patient', 'the client' or 'the informal carer', now enjoys more freedom of choice and independence – at least in theory. Complaints procedures and rights to redress in the case of inadequate service are increasing the degree of *empowerment* enjoyed by service users.

TOOLS AND TECHNIQUES USED IN MONITORING STANDARDS

Some measurement and evaluation tools are easier to develop and use than others, and some are more appropriate to certain service-user groups than to others. Examples of common tools and techniques include:

- patient-client-staff-satisfaction questionnaires and surveys
- a direct observation of health and social care; for example, observing the length of time a client has to wait before being seen by a social worker
- an analysis of recovery rates, particularly after surgery or hospitalisation
- interviews of staff and clients
- care conferences, for example between staff or between clients/service users, relatives and staff
- reviews or audits of nursing or social-work records
- focus groups – where a particular group of clients/patients is brought together to provide feedback on a predetermined topic. A group *facilitator* uses a framework of open-ended questions to elicit responses from group members about their

experiences and concerns. These responses are then summarised in writing by the group facilitator
- brainstorming sessions: such informal group techniques encourage active involvement and a creative approach to solving problems and assessing quality of care

Which appropriate tool or technique is selected will depend on issues such as time, resources, skills and access to the data source. Schroeder (1994) proposes that the following principles should guide the selection of your tool or technique:

- It has the potential to generate/produce the necessary data
- It respects issues of confidentiality and rights
- It fits in with the traits (or characteristics) of the group
- It is efficient in terms of time, sample size, population and staff availability
- It creates the least possible disruption in the given setting
- Knowledge and skill in its construction and use are available.

The quality of a service is a *relative* concept. When evaluating quality of care – whether it be nursing, social or medical care – the activity in question must always be compared to something else – either the same activity measured at another time, or a similar activity. Quality can be related to the achievement of specific targets, aims and standards. These standards should not be seen as fixed, as all quality initiatives imply continual improvement.

ACTIVITY

In work placement:

1 Find out how quality of care is measured and evaluated in the work setting.

2 Find out what aspects of care delivery are measured by the tools and techniques used.

3 Find out about:
   - option appraisal
   - performance indicators (PIs – sometimes called *quality indicators*)
   - resource allocation
   - mission statements
   - standards of practice

4 Prepare a written case study on quality assurance in care settings which is specific to your work placement, to present to your study group in college.

WHAT ARE THE KEY ASPECTS OF PERFORMANCE?

Two aspects of the process of care are important in this context: the *technical* and the *expressive*.

1 The *technical*: these are controllable inputs which the client expects to be appropriately provided during care. They include staff with appropriate training, the provision of suitable management, the availability of an acceptable range of facilities and the provision of appropriate supplies.
2 The *expressive*: this aspect relates to the interface between patients or clients and the staff who care for them. This is much harder to measure, but can be perceived by the patient as a degree of understanding and warmth in the attitudes of staff. These interpersonal skills are greatly influenced by the individual's state of mind and cannot be bought.

Technical skills without expressive skills will result in low-quality care, and vice versa. The two combined, however, result in the process of care-giving (see Figure 5.4).

QALYs

The concept of 'Quality Adjusted Life Years' of QALYs has been developed by York

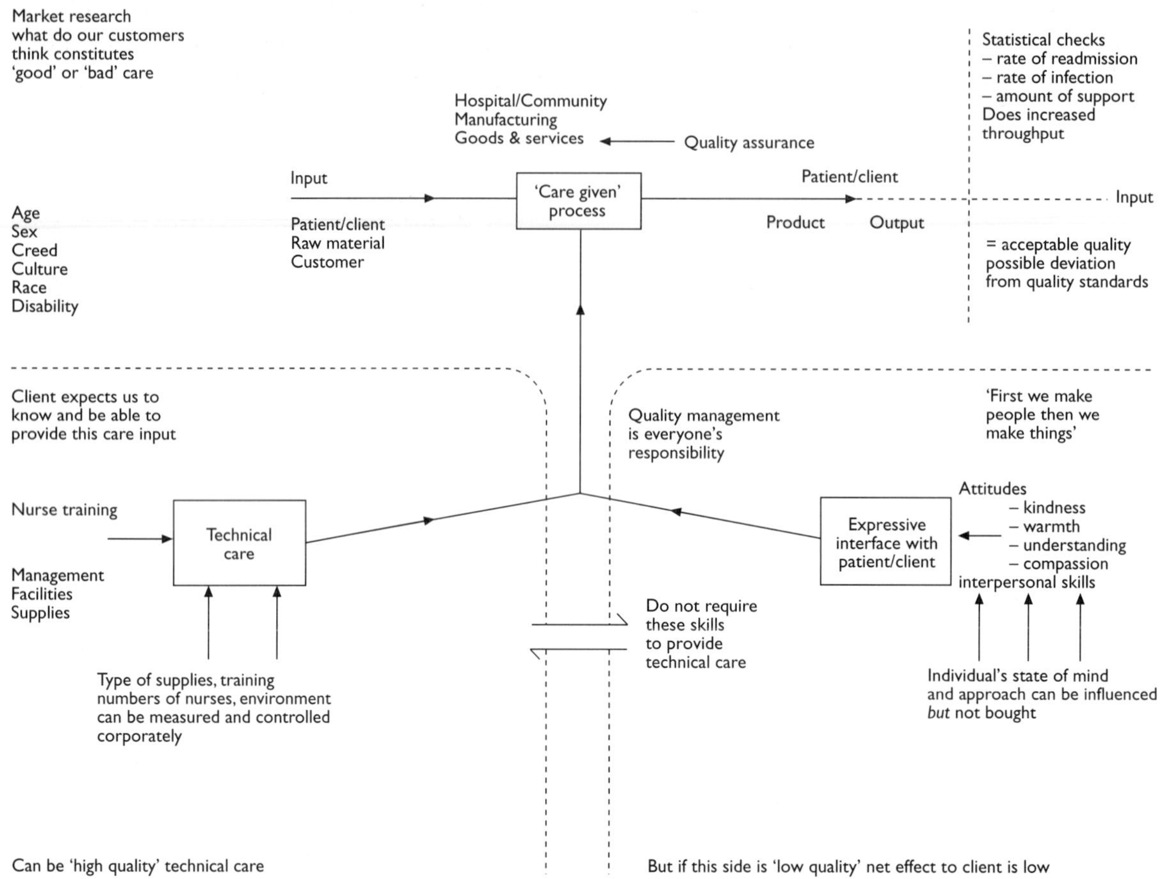

Figure 5.4 The technical and expressive aspects of the care process

University's Centre for Health Economics. It is a cost-benefit approach to the use of resources. New techniques mean that we can keep more people alive for longer and treat illnesses that we used to have to suffer. Decisions *must* be made about which treatments and operations should have priority, and these should be arrived at by more than a simple calculation of the financial costs.

An example of the QALYs system

A heart transplant patient, expected to live for at least 10 years in perfect health, is given a weighting of 1, which represents a *full* quality of life in each of those 10 years. Therefore:

$10 \times 1 = 10$ QALYs

A patient with leukaemia, expected to live for 10 years with only half the quality of life that perfect health would give – because of illness and frequent hospitalisation – is given a weighting of 0.5. Therefore:

$10 \times 0.5 = 5$ QALYs

Then, the cost of treatment is considered. If £100,000 provides *one* heart transplant, then this sum will provide:

1×10 QALYs $= 10$ QALYs

If £100,000 provides *five* leukaemia treatments, then this sum will provide:

5×5 QALYs $= 25$ QALYs

In this example, leukaemia treatment produces more benefit than a heart transplant and could determine the decisions that doctors have to make on prioritising. However, a dilemma remains: if money is not

Table 5.3 How QALYs are measured

A combination of two factors is used to evaluate someone's quality of life – disability and distress. The tables below show how each of these is assessed.

Disability Category	*Degree of disability*
I	No disability.
II	Slight social disability.
III	Severe social disability and/or slight impairment of performance at work. Able to do all housework except heavy tasks.
IV	Choice of work or performance at work very severely limited. Housewives and old people able to do light housework only, but able to go shopping.
V	Unable to take any paid employment. Unable to continue education. Old people confined to home except for escorted outings and short walks; unable to go shopping. Housewives only able to perform a few simple tasks.
VI	Confined to chair or to wheelchair or able to move around the house only with support from an assistant.
VII	Confined to bed.
VIII	Unconscious.

Distress	
A	No distress.
B	Mild distress.
C	Moderate distress.
D	Severe distress.

The distress measures were assessed by looking at factors such as pain, emotional status and satisfaction with life. Together this information is known as the Rosser Index, after the doctor who developed it. From these sets of information, a matrix has been developed. There are two fixed points on the matrix: 1 is healthy and 0 is dead. For example. IA on the matrix means that the person is very healthy, without disability or distres.

Distress *Disability*	A	B	C	D
I	1.000	.995	.990	.976
II	.990	.986	.973	.932
III	.980	.972	.956	.912
IV	.964	.956	.942	.870
V	.946	.935	.900	.700
VI	.875	.845	.680	.000
VII	.677	.564	.000	−1.486
VIII	−1.028	—	—	—

Source: The QALY Toolkit, C Gudex, P Kind, York University

spent on research and development of the newer transplant techniques, then medicine in that field will stand still and there will be no hope of *reducing* the costs involved above.

ACTIVITY

Look at Table 5.3, 'How QALYs are measured', and the extract below.

QALYs and the NHS

Normally, the authority's costings only involve financial elements, such as staff, medical and surgical supplies, and the maintenance of wards, theatres and laboratories. The outcomes are only measured in terms of extra patients or beds occupied. It is easy to put a value on all these items; little notice is taken of the improvements in patients' health, which is more difficult to assess.

The case study looked at the following: kidney failure, replacement of joints in the hand and arm, a new treatment for cystic fibrosis, and operations on people with curvature of the spine. The following data was obtained.

Treatment	QALYs gained per patient	Total cost	Cost per QALY
Haemodialysis	6.1	£55,354	£9,075
Cystic fibrosis	0.4	£3,290	£8,225
Kidney transplant	7.4	£10,452	£1,413
Shoulder joint replacement	0.9	£533	£592
Curvature of the spine —A	1.2	£3,143	£2,619
—B	16.2	£3,143	£194

Not all the figures in the table produce the cost per QALY result that might be expected. This is because part of the treatments involve one-off costs, but have benefits which are spread over a long period. Other treatments continue over many years and are therefore counted annually.

An additional problem is that the QALYs arising from a treatment vary according to factors such as the patient's age and condition. For example, there are two sets of data for curvature of the spine. They show how different the results can be when the same treatment is carried out on different groups of people.

The benefit to teenagers who simply suffer from this problem is not as great as performing the operation on people who have curvature of the spine as a result of neuromuscular illness.

(The Guardian *30 Oct 1990)*

- Is the QALY system a fair way of assessing the quality of life?
- Is it fair to ration treatment? (Consider the recent case of a heavy smoker being refused a heart transplant because, his doctor argued, his chances of a healthy life after the operation were greatly reduced by his smoking habit.)

CODES OF PRACTICE

A code of practice is not a legal document, but it gives direction and cohesion to the body for which it has been designed. A code of practice must cover areas of ethical concern, such as:

- confidentiality
- safety
- the use and abuse of privilege
- the refusal of gifts
- the use of qualifications for advertising purposes

In 1983, the first Code of Professional Conduct for the Nurse, Midwife and Health Visitor was published by the United Kingdom Central Council (UKCC).

CODE OF PROFESSIONAL CONDUCT FOR THE NURSE, MIDWIFE AND HEALTH VISITOR

Each registered nurse, midwife and health visitor shall act, at all times, in such a manner as to justify public trust and confidence, to uphold and enhance the good standing and reputation of the profession, to serve the interests of society, and above all to safeguard the interests of individual patients and clients.

Each registered nurse, midwife and health visitor is accountable for his or her practice, and, in the exercise of professional accountability shall:

1. Act always in such a way as to promote and safeguard the well being and interests of patients/clients.
2. Ensure that no action or omission on his/her part or within his/her sphere of influence is detrimental to the condition or safety of patients/clients.
3. Take every reasonable opportunity to maintain and improve professional knowledge and competence.
4. Acknowledge any limitations of competence and refuse in such cases to accept delegated functions without first having received instruction in regard to those functions and having been assessed as competent.
5. Work in a collaborative and co-operative manner with other health care professionals and recognise and respect their particular contributions within the health care team.
6. Take account of the customs, values and spiritual beliefs of patients/clients.
7. Make known to an appropriate person or authority any conscientious objection which may be relevant to professional practice.
8. Avoid any abuse of the privileged relationship which exists with patients/clients and of the privileged access allowed to their property, residence or workplace.
9. Respect confidential information obtained in the course of professional practice and refrain from disclosing such information without the consent of the patient/client, or a person entitled to act on his/her behalf, except where disclosure is required by law or by the order of a court or is necessary in the public interest.
10. Have regard to the environment of care and its physical, psychological and social effects on patients/clients, and also to the adequacy of resources, and make known to appropriate persons or authorities any circumstances which could place patients/clients in jeopardy or which militate against safe standards of practice.

11 Have regard to the workload of and the pressures on professional colleagues and subordinates and take appropriate action if these are seen to be such as to constitute abuse of the individual practitioner and/or to jeopardise safe standards of practice.
12 In the context of the individual's own knowledge, experience, and sphere of authority, assist peers and subordinates to develop professional competence in accordance with their needs.
13 Refuse to accept any gift, favour or hospitality which might be interpreted as seeking to exert undue influence to obtain preferential consideration.
14 Avoid the use of professional qualifications in the promotion of commercial products in order not to compromise the independence of professional judgement on which patients/clients rely.

(Hinchliff et al. 1989; reproduced by permission of the UKCC)

Heywood-Jones (1988) tells the story of an incident which infringed various clauses of the Code of Professional Conduct:

A staff nurse and auxiliary nurse were alone in charge at night on a 28-bedded medical ward. When they were asked to admit a patient from Accident and Emergency they pointed out that they had not the staff nor the experience to deal with the patient and indeed had made a formal complaint to the director of nursing services some months ago to this effect. Their protestations were not accepted then or now, and when – perhaps inevitably – a drug error was made and the patient died of an overdose, the nurses were disciplined and made subjects of complaint by the health authority. The doctor in charge was not treated in the same way, though the nursing hierarchy was eventually publicly criticised.

In this case, the senior nurse would have been within his or her rights to go to his or her superior, invoking the relevant clauses of the Code. The Code cannot be used as a document for defence when things have gone wrong, but it enables professionals to exercise their professional accountability.

Equal opportunities

The Black Report (1980) on inequalities in health strongly argued the need to improve the distribution of health service resources in order to match the greatest need with the most effective care. It suggested that there are two main reasons for the present state of unequal access to health care:

- There is *less provision* in some areas (e.g. inner cities) than in others in relation to the size of the population and the need for services
- The way in which existing services are organised is *not always appropriate* for the nature of the population they serve

Evidence suggests that, as a particularly disadvantaged section of the population, ethnic minority groups are likely to experience unequal access to health care for the same reasons as other disadvantaged groups, e.g. homeless people, people with disability, unemployed people, etc.

The Commission for Racial Equality (CRE) has produced a series of information leaflets for employers on equal opportunity policies, positive action and monitoring.

EQUAL OPPORTUNITIES POLICIES

An equal opportunities policy represents a commitment by an organisation to ensure that its policies do not lead to any individual receiving less favourable treatment on the grounds of

- sex
- marital status
- religious belief
- race
- disability
- colour
- ethnic or national origin

It does *not* mean positive discrimination in favour of black people. An effective policy will establish a fairer system in relation to:

- recruitment
- training
- promotion opportunities

Policy statement

Each employing organisation should set out a clear policy statement which can be made available to employees and service users. The statement should include:

- a recognition of past discrimination
- a commitment to redressing inequalities
- a commitment to positive action

The following is an example of such a statement:

THE CITY OF EAST LONDON AREA HEALTH AUTHORITY (TEACHING) EQUAL OPPORTUNITY POLICY

1 The City and East London Area Health Authority (Teaching) is an Equal Opportunity employer. No job applicant or employee will receive less favourable treatment on grounds of sex, marital status, religious belief, disability, race, colour, nationality, or ethnic or national origins. Therefore no employee will be disadvantaged by conditions or requirements which cannot be shown to be justified.
2 There may be certain posts which under the provisions of the Race Relations Act 1976 and Sex Discrimination Act 1973 will carry a Genuine Occupational Qualification; these will however be few and the need for such a classification will be determined at regular intervals and whenever such a post falls vacant.
3 It is acknowledged that it is essential to remain on guard against some of the more subtle and unconscious varieties of discrimination which may not easily be identified and that these may result from general assumptions about the capabilities, characteristics, and interests of minorities which may influence the treatment of individuals or groups.
4 Induction courses for new employees shall include a reference to the Authority's policy on equal opportunity.
5 Any employee who considers that he or she is suffering from unfair treatment on the grounds of sex, marital status, religious belief, disability, race, colour, nationality, or ethnic or national origins, may raise a complaint through the agreed procedure for dealing with individual grievances.
6 This policy will be reviewed by the Area Personnel Officer in the light of changing legislation or guidance from the DHSS, the Equal Opportunities Commission or the Commission for Racial Equality, through the established joint consultative machinery.
7 It is recognised that to ensure that this policy is fully effective it will be necessary to introduce personnel procedures that will guard against inadvertent discrimination. In endorsing this policy the AHA(T) authorises its officers to prepare and implement such procedures, subject to appropriate joint consultation.

(Mares et al. 1985)

Training should be provided to explain to all staff the implications of the policy and its practical consequences. The organisation must also provide information about the law on direct and indirect discrimination.

Any policy which attempts to promote equality is only effective if the individuals working in the organisation incorporate its principles into their individual practice. Some suggestions for the implementation of such a policy are:

- Always inform ethnic minority staff about training programmes and promotion opportunities, and encourage them to apply
- Encourage all staff to accept that racial and ethnic variations should not be ignored but rather recognised positively in the context of care
- All staff should be aware that attitudes or actions based on racial prejudice are unprofessional and unacceptable in the workplace
- Take up the interests of ethnic minority

staff and find out whether there are special needs for canteen, social or cultural facilities, religious holidays, etc.
- Try to ensure greater participation of ethnic minority staff in team meetings and case conferences. For example, include on the agenda an item on 'multi-racial and multi-cultural aspects of care'

ACTIVITY

Find out about the professional training available in your district in the health service. You may interview a nurse tutor, or obtain a copy of the curriculum.

- Is the multi-racial nature of British society built into the context of the whole course, or are the ethnic minority issues limited to a few sessions, often at the end?
- Are social and economic factors given as much consideration as cultural factors in assessing the needs and health status of different groups?
- What is the proportion of staff, and of patients, from ethnic minorities in your local district general hospital?
- What do you consider would be the best way of making nursing training more appropriate to the needs of a multi-racial society?

GENDER DIVISIONS IN HEALTH CARE

The Department of Health set up a Joint Working Party in 1991 to study the career progression of women in medicine. In 1990, women made up almost half the total number of house officers, and yet only 15% of consultants (i.e. those at the highest level) were women (see Figure 5.5). The Joint Working Party reported that change was necessary, and proposed a number of actions:

- good equal opportunity practice
- the monitoring of gender balance
- the restructuring of jobs

Nurses and midwives make up almost half the total workforce in the NHS (see Figure 5.6). Nine out of ten nurses are women; male nurses are concentrated in the specialities of mental illness, and men in nursing are more likely to be promoted quickly to senior posts in mental health, mental handicap and education.

The Royal College of Nursing (RCN) is aware of discrimination against women; this discrimination is partly the consequence of part-time work among female nurses, on which nursing heavily depends. Lesley Mackay, a sociologist, has documented nurses' feelings about discrimination against women with children, particularly those who work part-time. She quotes a staff nurse: 'Part-time nurses are considered as very much second-class members of the team, given no opportunity or encouragement to embark on further studies or courses. This appears to be management policy' (Mackay 1989).

ACTIVITY

During your hospital work placement, try to find out more about gender divisions in the NHS. You could compile a short questionnaire to find out the following facts:

- How many doctors in senior positions are female, and what specialities are represented?
- How many nurses are part-time workers? Is there a crêche in the workplace?
- What percentage of nurse managers is female?

The personnel department at the hospital should be able to supply you with this information; it is advisable to request this in writing, prior to your placement.

When you return to college, you may wish to debate within your class or group the issue of gender divisions in the NHS and their implications for good patient

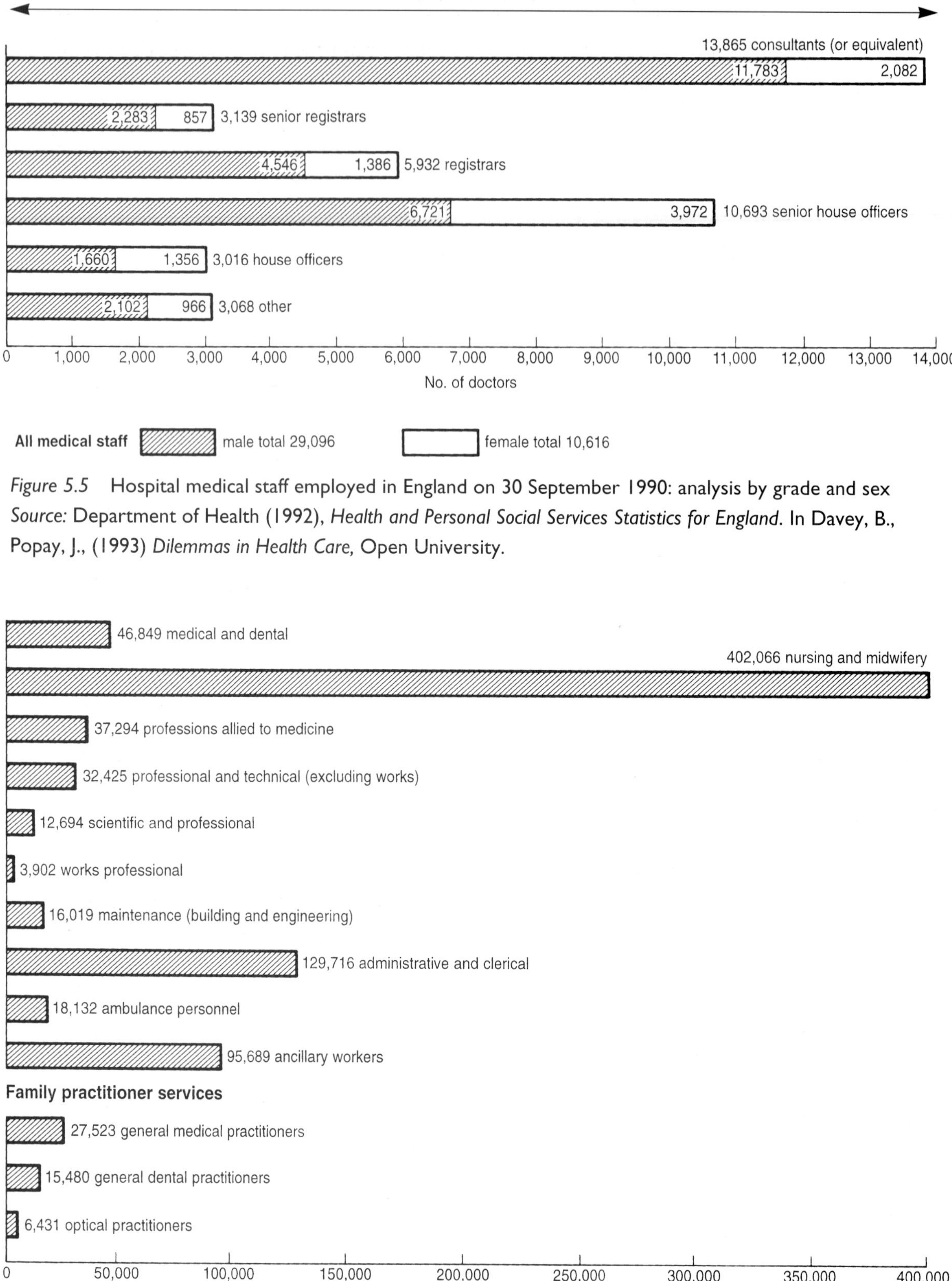

Figure 5.5 Hospital medical staff employed in England on 30 September 1990: analysis by grade and sex
Source: Department of Health (1992), *Health and Personal Social Services Statistics for England.* In Davey, B., Popay, J., (1993) *Dilemmas in Health Care,* Open University.

Total staff and practitioners 844,220

Figure 5.6 Numbers in different occupations in the NHS in England in 1990
Source: Department of Health (1992), *Health and Personal Social Services Statistics for England.* In Davey, B., Popay, J., (1993) *Dilemmas in Health Care,* Open University.

care, the organisation of management and the status of women within the health service.

Health and safety policies

Every employer has a duty to protect employees at work and to keep them informed about health and safety. In general, the employer's duties include:

- making the workplace safe and free from risks to health
- keeping dust, fumes and noise under control
- ensuring that plant and machinery are safe and that safe systems of work are set and followed
- ensuring that articles and substances are moved, stored and used safely
- providing adequate welfare facilities
- supplying the information, training and supervision necessary for the health and safety of employees

In addition, the employer must:

- draw up a health and safety policy statement, if there are more than five employees, and bring it to the attention of employees
- provide, free, any protective clothing or equipment specifically required by health and safety law
- report certain injuries, diseases and dangerous occurrences to the enforcing authority
- provide adequate first aid facilities
- consult a safety representative (appointed from among the workforce) about issues which affect health and safety in the workplace
- set up a safety committee if asked in writing by two or more safety representatives

There are other more specific duties concerning e.g. overcrowding and hygiene; these vary from one workplace to another.

The employee has legal duties too, which include:

- taking reasonable care of their own health and safety and that of others who may be affected by what is done or not done
- cooperating with the employer on health and safety
- not interfering with, or misusing, anything provided for the employee's health, safety or welfare

ACTIVITY

1 When on work experience placement, ask to see the organisation's health and safety policy document. Find out who was responsible for writing it and how staff are informed generally about issues in health and safety.

2 Find out what information and guidance is given in hospitals, nurseries and the community in relation to the risk of contamination by blood infected with e.g. hepatitis or HIV.

Professional development within care organisations

When the word 'profession' is talked about, most people think in terms of the traditional disciplines of law, medicine and architecture. Millerson (1964) cited certain key characteristics which define a *profession*:

- skill based on theoretical knowledge
- the provision of training and occupation
- organisation
- tests of the competence of members
- adherence to a professional code of conduct
- altruistic service

Recently, the occupations of nursing, teaching and social work have claimed professional status, chiefly by extending the length of training and by emphasising the academic principles and learning which underlie the caring professions.

> **ACTIVITY**
>
> Discuss the concept of professionalism and the definition of a profession:
>
> - Does it matter whether nursing, midwifery and social work are categorised as professions or occupations?
> - Are there other criteria which separate professions from occupations?

Professional development cannot be separated from *personal* development. A care worker needs a base of knowledge and skill to draw on, and also needs to be able to communicate with others whilst keeping in control emotionally (see p. 151 above for qualities of an effective carer).

CAREER PATHWAYS

The structure of care organisations is constantly changing, even if the work involved remains the same. Health and social care professionals have seen an expansion of their roles as a result both of increasing technological advances and of the continuing reorganisation of resources. Care organisations have a responsibility to their employees to provide opportunities for staff development. This may take the form of in-service training, a programme of lectures or conferences or day release for the individual to gain an extra qualification. A career pathway has the following features:

- studying for a specific qualification – examples: GNVQ, NVQ, nursing, social work, physiotherapy, occupational therapy, nursery nursing, etc.
- an assessment of the individual's current status and level of performance within the organisation – i.e. a staff appraisal and performance review (sometimes called an *audit*)
- opportunities for professional development: all care organisations should practise staff development and training with regard to equal opportunities and other appropriate policies
- advice on methods of progression and gaining promotion: ideally, such career guidance should be tailored to the specific personal and professional needs of the individual
- support for, and the facilitation of, change – for example, on completion of a course

The best method of finding out about professional development is to focus on the career that *you* have chosen. Even if you are not yet certain which career is right for you, try to choose one that interests you and arrange to complete the following research project, ideally as part of your work-experience programme. It would help to read through the section on research methods in health and social care in Chapter 8 of Thomson et al. 1995.

> **ACTIVITY**
>
> *Investigating personal and professional development*
>
> 1 Having identified a career, find out and list the qualifications necessary to be accepted for training. Then construct a brief questionnaire to find out what *personal qualities* are thought to be necessary in your career role – use a ranking system for each quality described. Present your results in the form of a bar graph or pie chart.
>
> 2 Identify and describe the staff development and training programme which exists within the care organisation to support the individual's career. Then, explain the role of the relevant professional bodies – examples include The Chartered Society of Physiotherapists, the UKCC for nursing, midwifery and health visiting, and the Central Council for the Education and

Training of Social Workers (CCETSW) for the training of social workers. Consider particularly the professional body's function in:

- determining the standards to which its members work
- maintaining those standards and monitoring the competence of its members
- providing training and examining opportunities for its members

Communication between care organisations

In the fields of health and social care services, there is an increasing need for organisations to collaborate effectively with each other. Many problems do not fit neatly and exclusively into one department. An elderly person might have needs which can be addressed by statutory bodies (e.g. hospitals and social service departments), voluntary bodies (e.g. a self-help group such as the Parkinsons's Disease Society) and private-sector agencies (e.g. private residential homes). Communication, whether formal or informal, is an important factor in the effectiveness of this kind of collaboration.

Communication within care organisations

Most business organisations are *hierarchical* in structure. Those at the top of the hierarchy take the most important decisions, and are rewarded by the highest salaries, and they communicate their decisions downwards through a *chain of command*.

The number of levels within the hierarchy can vary a great deal, and the fewer there are, the greater the efficiency of communication. Information can flow in three directions:

- downwards from top to bottom
- upwards from bottom to top
- sideways at various levels

Whatever system of management is used, a large amount of information must flow down the hierarchy, from top management to the ward cleaners. Research has proved that such downward communication can be very inefficient, with only 20% of information reaching the bottom of the pyramid.

Communication from the bottom upwards has two important functions:

- to feed back information on what action has been taken on messages sent downwards
- to alert the decision-makers to the feelings and attitudes of those lower down the organisation, so that they can devise realistic strategies

LINE MANAGERS

Many large organisations with grouped specialities use a system of *line authority*. Line managers are directly responsible for achieving the organisation's objectives, and exert direct authority over their subordinates. Line authority flows through the chain of command from the apex to the base. The chain of command is illustrated by means of an *organisation chart* (see Figure 5.7).

- Each position in the line system shows points of contact between the manager and the subordinates, showing the authority of its occupant and to whom that person is responsible
- Vertical communications proceed only through the line system

COMMUNICATION NETWORKS

Small-group networks are communication networks comprising five members. Much research has been carried out to examine the efficiency of communications within certain structures:

- The *circle* (see Figure 5.8(a), p. 177): this is the best system for matters requiring several comments and opinions. Morale tends to be high because there is greater participation, but decisions are arrived at more slowly than with other systems

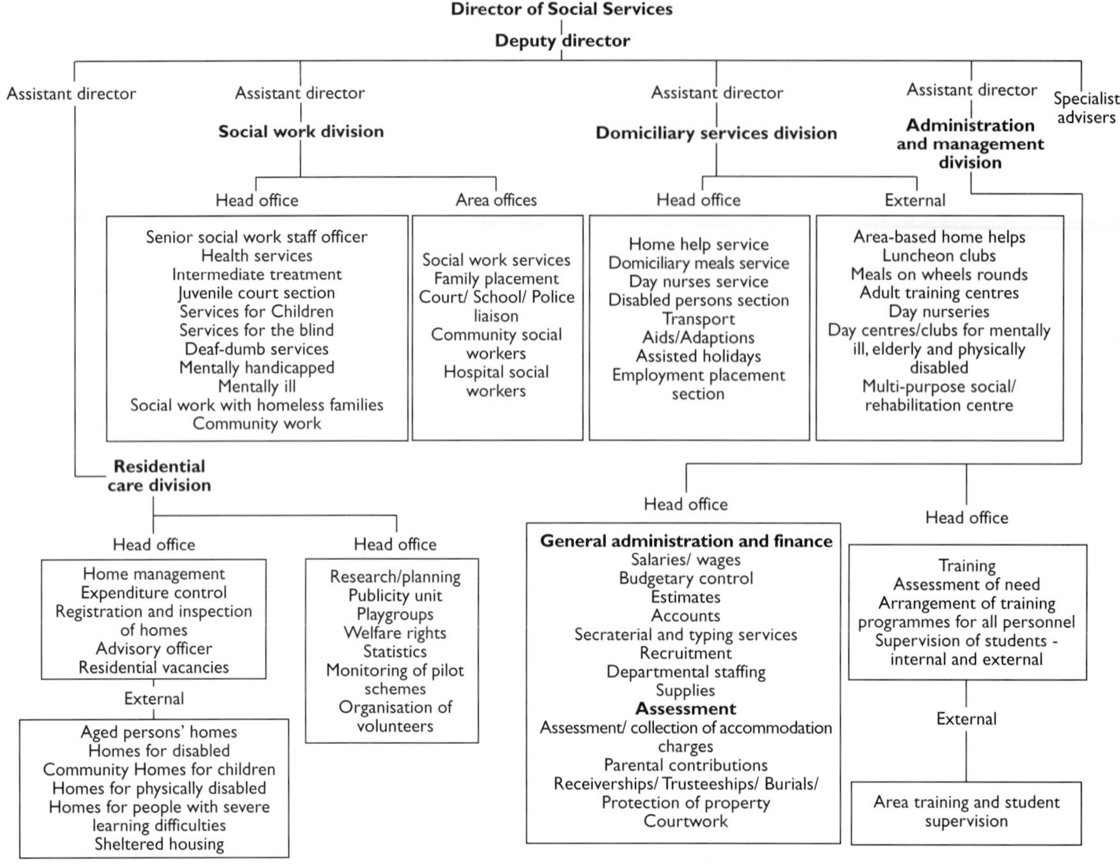

Figure 5.7 One possible organisational structure for a local-authority social-service department
Source: Hall, P. (1983), *Social Services in England and Wales,* Routledge.

- The *wheel* (see Figure 5.8(b)): this is effective for completing routine tasks, since messages can be transmitted between any pair of members in at most two steps; decisions are arrived at more quickly
- The *all-channel system* (see Figure 5.8(c)): this is best when dealing with complex problems, as everyone is able to communicate with everyone else
- The *chain* (see Figure 5.8(d)): this is appropriate where instructions need to be implemented quickly and little communication between members on the same level is required

NEGOTIATION

Within any health care organisation, there is a variety of personnel: patients, doctors, nurses, administrators, porters, cleaners, physiotherapists, social workers etc. They are all working towards the same goal, i.e. to restore and maintain patients' health. These groups bring together different personal backgrounds, different views and perspectives on health, and different types of training. However, differences of opinion will regularly emerge on matters of patient care and organisational policy; e.g. there may be competition between two different medical departments for the same set of resources; for example, when each needs to buy a piece of equipment that each feels is vital for better patient care. *Negotiation* is usually an informal process used by the parties involved in a dispute to maintain social order. It is carried out by:

- diplomacy
- bargaining
- cooperating
- a process of give and take

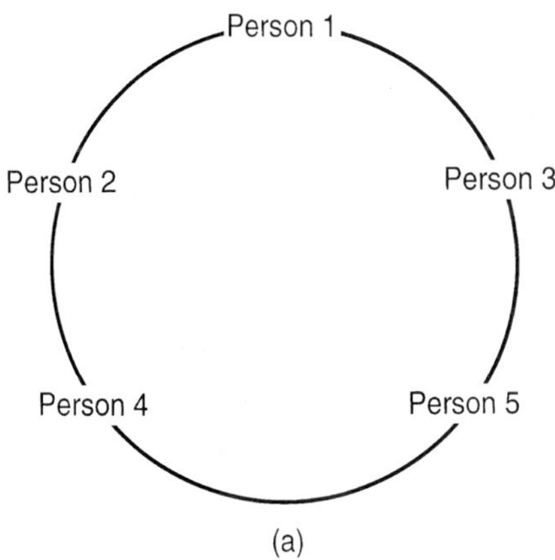

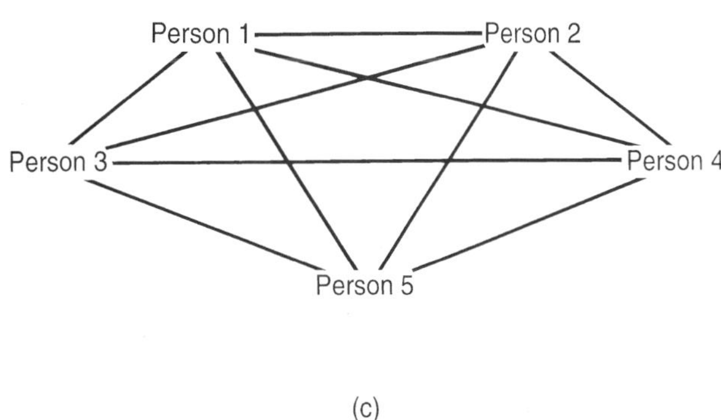

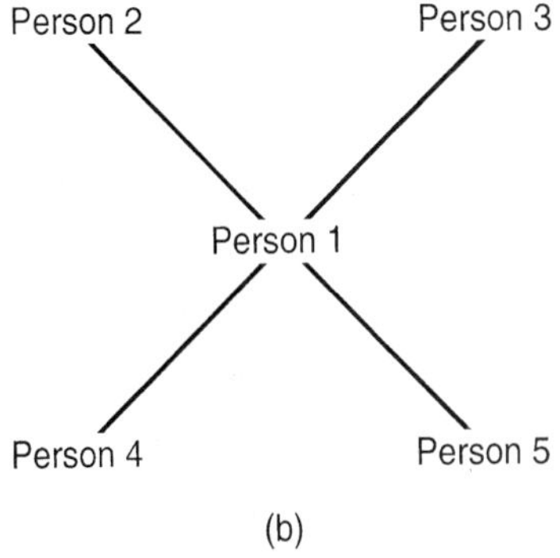

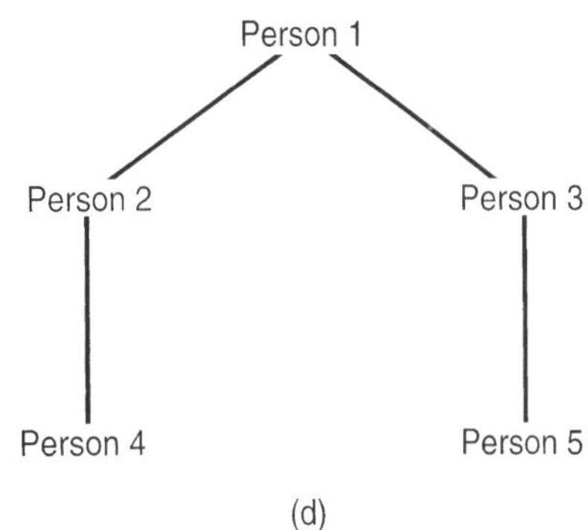

Figure 5.8(a) The circle system
(b) The wheel system
(c) The all-channel system
(d) The chain system

- the withholding of information

Only if these methods fail does the care worker seek to apply more formal rules and procedures.

The voluntary sector

Charities and trusts are legally recognised non-profit-making bodies that are bound by their contracts to dispense money for defined purposes:

- education
- research
- welfare

Charities rely on three main sources of income to a varying extent:

- voluntary donations from the general public and from institutions
- investment income from trusts
- charges for services they provide

Medical and health charities receive substantially more money from the public than any other area of charitable activity (see Figure 5.9).

In terms of resources for care organisations, many charities provide equipment for 'their' adopted group, and some deliver health care directly to those in need, e.g. the National Society for Cancer Relief funds the Macmillan terminal care nurses.

The private sector

Although private health care is far less developed in the UK than in most other Western European countries, there are now

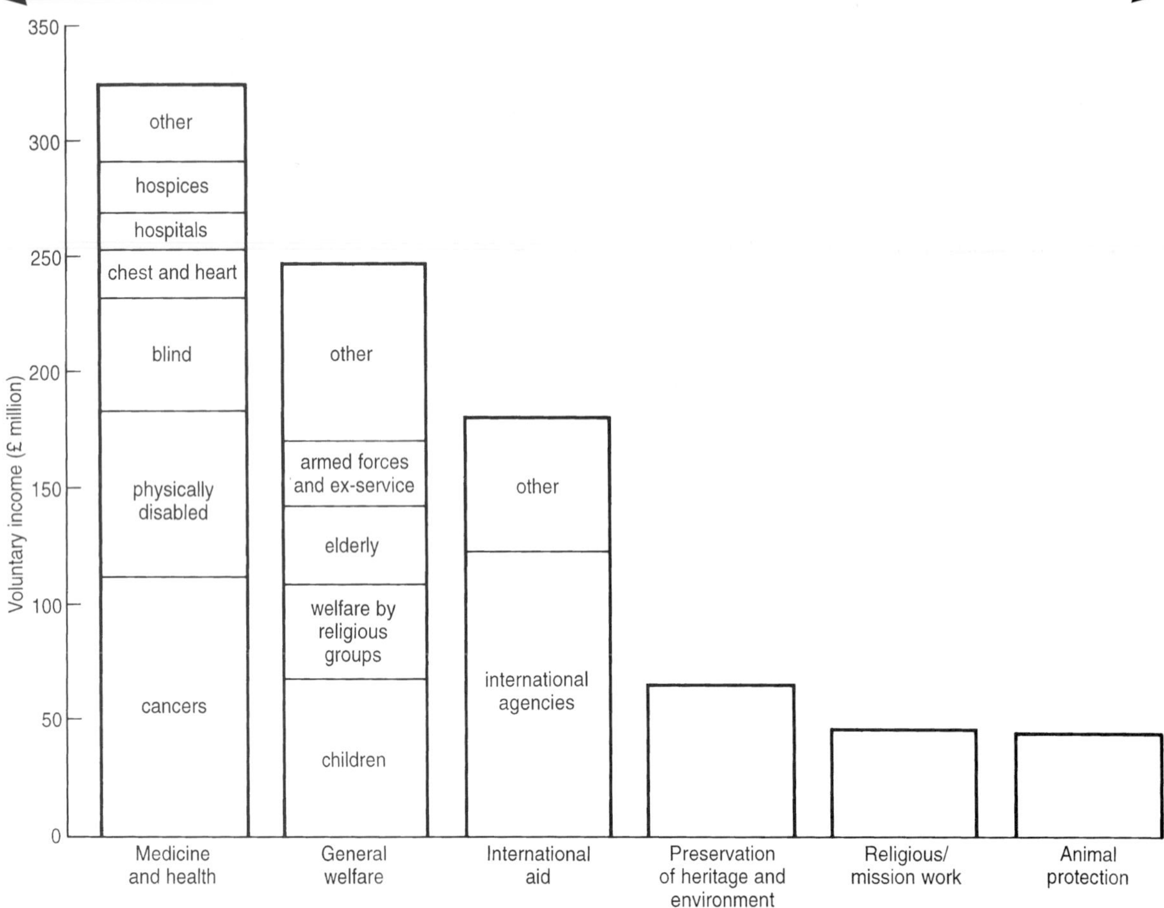

Figure 5.9 Charities attracting the largest voluntary donation, 1987–8 (based on the 200 charities with the largest voluntary incomes)
Source: Davey, B., Popay, J., (1993) *Dilemmas in Health Care,* Open University.

about 200 private hospitals with surgical facilities, in addition to several thousand nursing and residential homes. The resources available in these private organisations are the same in respect of medical treatment as in the NHS; and most doctors who work in private practice are also NHS consultants. The extras, which are largely paid for from private health insurance schemes, are the guarantee of privacy and a better choice of diet. The environment tends to be more akin to a hotel in some of the newer establishments.

Pressure groups

There are many support groups and pressure groups representing the interests of particular health service users. Three examples are:

- Action for Sick Children (previously NAWCH: the National Association for the Welfare of Children in Hospital) has campaigned successfully for the right and resources to allow parents and relatives to stay with children when the latter are admitted to hospital
- The National Childbirth Trust has championed the rights of a woman to decide on the method of birthing most appropriate for her
- MIND have campaigned for better services for people who are mentally ill

ACTIVITY

There are many more voluntary organisations which represent the interests of particular health service users. In groups, choose one such group and research the following information:

- What is the main function of the organisation?
- How does it ensure that it meets the needs of its client group?
- What difference, if any, has it made to statutory provision in its own area? (This may be in the care of direct health care provision, bio-medical research, staff training, etc.)

When you have found out all you can, present your findings to the whole group and place the research in a 'fact file' for the use of others.

REFERENCES AND RESOURCES

Aggleton, P. (1990), *Health*, London: Routledge.

Allen, I. (ed) (1990), *Care Managers and Care Management*, London: Policy Studies Institute.

Bond, J. and Bond, S. (1986), *Sociology and Health Care* Edinburgh: Churchill Livingstone.

Burton, G. and Dimbleby, R. (1988), *Between Ourselves: An Introduction to Interpersonal Communication*, Ch. 5, London: Edward Arnold.

Davey, B. and Popay, J. (1993), *Dilemmas in Health Care*, Milton Keynes: Open University Press.

Department of Health (1992), Patients' Charter, Norwich: HMSO.

Frankl, V. (1983), *Man's Search for Meaning*, New York: Pocket Books.

Handy, C. (1985), *Understanding Organizations*, Harmondsworth: Penguin.

Heywood-Jones, I. (1988), 'The buck stops here', *Nursing Times*, vol. 84, no. 17, pp. 50–2.

Hinchliff, S., Noma, S. E., and Schober, J. E. (1989), *Nursing Practice and Health Care* London: Edward Arnold.

Mackay, L. (1989), *Nursing a Problem*, Milton Keynes: Open University Press.

Mares, P., Hailey, A. and Baxter, C. (1985), *Health Care in Multiracial Britain*, London: HEC/NEC.

Milgram, S. (1963), *Obedience to Authority*, New York: Harper & Row.

Millerson, G. (1964), *The Qualifying Associations*, London: Routledge & Kegan Paul.

Oliver, R. W. (1993), *Psychology and Health Care*, London: Bailliere Tindall.

Pedler, M., Burgogyne, J. and Boydell, T. (1986), *A Manager's Guide to Self-development*, London: McGraw-Hill.

Schroeder, P. (1994), 'Improving quality and performance: concepts, programmes and techniques', in *Mosby Year Book*, St Louis.

Schein, E. (1969), *Process Consultation*, Reading, Massachusetts: Addison-Wesley.

Thomson, H. et al. (1995), *Health and Social Care for Advanced GNVQ*, 2nd edn, London: Hodder & Stoughton.

Townsend, P. and Davidson, N. (1988), *Inequalities and Health*, London: Penguin.

USEFUL ADDRESS

Central Council for the Education and Training of Social Workers (CCETSW)
Derbyshire House
St Chad Street
London WC1H 8AD
Tel.: 0171 278 2455

Useful sources of careers information in the UK

Chiropodists:
Society of Chiropodists
53 Welbeck Street
London W1M 7HE
Tel.: 0171 486 3381

Institute of Chiropodists
91 Lord Street
Southport
Merseyside PR8 1SA
Tel.: 01704 546141

Dietician:
The British Dietetic Association
7th Floor
Elizabeth House
22 Suffolk Street
Queensway
Birmingham B1 1LS
Tel.: 0121 643 5483

District nurse, health visitor, hospital nurse, midwife:
English National Board for Nursing
Midwifery and Health Visiting
ENB Careers Service
PO Box 356
Sheffield S8 0SJ

National Board for Nursing, Midwifery and
Health Visiting for Scotland
22 Queen Street
Edinburgh EH2 1JX
Tel.: 0131 226 7371

Health Service Manager:
National Health Service Training Directorate
St Bartholomew's Court
18 Christmas Street
Bristol BS1 5BT
Tel.: 0117 9291 029

The Scottish Health Service Management
Development Group
Scottish Health Service Centre
Crewe Road South
Edinburgh EG4 2LF
Tel.: 0131 332 2335

Homoeopath:
British Homoeopathic Association
27a Devonshire Street
London W1N 1RJ
Tel.: 0171 935 2163

The Society of Homoeopaths
2 Artizan Road
Northampton NN1 4HU
Tel.: 01604 21400

Housing officer:
Institute of Housing
Octavia House
Westwood Business Park
Westwood Way
Coventry
Warwickshire CV4 8JP
Tel.: 01203 694433

Institute of Housing in Scotland
6 Palmerston Place
Edinburgh EH12 5AA
Tel.: 0131 225 4544

Occupational therapist:
The College of Occupational Therapists/
Occupational Therapy Training Clearing
House/British Association of Occupational
Therapy
6/8 Marshalsea Road
London SE1 1HL
Tel.: 0171 357 6480

Physiotherapist:
The Chartered Society of Physiotherapy
Central Applications Office for Diploma
Courses in Physiotherapy
Room 422
Foulton House
Jessop Avenue
Cheltenham
Gloucestershire GL50 3SH

North London School of Physiotherapy for the
Visually Handicapped
10 Highgate Hill
London N19 5ND
Tel.: 0171 288 5959

Probation officer:
Central Council for Educational and Training
in Social Work (CCETSW)
Derbyshire House
St Chads Street
London WC1H 8AD
Tel.: 0171 278 2455

Probational Service Division
Room 442
Home Office
50 Queen Anne's Gate
London SW1H 9AT
Tel.: 0171 273 2675

Psychologist:
British Psychological Society
St Andrews House
48 Princess Road East
Leicester LE1 7DR
Tel.: 0116 2549 568

Social worker (field/residential)/care assistant:
Central Council for Education and Training in Social Work (CCETSW)
Derbyshire House
St Chads Street
London WC1H 8AD
Tel.: 0171 278 2455

CCETSW Information Office
78–80 George Street
Edinburgh EH2 3BU
Tel.: 0131 220 0093

Speech and language therapist:
The College of Speech and Language Therapists (CSLT)
Harold Poster House
6 Lechmere Road
London NW2 5BU
Tel.: 0181 459 8521

Teacher: special educational needs:
Teacher Training Agency
Communications Centre
PO Box 3210
Chelmsford
Essex CM1 3WA
Tel.: 01245 454454

Scottish Office Educational Department
Careers Service Branch
Room 5/32
New St Andrew's House
St James Centre
Edinburgh EH1 3SY
Tel.: 0131 224 4692/8

Volunteer organiser:
Volunteer Centre UK
29 Lower King's Road
Berkhamsted
Hertfordshire HP4 2AB
Tel.: 01442 873311

Volunteer Development Scotland
80 Murray Place
Stirling FK8 2BX
Tel.: 01786 79593

Youth and community worker:
National Youth Agency
17–23 Albion Street
Leicester LE1 6GD
Tel.: 0116 2471 200

Scottish Community Education Council
West Coates House
90 Haymarket Terrace
Edinburgh EH12 5LQ
Tel.: 0131 313 2488

6

ANALYSING SOCIAL POLICY

INTRODUCTION

Studying the development and administration of social policy in isolation from its effects may seem rather like being given the task of setting up a huge public firework display, placing all the fireworks, lighting a few touchpapers and then being hurried away to organise refreshments, so missing the display and being unable to judge how it has affected the assembled crowds.

The aim of this chapter is to look at how social policy in the UK and the European Union has developed, and to study the ways in which social care, health and education services are provided. It would be pointless, however, to study social policy without an additional understanding of its impact on people's lives. You should therefore consider reading this chapter in association with Chapter 7 on social change and welfare provision. That chapter considers some of the social and demographic changes which have taken place over the past 150 years in the UK, and which have affected the way in which social policy has been made over that period. The first part of this chapter, in turn, is intended to help you investigate the *historical context* of social policy in the UK. What was life in the UK like in the nineteenth and earlier parts of the twentieth century? What approaches to social policy developed in those periods? What key influences helped to form those approaches?

HISTORICAL ASPECTS OF SOCIAL POLICY

If you have not studied social and economic history before, you may feel a little daunted by the prospect of investigating it now. You may even be wondering why it should be necessary to look so far back into British history. Why should people's lives in, say, 1895 be relevant to life in the 1990s? The simple answer to this question is that your study of the historical development of social policy should help you to better understand social policy in the UK *today*. History promotes 'our understanding of the past in the light of the present and of the present in the light of the past' (E.H. Carr 1977, p. 107).

While this chapter will give you a broad overview of the historical development of social policy in the UK, your enjoyment of and interest in this subject will be much greater if you supplement your study with the use of a wider range of resources. These might include:

- relevant social and economic history textbooks
- films and TV programmes set during the period
- contemporary sources from the period such as novels, newspaper and other official reports, and extracts from the writings of social reformers
- local history societies and resources, which may be able to illustrate how broader societal changes affected the area you live in

- family histories of people in your class, if available
- local museums and archives

THE SOCIAL CONDITIONS OF NINETEENTH-CENTURY BRITAIN

By 1800 the UK was entering a period of rapid industrialisation through key changes to existing technologies in industry and agriculture, the organisation of the manufacturing sector into a factory system and the availability of capital via the growth of the joint-stock company. Industry steadily expanded in the second half of the nineteenth century, and there was an estimated tenfold increase in industrial output between 1820 and 1913. The country was changing from a mainly agricultural society to one in which *urbanisation* (the growth of towns and cities), new transport systems (road, rail and canal) and new farming techniques and machinery were transforming the landscapes and the lives of the people. As a result of the scale of the changes that occurred, this period, from approximately 1750 to 1900, has become known as the age of the 'Industrial Revolution'.

ACTIVITY

1 Find out what is meant by the terms 'factory system' and 'joint-stock company'.

2 Find out if any industries or companies in the area in which you live originated in the period 1800–1900. Investigate the possibility of a representative from any such business talking to your group about its history.

These changes had important effects on the way of life of working people, as well as influencing the *social conditions* in which they lived. One of the most dramatic changes concerned the extension of the aforementioned *factory system* of industrial organisation. In many areas this meant that the workshop or domestic system of production (where a master workman, and often his family, worked for himself or as an employee of another craftsman, such as a shoemaker, who supplied him with his raw material and paid him 'by the piece' for the work done) declined. The population of many districts became dependent for employment on a single factory-based industry such as cotton-spinning.

ACTIVITY

Why do you think that the factory system of production was more successful than the domestic or workshop system?

The wages in the new factories were sometimes higher than could be earned in the domestic system, but the hours and conditions of work were strictly regimented and determined by the factory owner. Furthermore, the factory machinery kept the employee constantly at work. Working conditions in the factories were, with a few exceptions, generally very poor – with children (especially orphans or paupers) exploited as child labourers – and fluctuations in trade and in the fortunes of the factory owners made workers very vulnerable to unemployment. Some of the hardships experienced are touched upon in the following song which came from that period:

THE TRADESMAN'S COMPLAINT

You Englishmen where'er you be, come list to what I say:
Our English pride in commerce now is fast fading away.
Distress of trade some thousands feel, for they know not where to go,
And many are forced to beg or starve for they have no work to do.

For many years trade has declined, but ne'er so much as now,
For thousands they can get no work and wages are so low;
There's spinners, weavers, clothiers, and stocking-makers, too,
Are wandering through the country, not knowing what to do.

In Nottingham and Manchester, in Bolton and in Hyde,
There's thousands who once worked for bread now cannot bread provide;
In Bury, Rochdale, Dukinfield, Stockport and Ashton, too.
Great numbers are working on short time and more have no work to do.

Through Lancashire and Yorkshire and all old England o'er.
Nought else but poverty does appear among the labouring poor;
Their bread is scarce, their clothes are rags, their naked skin peeps through;
'Twas different when their wage was good and they'd plenty of work to do.

The labourers of England once lived on pudding and beef,
But now the times are altered, which fills their hearts with grief;
No more the pudding and the beef their dinner tables show,
But gruel and taters are their fare now there's no work to do.

Now let us hope the times will mend, but this is vain, I fear;
Instead of better they're getting worse, each and every year.
But if the Corn Laws are repealed and we get work to do,
Then with Free Trade we will rejoice and get good wages, too.

(Palmer 1974, p. 214)

Most working-class people in the nineteenth century were therefore likely to experience poverty at some time in their lives. Since there was no modern system of social security, most, when unable to find work, were forced to rely on the earnings of their children, family and friends, and on credit from local tradesmen. The problem of irregular and low earnings was compounded by the incidence of large families to feed. If the chief breadwinner became sick or died, wives and widows were left with dependent children. Sometimes it was impossible for women to manage alone; and the children might be left in a 'baby farm' where mothers paid to have their children looked after by the person who ran the 'farm'. Alternatively, there were workhouses, established as a result of the Elizabethan Poor Laws. Poor children and families could be housed in these. The Poor Laws, in theory, also provided 'outdoor relief' (goods or money) to the poor, and each parish was responsible for appointing officials who administered this relief. However, what was given was often insufficient, and elderly people, in particular, often experienced poverty when they could no longer earn a wage, and became dependent upon their children and families.

Despite all these difficulties, it was the opinion of many wealthier people in the nineteenth century that the root causes of poverty were intemperance and idleness. Many thought that poverty should exist for some as an incentive for others to find work. Indeed, the Victorians seemed to believe that 'the poor are always with us'. Certainly, poverty, although by no means a new phenomenon in the countryside, was now exacerbated by the rapid growth in the towns. Older towns grew, until in some areas they merged into each other, becoming **conurbations**. Small villages in turn became new towns: many 'industrial villages' grew up closely together in clearly defined areas, forming regions of relatively dense population without civic and commercial town centres. In the nineteenth century, rows and rows of terraced brick houses were built for working people – many very small, built closely together and lacking in basic sanitary facilities and gardens. In 1842 Edwin Chadwick produced a report on the sanitary condition of the labouring classes. This:

> ... gave a painfully vivid picture of men, women and children living in overcrowded lodging houses, damp cellars and unventilated back to back houses. In streets, yards and courts their refuse accumulated in stinking piles. They collected polluted water from pumps, rivers, ponds and wells. They hung out washing across narrow, smoke-laden streets.
>
> *(Brendon 1994, p. 83)*

Vyvyen Brendon also notes that it was quite common in the 1840s for Parliament to suspend its sittings because of the unbearable stench from the Thames, which at that time received most of the sewage of the almost two million inhabitants of London (Brendon 1994, p. 83). Londoners drew water from the Thames to drink.

ACTIVITY

Use a class or group brainstorming session to investigate what knowledge, images and impressions of the 'Industrial Revolution' you and your class share. Has anyone read any nineteenth-century novels such as *Oliver Twist* or *Jane Eyre*? Has anyone visited museums of this period or studied local history?

Use this session to decide upon areas which require further investigation. These could include:

- child labour in the factories, mines and farms
- disease, illness and medicine (in the nineteenth century, cholera, tuberculosis, typhoid, diphtheria, meningitis, polio and smallpox were all a much greater danger to health than they are today)
- crime and the police
- housing and urban growth
- sanitation and water supplies

APPROACHES TO SOCIAL POLICY: GENERAL BACKGROUND, 1800–1948

The response to the social conditions of nineteenth-century Britain set the scene for later developments in twentieth-century social-policy-making. In what follows, the period 1800–1948 will be divided into three parts: 1800–1906, 1906–39 and 1939–48, and general developments and influences on policy-making will be considered briefly. This will be followed by a more detailed historical examination of social policy developments in six areas:

- health
- personal social services
- education
- youth services
- social security
- housing

1800–1906

By the mid-nineteenth century, the overriding public attitude towards poverty was that *pauperism* or *destitution* was undesirable because the poor might then pose a threat to the social order: they could become a social menace whose actions could be unpredictable. The Elizabethan Poor Law, which still provided the main source of aid to the poor, required that each parish had to relieve poverty within its own boundaries, and had to appoint two Overseers of the Poor annually to administer this relief. However, the money for this 'poor relief' had to be raised from the people of the

Table 6.1 Key events and social policies in the period 1800–1906

Key events		Social policies	
1837:	accession of Queen Victoria	1834:	Poor Law Amendment Act – workhouses for the 'able-bodied' poor
1838:	People's Charter	1848:	first Public Health Act
1946:	repeal of the Corn Laws	1850:	Factory Act establishes a $10\frac{1}{2}$-hour day
1848:	revolutions in Europe	1870:	Elementary Education Act establishes the board schools
1851:	Great Exhibition	1875:	Artisans Dwellings Act – to promote slum clearance
1854:	Crimean War	1880:	Education Act
1867:	Second Reform Act	1883:	Diseases Prevention Act – non-Poor Law hospitals
1899:	Boer War	1890:	Housing of the Working Classes Act
1901:	death of Queen Victoria; accession of Edward VII	1891:	free elementary education
		1902:	Education Act sets up local education authorities and state secondary education
		1905:	Unemployed Workmen's Act

parish itself. It was only rarely that enough money could be raised in this way. What help there was took the form of 'indoor relief' to paupers living in the parish workhouse, or 'outdoor relief' – money or goods given to paupers living at home.

This system could not cope with the rising numbers of unemployed people in the nineteenth century, and in 1834 a Report of the Royal Commission on the Poor Laws provided the impetus for the Poor Law Amendment Act 1834. This act offered maintenance in a workhouse to all those who applied for 'relief'. Their lives would be regulated and made less comfortable than the lives of those who chose to stay outside and fend for themselves. This scheme of 'less eligibility' was designed to be a self-acting test of destitution which would distinguish between the 'deserving' and 'undeserving' poor. Those in genuine need would, it was assumed, accept the workhouse rather than starve. Workhouses were to be paid for out of the parish rates, and the ratepayers elected local Boards of Guardians to run them.

The Commissioners recommend diets for the paupers; women's rations are shown in brackets and breakfast is the same each day

Sundays, Tuesdays and Thursdays:

Breakfast	6 (5) oz. bread, $1\frac{1}{2}$ pints gruel
Dinner	5 oz. cooked meat, $\frac{1}{2}$ pound potatoes
Supper	6 (5) oz. bread, $1\frac{1}{2}$ pints broth

Mondays, Wednesdays and Saturdays:

Dinner	$1\frac{1}{2}$ pints soup
Supper	6 (5) oz. bread, 2 oz. cheese

Fridays:

Dinner	14 (12) oz. suet or rice pudding
Supper	6 (5) oz. bread, 2 oz. cheese

from the first Annual Report of the Poor Law Commissioners (1835)

(Brendon 1994, p. 43)

Michael Rose argues (1986) that while this new scheme was no solution to poverty and was strongly opposed by many people, it was less inhumane than some have suggested. Nevertheless, partly because of strong local opposition to the building of more workhouses, the system of 'outdoor relief' continued in many areas and by 1850 only 110,000 paupers, out of a total of 1 million, were workhouse inmates – and many of these were the old and sick who had nowhere else to go (Brendon 1994, p. 39).

Figure 6.1 Dinner time at Marylebone workhouse

Brendon suggests that the Poor Law Amendment Act

> succeeded in that it brought down Poor Law expenditure from £7 million in 1834 to £4.5 million in 1844. It also created a lasting fear of the workhouse and made poverty seem a disgrace. After the Act, as before it, poor people continued to manage as best they could, relying more on the help of family and neighbourhood than on statutory aid.
>
> *(Brendon 1994, p. 39)*

M.A. Crowther, in his book *The Workhouse System 1834–1829*, suggests that from 1869 to 1914 increasing amounts of public money were spent on building larger and larger institutions. These included workhouses, but money was also spent on new administrative blocks, nurses' homes, children's homes and other specialised institutions. Charities also seemed enthusiastic to build hospitals, residential homes (e.g. Dr. Barnardo homes) and hostels for the destitute (e.g. the Salvation Army). Gradually, there was a change in attitude towards institutions. On the one hand, they could still be intended to provide a punitive and deterrent regime, based on firm discipline, such as was the case with the workhouses and prisons, but on the other hand they could be built with the belief that the poor and unlucky might enjoy better facilities than they did in their own homes. Moreover, institutions might provide 'care', 'treatment and cure', a substitute family life or the opportunity to reform one's character and behaviour. Crowther argues that in the nineteenth- and early-twentieth-century, such institutions, whatever their purpose, were rarely successful because insufficient money was spent on them and because inmates' responses to institutional life were not always in line with what the providers intended.

ACTIVITY

Current debates about care in the community are still concerned with the effectiveness and cost of institutions for the mentally ill, the elderly, the sick and children. Are there still any justifications for housing people in institutions? Are institutions successful in achieving any of the aims which the Victorian and Edwardian reformers had for them?

The elderly, the sick and orphaned children were not really helped by the Poor Law Amendment Act, nor by the philosophy of 'self-help' which lay behind it. Middle-class Victorians were strongly influenced by the view that work, thrift, respectability and above all self-help would benefit the whole society. All things were considered possible if individuals worked hard, saved, led sober and well-behaved lives and did not rely on others. A popular proponent of this view was Samuel Smiles who, in two books *Self-Help* and *Thrift*, argued that hard work and saving was the answer to poverty.

ACTIVITY

To what extent do you think that these Victorian ideas still influence people today? Organise a debate in your class based around these ideas. For example, you might wish to discuss whether the UK today is facing a decline because the idea of self-help appears to have gone out of fashion.

Alongside this idea of self-help was the great middle- and upper-class Victorian concern with 'charitable works' and philanthropy, a concern which some historians argue often benefited the giver more than the receiver.

ECONOMICAL AND SUBSTANTIAL SOUP FOR DISTRIBUTION TO THE POOR

I am well aware, from my own experience, that the charitable custom of distributing wholesome and nutritious soup to poor families living in the immediate neighbourhood of noblemen and gentlemen's mansions in the country, already exists to a great extent; yet, it is certainly desirable that this excellent practice should become more generally adopted, especially during the winter months, when their scanty means of subsistence but insufficiently yield them food adequate in quantity to sustain the powers of life in a condition equal to their hard labour. To afford the industrious well-deserving poor a little assistance in this way, would call forth their gratitude to the givers, and confer a blessing on the needy. The want of knowing how to properly prepare the kind of soup best adapted to the purpose has, no doubt, in a great measure, militated against its being more generally bestowed throughout the kingdom; and it is in order to supply that deficient knowledge, that I have determined on giving easy instructions for its preparation.

NO. 239. HOW TO PREPARE A LARGE QUANTITY OF GOOD SOUP FOR THE POOR

It is customary with most large families, while living in the country, to kill at least some portion of the meat consumed in their households; and without supposing for a moment that any portion of this is ever wasted, I may be allowed to suggest that certain parts, such as sheep's heads, plucks, shanks, and scrag-ends, might very well be spared towards making a good mess of soup for the poor. The bones left from cooked joints, first baked in a brisk oven for a quarter of an hour, and afterwards boiled in a large copper of water for six hours, would readily prepare a gelatinized foundation broth for the soup; the bones, when sufficiently boiled, to be taken out. And thus, supposing that your copper is already part filled with the broth made from bones (all the grease having been removed from the surface), add any meat you may have, cut up in pieces of about four ounces weight, garnish plentifully with carrots, celery, onions, some thyme, and ground allspice, well-soaked split peas, barley, or rice; and, as the soup boils up, skim it well occasionally, season moderately with salt, and after about four hours' gentle and continuous boiling, the soup will be ready for distribution. It was the custom in families where I have lived as cook, to allow a pint of this soup, served out with the pieces of meat in it, to as many of the recipients' families numbered; and the soup was made for distribution twice every week during winter.

(Francatelli 1852)

Whether or not changes of the period 1880–1850 paved the way for greater social progress after that period is the subject of much heated historical debate. However, there had been little real improvement in the great social concerns of poverty, illness and high levels of crime by the 1860s. A main reason for this was the prevalent and influential Victorian idea of 'laissez-faire'. Supporters of this idea believed in allowing industries and businesses to establish their trade freely without state-imposed restrictions, quotas, regulations and prohibitions. This served to excuse governments from acting so as to enforce improvements in welfare.

A CLASSIC STATEMENT OF THE *LAISSEZ-FAIRE* THEORY

It cannot be denied that there is more busy, prying, laborious benevolence in England than there is in any country under the sun . . . Instead of any longer contenting ourselves and soothing our consciences with idly nibbling at the outskirts of a vast and growing mischief in our social state, – let us have the courage and candour to go at once to the origin of the evil – to strike at the source of that malady which has so long withered up the physical energies and moral virtues of our people. Let us unfetter the springs of the national industry, in the full confidence that, if we do so, it has an expansive elasticity within it, sufficient to absorb into profitable employment all those numbers whom it is now the fashion to consider as redundant . . . Under a system of unrestricted freedom, the field of employment is capable of this indefinite enlargement.

from an article in *Edinburgh Review* (1844).

(Brendon 1994, p. 15)

From the mid-nineteenth century, however, the state did begin to take more action to redress these ills, and the belief in freedom from *state* intervention slowly ebbed. Collectivist ideas, i.e. those which suggested that the state should create adequate conditions and opportunities for the fulfilment of each individual, began to take root. These were stimulated by the many political uprisings, rebellions and social movements of the nineteenth century such as the Chartist movement, the cooperative societies and the rise of the trade unions.

From 1850 to 1906, a series of Public Health Acts meant that large towns began to make adequate provision for water supplies and sanitation. The Local Government Act of 1888 set up elected county councils, and some progress was made towards setting up a national system of elementary education. However, it was not until the period 1906–14 that the problem of poverty was more seriously addressed. The Liberal government of 1905 laid some of the foundations for the post-1948 welfare state. Lloyd George, who became chancellor of the exchequer in 1908 (and later prime minister in 1916–22) successfully advocated social reforms which included:

- infant welfare clinics
- school meals to schoolchildren
- medical examinations of children in elementary schools
- Juvenile Employment Bureaux to help school leavers find suitable jobs
- the introduction of borstals and probation courts for young offenders
- old-age pensions to the over-seventies, paid in weekly payments from post offices

- National insurance schemes against unemployment and sickness

The main liberal social reforms of the period 1908–14 comprised:

- The Education Acts 1907, 1908
- The Children's Act 1908
- The Old Age Pensions Act 1908
- Trade Boards – from 1909 onwards
- The Labour Exchange Act 1909
- The National Insurance Act 1911

These reforms were brought about by:

1 a growing awareness of poverty in late-Victorian and Edwardian Britain;
2 an ideological belief in reform on the part of 'New Liberals' like Churchill and Lloyd George;
3 a political need to boost Liberal support following the failure of legislation on other matters and by-election defeats in 1908;
4 the threat of the socialist reform programme of the Labour Party gaining popular support if the Liberals failed to act.

ACTIVITY

1 You may not be lucky enough to have relatives or friends old enough to remember the introduction of old-age pensions or national insurance schemes in the first decade of the twentieth century, but there are many oral-history accounts of these years. Contact local history societies who may be able to help you to find some of these accounts, or approach history teachers in your school or college for help in finding appropriate books and materials.

2 Find out more about the introduction of old-age pensions. Why can this piece of policy-making be considered particularly important?

1906–1939

By 1914 the working class could gain more support from the state. Many more were insured, council housing had begun to be built and a hospital system had started. However, in the period 1906–39 overall, few of the changes in social policy had been thoroughly planned; most were just a response to the high levels of post-war unemployment. Anne Crowther suggests that in the period 1914–39

- the First World war stimulated a concern for 'national efficiency' in two ways:
  1 There was a concern to maximise output in the war industries. The Factory Acts were suspended so that women and young people could work longer hours in the factories.
  2 There was a concern to 'preserve the national stock' by protecting the health of mothers and children. Local authorities were encouraged to improve their services towards mothers and babies by setting up clinics, home visitors, hospital treatment and food for the needy
- most government spending on social services was directed towards measures to alleviate high unemployment as soldiers returned from the trenches of the First World War. By 1921, two million men were out of work. Unemployment insurance was extended in 1926 to cover everyone earning less than £5 a week, except for farm labourers and domestic and civil servants. Having said that, the household 'means tests' used to establish how much assistance should be given to the unemployed still retained the ethos of the Poor Law. These tests demanded details of a family's total income, including savings – however small – and money earned by wives and children. The family, not the state, still had first responsibility for the care of its members
- the attention given to dealing with unemployment after the First World War

Table 6.2 Key events and social policies in the period 1906–39

Key events		Social policies	
1914–18:	First World War	1906:	school meals for poor children
1930–33:	economic depression	1907:	school medical inspections; scholarships to secondary schools
1936:	Jarrow Crusade	1908:	Children Act – concerned with the protection of children and the setting-up of Juvenile Courts, and establishes the probation service; non-contributory old-age pensions established
1939:	outbreak of Second World War	1909:	Peoples' Budget – graduated taxation; trade boards established; labour exchanges set up
<u>Governments</u>		1911:	National Insurance Act
1906–15:	H. H. Asquith (Lib. and Coalition)	1918:	Representation of the People Act Education Act – school-leaving age raised to 14;
1915–19:	D. Lloyd George (Coalition)	1919, 1923 & 1924:	Subsidised Housing Acts – local-authority council housing
1922:	A. Bonar Law (Con.)	1920:	Unemployment Insurance Act – unemployment insurance extended to most workers and their dependants
1923:	S. Baldwin (Con.)	1925:	contributory old-age, widows and orphans' pensions
1924:	J. R. MacDonald (Lab.)	1926:	Hadow Report – recommended state secondary education for all
1924:	S. Baldwin (Con.)	1928:	women over 21 allowed to vote
1929:	J. R. MacDonald (Lab.)	1929:	Local Government Act – abolished Poor Law Unions and Guardians of 1834
1931:	J. R. MacDonald (Nat.)	1931:	'Means Test' brought in
1935:	S. Baldwin (Nat.)	1934:	Milk Act Unemployment Assistance Board for the long-term unemployed
1937–39:	N. Chamberlain (Nat.)		

diverted policy-making and money away from the elderly, education and housing. However, the building of cheap council houses *was* given some encouragement by government subsidies to local authorities

- while local government still played the major role in the implementation of social policies, there was gradually more centralised control. New governmental and civil-service bureaucracies began to emerge and to shape policy, e.g. the Ministry of Labour and the Ministry of Health. In tandem with this, several interest groups began to exert more organised pressure on central government departments, e.g. the British Medical Association and the Trades Union Congress
- public pressure for changes in social policy tended to be centred around the issue of unemployment (e.g. the Jarrow Crusade), but there was a growing general public concern with social policy. This pressure on the government was intensified by the extension of the electorate (those who could vote in elections) during this period. In 1918 the Representation of the People Act was passed, giving all men over 21 (except peers, lunatics and criminals) the

right to vote after six months' residence in a constituency; women over 30 were also given the vote if they or their husbands owned or occupied any property or land; and out of a total electorate of 21 million, 8.5 million women now gained the right to vote for the first time. 1918 saw the first general election in which women voted. Women could also become MPs in 1918, and in 1919 they could hold government posts. In 1928, the right to vote was extended to all women over 21.

1939–48

The Second World War of 1939–45 interrupted peace-time policy-making. During this war, the process of evacuation, whereby children and families were made to move away from areas close to probable air-raid targets to safer country districts, constituted a social policy of a kind. It certainly revealed to many better-off citizens in the UK that large numbers of families had been living through the 1930s in poverty and hardship. The coalition government of the war years made some efforts to alleviate the social problems faced by the population and exacerbated by the war. Among these were:

- supplementary (extra) pensions for old people and widows (1940)
- an easing of the means test so that financial help could be given to more people
- school milk, vitamin foods and milk for infants were provided free for all
- home helps for the sick and the elderly

In June 1941 the government ordered a Special Committee of Inquiry to undertake 'a survey of the existing national schemes of social insurance . . . and to make recommendations'. The chairman was Sir William Beveridge. In 1942 the resulting Beveridge Report proposed measures to deal with '5 giants on the road to reconstruction and social progress':

1. *Want:* a complete system of social insurance for all citizens – in return, flat-rate benefits would be paid to all citizens if they were sick, unemployed or retired. There was to be no means test.
2. *Disease:* a new national health service.
3. *Ignorance:* more and better schools.
4. *Squalor:* more and better houses.
5. *Idleness:* unemployment curbed by tighter government control of trade and industry.

Table 6.3 Key events and social policies in the period 1939–48

Key events		Social policies	
1939–45:	Second World War	1940:	school milk and meals for all
		1941:	national milk scheme and vitamin foods for young children; Unemployed Assistance Board becomes Assistance Board; supplementary pensions introduced
Governments			
1939:	Neville Chamberlain (Nat.)		
1940:	Winston Churchill (Coalition)	1942:	Beveridge Report on social insurance
1945:	Winston Churchill (Con.)		
1945–48:	Clement Attlee (Lab.)	1944:	Butler Education Act – provides secondary education for all
		1945:	Family Allowance Act
		1946:	National Health Service Act; New Towns Act; National Insurance Act; National Assistance Board; Children Act; Industrial Injuries Insurance Act
		1948:	5 July, 'The Appointed Day' – official beginning of the post-war welfare state

Figure 6.2 Sir William Beveridge – architect of the welfare state

Beveridge's plans were not adopted immediately or in full by the governments of the day but they did form the basis for many of the reforms following 1948 – discussed more fully in the next section. Aneurin Bevan, Labour's minister of health 1945–50, was responsible for health and housing policy, and worked towards the creation of a free health service. The National Health Service came into operation on the same day as National Insurance and National Assistance: 5 July 1948, 'The Appointed Day'.

CHANGES IN THE APPROACH TO SOCIAL POLICY: DETAILED HISTORIES OF DIFFERENT SERVICES

Health: context and background

In the nineteenth century the most important area of state involvement in the provision of health services was that of public health legislation. The 1848 Public Health Act provided the basis for the provision of adequate water supplies and sewerage systems. The period between 1900 and 1930 saw an increasing state concern with levels of public health, and in particular with the fitness of mothers and young children. Midwifery and health-visiting services expanded during this period. In 1911 the National Insurance Act provided for free care from GPs for certain low-paid workers and for those who now paid contributions to the insurance scheme. Financial support during periods of sickness and unemployment could be claimed.

The public provision of hospitals grew out of the workhouses provided under the Poor Law, and by 1939 local authorities were responsible for a large range of hospitals.

The National Health Service was introduced in 1948 as one area of welfare expansion pioneered by the Beveridge Report and fought for by the then Labour minister Aneurin Bevan. It is now a central part of the country's 'health care system', but is not the only agent or organisation which provides health care. (See Thomson et al. 1995, Chapter 5, for further information on developments after 1948.)

Personal social services: context and background

The social conditions of many people's lives in the eighteenth and nineteenth centuries were changed by the processes of industrialisation and urbanisation. The 'social problems' which arose (poverty, child labour, high mortality and morbidity rates, crime and prostitution) were seen by some to be soluble if people could be *reformed* – i.e. their behaviour and attitudes changed. By the late nineteenth century there were also concerns about a widening chasm between the experiences and material conditions of the working class and those of the upper and middle classes. There was a worry about a 'loss of community' and fear of the possibility of social revolt and the breakdown of common values.

Nineteenth-century reformers and charitable workers (women, in the main) worked to provide an uplifting moral example; to encourage people to become independent of the material assistance of others wherever possible. Social work during this period was dominated by middle-class values, and one of the most prevalent of these was the aforementioned notion of a distinction between the 'deserving' and the 'undeserving' poor.

In the earlier part of the twentieth century, this tendency to view social problems in an individualised way influenced the emerging social-work profession. Two particular approaches to 'helping people' developed:

1 the 'casework' method, where social workers focused on the uniqueness of each family and individual and their circumstances. The growing science of psychology was used to provide theories and explanations of behaviour;
2 the idea of the professional social workers as the 'gatekeeper' to other resources – financial, material, services. The social worker was to use his or her greater knowledge to 'assess' the needs of individuals, families and children and provide whatever was necessary to help people function more effectively.

As a result social workers in the second half of this century have had to address twin aspects of their role. They have been increasingly expected to provide *care* and *control*: to give personal help to people and to exercise the power to make decisions about the direction of other people's lives. (See Thomson et al. 1995, Chapter 5, for further information on developments after 1948.)

Education: context and background

In the nineteenth century in the UK, most children received no formal education or 'schooling' at all. Until the expansion of secondary schools in the 1940s, elementary schools provided the only form of education received by the vast majority of people in this country. Mass, compulsory schooling until the age of 16 is therefore a relatively recent phenomenon.

Many early advocates of extending education to the children of working-class families believed that schooling would teach the values of obedience to authority and hard work. Children disciplined and controlled in this way would thus be easier to manage as adult workers in the new industrialised UK. The first organisations to provide an elementary education to working-class children by building schools and employing teachers were voluntary Church bodies: the Anglican National Society for Promoting the Education of the Poor in the Principles of the Established Church (set up in 1811) and the non-conformist British and Foreign Schools Society (set up in 1814).

In 1833 parliament voted to provide money to build more elementary schools, and these funds were paid mainly to the existing Church education societies. In 1846 a pupil-teacher system was introduced where suitable young people, normally previously educated in elementary schools, were selected at the age of 13–14 to become *apprentices* or *pupil-teachers*. After a five-year period with examinations at the end, they became teachers in their own right.

In 1862 Robert Lowe, Vice-President of the Committee of the Privy Council for Education, replaced the old system of government grants to elementary schools with a payment-on-results system; schools could now earn 12 shillings (60p) for each child over six who attended a certain number of times in a year. However, part of this money was deducted if the child failed examinations in the 'Three Rs'. This had the effect in most schools of narrowing the curriculum and emphasising *drill* and *rote* learning.

By the 1870s the pace of growth in the education system began to increase. By 1869 over 1,000 new elementary schools had been opened, and in 1870 W.E. Forster produced the UK's first major Education Act. This:

- increased government aid to all elementary schools
- set up school boards in boroughs where there were not enough existing Church school places for all children. These boards were given powers to equip, provide, maintain and staff elementary schools. They could also raise local rates to finance these activities. In effect, they were the first *local education authorities (LEAs)*

In 1880 attendance at elementary school was made compulsory for all children, and by the 1890s some school boards had begun to set up 'higher grade schools' which were like secondary schools. Nevertheless, most secondary schools in the country at this time were still private, fee-paying schools catering almost exclusively for children of the upper and middle classes.

In 1899 a Board of Education Act was passed which in effect established the first central government department of education, the new Board of Education. In 1902 another Education Act was passed abolishing the school boards and transferring their powers to the new local education authorities covering the whole country (around 300 at the time). These local authorities were also responsible for secondary education, and they started in some areas to build their own secondary schools, which remained fee-paying and academic in their curriculum. In 1907, however, all secondary schools had to offer 25% of places to able pupils from elementary schools.

In 1918 the school-leaving age was raised to 14 years of age. Local education authorities now had to make provision in separate schools or classes for children over the age of 11.

It is generally agreed that, in the first half of the twentieth century in the UK, the most important and influential piece of legislation relating to education was the 1944 Education Act (the 'Butler Act'). This abolished the old Board of Education which dated from 1899, replacing it with a new Ministry of Education. Local education authorities now had new statutory duties. They had to organise school provision into three separate stages: *primary*, *secondary* and *further*. Fees were abolished in secondary maintained schools, and the school-leaving age was raised to 15 (and then to 16 in 1972). The Act laid down that children should be educated according to their aptitude and ability, and LEAs were encouraged to adopt a 'tripartite system of schools' to cater for the perceived different ability and aptitude levels of children. These three types of school, *secondary modern*, *technical* and *grammar*, were supposed to have 'parity of esteem', i.e. to be considered equally good but different. The grammar school catered for the 'academic child', the technical for the technically gifted and the secondary modern for all the others. In most areas technical schools did not really develop, and selection into the grammar schools was on the basis of an 'eleven-plus' examination, an intelligence and aptitude test taken at the end of primary school.

Not everyone was convinced that the three (or, in most places, two) types of school did have 'parity of esteem'. GCE examination courses were not even offered to students in the secondary modern schools until the late 1950s, and the grammar schools were generally considered to have higher status, better resources and more highly trained teachers. There was also controversy over the use of the eleven-plus test.

By 1963, in response to these criticisms, a number of local education authorities were working on schemes for at least some comprehensive schools to be set up in their area. These schools offered places to all, irrespective of ability. The Education Act 1964 encouraged further moves in this direction, enabling LEAs to transfer pupils from one stage of education to another at ages other than 11, making *middle schools* possible.

In 1965, the Labour government set out its plans for the reorganisation of secondary schools, in Circular 10/65. It wanted to end selection at 11 and introduce comprehensive schools throughout the country. Over the next 10 years successive Conservative and Labour governments battled to halt or speed up the process of reorganising secondary schools into comprehensives. By the mid-1980s, excluding the independent sector, the vast majority of children of secondary school age attended comprehensive schools, with only 10% of the total in grammar and secondary modern schools in those LEAs which had managed to hang on to the old system.

In 1972 the Local Government Act (effective from 1974) brought in a new system of local government in England and Wales. More control over education began to be transferred to the Department of Education and Science and to the governing bodies of individual schools. The 1944 Butler Act had in fact given more potential power and direction to central government over education, but these powers had not been much used. However, in the 1970s the drive to reduce public expenditure, to respond to significant criticisms of the education service (e.g. in the Black Papers of 1969–77 and in the Great Debate initiated by Prime Minister James Callaghan in 1976) and to respond to an apparent increase in the demand by parents and educational professionals for greater participation in educational decision-making (e.g. as expressed in the Taylor Report of 1977) led to central government extending its powers in educational policy-making. This was mainly achieved through a series of very significant Education Acts, whose most important provisions are summarised below.

1 Education Act 1980
   - Introduced a new system of assisted places at independent schools
   - Removed the compulsion on local authorities to provide schools with meals but restored the right for LEAs to provide milk for children over eight
   - Laid down that there must be parent and teacher governors on each governing body; each school was to have its own governing body unless the LEA felt that two schools could share one
   - Introduced new rights for parents and a Parents' Charter. Parents could now choose schools for their children within reasonable limits of 'efficiency' and 'economy' for the LEA involved. Parents could also appeal against decisions to a local Appeals Panel
   - LEAs were required to undertake additional consultation with the public over school closures, and were asked to take surplus school places out of use

2 Education Act 1981
   - The sole concern of this Act was special education

3 Education Act 1986
   - Reduced the dominance of LEA representatives on school governing bodies and gave more places to teachers, parents and community representatives
   - Laid down procedures for the organisation and function of governing bodies
   - Abolished corporal punishment in schools

4 Education Reform Act 1988
   - Further increased the powers and authority of governing bodies
   - Removed polytechnics and colleges of higher education from the control of LEAs. These were now funded by a new funding council which made them more accountable to central government
   - Altered the funding arrangements for universities

- Abolished the Inner London Education Authority, transferring powers for education to the 12 inner London boroughs and the City of London
- Introduced the National Curriculum of three core subjects and seven foundation subjects, with key stages of study ending at 7, 11, 14 and 16. Applied to all maintained schools but not to the independent or private sector
- Encouraged schools to 'opt out' of the LEA system and apply for grant-maintained status, funded by central government. Parents were to be balloted on whether their schools were to become grant-maintained
- Allowed schools to increase their enrolment numbers
- Allowed schools to control most of their own finances via a system called *local management of schools*
- Gave the secretary of state powers to establish City Technology Colleges
- Allowed schools to charge parents for some activities, such as music tuition

5 Education Act 1993

- Made it even easier for schools to obtain grant-maintained status by requiring governing bodies to carry out yearly ballots
- Set up 'hit squads' of government-appointed inspectors to help failing schools improve
- Allowed the incorporation of sixty-form colleges and further-education institutions, which were now to be centrally funded by the Further Education Funding Council
- Transferred some of the existing powers of LEAs to a new Funding Agency for Schools. This was launched in April 1994, and has the following duties: the financial monitoring of and calculation and payment of grants to grant-maintained special schools, and ensuring the provision of sufficient school places in certain LEAs

It will not be difficult for you to find plenty of evidence for the considerable controversy which these changes have brought about. You could explore further some of the key current debates which are outlined below.

Defenders of the changes believe that:

- the choice of schools for parents has increased
- standards in schools have been raised because schools compete for pupils
- the powers of teachers, unions and local authorities in education have been reduced, and that this is a good thing because their work is now managed and controlled more carefully

Critics of the changes believe that:

- the increased centralisation of power in the hands of the Secretary of State for Education is damaging the education system
- there has been a loss of democratic control and of effective local planning for educational needs
- the cause of underachievement is inadequate resources, and that this issue is not being addressed

Youth services: context and background

Although methods of delivery are changing, the youth service in Britain is part of the education system, traditionally organised through a partnership between local authorities and voluntary organisations. These voluntary organisations range from uniformed bodies such as the Girl Guides, with roots stretching back into the nineteenth century, to newly formed, independent groups. The precise nature of the work that the youth service does is therefore decided at a local level or within individual voluntary organisations.

The National Youth Agency publishes two excellent short guides: *What is the Youth Service?* and *Becoming a Youth Worker*. (For the agency's address, see the 'Useful Addresses' section at the end of this chapter.) The following is an extract from the first of the guides mentioned above which gives a brief history of the youth service.

The origins of the youth service lie in the late 19th century, when a large number and range of clubs for young people were established out of a sense of humanitarian duty to respond to the grim conditions in the new industrial age.

More voluntary youth organisations developed during the early 20th century. In 1939, the government recognised the value of youth organisations and urged the setting up of local youth committees.

In 1944, a duty was placed on local authorities to secure provision for the 'social, physical and recreational training and leisure time activities' in cooperation with voluntary organisations.

The Albermarle Report, produced for government in 1960, identified the notion of social education through leisure. The report called for a massive building programme of youth clubs, projects for working with 'unattached' youth, and a crash programme of training for youth leaders.

Nine years later, the Milson-Fairbairn Report broadened the focus of youth work and emphasised young people's involvement in the community.

The 1982 Thompson Report confirmed social and political education as the fundamental purpose of the youth service.

Other non-governmental reports have also helped shape the youth service. The Hunt Report in 1967 addressed the youth service's role in meeting the needs of 'young immigrants'. This and subsequent reports in the 1970s saw the role of the service as helping young Black people integrate into white society and so rejected separate youth provision for young Black people.

It was not until the 1980s that reports such as *In the Service of Black Youth* by Gus John and *The Fire Next Time* from the Commission for Racial Equality began to point out this approach ignored the discrimination faced by young Black people and did little to meet their needs. Independent, community-run provision with relatively little contact with the formal youth service has been one result.

In the mid-1980s the service was influenced by a series of reports from the National Advisory Council for the Youth Service. These focused attention on broad issues such as the greater participation of young people in decision-making, and on specific areas such as work with girls and young women, work with young people with disabilities, and work with young people in rural areas.

Most recently, three ministerial conferences have continued this work. Their aim has been the development of the youth service into a more coherent education service, with greater common purpose, and clearer indications of what it seeks to achieve.

(NYA, What is the Youth Service?)

Employment

See Chapter 7 pages 267–68 for further information.

Housing: context and background

In the nineteenth century in the UK, the population grew rapidly. In England and Wales it grew from 9 million in 1801 to 18 million by 1851. The process of urbanisation saw people move to the towns and cities, and in these areas the shortage of and demand for housing was acute. Before the First World War most households in the UK rented their homes from landlords. Private ownership of housing was comparatively rare and confined mainly to the upper and middle classes. Rented housing for the working class was of notoriously low quality, and some of the early charitable housing associations came into being to provide decent low-cost housing. However, the problems were too severe to be dealt with in this way alone, and by the 1930s local authorities were building 'council housing' for rent, adding another means of access to housing for those on low incomes. By 1939 councils had built more than a million homes – a tenth of the total housing stock. The governments of the time were also encouraging a programme of private house-building. Thus, three broad sectors of housing became available to people:

- the public rented sector
- the private rented sector
- owner-occupation

By the 1950s there was increasing public dissatisfaction with the quality of public rented housing. High rents in the private sector and destruction and damage to housing during the Second World War prompted an increased postwar demand for housing. Between 1945 and 1965, councils built nearly 3 million homes, a million more than the private sector, many of them in high-rise estates. Council-house building declined, however, after 1968.

In 1957 the Conservative government introduced a Rent Act. This:

- removed rent controls and security for tenants
- accelerated the decline of the private sector
- led to some harassment and exploitation of tenants

In 1965 the Labour government passed another Rent Act reintroducing controls and 'security for tenants'. This gave rise to the system of 'fair rents'.

Since the late 1970s, housing has been one area of social expenditure where the government has achieved a real cut in the housing budget (by about half since 1979). Conservative governments up to 1994 have tried to encourage people into owner-occupation and to minimise the role of local authorities in the provision of housing. Several recent pieces of legislation illustrate this tendency, and are briefly summarised below:

1. Housing Act 1980: this allowed council-house tenants to buy their own homes at substantial discounts. The Act also restricted or removed some of the rights tenants had previously enjoyed if renting from a private landlord.
2. Social Security and Housing Benefit Act 1982: housing benefit was now paid to claimants by local authorities rather than under the social security system.
3. Housing and Planning Act 1986: this made the procedures for buying council property easier.
4. Housing Act 1988: this Act reduced government controls over rent-fixing in the private sector of housing. It also created Housing Action Trusts to take over and improve run-down council estates, and identified housing associations as the form of 'social housing' preferred by the government.
5. Local Government and Housing Act 1990: this prevented local authorities from subsidising the rents of their tenants. It also placed controls on the income from sales of council housing under the 'right to buy' scheme.

By the end of 1992 more than two million public-sector tenants in the UK had made applications to buy their homes, with nearly seven in ten making a purchase: 65,000 council homes were sold in 1992 (*Social Trends* 1994).

CONTEMPORARY SOCIAL POLICY

Social policy can first be studied as a discipline in itself – that is, as the ideas developed by academics and researchers in colleges and universities; the ideas promoted by key policy-makers in government and by MPs, civil servants, the political parties and other political organisations; and the ideas for social change developed by pressure groups and other interested organisations. The discipline of *social administration* is the study of these ideas. One of the aims of people working in this subject area is to collect facts and evidence about issues such as homelessness, poverty, illiteracy, etc. with the aim of trying to persuade governments to improve or alter their welfare provision. Rational ideas, it is hoped, will persuade governments to change what they are doing.

During the course of your studies you may well meet people in the health and social care services who are involved in the process of producing social policies, or who are using studies to inform and improve what they do. In talking to them, it will be interesting to explore the extent to which people think ideas can be a force for change. How much do you think you have been influenced already by the various arguments for and against the existence of a welfare state?

Social policy can also, however, be studied as the development and administration in practice of state welfare policies. That is, what exactly has been done, and how and why? Whose ideas have had the most influence? Who has had the power to initiate and administer various social policies? What political structures and processes have been involved? What economic and social changes have prompted particular policy changes? Not only is there an interest here in the institutions and organisations involved in service delivery and their history and development, but questions can also be asked about who benefits from those services.

Each of these key themes will be returned to in this chapter.

The study of social policy involves contributions from sociology, politics and economics. Students with some previous experience of studying these three subjects will find it easier to understand some of the concepts and terminology used in this chapter. Those with no previous study of these subjects are strongly advised, before starting their study of social policy, to familiarise themselves with the following:

- the basic workings and procedures of the British parliamentary system (MPs, the prime minister, elections, the role of parliament, central and local government, the cabinet, right-wing/left-wing, citizenship, statutory legislation)
- some key economic concepts; recession, the market economy, investment, collective bargaining, ERM, the global economy, inflation, interest rates, privatisation, the labour market, the trade deficit, demand and supply, GDP, import/export, industrial output, decentralisation, budgets, capital
- a few sociological ideas: the state, capitalism, racism, sexism, feminism, the nuclear family

This may all seem rather daunting. The academic study of social policy can, at first sight, seem rather remote from the daily realities of people's lives. However, if you are wondering what social policy has got to do with your life, the lives of your family and friends and your possible choice of career, look at Figure 6.3.

Does social policy now seem so unrelated to the issues that we talk about in our homes and with our friends and that we see dramatised on TV and in the cinema?

Social policy is essentially concerned with questions about:

- how needs are defined or met – or both
- what limits there are on our behaviour
- who makes the relevant decisions

Factors affecting the development of social policies

Your nine-month-old baby will not sleep through the night. Instead, she wakes up every hour or two and cries. She will not go back to sleep without being breast-fed or rocked to sleep again in your arms. You are becoming totally worn-out by never being able to sleep for more than an hour or so at a time. One response to a situation like this would be to muddle on, getting increasingly tired, until your daughter's sleep patterns eventually change. But there would be risks. You might become so stressed that you become ill or even hit or shake your daughter.

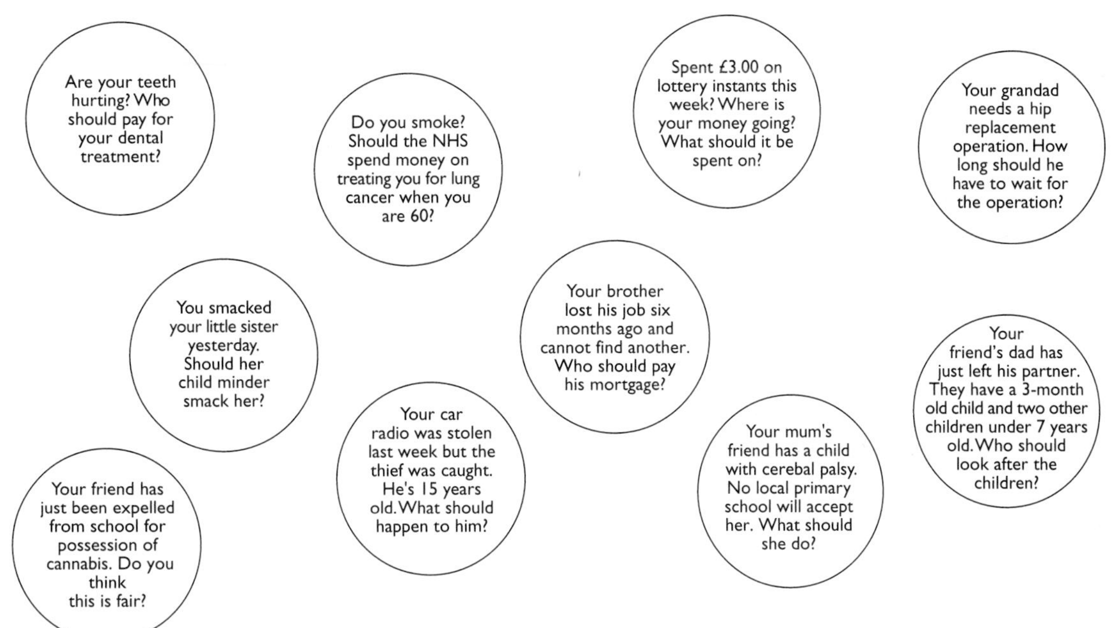

Figure 6.3 What's social policy got to do with *my* life?

One solution to the situation would be to consider possible strategies that could change the pattern of her sleep. These might include letting her sleep in the same bed with you, not picking her up when she cries but offering reassurance with your voice, or trying to stop breast-feeding.

Social policies arise in much the same manner. A problem is perceived and defined by a particular group or individual, and if the situation is considered intolerable, a response may be made. The response may not necessarily be successful, and several different responses may have to be experimented with. Moreover, solutions may be found which could suit some people in society better than others. In the UK, it is central and local government which have the greatest powers to define social problems and formulate responses. In doing so, they may have to respond to changing demographic and social conditions, such as a rise in unemployment or a fall in the death rate. In Chapter 7 we consider the impact of such changes in detail.

THE MASS MEDIA

Another key factor which influences governments in the decisions they make is the response of the *mass media* to public issues. The media has considerable power today to publicise incidents and events to enormous audiences and to set the context in which these events may be interpreted; and it has, on occasion, been accused of sparking off a 'moral panic' about certain issues, which has then resulted in particular responses by the government. On other occasions, however, when it highlights social issues and stirs up public debate and opinion, the media is often seen in a more favourable light. Two recent examples illustrate these points.

1 In November 1994 Ian Kay killed John Penfold, a Woolworth trainee manager at Woolworth's Teddington branch in west London. He pretended to buy a packet of crisps, then thrust a knife more than four inches into Mr Penfold's chest before escaping with £165 from the till. Kay had been granted home leave from prison but absconded, embarking on a series of robberies which ended in Mr Penfold's death. This incident received enormous publicity at the time.

Home leave and temporary release from

prison had, until November 1994, been widely used by the Prison Service to ensure that low-security inmates maintained family ties, were prepared for release by undertaking outside work or community-service projects, or were allowed, for compassionate reasons, to attend such occasions as family funerals. Following this incident, Michael Howard, the then home secretary, announced changes to this provision. He ended the automatic right to temporary release and introduced a much more rigorous risk assessment to be carried out before a prisoner is released, as well as creating a criminal offence of failing to return on time. These changes came into effect in March 1995, and cut by 40% the number of prisoners given temporary release in the following year.

QUESTION

Was there any link between the media publicity for this crime (and another similar case at the time) and the actions of the home secretary?

2 The television series *Brookside* has, over many years, highlighted a number of sensitive and controversial social issues.

ACTIVITY

Read the letter below from the writer of the series, Phil Redmond. Do you think TV series like *Brookside* can have any effect on the way policy is made in this country?

BROOKSIDE, THE OMNIBUS EDITION FEATURING REAL-LIFE HUMAN DRAMA

For the past few days the fictional Brookside has found itself once again linked to the tragic realities of life. This is not an uncommon occurrence, as there is always somebody ready to use television as the scapegoat for all society's ills. This time it is the case of Mary Smith, recently set free after killing the grandfather who abused her and threatened to abuse her younger sister as he had done to her.

The similarities to Brookside were obvious. This was the same motive we used in the recent storyline when Mandy and Beth Jordache were jailed for murder after discovering the father was starting to abuse the younger daughter, Rachel. Mary Smith stabbed her grandfather; Mandy Jordache stabbed her husband. Immediately the link was established and Mary Smith became the 'Brookside copycat killer' in tabloid headlines.

This was, as usual, a crass simplification of a complex issue. The headlines obscure the point that alongside the widely quoted diary reference to the Brookside storyline the police also found a number of press cuttings in her bedroom about child-abuse victims taking their revenge. Why, then, were there no 'newspaper copycat' headlines? The answer of course is that it would be tantamount to shooting the messenger. Yet who is to say in what guise the messenger arrives?

The Jordache trial, although fictional, served to highlight the issue of domestic violence and abuse that many women like Mary Smith endure. Months after the transmission we are still receiving many letters from women outlining the suffering they have experienced but always expressing their support for what we did.

By highlighting this issue we hoped to contribute to a long and continuing debate about the law surrounding this issue, which seems to revolve around the definitions of provocation and diminished responsibility, but at its centre is the definition of murder. Is someone like Mary Smith really in the same bracket as a professional hitman or terrorist? In this case the Court seemed to think not, backed, I suspect, by the unequivocal support of the police, who have said that they 'wholeheartedly agree' with the decision and feel 'Mary Smith was the real victim'.

It is not our place to try and change the law. Though we can, like newspapers, try and reflect the harsh realities of life.

(Phil Redmond in the Guardian, *21 July 1995)*

PRESSURE AND INTEREST GROUPS

Of enormous importance in influencing the making of social policy is the work of hundreds of public and pressure groups directing their energies around particular interests in this country. Many of these are well-known and long-established, such as Shelter and the Child Poverty Action Group. Others are locally or regionally based, but a further growing and interesting source of pressure is from groups set up or coming together over specific local or environmental issues. Some of these groups are interested in taking direct action (e.g. the protesters against the M11 road link, animal-rights protesters), some are interested in more traditional campaigning to save or protect threatened services and facilities, and some are interested in self-help and self-sufficiency projects.

Among the strategies pressure and interest groups can use to influence policy-making are:

- the 'lobbying' of government ministers and civil servants
- the use of the media to highlight their ideas
- direct action
- appeals to, and the involvement of, the public
- research, and the publication of reports

ACTIVITY

1 You may be fortunate enough to get a work-experience placement in a pressure or interest group. If so, ask questions about the extent to which the group regards itself as successful in influencing policy-making.

2 There are likely to be a number of local groups campaigning in your area. Use local newspapers to investigate any current issues, and invite a representative from a local group to talk to your class about their campaign.

Finally, while social policy in the past has not always been planned (it is often a response to emergencies or rapid social change) it does often seem motivated by particular sets of ideas and beliefs (*ideologies*) about people and their behaviour and motivations, and about society and how this ought to work. These ideologies are discussed in depth on pp. 244–48.

The relationship between local and central government

What local government can do to create social policies is extremely limited. Local government can only do what parliament permits. How can local, decentralised governments respond constructively and democratically to the specific needs of people in their areas and communities? Can they do this more effectively than central government? What powers should local government have in this respect?

Since 1979 Conservative-led local authorities have tended to argue that the best way to respond to local needs is to treat the citizen as a 'customer' – to contract out and privatise as many council services as possible so that the 'customer' has a choice. Services, according to this model, can be provided in a competitive market, and council administration costs are reduced, making it possible to charge local electors lower taxes (council tax). For example, encouraging local schools to 'opt out' of local authority control reduces the cost for the local authority of administering those schools. Central government policies have tended to support local authorities which have pursued these aims.

Labour- and Liberal Democrat-led local authorities maintain an ethos of public service, decentralisation and the empowerment of groups and localities. This, they argue, is the best way to ensure that local people are involved in discussions about what social policy decisions should be taken.

Central government policies have tended, since 1979, to conflict with this approach, making it more difficult to implement and sustain.

There is a shifting balance of power between central and local government. Is central government becoming more powerful and local government less so? What functions is local government acquiring or losing? These are questions which are considered in Chapter 7.

ACTIVITY

1 Does it matter whether services to people are decided locally or nationally? What differences in policy might occur if services were provided locally rather than centrally?

2 Using a local newspaper, make a list of social policy issues which currently seem important to people in the area in which you live. You might look at the letters pages, news or features pages or editorial comments. From your list choose one or two issues in which you are most interested. Could these issues best be tackled by central government or by the local authorities or councils where you live? Then carry out a small-scale survey of public opinion on these issues, concentrating on those questions which ask people whether they think the issues should be dealt with locally or nationally.

MODELS OF SOCIAL POLICY PROVISION AND THE WELFARE STATE

There have been important changes in the organisation, structure and 'delivery' of health and care services. What has influenced these changes? Some people observing and trying to describe developments since the nineteenth century have found it useful to try to summarise and classify different perspectives on social policy and welfare provision. They have looked at the ideas and values which lie behind a particular set of views (political ideologies) and have tried to explain how these have affected the direction which social policy-making has taken. Usually, these sets of ideas or perspectives involve attempts to explain social problems and devise appropriate solutions to them. In essence, these models of social policy provide different views on exactly where the burden and balance of responsibility for health and care provision should lie in any society.

Students may find studying this area quite difficult as different writers on social policy use different systems to classify and describe models of social policy. In this summary, I shall use Fiona Williams's classification from her *Social Policy: A Critical Introduction* (1989).

Four models of social policy will be described:

- anti-collectivist/market models
- non-socialist welfare collectivists/liberal collectivists/the mixed economy of welfare
- the Fabian socialists (universalist models)
- the political economy of welfare

These outlines will be followed by feminist and anti-racist critiques of these models.

Anti-collectivist/market/selectivist/individualistic models

Right-wing Conservative governments have believed that state intervention in society should be reduced. According to this approach, people should become more responsible for themselves and their families – they should 'stand on their own two feet'. The family and community should be the main source of care for children, the elderly and the infirm. State welfare is seen to limit individual freedom and choice, and leads to more demands on government than it can afford to pay for or administer. The real objective of state welfare is ultimately to make people do without it. These arguments suggest that people should not rely on the 'nanny state'.

The way to reduce the cost of the welfare state is to promote *selectivist* health and welfare policies where the benefits of the policies are available only to those assessed as in need of them. *Universalist* policies, i.e. making services and benefits available to all, should thus be discouraged.

The term 'the New Right' has come to be used to describe the ideas of the Conservative governments led by Margaret Thatcher and John Major since 1979. New Right ideas involve the belief that:

- people lack choice if there is no readily available alternative to the state provision of services
- state welfare services become wasteful and inefficient when they are faced with no competition or are not controlled by principles of cost-effectiveness
- the more people get the more they expect
- state bureaucracies have created self-interested groups of professional workers and administrators who want the growth in the welfare state maintained because it is in their interests – it provides them with employment
- the welfare state is morally disruptive: it saps people's will to find work and to provide for themselves
- the state is incapable of the efficient running of mass welfare schemes, e.g. insurance, pensions; private companies competing with each other in the marketplace could exercise these functions much more efficiently
- the role of the state should be as a 'purchaser' of services for people rather than as a direct provider and financier of those services. State provision should be replaced by independent providers competing in 'internal' or 'quasi'-markets

Non-socialist welfare collectivists/liberal collectivists/the mixed economy of welfare

These ideas originated with the Liberal Party in the early twentieth century and were taken up by figures such as Beveridge and Keynes and politicians of more recent years such as David Owen.

Liberal and social democratic (and more moderate Conservative) approaches have argued for a 'mixed economy of welfare' – a partnership between individuals, families, industry and the state in the provision of health and care services. Families and individuals cannot always function alone. They sometimes need professional support and help – financial, emotional and practical. There are times when state-employed professionals must 'step in' for the sake of those vulnerable either to the 'downside' of capitalism, such as unemployment and poverty, or to the 'bad' in people, e.g. children at risk of abuse. There is a belief here that capitalism and free enterprise is the best way to ensure people have freedom, but that welfare services are necessary to ensure political stability and the smooth maintenance of capitalism. Hence there is a belief in:

- the direct public provision of welfare benefits and services
- the commitment to universal access to those services (but only at a minimal level)
- some 'targetting' of certain services to particular individuals or groups, i.e. some selectivity
- the role of the state in supporting the activities of voluntary agencies and self-help groups

The Fabian socialists: universalist models

This movement dates from early Fabians, such as the Webbs, and postwar writers such as Crosland and Titmuss. The dominant values of these writers are equality, freedom and fellowship. They argue that capitalism is unethical, unjust and undemocratic, but that it can be transformed and changed. Government action can play a part in this process, and the welfare state is one of the main ways in which this transformation can be achieved. There is thus a belief that:

- the welfare state can be a springboard for change – a progressive force which can encourage the gradual development of citizenship rights
- universal services should be provided by the state, with some positive discrimination for areas or groups defined as being in greater need
- social change is generated by the state's action. If the state is seen to be just and altruistic, people will follow the 'good example' set

More radical versions of this policy model suggest that:

- social policy is more important than economic policy and should certainly not just be a reaction to economic policy, dealing with the problems of capitalism as 'side-effects'
- social and economic policies need to be unified through a democratic, decentralised process of social planning according to need
- any analysis of social problems must take into account the class structure of society
- the assertion of socialist values can change capitalism

The political economy of welfare

This model applies Marxist economic and political theory to the development of the welfare state in the twentieth century. It suggests that the state should be highly committed to people's welfare but that people's values will change only when the economic organisation of society changes. Collectivist values will arise out of the struggle by the working class to achieve more power. Until this occurs, this perspective suggests that the welfare state in capitalist societies is:

- on the one hand, used by the state to have more control over its workers
- on the other hand, also partly the outcome of struggles by the working class to improve social and economic conditions for themselves

The feminist critique

Feminists suggest that welfare legislation has tended to reflect patriarchal attitudes in society. The 'caring' role of women within families (as mothers and as carers for the elderly or disabled) is assumed to be part of their 'normal' duties and responsibilities, and as such the state has tended to feel it should not subsidise women in these positions. There has been a reluctance by governments to replace the unpaid work of women within the family with health/welfare institutions and provision.

The anti-racist critique

This perspective identifies the welfare state as part of institutionalised racism in society which denies black people's access to benefits and provision, reproduces the racial division of labour within the welfare state and uses welfare agencies to police black people and immigrants. The state is seen as an agency of social control, coercing people into situations which may not necessarily lead to their receiving better health and care services.

AN EXAMPLE OF SOCIAL POLICY-MAKING: THE CHILD SUPPORT ACT 1991

In October 1990 the government issued a White Paper called *Children Come First* which discussed the rights of lone parents (who are mainly women) who are on benefits. This paper was a response to a perceived public concern about the numbers of lone parents in society; the proportion of them who are receiving income support (about three-quarters); and the 'problems' of caring for children from lone-parent families. The government wished to recoup the rising costs of paying benefits to nearly 900,000 single parents who receive little or no maintenance from their ex-partners. The White Paper also reflected an ideological debate in government circles about the 'moral status' of lone-parent families, their dependence on the state and their 'disruptive' influence on society. Lone-parent families were seen by followers of 'New Right' ideas to be a deviation from the desired 'norm' of a two-parent nuclear family.

The White Paper set out proposals for a new system of securing maintenance for children. With only very minor changes (the Child Support Bill received all-party support in the House of Commons), this formed the basis of the 1991 Child Support Act which came into force in April 1993. The Act:

- created a new child-maintenance system designed to replace the previous system
- created the Child Support Agency which, from April 1993, had responsibility for the assessment, review, collection and enforcement of child-maintenance payments

The formula used for the calculation of the payments takes into account what the absent parent has to pay in essential expenses such as housing costs, tax and national insurance. Under this new system, which is supposed to act as a buffer between absent parents and persons with care of a child, and to ensure that maintenance is actually paid, anyone who has a national-insurance number can be traced and made to pay, whether or not they have access to the children involved. Tony Newton, former Secretary of State for Social Security, said in November 1990 that 'Maintenance reform is a key part of the government's strategy to help lone parents and their children achieve a better standard of life.'

Any parents in receipt of benefits (e.g. income support) must cooperate with the agency to provide the information needed to help trace any absent parent and to assess and collect any maintenance owed (unless they have reasonable grounds to believe that to do so would put them or their children at risk from the absent parent). If they do not cooperate, their benefits will be reduced. However, if maintenance is paid, those on income support have their benefits reduced pound for pound by whatever payments are received. Lone parents who do not rely on state benefits do not have to cooperate with the Agency and do not risk any other source of their income being affected if maintenance payments are made.

The Agency was given a budget of £114 million in 1993/4, and will have a budget of £184 million in 1994/5. It employs 5,900 staff, but this will rise to 6,600 in 1995.

Since the Agency has started work, it and the social policy ideas behind it have attracted a great deal of both support and criticism. Some of the key arguments on each side follow here.

Arguments in support of the Agency

1. Men who father children out of wedlock should be forced to help bring them up. The work of the Agency is supported because it is seen as a more effective way of ensuring that men meet their responsibilities. The Agency and the Act therefore have a practical and a moral role: to change people's situations but also to 'warn' men of the consequences of irresponsibility.
2. For women who want maintenance, the new system should be an easier and fairer way of ensuring that it is paid than chasing absent fathers through the courts.

Arguments against the Agency

1. Lone parents receiving state benefits do not benefit financially from the Agency's work

as their benefits are reduced if maintenance is paid.

2 Lone parents and their children should not be seen as a 'drain' on the country's resources; they should be given greater material and social support.
3 The Agency supports the New Right model of welfare in emphasising that people have private financial responsibilities rather than that the state has a public responsibility for all children. The 'real' aim of the Agency is to reduce the social-security bill.
4 For absent parents who live long distances away from their children, the enforcement of maintenance payments may make it difficult or even impossible financially for them to travel to see their children.
5 Parents with the care of children are having previously flexible and informal agreements with ex-partners and husbands overridden by the Child Support Agency.
6 The Agency has made 'clean break' divorce settlements (where a father allows his ex-wife to keep the family home in return for no, or a low rate of, maintenance payments) impossible to sustain.

In response to some of these criticisms, the government made some limited changes to the work of the Agency which mainly allowed absent parents with second families a longer time in which to pay maintenance bills. However, these changes were still viewed by some as insufficient, and complaints to the Agency continued to made. In July 1994 management consultants were called in to review the performance of the Agency. In May 1995 the Child Support Bill, aimed at remedying problems with the Child Support Agency, cleared its Commons stages. This Bill allows a new appeals system for financial settlements and a recognition of 'clean break' settlements.

A new problem faced by the Agency in 1995 is a rise in unpaid maintenance: the Agency is owed £438 m, and parents £87 m.

ACTIVITY

1 Carry out further research into the past work and current progress of the Child Support Agency. It has had a high profile in the media since its introduction, so if you have access to a relevant CD-ROM system or to past copies of newspapers, you should not find it too difficult to look more closely at the development of this particular social policy.

2 Which of the models of social policy outlined on pp. 204–206 most closely relates to the ideas and principles behind the Child Support Act 1991?

3 *Groupwork exercise*
One group of students who understand the ideas and principles behind the Child Support Act 1991 should agree to defend and support the Act (even if only in a 'role-play' mode). The rest of the class should then be split into groups, each choosing to adopt the perspective of one of the other social policy models. Each of these groups should prepare a statement explaining why, from their perspective, they agree or disagree with aspects of the Child Support Act. Those students representing support for the Act should then respond to these statements in turn, defending their position if necessary.

4 The exercise described above can be adapted to provide an active approach for researching and debating the ideas behind other social policies, specific legislation or 'blueprints for reform' such as political party manifestos.

THE ROLE OF GOVERNMENT IN THE FUNDING, DEVELOPMENT AND REGULATION OF SOCIAL POLICY

When governments (central or local) want to make or change social policy, how is this done? The purpose of this section is to explain, as simply as possible, some of the processes involved in intervention by the state in the lives of individuals.

Policy can be defined as a set of ideas and proposals for action culminating in a government decision. To study policy, therefore, is to study how decisions are made.

(Jones et al. 1994, p. 535)

When a new government comes into power after a general election, it will normally have a number of policies it wishes to put into effect, and these include social policies. During the course of a government's term of office, there may be particular circumstances which arise which also provide the motivation to formulate and implement policies.

The funding of social policy

Who determines how much money can be spent on making and implementing social policies? Welfare spending in general is by far the largest part of public expenditure in the UK. The prime minister, the cabinet and the treasury have to make the key decisions about how much should be spent on which policies. The resources to pay for welfare and social policy come from:

- the taxes (income tax, VAT, etc.) raised by central government
- the transfer of payments to people from central and local funds (e.g. in the form of social-security benefits)

ACTIVITY

Although this may be simplifying the debate a little, there have been several key arguments about the funding of social policy and the welfare state:

- Some people argue that people would be prepared to pay more for welfare state provision through higher taxes
- Others suggest that the government should transfer some of the money it currently spends on other areas, such as military spending, to welfare services
- A third argument suggests that since the largest part of welfare spending is the social security budget, the government could save money in the long run if it took measures to reduce unemployment
- Other arguments suggest that there will have to be some redistribution of wealth from the rich to the poor

Conduct a class debate around these issues or invite in speakers from the main political parties to give you their views on the subject.

THE RESOURCING OF SERVICES

Since the beginning of the 1980s, the growth in spending on welfare policies has been restrained, but overall, 'social spending' has remained high, largely to meet the costs of mass unemployment. The government has attempted to 'target' social-security benefits and services on those considered most in need and most deserving; and they have attempted to apply stricter controls over who is applicable for means-tested benefits. However, the groups which the government considers most in need do not always correspond with those groups who have seen the least improvement in their living conditions and income, such as the long-term unemployed and one-parent families.

The 1990 British Social Attitudes Survey revealed a 'long-standing preference for increased spending on the mass-consumed (and most expensive) services (health, education and pensions), and a lower level of support for social security benefits, which were seen to be directed towards a 'less-deserving' minority (Pierson, in Dunleavy et al. 1993, p. 260).

ACTIVITY

It is difficult to keep up to date with evidence of the overall expenditure on public services, but information on this can be obtained from the relevant government departments. There has been a very heated public debate over the past 20 years about whether enough money is spent on the health and care services. Many people working in health and care organisations will have interesting views about the resourcing of services. Carry out a series of interviews or a small-scale survey to investigate public perception of this issue.

The regulation of social policy

Current legislation gives some health and social care workers:

- statutory powers, i.e. parliament has passed laws which require certain services to be delivered in certain ways. For example, social workers can and must follow certain procedures in relation to people with mental illnesses and to children
- the control of resources. For example, the NHS and Community Care Act 1990 makes social-services departments the lead agency in community care provision, and local authorities now handle and use resources to pay for private and voluntary sector residential accommodation for old people. Fund-holding GPs may now have greater scope to provide medical services for their patients in some circumstances, whilst hospital specialists may find the range of treatment for their patients restricted by financial constraints imposed as a result of the 'internal market'
- obligations to fulfil. For example, secondary schools in the UK are obliged to implement the National Curriculum, observe the regulations for religious worship in schools and set the Standard Assessment Tests

Therefore, legislation can both circumscribe what health and care workers do and give them additional powers in relation to service users – it thus has an enabling, constraining and compelling role. Laws are intended to provide a framework for the delivery of services to the public. In theory they lay down what can or cannot be done. However, almost all laws passed in parliament are *debated* before, during and after their enactment. Many are and remain highly controversial, others are complex or little understood or recognised, and a few are all but completely ignored. Therefore, the legislative process itself is not enough to ensure that services are 'delivered' in the ways intended in the legislation. Most workers in health and care organisations receive some training in legislation relevant to their work, but there may be many constraints on the way in which legislation is implemented. These include:

- a lack of adequate resources to put the law into effect
- a lack of knowledge about the legislation
- confusion about certain aspects of the legislation
- non-compliance with the legislation
- a lack of suitable procedures in place to implement the legislation or to *check* that it is being implemented

ACCOUNTABILITY

Parliament makes the legislation; the judges (in the courts) then interpret and apply it. Therefore, legislation does provide an opportunity for service users to take steps if they feel that there have been faults in the way those services were provided. The ways in which complaints can be made vary from service to service, as do the chances of a successful outcome. There are many ways of protesting:

- written complaints to the provider of the service, e.g. a letter to a consultant at a hospital, which may have its own internal complaints procedures and systems
- the use of an appeals system, if one exists (as in some aspects of the education system)
- personal injury litigation, with the aim of claiming compensation through the courts
- complaints to an MP
- complaints to the ombudsman

ACTIVITY

Investigate each of these forms of complaint in more detail, trying to find recent examples wherever possible.

Ultimately, governments are accountable for their policies through the ballot box. If their policies are unpopular, they can lose general or local elections.

The regulatory role of the state

An interesting area of study would be the relationship between the state, parents and the paid carers of those parents' children. A well-publicised case of 1994 has been that of a childminder, Ann Davis, in Sutton, Surrey. The local authority refused to register Ms Davis as a childminder because she refused to sign an agreement with the authority that she would not 'smack' the children in her care. She took the local authority to court, arguing that she had the parents' permission to smack their children if necessary and that she therefore should not be refused registration.

Under the Children Act 1989, inspectors employed by the local authorities which register childminders must satisfy themselves that the childminder and those living with them are 'fit persons' on 'suitable premises', with adequate equipment, proper records and set limits on the number of children cared for. Authorities may also set 'discretionary requirements' associated with a good quality of service, and it is under this power that 'no smacking' rules have been introduced in accordance with the Children Act guidance.

The court found in Ann Davis's favour and ruled that she should not have been refused registration, leading to some current confusion about what childminders may or may not do. The National Childminders Association wants to stay with the 'no smacking' rule.

ACTIVITY

Talk to childminders and parents about the implications of the Ann Davis case. To what extent do they think that childcare arrangements should be a 'private matter' between parents and minders? How far should local authorities or central government attempt to regulate or control these arrangements?

MAIN FEATURES OF CONTEMPORARY SOCIAL POLICY

There are some current features of social policy which it is impossible to avoid. Many of these issues arouse strong feelings among people working in health and care services, and all are controversial. The purpose of this short section is to explain some of the concepts involved in these debates so that students can recognise the arguments being used when talking to others, carrying out research or studying the delivery of social services.

The Conservative Party initiated significant changes in social policy in the 1980s, and key aspects of the Party's ideas are still being developed and implemented as part of their radical legislative programme. The issues described here reflect some of those ideas and have been put on the current policy agenda by that programme (although many do have roots which stretch further back into the history of social policy-making). It is therefore worth considering whether these are the only issues that you think ought to be raised.

ACTIVITY

In your discussions with people working in health and care contexts, and from your own experiences, consider whether these *are* the important issues.

Charters

The Citizen's Charter is the result of the personal initiative of John Major as prime minister. Announced in 1991, it aimed to emphasise and raise the quality of service delivery. The scheme covers all government departments, the NHS, nationalised industries, privatised utilities, local government and the universities. Organisations are encouraged to emphasise prompt service, openness, consumer research and a stronger voice for citizens. Service targets and methods of redress are published, and a Charter Mark of Excellence can be awarded. Some 'mini-charters' have also been published, such as the Patient's Charter and the Parent's Charter.

Shifts in accountability, centralisation and empowerment

If you smash a china mug accidentally when shopping in a gift store, you expect to be asked to pay for it. In the same way, those who have the public power to make and enforce social policies need to work in ways in which they can be held responsible for the consequences of their actions if necessary. People can often feel powerless to challenge or change the laws and policies which affect their lives, making it even more essential that those who control public institutions and services should be:

- required to give an account to the public of their exercise of power, i.e. required to explain what they are doing and why
- able to be brought to account by the public, i.e. procedures should exist to penalise those who persist with illegal, damaging or inappropriate policies and practices

In practice this might mean that there should be effective measures to deal with cases where:

- governments are acting secretly or illegally and withholding information or resources from people
- health and welfare professionals are acting dangerously or irresponsibly
- organisations are not complying with the law

Some writers have argued that the increasing centralisation of the organisation and funding of health and welfare services in fact makes it more difficult for accountability to be possible (Stewart 1995). Services are now less likely to be the responsibility of locally elected councillors but are more likely to be controlled by members of boards, associations, corporations and semi-autonomous agencies or *quangos*. These people are generally appointed by the government, and it is difficult for the public to know, or take any interest in, who they are or what they do.

Another problem in the new health and welfare market is that accountability is linked with contracts for work or services purchased. What standards of work should be written into these contracts? What happens if the contracts are not met or the work is unsatisfactory? How can the public influence or play a part in these decisions? The Citizen's

Charter is intended to 'empower' the 'customers' of health, education and care services, i.e. it is meant to extend the freedom and rights of patients, parents etc. It is meant to make it easier for people to complain about unsatisfactory services and to achieve 'compensation' if complaints are justified.

However, the term 'empowerment' has also been used in a rather different way by other people working in health and care organisations. For many, empowerment means ensuring that people have a voice in controlling standards and services themselves – that people with disabilities, for example, should be able to make their own decisions about what needs they may have and how those needs should be met. In this use of the term, people require 'empowerment' because, in various ways, they are oppressed by the structure of the society in which they live. For some writers (e.g. Ward and Mullenden 1993), self-directed group work, where people with similar needs decide on their own goals using the help of professionals if required, is a way of raising consciousness and working collectively and efficiently. It also avoids the assumption that the answer to problems lies only with the individual.

Privatisation and market forces

Private health and welfare organisations are not new. What has happened since the 1980s is that the government has encouraged more private provision of services in areas where they already existed and new private provision of services in sectors where the previous provision was entirely state-run.

People wanting private operations should shop around, haggle and ask for no-frills packages, as costs between hospitals in the same region can vary by thousands of pounds, the Consumers' Association says today.

Its magazine *Which? Way to Health*, found in a survey that among 10 hospitals in the West Midlands and South Yorkshire a hernia repair cost from £1,470 to £738; among 10 in Essex varicose vein surgery cost from £1,544 to £567; and among 10 in Greater London a hip replacement cost from £8,281 to £5,320.

(The Guardian, *7 December 1993)*

The purchaser/provider

In the business and industrial sector of the economy there is a reasonably clear distinction between a purchaser and a provider. If I wish to purchase a pound of apples, I must go to a provider – a supermarket or greengrocer. If the apples are bruised, soft or too expensive, I will in future be more likely to buy them from another provider – a different shop. The shop which provides the best apples at the best price will, in theory, attract the most purchasers (customers). The Conservative government believes that such competition between providers improves, through 'market forces', the quality of services or products they offer.

Can this approach be applied to health welfare and other care services? The Conservative government believes that many of the existing social services can and must be split into different sectors of 'purchasers' and 'providers'. The split is not as simple as in the case outlined above, however. In most cases the purchasers will not be the public but professionals such as GPs and social workers, who will purchase services on their behalf – rather like allowing someone else to buy that pound of apples for you. The principle here will be that only the professional can really assess what the needs of the person are; it would not be appropriate for the potential patient or client to make their own decisions. It will be the professionals, too, who have the money to pay: they control the purse. However, in some areas of social policy, the government does intend to try to give the public more direct 'purchasing' power, as in its suggestions that students in further and higher education should be allocated education vouchers which they could spend on a range of courses.

SOCIAL POLICY IN THE EUROPEAN UNION

Why study social policy in the European Union?

Your study of the historical development of, and current issues in, social policy and administration in the UK will have revealed some interesting conflicts and differences in perspective over the ways in which governments take action in the fields of personal and family income, education, health care, crime, housing and personal social services. You will have been able to relate some of these discussions to your experiences on work-experience placements, to your own employment experiences and to current debates both in the media and among colleagues, fellow students, family and friends. The relevance of some of these issues will, hopefully, be clear to anyone intending to work in a health- or social-care-related context. However, unless you have strong personal links with others in another European country, or speak or are studying another European language, or intend, eventually, to try to find work in another European country, you may be wondering what the relevance of studying social provision in the European Union (EU) is.

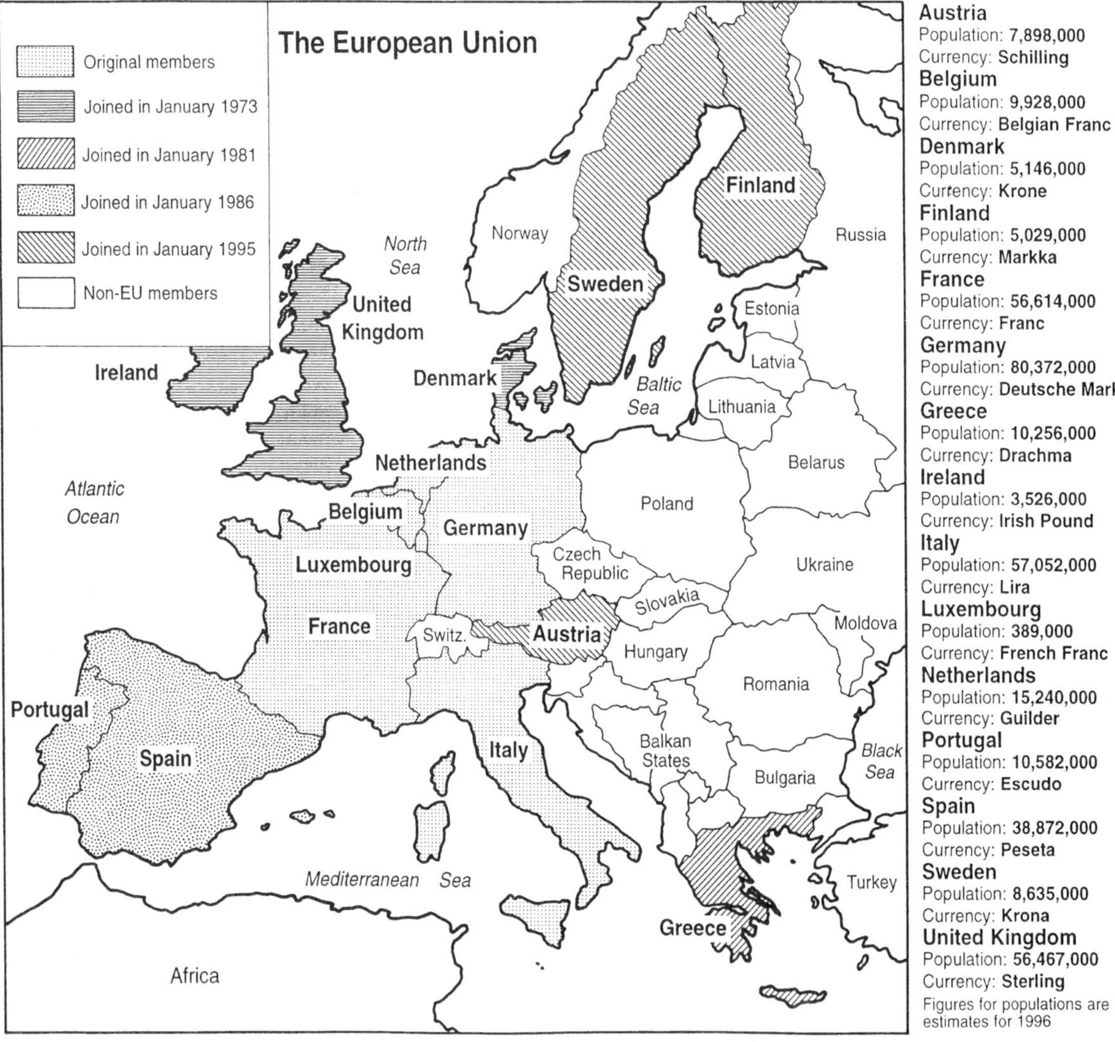

Figure 6.4 A map of the European Union
Source: The *Guardian*, 28 February 1995.

Figure 6.5 Headlines from the European Union

Although you may be forming or may have formed particular political views and perspectives as regards British politics, and may have a greater or lesser understanding of the British political system, the workings of the European Union may be less well understood because they appear to have little observable influence on our lives.

ACTIVITY

In your class, use a brainstorming exercise to:

- establish whether there are students in your class who speak other European languages besides English
- see if anyone has lived or worked in another European country
- find out what people generally understand by the term 'European Union'
- discuss whether people regard themselves as 'European' or 'British'. What do these terms mean to people?

There are several important reasons for studying social provision in Europe:

1 Comparative studies of the social policies in European countries can highlight differences and similarities in organisations and practices in each country. Can we learn from the best practices of other countries? Each welfare state in Europe has been uniquely shaped by the cultural, social, political and economic context within that country. What are its strengths and weaknesses? What are people's experiences of health and care provision in these countries? Could practices which have developed elsewhere be put into practice in the UK?

2 The European Union, although initially intended to be a mechanism for ensuring economic and political union in Europe – bringing European people 'closer', ensuring peace in Europe, preserving parliamentary democracy and developing a firm economic base for the free movement of goods, services, people and capital – has, despite resistance from some national governments, been able to exert some influence over the pattern of social policy development in the member countries. There has been a 'Europeanisation' of some policy- and decision-making. The conflicts and differences of perspective over social policy referred to at the beginning of this chapter are now reflected at a European as well as a national level. How much future influence will the European Parliament and the European Commission have over the development of social policy in the UK? Will this be advantageous or not?

3 A study of changes both in the groups of people requiring health care and welfare services and in the patterns of need in different European countries can highlight social trends which cut across national barriers. For example, there has been a growth in the numbers and proportion of very elderly people in Europe as a whole. The number of people in Europe aged over 65 will have almost trebled from 34 million in 1950 to 97 million by 2025, and the percentage of pensioners in the population will have almost doubled from under 9% to over 20% over the same period.

There are also Europe-wide high levels of unemployment. Current estimates suggest that there are at least 18 million unemployed people in the 15 European Union countries.

A third example is that new patterns of poverty, marginalisation and exclusion in the Europe of the 1990s affect much wider sections of the population than before. People of working age have overtaken pensioners as one of the largest groups of people in poverty in Europe, and this group particularly includes lone-parent families.

Can 'solutions' to these problems be found at national levels only? For example, if nearly 50 million (15%) of the population of the 15 European Union countries are too poor to consume goods and services offered to the 'marketplace', what will be the impact on the businesses and economies of these countries? The cost of public spending to support a large number of largely, unemployed, migrant and poor people is a problem which affects all the countries. The working-age labour force in Europe of 133 million is already less than half the total population.

Fundamental issues such as these pose major economic, social and moral questions for the emerging European market and community, and are at the heart of the battle of competing ideas, interests and values within the welfare systems of the member states (see Bennington and Taylor 1993).

4 From a personal point of view, you may be considering looking for future employment in another European country. The opportunity you have here to investigate social provision in other countries should therefore be helpful to you.

What is the European Union? How has it come about?

The European Union is a group of 15 countries, in western Europe and Scandinavia, representing some 370 million citizens from the Arctic Circle to the Adriatic Sea. Treaties are the major legislative forms which determine membership of the European Union and major changes to its workings. In 1957, under the Treaty of Rome, six nations, Belgium, France, Italy, Luxembourg, West Germany and the Netherlands, who in 1952 had originally joined together to regulate their coal and steel industries, formed the European Economic Community (EEC). This union had several aims:

- to strengthen peace in Europe
- to achieve economic integration and harmonise economic development
- to achieve the closer union of people in Europe

Some Articles of the Treaty of Rome formed the basis for agreement on Community social politics as well as economic ones (e.g. Articles 117–28).

In 1973 the UK, Ireland and Denmark joined the EEC; Greece joined in 1981 and Spain and Portugal in 1986.

In 1987 the Single European Act was passed in the European Parliament. This amended the Treaty of Rome, and its broad intention was to create a Europe-wide free-trade area by 1993. It gave authority to the European Commission to act in new areas, such as the environment, and it generally highlighted the will of the European Community to act in the area of social as well as economic policy. The 12 member states were to 'protect and improve the quality of the environment, to contribute towards protecting human health', and to ensure a prudent and rational utilisation of natural resources. The Act allowed for work, health and safety measures to go through the European Parliament on a majority vote. Social security, migrant workers' rights, equal opportunities and worker participation measures can only be passed in the European Parliament by a unanimous vote.

In 1992, the UK, with the other 11 members of the European Community, signed the Maastricht Treaty. The purpose of this treaty was to bring about a more unified Europe. The treaty had five main objectives:

- a closer European Union (EU) with more cooperation between governments
- a common foreign and security policy among all member states
- all EU members to have the same home affairs and justice policy – the same laws applying in the UK, France, etc.
- a single European currency controlled by a European central bank to be made possible by 1999
- European citizenship: all nationals of the EU to share the same rights and to have free right of travel across the community

It also gave greater powers to the European Parliament and entitled it to make decisions relating to people's conditions of work and the treatment of children.

The Social Chapter

The UK refused to accept or to sign one part of the Maastricht Treaty which is now known as the Social Chapter of that treaty. The Social Chapter intends to give the European Union the power to enforce certain social rights and obligations regarding conditions of work for employees. It aims to set minimum conditions for workers across Europe. It includes a range of measures such as the rights of workers to have a say in the running of their companies; additional job-creation schemes; equal opportunities for men and women at work; increased spending on training; improvements in health and safety at work; a minimum income for elderly people; freedom of association; and collective negotiations with employers.

There was an enormous debate in the UK about the Conservative government's refusal to accept the Social Chapter of the treaty. Some of the arguments were as follows:

- The 'Euro-sceptics' (mainly Conservative Party members and MPs) campaigned against any further involvement of the UK in the European Union. Many of them would like to see the UK withdraw its membership entirely
- Most Conservatives and some business-sector figures argued that the Social Chapter would mean that employers would be forced to make more workers redundant as it would cost them more to keep the ones they had. They suggested that productivity would be harmed by giving too many (expensive) rights to workers and employees. European businesses would be unable to compete with Third World businesses that pay their workers less.

- The Labour Party, the Liberal Democrats and many trade unions argued that the Social Chapter was weak but would go some way to providing greater protection on working conditions and wage levels. For example, under the Social Chapter, some directives that had been blocked by the UK government, e.g. a proposal for European works councils, could be voted through under qualified majority voting.
- Others argued that the Social Chapter was such a cautious and generalised set of statements about the rules under which the EU states could lay down policy on social affairs that it was not worth all the fuss and bother.

Nevertheless, for many of the EU nations, the Social Chapter proposals represent little difficulty as they merely confirm what is already happening in those countries. For example, the EU would like to see a maximum working week (excluding overtime) of no more than 48 hours. Nine out of the 12 countries already have a maximum working week of 48 hours or below, and only three, the UK, Ireland and Denmark, set no limit on the maximum hours worked.

The enlargement of the EU

In May 1994 the European Parliament voted overwhelmingly in favour of admitting Norway, Sweden, Finland and Austria to the European Union. Each of these countries held a national referendum on whether or not to join the EU in 1995, as full members. Austria, Sweden and Finland joined the EU officially on 1 January 1995. Norway voted against joining the EU, after holding a referendum in November 1994. It is calculated that the three newcomers will pay nearly £1 billion a year more into the EU budget than they will receive in spending benefits from Brussels. This surplus could be used to reduce Britain's contributions to the EU budget, as well as to boost aid to the poorer southern-region European members. It is also likely that the membership of these three countries, which at the moment have social democratic governments who support the Social Chapter, will put even more pressure on the EU to give the environment and social policy higher priority. The UK may face even more opposition for its stance against the Social Chapter.

Federalism, regionalism and nationalism

With the potential involvement of more European states in the EU (other countries such as Poland, Hungary and the Czech Republic also want to join), some people are concerned that Europe will become a federation of *regions* rather than nation states, i.e. that the European Parliament will become more centrally powerful, national governments less powerful and the regions more important. The European Parliament has already a Committee of the Regions set up by the Maastricht Treaty.

In 1996 the EU will review its whole role at an intergovernmental conference. This will be a crucial time for national governments who may wish to try to redefine the extent of their powers in relation to the powers of the European Parliament.

How is the European Union organised?

There are several key institutions in the EU which, between them, are responsible for the establishment of policy and the enactment of Community law. There is:

- the Council of Ministers
- the European Parliament
- the European Commission
- the European Court of Justice
- the European Council
- the Economic and Social Committee

THE COUNCIL OF MINISTERS

The Council of Ministers is based in Brussels, Belgium. It makes the major policy decisions in the EU. It is made up of one government minister from each of the member states; which ministers attend depends on the topic being discussed. The Council of Ministers meets privately and on a regular basis.

The presidency of the Council rotates every six months between member states, in alphabetical order. The president sets the agenda and chairs the meetings.

The Council of Ministers considers European Commission proposals and tries to negotiate to reach an agreed position on them. After the European Parliament has discussed any proposals, the Council of Ministers than makes the decision whether or not to adopt these proposals. After this, it is the role of the European Commission to ensure that the proposals in question are put into action.

The ministers make decisions by unanimous agreement, qualified majority voting or simple majority voting, depending on the subject under discussion. They are the most powerful body of the EU.

THE EUROPEAN PARLIAMENT

The European Parliament sits at Strasbourg, in France. It held its first elections in 1979, and the latest elections were held in June 1994. At present it has 626 representatives, called Members of the European Parliament (MEPs). More than 80% of MEPs were male in 1993. The MEPs are elected by political affiliation every five years in Europe-wide elections covering up to 200 million voters. All nationals of the member states over 18 years old are also citizens of the EU and have voting rights and rights to stand in European and local elections in the member state where they live. Voters must be registered as electors.

The number of MEPs per country is decided by the population size of the country. In the June 1994 elections these were:

UK	87
Northern Ireland	3
Ireland	15
France	87
Portugal	25
Spain	64
Italy	87
Belgium	25
Luxembourg	6
Netherlands	31
Denmark	16
Germany	99
Greece	25

When Sweden, Austria and Finland joined in January 1995, their MEP allocation was 22, 21 and 16 respectively.

The European Parliament considers and comments upon new proposals (published in White Papers) put forward by the European Commission. Depending on what these are about, it has rights to put forward amendments (changes). It also approves a yearly budget to pay for the work of the EU institutions and organisations. In addition, the European Parliament considers plans for new laws put forward by the Council of Ministers. The European Parliament is the world's first and only existing democratically representative body which crosses national boundaries.

Some people have suggested that to date, the European Parliament has been little more than a 'talking shop'. Certainly, MEPs have been reluctant to use their limited powers to disrupt the proposals and policies of national governments if these have been in conflict with the intentions of the European Parliament.

How representative of their electorate can MEPs be?

MEPs have such huge constituencies (in population size) that it is difficult to see how they can represent all the wishes of their electorate (the people who vote for them). In the 1994 elections, the turnout at the voting stations across Europe was, on average, only 56.5% of the electorate.

For the June 1994 election, three organisations, Charter 88, the European Movement and the Electoral Reform Society, organised nationwide Democracy Days where people could meet their MEPs and question them about their vision of Europe.

The political parties also publish manifestos, which are statements of their intentions if voted into power. Voters can make themselves more aware of the differences in the approaches of potential candidates in elections to the European Parliament by reading these.

ACTIVITY

Find out who your MEP is. Giving plenty of notice, invite him or her into your school or college to talk to you and answer your questions. If this cannot be arranged, send a list of questions to your MEP, explaining your interest in their work and how the information they give you would be useful. A list of British MEPs can be obtained from the European Parliament UK Office; see the 'Useful Addresses' section at the end of this chapter.

In the June 1994 Euro-elections, the UK Conservative Party won 18 of the country's 87 seats in the European Parliament. Labour won 62 seats, the Liberal Democrats two seats and the Scottish Nationalist Party two seats

THE EUROPEAN COMMISSION

The European Commission has its headquarters in Brussels. It is one of the four governing institutions of the European Union. The Commission makes proposals for EU legislation. It has 20 Commissioners nominated by member-state governments (they are not elected). It is bound to act independently and in the interests of the EU as a whole. The Commission administers EU funds and subsidies, manages and implements policies and makes sure that they are put into effect.

The presidence of the Commission

Jacques Delors, Commission president from

Figure 6.6 The European Parliament

1985 to January 1995, had been a very influential figure in the work of the European Commission over the past decade. Among his beliefs were:

- the need to convince European citizens that even the most powerful nation is no longer able to act alone
- the need to reform the EU to cope with up to 20–25 new members
- the need for the EU to have a clear social policy and for workers to have social rights, protection at work and the opportunity for education throughout their lives

ACTIVITY

In January 1995, Jacques Santer of Luxembourg became the new President of the Commission. He was appointed by the Council of Ministers. Find out what beliefs and policies, especially in the field of social policy, he has.

Examples of the work of the European Commission

1 *The 1994 White Paper: European Social Policy – A Way Forward For The Union.* In November 1993, having appealed for contributions and comments from interested parties in the member states, the Directorate-General for Employment, Industrial Relations and Social Affairs within the European Commission issued its Green Paper on social policy. This was a consultative document meant to launch a wide-ranging debate about the future direction of social policy. The intention was that after inviting responses to this Green Paper, the Commission would put forward specific proposals on social policy in a White Paper which would be prepared in 1994 and be debated in the European Parliament. This debate would form the basis for a new EU social action programme to be ready by January 1995.

The White Paper on social policy argues that economic and social progress in Europe must go hand-in-hand. It suggests that much of Europe's influence and power has come precisely from its capacity to combine wealth creation with enhanced benefits and freedoms for its peoples. It asks several key questions:

- Is there a route back to full employment in Europe?
- Should the welfare state be given a new role? If so, what should this be?
- How can equality of opportunity for all people be promoted?
- Can the European Union establish a constitutional (i.e. legal and written) basis for the fundamental social rights of citizens?

2 *The European Commission White Paper: Growth, Competitiveness and Employment (December 1993).* This White Paper was intended to address the issues of unemployment and the declining competitiveness of industry. It proposed:

- to provide additional funding to ensure the survival of priority EU projects in these areas
- to reduce the number of unemployed significantly and to create up to 15 million jobs by the end of this century
- to support job-creation options such as deregulation in the labour market and help for small businesses
- a European network for electronic mail and interactive video
- transnational European networks to coordinate investments in high-speed trains, roads, airports and gas and electricity installations
- a guarantee that all school-leavers should have a job or training place up to the age of 20
- the encouragement of work-sharing, shorter working weeks and partial employment

It was estimated that up to three million new jobs could be created in: home-helps for the elderly and disabled; health care; minding

Figure 6.7 In the European Union, economic and social progress go hand in hand
Source: Green Paper European Social Policy – Options for the Union, Commission of the European Communities, 1993.

pre-school children and looking after children before and after school; assistance to young people facing difficulties; providing security in blocks of flats; the renovation of run-down areas; and a variety of environmental-improvement schemes. All this would amount to a new 'social economy'.

ACTIVITY

1 Try to obtain copies of the two documents outlined above (and any updated proposals relating to them which have been made since this book was written). Write to the Commission of the European Communities (see the Useful Addresses at the end of the chapter).

2 There are many issues worthy of discussion and debate here. Pick out your own or choose from the following questions
- Could unemployment in Europe be alleviated if people were willing to work a shorter week for less money?
- Can wealth creation go hand in hand with social progress?
- What proposals would you like to see the European Commission put forward to the European Parliament in terms of social policy?

THE EUROPEAN COURT OF JUSTICE

The European Court of Justice sits in Luxembourg. It is composed of 13 judges (one from each member state and one more) assisted by six advocates-general. The court considers any infringement of Community law or question of interpretation. Rulings are final on European law, which takes precedence over national law.

The judges are appointed for six years by the consent of the 15 member states. The court can quash any Commission measure.

THE EUROPEAN COUNCIL

The heads of government of member states and the presidents of the European Parliament and the European Commission meet at least twice a year as the *European Council*. The Council discusses major community issues and political cooperation. The talks are intended to give an overall 'direction' to the Community's work.

THE ECONOMIC AND SOCIAL COMMITTEE

This meets in Brussels. It is a consultative body with 189 members, 24 from the UK, who represent employers, trade unions and other groups such as farmers and consumers.

How are we affected by European law?

WHO PAYS FOR EUROPEAN UNION INSTITUTIONS?

Money is raised for the EU on customs duties and levies on goods entering the Union. These monies are forwarded to Brussels. A proportion of Value Added Tax (VAT) also goes to Brussels, as does some of the gross national product of each member state. In 1991 the EC budget was 55,000 billion ECUs (European Currency Units) – the equivalent of £38 billion. This represented 1% of the gross national product of the 12 member states.

ACTIVITY

Use the financial papers of a quality newspaper to find the current value of ECUs in pounds sterling.

HOW IS COMMUNITY LAW MADE?

Regulations must be enforced by the member states and have immediate effect. These regulations prevail over national laws. They are made by the Council of Ministers, or more rarely by the European Commission: see Figure 6.8.

An interesting example of these regulations are the Unfair Terms in Consumer Contracts Regulations which came into force in the UK in July 1995. These make it much more difficult for businesses such as banking, insurance, travel and telecommunications businesses to include 'small print' terms in their contracts which are unfair to consumers and customers: many such 'get out' clauses will now become illegal. For example, tour operators who have, in the past, put written clauses in their contracts which allow them to cancel or alter the tour more or less at will, with no greater obligation than to refund money paid in advance, may now have to pay compensation for the customer's cost of a similar holiday with another company, even if this is greater than the cost of the cancelled holiday (*Money Guardian*, 24 June 1995).

Another example, from the area of consumer protection and food safety, are the EU regulations concerning food labelling. Legislation has been enacted to ensure that there is a uniform system of labelling applied throughout the Community on food products. See the following extract.

THE PURPOSE OF FOOD LABELLING

The prime aims of the legislation are:

1 To inform and protect the consumer regarding 'any words, particulars, trade marks, brand names, pictorial matter or symbols relating to a foodstuff and placed on any packaging, document, notice, label, ring or collar accompanying or referring to such foodstuff'.
2 To ensure that the label does not mislead the consumer as to the nature, identity, properties, composition, quantity, durability, origin, or method of manufacture or production of the food product.
3 To ensure that the label does not attribute to the foodstuff effects or properties which it does not possess nor suggest that the foodstuff possesses special characteristics, when in fact all other similar foodstuffs possess such characteristics.

(Food Safety Advisory Centre 1995)

Directives apply to some or all member states but *national* governments can decide how to put them into effect. One such directive has recently been concerned with maternity pay. To meet EU standards, the UK has had to increase and simplify maternity payments.

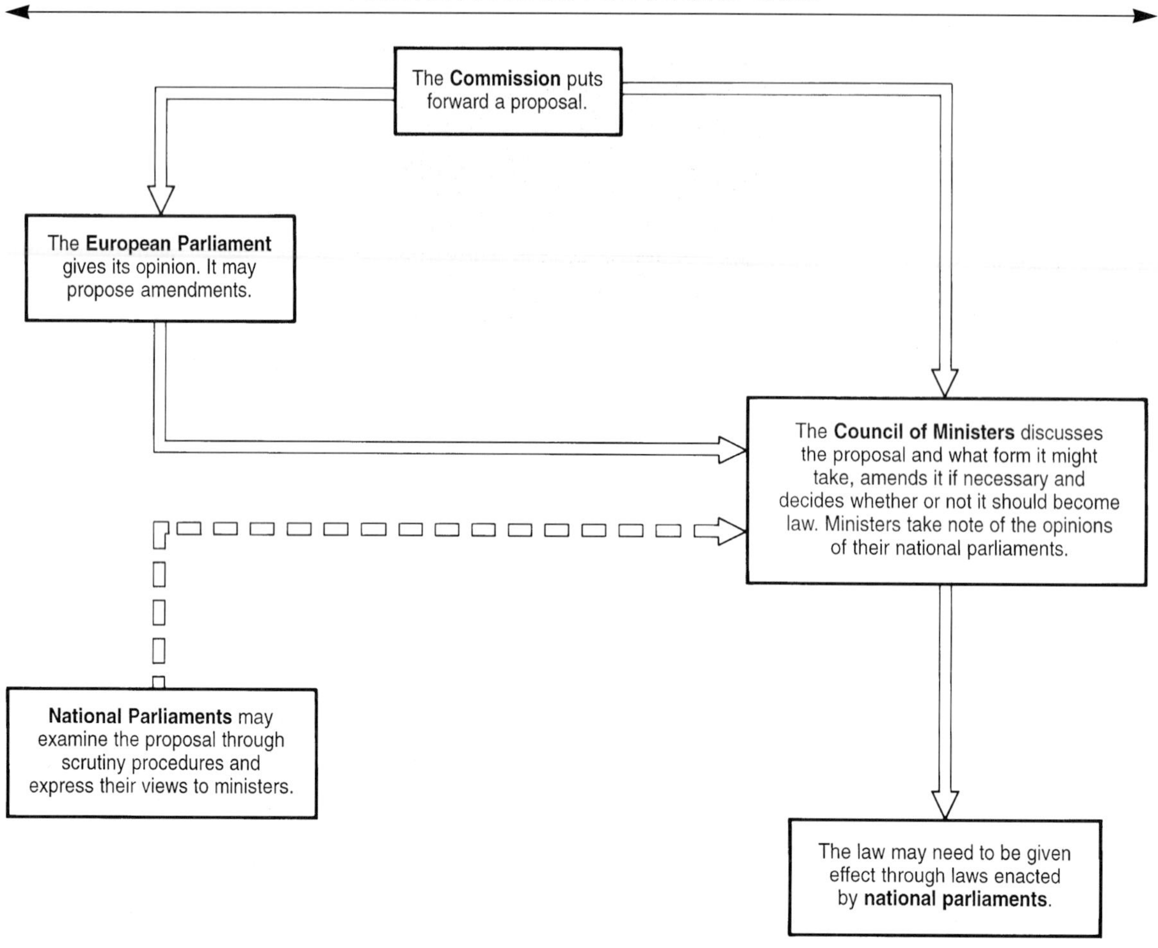

Figure 6.8 How Community law is made
Source: Britain in Europe, the Foreign and Commonwealth Office, 1992.

The government expects about 285,000 working women to benefit from the changes which will be in place by 16 October 1994.

Decisions apply to individual persons, corporations or member states, and are binding on them. They must be carried out as directed. These decisions are the result of the deliberations of the Council of Ministers.

Recommendations and *opinions* have no binding force, but represent the view of the Commission or the European Parliament.

ACTIVITY

Find further examples of how European regulations, directives, decisions, recommendations and opinions may be affecting the social, consumer and employment rights of people in the UK.

Social policy and the European Union

Why should the European Union have anything to do with social policy? How does this affect us, in the UK? To understand the answers to these questions, we must return to the central reasons for the creation of the EU (formerly the EC and the EEC). Figure 6.11 shows the two main elements of the founders' aims. Together, these elements were to be the basis for a single European market to allow:

- the removal of physical barriers to trade and movements between countries (e.g. customs posts/passport checks)
- the removal of technical and legal barriers restraining the free movement of goods and provision of services
- the reduction of fiscal disparities (e.g. taxes on alcohol and cigarettes)

To create a single economic region where goods, services, people and capital could move freely, and where national economies could grow strongly.
To create a political union.
To ensure peace in Europe.
To preserve democracy and to develop the integration and closeness of its peoples.

Figure 6.9 Reasons for the creation of the EU

- the freedom of people to work where they like; the mutual recognition of qualifications and the right of establishment and residence
- the removal of discriminatory and protective national public procurement and supply policies
- the freeing of all capital movement
- a legal and economic environment for the growth of economic activity and partnerships

With the move towards and final creation of this single European market in 1993 came a growing recognition among some member states that the measures put into place may be advantageous for some people but may have serious adverse consequences for others such as

- the unemployed
- people with disabilities
- the illiterate
- the homeless
- the very old
- the very young
- women

WHY MIGHT PROBLEMS OCCUR?

Two examples illustrate the way in which a potential gain for some in the EU might mean a potential loss for others.

1 The freedom of people to work where they like within Europe may result in workers in some areas feeling threatened by the potential loss of jobs in their communities and countries to workers from other countries.
2 The freedom for companies to set up businesses and employ workers from anywhere in Europe may mean that they will relocate their industries to areas of the EU where average wage levels are lower. Countries which give their workers the least protection in terms of working conditions and pay levels are therefore likely to be the most attractive to employers. Workers and union leaders in the richer 'north' of the EU fear 'social dumping' whereby the creation of a more competitive and integrated European market could widen existing disparities between the regions, polarising the labour market between the 'haves' and 'have-nots'.

THE SOCIAL CHARTER/SOCIAL ACTION PROGRAMME

In 1988, therefore, a new social dimension to the single European market began to be discussed in the EU. This included attention to:

- consumer protection
- workers' rights to fair wages
- adequate social protection
- freedom of association and collective bargaining
- the rights of the young, the disabled and elders
- safety in the workplace
- equal opportunities for men and women
- skills training
- health and care programmes
- environmental programmes
- famine relief

In 1989 11 member states (excluding the UK) signed the Social Charter. This was an expression of broad support for some of the above-mentioned aspects of social policy. This Charter was the foundation for the European Commission's 1990 Social Action Programme, which was initiated to put the principles of the Social Charter into effect.

The Social Action Programme had three objectives:

- to define, legally, the social rights of workers
- to give financial support to training and employment measures
- to encourage networks and partnerships of those involved in social policy in Europe, and to promote the exchange of information, experience, innovation and good practice and policies.

WHAT HAS THE SOCIAL ACTION PROGRAMME ACHIEVED?

1 There has been relatively little legislation arising out of this programme, but in the past few years, various EU directives have begun to create Community rights against sex discrimination, rights related to health and safety at work and rights protecting workers under labour law. Some of these rights may be enforced in national courts and in employment tribunals without the need to go to the European Court of Justice in Luxembourg.

2 The European Commission has used its European Social Fund, now known as the European Structural Fund, for training and employment measures. From 1989 to 1993 more than 21 billion ECUs were spent in this way.

3 Many of the programmes and projects arising from the Social Action Programme tried to identify and evaluate innovative action and to organise exchanges of experience in tackling long-term employment, local development, the integration of people with disabilities and specific health-research programmes such as cancer research.

In October 1994 the European Commission set up a new Community action programme on Aids and other communicable diseases which will run for five years and be funded to the tune of 50 million ECUs. A further budget of 30 million ECUs were given, in June 1995, to an education programme to encourage healthier lifestyles.

In 1995 the European Commission published a new three-year programme which will replace the Social Charter Action Programme. Among its proposals are:

- to focus on job creation
- to make further progress over the issue of parental leave
- to examine employee consultation practices in workplaces
- to establish a fourth equal opportunities action programme
- to write a Code of Practice for employing people with disabilities

ACTIVITY

A new programme in the field of education and vocational training will have begun in 1995, and will last for five years. This programme, the Leonardo Da Vinci Action Programme, may offer opportunities for students on GNVQ Health and Social Care courses (among others) to set up exchange programmes with similar students in other

European countries.

1 Contact the European Commission for more information on the programme.

2 Investigate the possibilities of work-experience placements in other European countries. (1996 is the European year for life-time education and training.)

The Maastricht Treaty was an attempt by the EU to *formalise* the inclusion of a social-policy dimension in the EU. The UK has refused to sign the 'Social Chapter' of this treaty. The first Directive passed, in September 1994, under the Social Agreement at Maastricht (to establish European Works Councils) will thus apply to all member states except the UK. The European Commission is now attempting to promote its social policies in other ways than through the treaty (e.g. in the White Paper discussed on p. 221). The Commission prepares the ground for future regulatory action and policies, setting standards to be adhered to in the member states.

National governments are most likely to support the social-policy dimension of the EU if the costs can be passed on to employers. If this dimension involves massive government expenditure or any significant redistribution of income and wealth, national governments will tend to resist the measures: if governments had to raise more taxes to pay for these measures, they would risk electoral unpopularity. Hence the purpose of social policy in the EU is still, at heart, to smooth the way for the implementation of the single market – to offset its less positive aspects.

The role of the Commission could be described as that of expanding the frontiers of the possible. Making use of its bureaucratic skills, building upon EC declarations, instituting social programme, setting up observatories and carrying out research projects, the Commission is continually preparing for the next opportunity to create new policies.

(Cram 1993)

The main aims of the *social dimension* in Europe can thus be summarised as:

- a desire for the fuller insertion into society of those groups within it who have become marginalised, e.g. the poor, people with disabilities, the unemployed, and the illiterate. Jacques Santer has identified poverty, unemployment and exclusion (from society) as the three great social challenges facing the EU
- a desire for *social cohesion* – for measures which would encourage social stability
- a desire for *common social rights*, especially in relation to fair wages, conditions of work, education and training, freedom from discrimination, consumer rights and health and care
- a desire for a *common European identity*, the reduction of national barriers and the promotion of mutual cooperation and understanding

Models of social policy and the welfare state in the European Union

The ways in which governments take action in health and social care, in housing, education and training, and in income support and employment change over time. Social policy is affected by:

- the political parties in power, and their ideas
- the ways both in which people are employed and in which wealth is created
- the status and roles of men and women, ethnic minorities and social class groupings
- the organisation of government and its response to problems of social control, order and integration
- pressure and interest groups

While each European country will have its

own unique history and political, social and economic culture, over the past 25 years there has been a great deal of interest in comparing the welfare states and social policies of European countries.

DID YOU KNOW? ...

In *Germany* the rights of parents in law are stronger than the rights of children, but there is great emphasis put upon intensive support for families with problems. In some areas of Germany, such families can be given up to 15 hours of support a week from psychologists or social workers.

In *France*, children have few rights in child-protection proceedings – parents come first – but there are 'children's judges' who work with the view that disadvantaged circumstances may be the reason for youth crime. Each children's judge has a team of educators who provide therapy for children at risk – and for their families too if necessary.

In *Denmark* the government guaranteed that every child will be entitled to a nursery place by the end of 1995.

Some attempts have been made to *classify* the social policies and welfare states of European countries into 'types' or 'models'. These comparisons have involved looking at:

- the benefits systems of the countries
- their political ideologies
- their health-care and family policies
- their economic systems and policies

The models in questions, explained briefly below, are most helpful for the ways in which they highlight differences and similarities between the countries. They do not, however, provide neat and tidy descriptions of all European countries and their welfare states. The pace and complexity of social change in Europe means that, at best, these models should only be used as reference points for further study.

THE SOCIAL DEMOCRATIC MODEL

Here, social policies will tend to be built on ideas of equality, cooperation and concern for others. Comprehensive welfare is provided from public funds, and high levels of taxation are common.

Until the 1990s, Sweden was a good example of a country with a welfare state based on this model. However, economic crises in the past few years have led to cuts in both taxation and public spending.

THE INSTITUTIONAL/ CORPORATIST SOCIAL MARKET MODEL

Here, social policies will tend to reflect a belief that the institutional provision of state aid for employment and income security should be complemented by help and support for individuals from corporations, businesses, trade unions and people's own families. There will be insurance-based benefits related to salary levels, so that pensions, unemployment benefit and other social insurance benefits will be closely earnings-related.

Germany has a welfare state which strongly reflects this model: the state interferes as little as possible in the workings of the market economy, and there is a strong emphasis upon individual and family responsibility for health and social care.

THE RESIDUAL MODEL

In this model of the welfare state, welfare policies only exist as a 'safety net' to catch those who have been unable to find assistance by any other means. The state plays virtually no role in providing welfare or in forming social policy, and it does not interfere in the market economy.

No European country as yet has moved wholesale towards this model, but many argue that the 'New Right' governments in countries such as the UK are attempting to move in this direction.

Social policies on employment and unemployment in the European Union

UNEMPLOYMENT IN THE EU, IN THE UK AND IN THE FEDERAL REPUBLIC OF GERMANY

In 1994 unemployment in the EU as a whole stood at around 17–18 million – approximately 10–11% of the population. More than half of the unemployed had been out of work for 12 months or more. While unemployment in the UK has dropped since 1993, the UK (with Italy) has the lowest long-term gain in employment of all the member states and the lowest gain in gross national product over the period 1989–94. A recent survey of Europe's most prosperous 117 cities found that the UK has only four cities (London, Norwich, Edinburgh and Brighton) in the top 50, while 15 are in the bottom 50 and 8 in the bottom 20 (Bennington and Taylor 1993).

In the 1970s, 1980s and early 1990s in the UK, the economy has suffered periods of recession or slump followed by brief periods of growth or boom. In the periods of slump people cannot afford to buy goods or services, so the demand for them falls and employers make more workers redundant or take on fewer new employees. Unemployment rises during these periods. Unemployment in the UK is measured by the number of people out of work and eligible to claim state benefit, and is, at the time of writing, around 2.7 million adults. It is falling slightly at the moment, as Figure 6.10 on p. 230 indicates.

In February 1994 Germany announced that the number of people out of work had risen above 4 million for the first time since 1933. This is partly a result of the reunification of East and West Germany in 1990.

Most research shows that unemployment tends to hit women harder than men through the EU countries: their unemployment rates are higher than those of men.

According to the International Social Attitudes Survey 1993 (reported in the *Guardian*, 1 December 1993), only about 4 in 10 of the British workforce felt happy in their work. More than most workers in the countries surveyed, they tend to feel insecure, find work stressful, fret over inadequate income, feel their work is not useful to society and then come home feeling exhausted.

A PROBLEM SHARED IS A PROBLEM HALVED?

What can member states of the EU such as the UK and the Federal Republic of Germany (FRG) do to tackle the problem of unemployment and achieve better conditions of work for people? The way in which each country will approach employment issues depends upon a number of factors, including:

- the specific nature of the problems in that particular country
- existing internal approaches towards social policy and the welfare state
- the general move towards the single European market and the problems that that creates for all European countries
- their approach to the social policy and social provisions of the EU

Each of these points will be considered briefly in relation to Germany and the UK.

The UK: key issues in employment and unemployment

- Unemployment stands at around three million
- British governments tend to believe that the recruitment, shedding and training of the labour force should be employer-led
- Employers in the UK frequently argue that there is a 'skills gap' – a shortage of skilled labour and an oversupply of unskilled labour
- Women's paid employment in the UK is growing. There are high levels of occupational segregation – i.e. women are concentrated in particular (usually low-paid and lower-status) occupations.

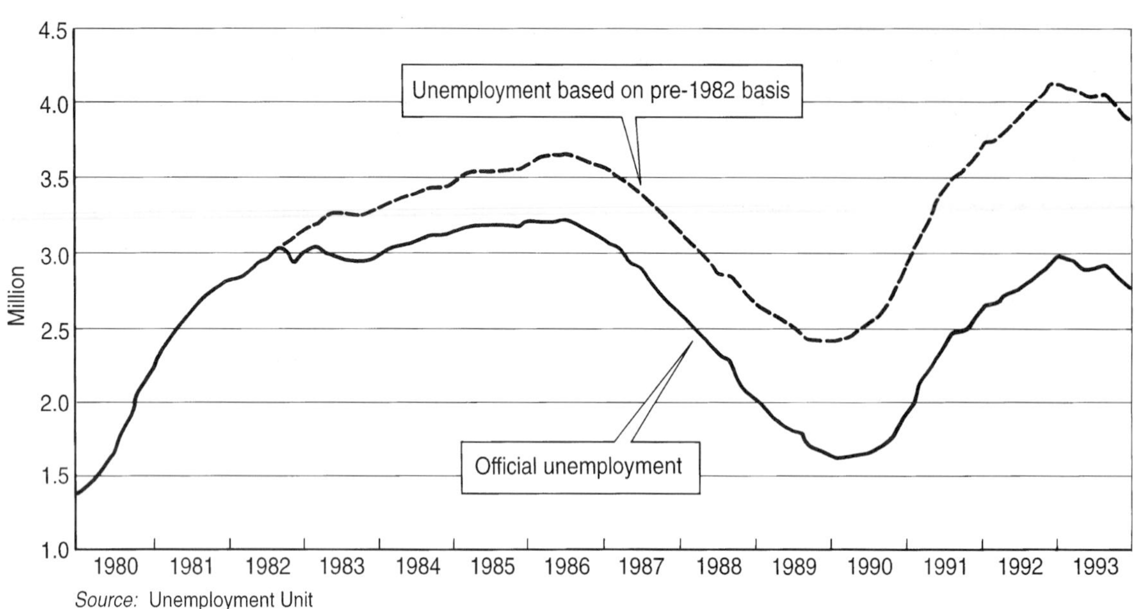

Figure 6.10 The number of unemployed in the UK
Source: The *Guardian*, 15 February 1994.

Women's earnings are still lower on average than men's

- In the UK, black workers are more likely than white workers to be in low-status, low-paid occupations, and to experience unemployment
- In 1988 the government removed income support for unemployed 16- and 17-year-olds
- The labour market in the UK is currently polarised into 'work-rich' and 'work-poor' households; 15% of working-age households in the UK have no earnings, and 55% have at least two earners. Those in permanent full-time work are enjoying rising 'real wages', while those unemployed are feeling the effects of a reduced relative value of the social-security benefits they receive
- Employees in the UK have the longest working week in the EU. Men in the UK work the longest of all, but the UK is the only member state where women work more than 40 hours a week on average (EC Briefing WE/3/95, 26 January 1995)
- Less than 50% of the working population in the UK has a full-time, long-term job with a traditional employment contract. One million people have more than one job. Part-time work has more than doubled in the last 15 years, and so has self-employment. Temporary employment and fixed-term contracts have significantly increased (*Guardian Careers*, 22 April 1995)

Germany: key issues in employment and unemployment

- Unemployment stands at around 4 million
- The short-term unemployed in Germany (if they have paid all national-insurance contributions) receive 68% of their previous earnings for up to a year. There are means-tested benefits for others at lower levels of pay. About 15–20% of the registered unemployed in Germany receive no social-security benefits from the state. These are usually married women, young people and migrant workers
- Germany views youth training schemes as one of its priorities
- Trade unions in Germany have struggled in particular for a shorter working week of 35 hours
- Women are discriminated against in social insurance and pension schemes because of their assumed dependent status in the household (on their husbands)

- The unemployment rate for women is significantly higher than for men. Women tend to be deployed as cheaper, more flexible substitutes for men in the labour force
- Settled 'foreign' workers in the FRG, originally actively recruited by Germany as *Gastarbeiterk* or 'guestworkers', now number about 4.5 million – around 7.5% of the total population. The largest group of these are of Turkish origin. These workers face institutional and racial discrimination in Germany; legislation passed in 1969 stated that German citizens must always be given preference over a 'foreigner' when a job vacancy is filled. There is no equivalent in Germany to the UK Race Relations Act. In 1990 a new immigration law in Germany was passed which may improve the legal right of abode for long-settled foreigners

SOCIAL POLICY IN THE UK

(For a fuller discussion of this topic, please refer back to p. 199.)

To understand the present position of the British government towards the social provisions of the EU, it is necessary to remind ourselves briefly of the current struggle between two ideologies or models of the welfare state.

Most writers agree that the UK, in the years immediately following the end of the Second World War, was characterised by a 'mixed economy of welfare' and a liberal-collectivist ethos in social policy-making. It had lower levels of welfare expenditure than many other European states but a more egalitarian ethos and more emphasis on the direct, public provision of services.

During the late 1970s and 1980s, advocates of this universalist approach to the welfare state found themselves in increasing opposition to the Conservative governments of the time which sought to dismantle some of the state provision of welfare, reducing welfare spending where they could and replacing it with a mixture of private, charitable and state provision in which the state becomes the regulator of privately provided welfare, controlling standards and encouraging the diversification of services – in essence, providing no more than a safety net for those in desperate circumstances lest it encourage dependence.

SOCIAL POLICY IN GERMANY

The Federal Republic of Germany came into being in 1949 with a strong written constitution called the Basic Law (*Grundgesetz*). In Germany, as in the UK, there have been two dominant approaches to, or models of, welfare:

- The idea of the welfare state (*Wohlfahrtsstadt*) is for some a negative idea, implying dependence and an interfering 'busy-body' state
- On the other hand, there is in the Basic Law the idea that the state should also have a 'general commitment to providing income and employment security . . . complemented by an emphasis on the obligations of private associations or groups (above all employers and trade unions), families and individuals to support themselves. There is no question of any commitment to equalising welfare outcomes, or even of an ambiguous welfare safety net' (Ginsberg 1992, p. 68)

This second approach is sometimes referred to as an *institutional* or *corporatist* model of welfare: a social-market-economy approach. There is an overwhelming emphasis here on individual and family self-help as social insurance, with direct state welfare as a last resort. Those not in employment have fewer and weaker rights. For example, there is an obligation in law for families to pay for the care of their elderly relatives if they are not providing it themselves.

PROBLEMS CREATED BY THE MOVE TOWARDS THE SINGLE EUROPEAN MARKET

The single European market aims to create a more flexible workforce in Europe, i.e. more people on temporary, fixed-term contracts, in part-time posts or self-employed occupations. This idea of flexibility is meant to help industries take on or shed staff according to their changing requirements. Job security, i.e. the protection of workers in employment against redundancy or dismissal, is thus weakened.

The single European market, in allowing companies to set up businesses and employ workers from anywhere in the EU, is encouraging the relocation and restructuring of industries – sometimes in poorer areas or regions of Europe where lower wages are the norm and workers can therefore be paid less. Workers and union leaders in the richer 'north' of the EU have, as already mentioned, feared that this 'social dumping' would increasingly occur, causing the twin problems of skill shortages and recruitment difficulties in some areas and the marginalisation of a pool of casual, low-paid workers in others. Women and black and ethnic-minority workers are particularly vulnerable to these pressures.

Women are affected because of:

- their caring and family responsibilities and the general lack of child-care provision; and they cannot always move around the EU for training
- the lack of recognition of women's qualifications
- their current structural position in the labour market
- their lesser involvement in trade unions, collective bargaining and decision-making processes in the workforce

Black, ethnic-minority and migrant workers are affected because:

- they already face a growing wave of racism/neo-Nazism within Europe, where, in a time of recession involving competition for jobs and housing, they become a scapegoat for people's fear and anger
- some member states, such as the UK, are attempting to 'strengthen their borders' against immigrants, refugees and asylum-seekers from the Third World and other parts of Europe. These people have in the past taken very low-skill, dangerous, unsocial or menial work. (Will black, ethnic-minority and migrant workers be increasingly forced into these occupations, further exacerbating their position?)

A preliminary study on the impact of 1992 [the single European market] on black and ethnic minority women in the UK has revealed that they may be particularly disadvantaged by the introduction of a single market. For example, they are disproportionately represented among 'atypical' employees (the national Homeworking Unit estimates that more than 50% of UK homeworkers are black and ethnic minority women), and are also disproportionately concentrated in the textile, electrical engineering and electronics industries, which are likely to be affected by relocation and changing markets.

(Bennington and Taylor 1993, p. 124)

CURRENT EU SOCIAL POLICY ON EMPLOYMENT ISSUES

Current EU proposals on employment and unemployment are:

- to strengthen equal-opportunities, sex-discrimination and equal-pay legislation by encouraging member states to take up job classification and evaluation schemes as a basis for a code of practice in implementing equal pay for work of equal value
- to encourage governments to provide financial and training assistance to workers worst affected by industrial restructuring
- work-sharing schemes
- new training systems
- encouraging small businesses and self-employment
- to produce an annual report on 'employment in Europe'
- to try to implement specific programmes in

areas of the EU, for example a Community programme in favour of the long-term unemployed which was launched in 1987
- to commit EU member states to ensuring the right of every worker to an equitable wage (the EU has not yet called for a minimum wage), regardless of sex, race, religion, ethnic origin or nationality
- to give workers a statutory right to representation when jobs are threatened (by a ruling of the European Court of Justice, March 1994): the British government may now have to introduce legislation to re-establish collective bargaining in industries and services where employers have ceased to recognise unions and put staff on personal contracts; this may aid both workers in the health service and local authorities who had to accept pay cuts and worse conditions of service as a result of the privatisation and contracting-out of jobs

EQUAL OPPORTUNITIES FOR MEN AND WOMEN

Over half the people in the European Union are women, and more women than ever before are involved in paid work. However, most women are still in lower-paid jobs and are underrepresented in many sectors and levels of industry, the professions and public service. They do not, as yet, play an equal role with men in political decision-making.

What social policies has the European Union supported in this area?

1. Article 119 of the 1957 Treaty of Rome committed member states to the principles of 'equal pay for equal work' between men and women.
2. In 1976 European Community directives were established on equal treatment for men and women in access to employment, training, promotion and working conditions.
3. In 1992 rights to maternity leave and pay, and a guarantee of adequate health and safety at work for pregnant women and nursing mothers were agreed.
4. Ministers have also agreed other recommendations and resolutions, including ones concerning positive action, vocational training, child care, combating unemployment, equal opportunities in schools and sexual harassment at work.
5. There have been three Action Programmes on equal opportunities launched by the European Commission. A fourth Equality Action Programme will come into force in January 1996, and will run until the year 2000. This will focus on measures to 'de-segregate' the labour market, to establish a code of practice on equal pay and to try to ensure that women are treated equally in the social-security systems of the member countries.

There is plenty of published material for a fuller study of the role of the European Union in the promotion of equal opportunities. The Equal Opportunities Commission (see the 'Useful Addresses' section at the end of the chapter) and the European Commission both publish useful guides. See 'References and Resources' at the end of this chapter for more information.

THE CURRENT GERMAN GOVERNMENT AND EU SOCIAL POLICY

The German government is a signatory to the Social Charter and the Social Chapter of the Maastricht Treaty. However, this does not mean that it accepts all EU proposals; in early 1994, for example, it expressed unease about a Commission policy document on immigration and asylum which proposed easier access to citizenship for entrants to EU states.

THE CURRENT BRITISH GOVERNMENT AND EU SOCIAL POLICY

Among Conservative MPs there are two main responses to the EU and its social policy. Those who came to be known as the 'Tory rebels' oppose all dealings and involvement with the EU and see the existence of the Union as a threat to national sovereignty. Pro-European Conservatives generally agree that the EU should not be much concerned with social policy. They argue that these decisions should be decided *nationally*, not on a European level. They believe that, where possible, employers and employees should settle employment conditions themselves, without regulation from parliament. Excessive regulation from the EU, they argue, would undermine the competitiveness of British industries. The British governments objected to many aspects of the proposals of the 1990 Social Action Programme, such as worker participation in company management, the concept of 'decent' wages and a minimum income for the poor. It is not a signatory to the Social Chapter of the Maastricht Treaty.

ACTIVITY

Choose two member states of the EU. (It would make sense to choose the UK as one of these because of the greater availability of information.) Then choose a small number (two or three) of health or social care (or both) occupations upon which to focus, e.g.

- nursing
- teaching
- social work
- occupational therapy
- speech therapy
- physiotherapy

Use interviews with workers and secondary sources such as books, newspapers, journals, trade-union literature, careers-advice literature etc. to answer the following questions concerning employment in your two chosen countries in the occupational areas you have chosen:

- What routes to training currently exist for these occupations?
- Is there competition for jobs in these occupations?
- Do all those who train get jobs?
- What are the current levels of pay for different grades of work in these occupations?
- What kinds of contract can workers be employed on (e.g. 'flexible', part-time, job-share, full time)?
- Can workers in these occupations usually opt for job-sharing contracts if they want to?
- Are there shortages of people to train in these occupations? Why? Or why *not*?
- What occupational benefits (national insurance, pensions, maternity, paternity, sick-pay, childcare/crêche facilities, private health insurance etc.) or other subsidies are available to people in these occupations?
- Are these occupations dominated by men or women, white or ethnic-minority workers? Which categories of worker are most likely to hold senior positions in these occupations?
- Is self-employment an option in these occupations?
- What proportions of workers are employed by the state, by private organisations and by charities and voluntary organisations in these areas?
- What are the views of people in these occupations towards their working conditions, pay and occupational status?
- To what extent do workers in these occupations take part in the decision-making and management processes in their workplaces?
- What trade unions exist to represent the views of workers in these occupations?

Some of these questions will be easier to answer than others. Possible sources of information might be:

- the relevant government ministries in the chosen countries, e.g. the Danish Ministry of Labour, the Danish Ministry for Social Affairs, the French Ministry of Labour, Employment and Vocational

Training, the Greek Ministry of Labour
- the modern-languages department in your school or college, which may be able to advise you about contacts or people to write to for more information in your chosen country

The role of a European Development Officer in a social services department

John Mitchell, European Development Officer for Kent Social Services Department (SSD), kindly agreed to respond to a short questionnaire for the purposes of this book. the questions put to him, and his responses, are printed below.

1 *Why do Kent Social Services employ a European Development Officer?*
My post is based on five policy objectives which were adopted by the Council in March 1992, following a research study into the implications of greater European integration for the Social Services Department. These are to:
(i) take advantage of European Union funding programmes to improve our services;
(ii) learn from social-services practice and provision in other countries in order to enhance our own;
(iii) identify opportunities to share our expertise with other countries;
(iv) ensure the department complies with EU regulations which affect us as a purchaser and provider of services, and as an employer, and to ensure we are involved in and influencing the development of social policy in Europe;
(v) prepare for the greater mobility of people in Europe and for the particular pressures on Kent as part of a transfrontier region.

2 *Which other SSDs currently employ a European Development Officer?*
Very few SSDs employ an officer specifically to develop 'European work'. Kent was, I believe, the first, and Hampshire has recently followed suit. However, a growing number of departments are becoming aware of the issues and have developed an operational function (e.g. giving lead responsibility to an existing social-services manager or ensuring that a corporate European Officer or team takes social services' interests into account alongside the other activities of the local authority). Several of the larger voluntary-sector organisations in the social care field have their own European Officer or section (e.g. Help the Aged, Age Concern, the Royal National Institute for Deaf People), and historically the voluntary sector has had stronger representatives at European level than statutory social care agencies.

3 *How can British health and social care organisations use EU funds?*
A small but increasing proportion of the European Community budget is allocated to 'social' policy objectives. These have a strong (but not exclusive) economic emphasis and are primarily concerned with tackling unemployment, stimulating economic development and getting people into the labour market. They also give rise to funding programmes, some of which are relevant to social care agencies. Kent Social Services has, for example, obtained European funds for:
- new services which adopt innovative approaches in the training, vocational guidance and employment of people with disabilities or mental health problems
- exchanging our knowledge and experience in various fields with social care agencies in other countries, e.g. child care and child protection (Romania), the management and delivery of social services (the Baltic states, the Czech Republic), work with

young offenders (France, Germany and Spain), care of elderly people (Holland, France, Ireland) and care and employment/training for people with severe disabilities (Holland, Portugal, Italy, East Germany, Ireland)

- bringing the benefits of greater European integration to the users of our services, e.g. involving elderly and disabled people in exchanges with other countries
- developing our strategic links with social services in northern France and in other areas/countries
- participating in European networks of organisations which are sharing good practice and influencing policy development at an international level

A number of new funds are coming up for which we will be making applications, e.g. to help fund new services for care leavers and other disadvantaged young people, to tackle poverty and to help people who misuse drugs, as well as to *prevent* drug use. The EC is becoming more involved in the health care field, and funds are or will become available for such activities as health promotion, combating cancer (including cancer research, prevention and treatment), Aids-related research and services and tackling drug dependency and abuse.

4 *Which EU regulations and directives do you think are having the most influence on social policy in the UK, particularly in relation to social work?*

A few EU regulations/directives are relevant to social work. One is the directive (or directives) relating to the mutual recognition of professional qualifications between the member states. This has resulted in social workers in several countries (the UK is not currently included as it does not meet the minimum standards for automatic recognition) having the freedom to move and practise throughout the union.

Several directives or European Court rulings have an influence on social-services organisations as purchasers of service and as major employers. For example, public purchasing directives, which are part of EU policies to stimulate free trade and competition between the member states, require local authorities to put larger contracts, for some of the services they wish to purchase form outside their organisations, out to tender on a European level. Failure to comply with these directives has resulted in some public authorities in the EU being taken to court by contractors who feel they have been unfairly excluded, with the result of losing time and money, and a great deal of hassle.

Several rulings and directives do affect or could affect us as an employer, e.g. directives on health and safety at work and recent European Court of Justice rulings on the employment rights of part-time workers.

5 *Can you give a good example of where Kent SSD is learning from innovative or good practice in Europe (and vice versa) in the delivery of social services?*

Kent Social Services is learning from, for example:

- 'Snoezelen', a Dutch model of care for people with learning disabilities, which uses sensory environments to provide appropriate stimulation and leisure, and to moderate challenging behaviour
- 'Hospital at Home', an innovative French approach to providing integrated health and social care services to ill people at home, as an alternative to in-hospital care
- user involvement in services for people with disabilities and mental health problems in Italy
- French approaches to prevention in child care and juvenile justice

We are sharing our experience and practice with a number of other countries, for example:

- Our counterparts in northern France have learned from our procedures and practice in developing their child-protection system

- Social-services organisations in the Scandinavian countries have looked closely at how we commission services from the independent sector
- Our practice in care management for elderly and disabled people is being studied closely by several other countries
- We are sharing our practice in residential care and family placement for children and adults with partners in France, Holland and Germany

6 *What directives and regulations would you particularly like to see the EU adopt in relation to social policy?* The nature of decision-making in the EU institutions means that radical policy developments are unlikely to suddenly emerge, although there is an incremental growth in EU social policy, which has been given fresh impetus by the Maastricht Treaty and a subsequent White Paper. The thrust of this policy is that increasing the competitiveness of the Union should not be achieved at the expense of social protection, and that particular effort will be needed to facilitate the social and economic integration of disadvantaged groups.

Personally, I would like to see policy objectives adopted at the European level which are concerned with

- facilitating exchanges of good practice and experience in a wide range of health and social care services between member states
- improving social and economic opportunities for disadvantaged groups (e.g. young people and families in need, people with disabilities or mental health problems, elderly people)
- encouraging greater emphasis on the prevention of poor-health and social problems
- facilitating both users' access to health and social care and social security where people in need travel between countries, and cooperation between services. This could be through funding programmes which support innovative approaches and from which independent and statutory health and social care agencies could benefit

Although much of EU social policy has until now focused on employment and the labour market, there is some evidence of a shift into areas of more direct relevance to the delivery of health and social services. The forthcoming Action Programmes for elderly people and on combating drug misuse are examples of this.

A number of national organisations and European networks in the social welfare field are hoping that the 1996 Intergovernmental Conference, which will review the Maastricht Treaty, will be an opportunity for greater European involvement in social policy. For example, one group of organisations is lobbying for a Treaty obligation on member governments in the EU to consider the rights of, and impact on, children when they make policies.

It is important to remember that Europe is not only about the European Union. Other institutions, like the Council of Europe and numerous European networks, are increasingly involved in issues affecting social services. Many social care organisations are, like Kent Social Services, forging their own links with their counterparts abroad, quite independently of the EU framework.

REFERENCES AND RESOURCES

Abbott, P. and Wallace, C. (1990), *An Introduction to Sociology: Feminist Perspectives*, London: Routledge.

Bennington, J. and Taylor, M. (1993), 'Changes and challenges facing the UK welfare state', *Policy and Politics*, vol. 21, no. 2.

Brendon, V. (1994), *The Age of Reform 1820–1850*, London: Hodder & Stoughton.

Carr, E.H. (1977), *What is History?*, Middlesex: Penguin.

Clarke, J. (ed) (1993), *A Crisis in Care: Challenges to Social Work*, London: Sage.
Commission of the European Communities (1993a), *European Social Policy: Options for the Union*, Green Paper, 17 November, Brussels: European Commission. (See also White Paper 1995.)
Commission of the European Communities (1993b), *Sources of European Community Funding*, London: European Commission UK Office.
Conservatives in the European Parliament (1993), *Older People in the European Community*, European Conservative Brief No. 1, London: Conservative Central Office.
Cootes, R.J. (1966), *The Making of the Welfare State*, Harlow: Longman Group.
Child Poverty Action Group (CPAG) (1994a), *National Welfare Benefits Handbook*, 24th edn, 1994/5, London: Child Poverty Action Group.
CPAG (1994b), *Rights Guide to Non-means-tested Benefits*, 17th edn, 1944/5, London: Child Poverty Action Group.
CPAG (1994c), *Child Support Handbook*, 2nd edn, 1994/5, London: Child Poverty Action Group.
Cram, L. (1993), 'Calling the tune without paying the piper? Social policy regulation; the role of the Commission in European Community social policy', *Policy and Politics*, vol. 21, no. 2, pp. 135–46.
Crowther, A. (1988), *British Social Policy 1914–1939*, London: Macmillan.
Crowther, M.A. (1981), *The Workhouse System 1834–1929 – the History of an English Social Institution*, London: Methuen.
Department of Social Security, *Facts and Figures 1994: Social Security*, London: HMSO.
Dunleavy, P. et al. (eds) (1993), *Developments in British Politics*, London: Macmillan.
EUROSTAT (1990), *Inequality and Poverty in Europe 1980–1985*, Rapid Reports: Population and Social Condition, 1990, no. 7.
Francatelli, C.E. (1852), *A Plain Cookery Book for the Working Classes*, London: Routledge (new edn, 1981).
Foreign and Commonwealth Office (FCO) (1992), *Britain in Europe*, London: HMSO.
Ginsberg, N. (1992), *Divisions of Welfare: a Critical Introduction to Comparative Social Policy*, London: Sage.
Ham, C. (1992), *Health Policy in Britain: the Politics and Organization of the National Health Service*, London: Macmillan.
House of Commons, *How Laws are Made*, House of Commons Education Sheets.
Jones, B. et al. (1994), *Politics UK*, 2nd edn, London: Harvester Wheatsheaf.
Lowe, R. (1993), *The Welfare State in Britain Since 1945*, London: Macmillan.
Moore, S. (1993), *Social Welfare Alive!* Cheltenham: Stanley Thornes.
Oppenheim, C. (1993), *Poverty: the Facts*, London: Child Poverty Action Group.
Outram, S. (1989), *Social Policy*, Sociology in Focus series, Harlow: Longman.
Palmer, R. (ed) 1974, *A Touch on the Times – Songs of Social Change 1770–1914*, Middlesex: Penguin.
Sharp, P. and Dunford, J. (1990), *The Education System in England and Wales*, Harlow: Longman.
Social Services Year Book (1993/4), Harlow: Longman Community Information.
Stewart, J. (1995), 'Accountability and empowerment in welfare services', in Gladstone, D. (ed), *British Social Welfare Past, Present and Future*, London: UCL Press.
Walmsley, J. et al. (1993), *Health, Welfare and Practice: Reflecting on Roles and Relationships*, London: Sage.
Williams, F. (1989), *Social Policy: a Critical Introduction*, Cambridge: Policy Press.

There is a steadily growing wealth of literature about services and practice in other European countries. If you are looking for books which provide a general round-up of provision in the EU, the following may be very useful (these references were provided by John Mitchell):

- Munday, (ed) (1993), *European Social Services*, 2nd edn, University of Kent. (This provides useful overviews of the policies, organisational framework and main provisions in each EU member state, with chapters written by relevant professionals from each country)

- Hill, M. (ed) (1991), *Social Work and the European Community*, London: Jessica Kingsley. (More comparative in nature, this book highlights different approaches between countries in services for different client groups, e.g. elderly people, children at risk, etc.)
- Cannan, C. et al. (1992), *Social Work and Europe*, BASW practice series. (This also looks at a number of countries, and includes an interesting analysis of European Union action in the social field, and of the role of social workers in different countries and settings)
- Cooper, A., Heatherington, R., Baistow, K., Pitts, J. and Spriggs, A. (1995), *Positive Child Protection: a View From Abroad*, Russell House Publishing. (One of the best comparative studies I have seen, this looks at the French and English child-protection systems and considers how the French experience provides a model for the development of practice in England in the light of the Children Act 1989 and the messages of subsequent research)
- Munday, B. (ed) (1993), *European Social Work Curriculum Material*, University of Kent/CCETSW. (A guide to literature published in English about social work in Europe)
- *Social Work in Europe Journal*. Recently launched by Russell House Publishing, subscription rates £20 for individuals and £50 for organisations, this journal promises 'news and views of relevant European policy, theory and practice', and I think this will be a useful and interesting source of material

USEFUL ADDRESSES

Child Poverty Group
1–5 Bath Street
London EC1V 9PY

Commission of the European Communities
8 Storey's Gate
London SW1P 3AT
Tel.: 0171 973 1992

Conservatives in the European Parliament
2 Queen Anne's Gate
London SW1H 9AA
Tel.: 0171 222 1720

Equal Opportunities Commission
Overseas House
Quay Street
Manchester M3 3HN
Tel.: 0161 833 9244

European Parliament UK Office
2 Queen Anne's Gate
London SW1H 9AA
Tel.: 0171 222 0411

European Parliamentary Labour Party
2 Queen Anne's Gate
London SW1H 9AA
Tel.: 0171 222 1719

Department of Employment
Caxton House
Tothill Street
London SW1H 9NE
Tel.: 0171 273 3000

The European Unit
Equal Opportunities Commission (EOC)
Overseas House
Quay Street
Manchester M3 3HN
Tel.: 0161 833 9244

National Youth Agency
17–23 Albion Street
Leicester LE1 6GD
Tel.: 0116 2471 200

7

SOCIAL CHANGE AND WELFARE PROVISION

INTRODUCTION

The first section of this chapter is intended to enable students to develop the critical and analytical skills to understand changes in the structure of the population, the consequences of social change and how social behaviour is influenced. Students are strongly advised to read this chapter in association with Chapter 6. They may also find it useful to consult more mainstream sociology texts for further explanations of key sociological ideas used here. Some are recommended in the 'References and Resources' section at the end of the chapter.

There is no attempt in this chapter to review the entire literature on all current social problems. The emphasis is rather on outlining the social and demographic changes which the UK is undergoing and enabling students to use their research skills to conduct further investigations of their own.

HOW AND WHY DO SOCIETIES CHANGE?

All people experience change in their lives. Becoming an adult, leaving school, starting or losing a job, beginning or ending a relationship – all these events in our lives involve change. These sequences of changes form the unique patterns of our lives and life-histories. Yet most of us will also have heard people talking about how 'society', 'the world' or 'the community around them' has altered. The implication here is that some aspect of the society or community in which they live has changed in such a way that it has affected them and others. This leads us to ask questions about how people's lives shape and are shaped by the immensely complex sets of relationships between the people around them to which we give the name 'society'. How and why do significant changes, that is, ones that affect many people at a time, occur in societies, in the organisations where we learn, work or play, and in the countless smaller groupings of people?

ACTIVITY

Interview someone at least 20 years older than yourself. Ask them to describe the ways in which they think society or their community has changed since they were a child. What changes do they think have been significant and why?

Ask them if they think that the changes they have described have affected their lives in any way. Why do they think that these changes have occurred in society?

It might also be interesting to ask your interviewee if they think there are any aspects of society which have not significantly changed in their lifetime, i.e. have remained relatively stable and continuous. Compare the results of your interview with interviews conducted by others in your class. Are there particular changes that are mentioned by *many* of the interviewees? What were these?

What changes do you think have occurred in society or in the community around you since you were a child? Write a short essay, asking yourself the same questions as you asked your interviewee above. In small groups, read and discuss each other's essays. What common areas of change did people in your group mention?

THE PRINCIPAL FEATURES OF SOCIAL CHANGE

All social change is important, whether it affects the lives of a few people or many. However, we might also be interested in why certain features of our society seem to show very little change – why they persist as features of that society. For example, we might ask:

- In what ways has the experience of poverty changed for people in the UK?
- Why is there still poverty in the UK?

We may also ask whether it is possible to distinguish between small and relatively minor changes in societies (such as, say, the introduction and use of new technology such as fax machines) and more key, core or fundamental changes, such as a change in the government or a war. We would need to ask what these more important changes would be and whether it is possible to categorise them around certain themes such as

- economic changes
- political changes
- social and cultural changes
- environmental changes

It may be possible, too, that a small number of changes in some parts of society will have greater consequences than a great many changes in other parts. Is there likely to be any change in society which is so fundamental that it causes change in every other part, like the ripples of a pond caused by a stone being thrown into the centre? In many cases, changes will affect some parts of society but not others – at least not directly.

There is considerable debate about what the causes and effects of social change are. Are we a healthier nation than we were a 100 years ago, for example? If so, is this due to the advances of medical science and better forms of treatment, or is it primarily due to improvements in our diet, in the sanitation of cities and in our general environment? Tackling such enormous questions as these has led to the production of competing theories among social scientists. Some have tried to provide evidence for their theories of such large-scale changes, while others have tended to concentrate on investigating social change through studies of smaller sections of society.

While we do not suggest that any of the following examples should be seen as more important than any other, there *are* some features of societies which can be seen as having the potential, at least, to cause significant social change, and these key features will be considered briefly.

Urbanisation and industrialisation

ACTIVITY

If you live in, or visit frequently, a town or city, ask yourself the following questions:

- What changes have you noticed in this town or city since your first association with it?
- Has it grown?
- Has the town or city centre changed?
- What new roads, buildings or housing have been constructed?
- Is there more or less traffic?
- Is it easier or more difficult to get around this town or city?
- Are there richer or poorer areas of the town or city?

- Are there new, out-of-town shopping centres or leisure facilities?
- What cultural and social events tend to bring people together in this town or city?
- What industries or businesses or services provide the most employment?
- What do you like or dislike about the way in which this town or city is changing?

Urbanisation refers to the development of towns and cities. People interested in urban studies ask the questions listed in the Activity above and many more about the ways in which life for people in towns and cities is changing. In the UK, the first set of urban changes involved the movement of people and jobs from the countryside to towns and cities as the industrial city grew out of the economic and social revolutions of the seventeenth and eighteenth centuries. The agricultural revolution pushed small farmers off the land and created the surplus of food necessary to feed the people who had moved to the new towns. The Industrial Revolution pulled these workers into new towns with the promise of jobs, better wages and new freedoms.

The transport revolution of the nineteenth century made it easier for people and goods to move quickly around the country. The population explosion of the nineteenth century then provided the markets for the new goods and services being produced. By 1901, 77% of the British population was living in towns and cities (adapted from Slattery 1989).

A second set of more recent urban changes has involved a movement out of cities to smaller towns, the suburbs, commuter villages and tourist and retirement centres. Cahill (1994) suggests that 'the major recent population movement has been out of cities towards the suburbs . . . and now increasingly to the countryside . . . many small towns greatly increased their population in the 1980s while the older urban areas recorded a net decrease in population.' This movement has in part been prompted by the greater mobility that car ownership gives; but this in turn has caused greater problems for those *without* cars. The easy use of facilities such as schools, hospitals and shopping centres relies increasingly on car ownership while inner-city urban areas decline.

ACTIVITY

These changes have an enormous number of implications for welfare-service provision. Among the issues which you may wish to research in more detail are the following:

- In towns and cities, who has the power and the finance to influence the development of the environment and the creation of jobs? Who decides what buildings shall be constructed? What will they be used for? Who will use them? How much influence do local people have over these decisions?
- How is the quality of people's lives affected by the urban environment? What services have to be provided to ameliorate the consequences of living in run-down, poorly served areas of towns and cities where there may be high rates of crime, vandalism, divorce, suicide, truancy, drug-taking, unemployment and overcrowded housing?
- When the urban environment is being planned and built, what account is taken of the needs of people for access to that environment? What measures could ensure safe and convenient access to public transport, public buildings, shops and work and leisure facilities for people with disabilities, people with young children, women alone and the elderly?

'Miss, I'm finding it hard to concentrate with the rats nibbling at my books'

Figure 7.1 Speaking out on poor-quality facilities in education!
Source: Cashtoons by Stan Eales (1992), Grub Street, London.

ACTIVITY

1 Do you agree that the processes of urban change are one of the most important features of peoples' lives in the UK today? Why, or why *not*?

2 How are the lives of people living in rural areas affected by changes in towns and cities?

3 Invite a speaker from a local history group to talk to your class about the ways in which urbanisation and industrialisation have, since the early nineteenth century, changed the area in which you live or study.

The economic organisation of societies

Western industrial societies such as the UK are capitalist societies. That is, the way goods or services are produced is geared towards the accumulation of wealth and profit – 'capital' – from the sale of those goods or services. In theory, that wealth is then used to expand production, make more things and, in doing so, employ more people. In a capitalist system of production, people do not work to produce all or most of what they need for themselves. Instead, they work for others to produce things which they may then buy with the wages earned from their work. Those people who own or control the means to produce things such as land, factories, skills and information, and who are successful in doing so, are often described as 'wealth producers' and in general enjoy the greatest wealth, power, income and status in capitalist societies.

The wealth of capitalist societies is thus measured by what it can produce. People working in health and welfare services rarely produce goods for sale, and the services they provide (unless they work in the private sector) are not generally bought directly by the people who use them but are paid for through taxation.

The ability of wealth producers to accumulate wealth and make profits is a driving force in social change in societies such as the UK. Put simply, recessions and slumps occur when the costs of producing goods for sale exceed the profit which can be made from that sale, or when the demand for certain goods falls. When this happens wealth producers may make their employees redundant, thus adding to the numbers of unemployed people in society.

People who are unemployed pay fewer or no taxes, thus reducing the total amount of money that the government can collect to spend on services such as health and welfare. At the same time, the government's 'bill' in social-security payments goes up. Such economic pressures can thus 'drive' governments in capitalist societies to attempt to reduce the amount they spend on health and welfare services. There is the further problem that the existence in society of large numbers of people with little money to spend reduces the demand for the goods and services produced by the wealth creators.

ACTIVITY

If possible, arrange an interview with owners or managers of private businesses or industries in your area (or invite one or two into your class to participate in a discussion). You do not have to choose people from health and care services, but if you do wish to focus on this area you could try:

- managers of NHS trusts
- owners/managers of private, residential nursing homes or nurseries
- private dentists
- private firms making aids for people with disabilities
- firms such as Securicor who provide services within the criminal-justice system

Among questions you might wish to explore with your interviewees are:

1 How important do your interviewees think that the economic organisation of society is to peoples' lives?

2 Do they approve of capitalist systems of production?

3 Do they see any alternatives to capitalism?

4 How has being a 'wealth producer' changed their lives?

5 Would they like to see any changes to the way we organise our society economically?

6 Do they approve of the 'privatisation' of health and welfare services? How do they think that this trend is affecting people in the UK today?

SOCIOLOGICAL PERSPECTIVES RELATING TO SOCIAL CHANGE

Explaining what social changes might have occurred, why they happened and what possible effects they may be having on people's lives is the task social scientists have set themselves. Sociologists, economists and political scientists have all been interested in these questions. However, as you may have found when you compared interviews in the Activity on page 000, people may have very different explanations for why the same things have changed. For example, many people may believe that 'there is much more crime nowadays'. However, one person may attribute this to children not being taught to respect authority and know the difference between 'right' and 'wrong', while another might suggest that crime is linked with rising levels of unemployment. Who is right?

Social scientists have also developed differing explanations for aspects of social change. These are based either on their particular view of 'society' or on evidence from research, or on a mixture of both. In reading about these theories of the causes of social change in the following sections, you will find it interesting to consider whether you or the person you interviewed in the Activity on page 240 have been influenced, consciously or unconsciously, by these theories.

Evolutionary theories

Based on the idea that societies change slowly over time, these ideas suggest that:

- over time, societies become increasingly complex in their structure and size, involving a greater variety of institutions and organisations. Just as more complex organisms in the biological world have a greater capacity than simpler ones to adapt to, and survive in, their environments, so the more complex a society is, the greater its chances of surviving
- like biological organisms, human societies compete for survival, and those which survive can be said to have made the greatest social progress. In the late nineteenth century and early twentieth century, a version of this theory called Social Darwinism (after the writings of Charles Darwin on evolution) claimed that Western societies had proved themselves to be 'superior' because they had dominated much of the rest of the world. This view has since been greatly criticised for its racist and Eurocentric associations
- each succeeding type of society in the gradual process of change is more effective in adapting to its environment than previous, simpler types

Structural–functionalist theories

Sociologists such as Talcott Parsons have suggested that the process of social change involves the progressive differentiation of social institutions, as societies develop from the simple to the more complex in their systems and structures. What is meant here is that areas of social life that were once interwoven become separate from each other. For example, before the beginning of the twentieth century in the UK, 'education' for most people was not carried out in separate institutions called schools: it was gained through experience in the family and the community, and through work. In the twentieth century it is more closely associated with the formal separate institutions of schools, colleges and universities.

This process of differentiation can be traced through the developments societies make in what Parsons called *evolutionary universals* – essential aspects of human society that help ensure its survival. Four such evolutionary universals are:

- communication and language
- religion
- kinship
- technology

Simpler societies will have structures where these universals are not organised and experienced separately from each other by the people involved. For example, religion may be an aspect of *family* and *community* life, and there may be no separate institutions, such as churches, with their own organisational hierarchies. More complex, industrial societies, according to Parsons, are more likely to survive because they have developed separate economic, political, educational, legal and religious systems; and communication is efficiently organised through the media.

Separating out areas of society in this way helps to ensure that systems for meeting people's physical needs, for setting common goals, for passing on agreed values, ideas and beliefs, and for avoiding damaging conflict between people are organised efficiently.

In this model of society, social change occurs when changes and developments in one institutional area such as 'the family' or 'the legal system' produce knock-on effects and changes in another. Thus, social change is seen as a gradual process.

Structural conflict theories

The best-known example of this type of theory is to be found in the writings of Karl Marx. Marx argued that the most basic survival needs of human beings for shelter, food and clothing are what determine their relationships with one another. The ways in which people attempt to use their physical and material world to provide for those needs can be called the *economic infrastructure* of society. An economic infrastructure could be the process of hunting and gathering; it could be domestic agriculture; it could be capitalism. Other aspects of societies – their political, legal and cultural institutions – arise out of this economic infrastructure and reflect its organisation. Thus, for hunter-gatherers, their religion and cultural beliefs will be closely associated with the ways in which they ensure their physical survival, whereas for people living in a capitalist society, ideas and beliefs are likely to support that particular way of organising the production of goods.

Marx suggested that social change 'can be understood through the ways in which, in developing more sophisticated systems of production, human beings progressively come to control the material world and subordinate it to their purposes' (Giddens 1989, p. 655). This process of control invariably involves clashes, tensions and struggles between groups of people for land, territory and the tools and the means to produce and buy essential items for survival. Human labour (work) is necessary to use the physical environment for survival, making the issue of who does what work all-important. Marx argued that social change is not gradual but occurs when these clashes and tensions become so acute that there is a movement towards the overall transformation of society – usually through a political and economic revolution. Thus, he predicted that in capitalist societies, the working class would become so powerless and poor and the upper class so powerful and rich that the conflict between them would produce a revolution which would transform the society from a capitalist to a socialist and, finally, into a communist one.

Interpretivist theories

Interpretivist sociologists are interested in the ways in which the actions and perceptions of individuals and groups can influence the social structures of societies. They look at the ways in which social actions, particularly those involving large numbers of people behaving in similar ways, could lead to large-scale social changes which cut across class, gender and racial barriers (e.g. the successful response to the introduction of the National Lottery). Max Weber was critical of all the theories of social change described above because he did not believe that any single factor (such as economics) could wholly explain the wide diversity of human social development. He suggested that a range of factors may be more useful in understanding particular instances of social change. Interpretivist theories are also particularly useful for their close observation of the smaller-scale changes in peoples' everyday perceptions of situations and of others.

Post-industrialist/ postmodern theories

These theories suggest that the UK, like many other Western societies, is moving towards a new type of structure beyond that of a merely industrial society. The prefix 'post' (meaning 'after') refers to the idea that we are leaving behind a society based mainly on the industrial manufacture of material goods towards a society where the *use of information or knowledge* is an equally important feature of the productive system. The service sector of the economy is the fastest-growing, and this has implications for the relationship between social change and social policy.

Michael Cahill (1994) has suggested that the information technology involved 'presents many opportunities which can be utilised to meet social need' (p. 3) but that for the poor, the disadvantaged and those with the least power in society, there are many barriers to the use of products such as carphones, cordless phones, electronic mail, fax machines, computers and word processors. His view of current social change is that new inequalities in society have emerged since the 1940s. These include unequal access to transport, shops and information technology (the more privileged own cars and so can shop in out-of-town superstores, own computers, etc.) which compounds a gulf between the two-thirds of British society who are in work and the one-third who are not. He argues that our consumerist society 'allows no thought for those without money: by definition they do not participate . . . what is becoming increasingly clear is that choice is very restricted for the poor and all the other groups who because of age or disability are excluded from participation in the consumer society' (pp. 191–2).

Cahill suggests that if we wish to study the relationship between social change, social policy and the provision of welfare services, we must look at people's everyday lives in a consumerist society. The ways in which people now communicate, travel, shop, work and play all concern social policy in its widest sense. Although studying these questions may not lead us into looking specifically at the development of social and welfare services such as the health or personal social services, it may point us towards an understanding of how, for example, a person's life may be more severely affected by the non-ownership of a car in an area where public transport has become unreliable and expensive than by, say, a small reduction in social-security benefits.

CONSUMERISM 'UNDERMINING WESTERN SOCIETY'

The rise of a 'shop-till-you-drop' culture throughout the developed world has led to increased crime and social tensions and diminished trust in governments, according to a book published today.

After the Gold Rush, the first book published under the auspices of the Henley Centre for Forecasting, one of Britain's leading research groups, argues that unless the West can rethink its attitude to consumerism and free itself from an 'obsession with shopping', it faces deepening inequalities, persistent high unemployment and growing environmental damage.

The book, written by Stewart Lansley on the 20th anniversary of the establishment of the centre, argues that the consumer dream has turned sour partly through failure to deliver the gains it promised and partly because it has degenerated into a rat-race . . .

In the first half of the post-war era, the building of a cohesive society was a central objective. But since the 1970s, income inequalities throughout the West have widened, unemployment has grown, welfare systems have been dismantled and an underclass of the young, the poor and the unemployed has arisen . . .

'Surveys may show that people would prefer to live in a caring, more co-operatively organised environment but that sort of society seems increasingly elusive. The trends of consumerism, of greater self-reliance, of corporate culture, of an increasingly privatised system of welfare are all pulling in the same direction – towards more competitive and divided ways of operating and living.'

Consumers seek status and identity through the goods they buy – expensive trainers, for instance – which help to distinguish them from others. This has created a 'leap-frogging' culture and turned consumption into a vicious cycle: hence the paradox that people 'do not feel better off despite increases in material living standards' . . .

(The Independent, *19 May 1994)*

The ideas described above can be studied in more detail by referring to most general introductory textbooks in sociology (see the 'References and Resources' section for some examples). At first sight these theories may seem rather remote from the study of welfare services and social change. How can they be used to explain how recent changes in the social structure of the UK might have affected welfare provision? One answer to this is that if relevant questions about these theories are asked, they can be tested against appropriate evidence, criticised, weighed up, rejected, modified or accepted. They provide a series of reference points around which we can sort out and arrange our own and other people's ideas on this subject.

Some of the questions which can be asked in connection with these theories are listed below.

1 *Evolutionary theories*
In what ways have welfare services developed, changed or become more complex? Will these welfare services survive longer the more complex they become? Are Western welfare services necessarily superior to those found in other cultures and societies? Are Western welfare services continuing to improve?
2 *Structural-functionalist theories*
Are Western societies still on a path of structural differentiation as far as welfare services are concerned? (The concept of 'care in the community' could be examined in relation to this theory.)
3 *Structural conflict theories*
To what extent are the rich becoming richer and the poor becoming poorer in the UK? How might such changes be affecting welfare provision? Is there any evidence of social tension between classes or other groupings in society?
4 *Interpretivist theories*
What other factors, besides class, power or structural differentiation, might be significant in explaining social changes which have an impact upon welfare provision? What ideas (e.g. feminism, equal rights) might be significant in affecting the way people behave and the attitudes they hold?
5 *Post-industrial and postmodernist theories*
What new inequalities are emerging in people's lives as a result of the changes that are taking place in the way we communicate, shop, travel, work and play? Are welfare services responding to these new inequalities?

ACTIVITY

Use the questions listed above as the basis for class discussion and individual research. Try to construct further questions of your own.

Significant factors determining social change

As you will have realised, 'social change' is a rather slippery concept. It does have some key features (industrialisation, urbanisation and economic organisation), but the relative significance of these is debatable. What causes societies to change? Is their organisation and structure the most important factor? Is the mode of production central? What part do ideas and actions play? Or is it information technology that is about to transform our world? All these features of change interact with other significant factors of change, some of which are discussed briefly below.

POLITICAL FACTORS

The ways in which societies develop are strongly influenced by their political organisation, i.e. who has the power to make decisions and what procedures and processes, wealth and military and physical strength underlie that power. War, for example, has a profound effect on the economy and social attitudes of societies.

In the exercise of power, governments have to respond to the views of pressure groups, trade unions, other political parties and the public. A change of government in the UK can be brought about, through the electoral system, by voting at, for example, a general election; smaller-scale political change (including influence on the legislative process) can also be brought about through public response to particular political issues. For example, public hostility to the Community Charge (poll tax) can be said to have had some impact upon its demise.

SOCIAL AND CULTURAL FACTORS

Our social attitudes and our cultural beliefs and behaviour can influence social change in society. Influences on those ideas and beliefs, such as the development of science and the apparent decline of religion, have greatly influenced how we think. The content of our ideas has changed. The mass media, demographic changes and changes in the ways in which we work, travel and play are all involved here.

ENVIRONMENTAL FACTORS

The physical environment can have an effect on the development of societies and the ways in which they are organised. Giddens gives the example of how the native Aborigine population of Australia remained as hunter-gatherers over thousands of years because the continent did not contain many indigenous plants suitable for regular cultivation, or animals which could be farmed for pastoral production (Giddens 1989, p. 657).

Factors such as the ease of communication between areas of a country, the availability of sea routes and the availability of rich agricultural land for food production can all affect the development of societies. In modern Britain, environmental features like the growth of towns and cities, the increased use of the car, the effect of pollution and the access which people have to space to play or live in are all issues which have an impact on social change. For example, it is increasingly the case that young children are now driven to school rather than allowed to walk because, ironically, the increased use of cars means that parents feel it is too dangerous to let children make the journeys themselves. In general, children's 'play time' seems to be more supervised by adults now than it used to be even 30 years ago because of the greater risks from traffic, the greater restrictions upon the amount of space available to them, and parents' belief that their children are more at risk from hostile strangers.

CARS – THE PROBLEMS

Today's children are confined by traffic. Since 1971, the proportion of 7–8 year olds allowed to travel to school without adult supervision has fallen from 80% to under 10%, largely because of the danger of motor traffic.

Motor traffic is the fastest growing contributor to global warming. It also produces much of our urban air pollution: World Health Organisation limits are exceeded in many British cities. Over 1,500 wildlife sites, including ancient woodlands, are still threatened by road-building.

(From 'Sustrans – paths for people')

(Sustrans is a registered charity – see the 'Useful Addresses' section at the end of the chapter.)

ACTIVITY

Use the schema provided below to classify all the examples of social change given into the box you consider most appropriate:

ECONOMIC CHANGES	Major: Minor:
SOCIAL CHANGES	Major: Minor:
POLITICAL CHANGES	Major: Minor:
ENVIRONMENTAL CHANGES	Major: Minor:

In pairs, compare your finished charts and discuss your results. What areas of agreement or disagreement emerge, and why?

Think of five other examples of change not included in the list provided. Where would you place them on the chart?

List of changes, actual or possible
Increasing car ownership
A general election won by the opposition political party
The invention of the domestic microwave oven
The invention of the contraceptive pill
Video games
The introduction of the National Curriculum in schools
The decline in church attendance in the UK
The invention of nuclear weapons
The creation and growth of the European Union
The *Power Rangers* TV series (and associated 'merchandising')
The invention of the microchip
The Mars bar
Rap music
The cashpoint card
The spread of HIV/Aids
The peace process in Northern Ireland
Bottle banks
Convenience 'frozen' meals
The introduction of GNVQ courses in schools and further education

KEY DEMOGRAPHIC TRENDS: SOCIAL CHANGE IN THE UK

When dramatic or far-reaching events occur in various parts of the world, there are often unmistakable consequences for the size and shape of the population in those areas. A war, a flood, a famine or the rapid spread of a contagious disease may kill or incapacitate certain groups of people in the population, leaving others with responsibilities for work and family care which were previously distributed in a different way. In the past few years we have seen how such events in countries such as the former Yugoslavia, Rwanda, Mozambique or Ethiopia have left people without homes, children without parents and the elderly and sick without medical care. It is all too obvious that in situations such as these, such events may mean that people's needs for care will also change.

In countries, such as the UK, which in recent years have not experienced such striking events, it is more difficult to gain a clear sense of how the size and shape of the country's population might be changing and how these changes relate to wider social changes. The purpose of this section of the chapter is to provide a summary of some of the most significant and interesting changes in the population of the UK, and to ask questions about how these changes might be affecting people's lives.

The unexpected growth and movement of the population of the UK in the nineteenth century gave birth to *demography*, the study of changes in population size, of the reasons for these changes and of their consequences. Governments began to collect and keep official statistics on how the population of the country was made up and where it lived. The first British census was carried out in 1801, since when a census has been carried out every 10 years, with the exception of 1941 (during the Second World War). The most recent census, therefore, was in 1991.

Later in this chapter, we will consider whether demographic changes may be affecting welfare provision. Many books about demography claim that information gathered in the way described above about the size, structure and nature of the population is useful to governments because it helps them plan welfare services. For example: 'Demographic information is very important, as it helps governments to predict and plan for the future needs of the society, such as the likely demand for schools, housing, hospitals and old people's homes' (O'Donnell and Garrod 1990, p. 241). Statements such as these have to be treated with great caution. Demographic trends may have an impact on welfare provision, but people disagree about the extent to which governments (local and national) have used the demographic information available to them to construct appropriate, rational or successful social policies.

When studying this and later sections of this chapter, it will therefore be helpful to keep the following questions in mind:

1 What broad demographic trends have occurred in the UK since the Industrial Revolution?
2 What are the most recent demographic changes, and why might they be occurring?
3 What examples can be found of governments using demographic information to plan welfare provision?
4 How successful have these policies been or are likely to be?

Between censuses, the census figures and statistics are used, together with annual estimates of births, deaths and net migration, to estimate the size and shape of the population.

While using the information in this book as a base for their studies, students are likely to want to update relevant statistics regularly. The Office of Population Censuses and Surveys (OPCS) produces a wide range of useful statistical publications on many health- and care-related subjects. Its quarterly journal, *Population Trends*, should be available in most good reference libraries, as will some other OPCS publications, such as the annual *General Household Survey*, and statistics on communicable diseases and abortion. Students will also be familiar with the annual publication *Social Trends*.

Interpreting statistics – problems with demographic data

When using demographic information, students should be aware that all statistics (especially estimates and projections) need to be treated with some caution, and that their reliability as valid sources of information does vary. For example, our knowledge of population changes during the period of the Industrial Revolution in the UK relies heavily on studies of parish registers of the Church of England. However, the civil registration of births and deaths did not commence until 1837, and the parish registers are therefore unlikely to be completely accurate and reliable sources of data.

On the other hand, the legal requirement which now exists in the UK to register all births, marriages and deaths means that statistics on age structure, fertility rates and birth and death rates are likely to be reasonably accurate (although there are still problems in interpreting changes and trends in the causes of deaths, since we cannot be absolutely sure that the 'cause of death' which is recorded on a death certificate is a completely true and objective judgement. There may be social pressures to disguise the causes of some deaths – for example, doctors in Catholic countries may be reluctant to record a death as a suicide).

In general, when considering demographic statistics, be alert to the following questions:

1 Who compiled them, and for what original purpose?
2 From what sample of the population were they drawn?
3 How reliable and representative of the whole population is that sample likely to be?

Changing patterns in the population

POPULATION SIZE

Table 7.1 clearly shows the pattern of population growth in the UK. The Industrial Revolution of 1750–1880 led to the fastest increase in the population. Since then, the population has still risen steadily but at a slower rate.

The resident population of the UK today was estimated to be 58.2 million in mid-1993, and it has grown at an annual rate of about 0.3% since 1984. The population of the UK is projected to continue increasing for about 35 years, rising from 57.8 million in 1991 to 62.2 million in the year 2027, after which deaths are expected to exceed births (*Social Trends* 24, p. 22).

ACTIVITY

1 Carry out further research into why there was a 'population explosion' during the Industrial Revolution in the UK.
2 After the year 2027 the population of the UK is likely to begin to decline. Why is this likely to happen?

THE AGE STRUCTURE AND SEX DISTRIBUTION OF THE POPULATION

In the eighteenth century in the UK, many people, infants in particular, were dying prematurely. This was mostly caused by endemic and epidemic infectious diseases or harvest failure, or both. In the nineteenth century people in the UK tended to have a diet less heavily concentrated on a single foodstuff, such as bread grain, so harvest failure became less important as a factor in explaining early death in the population (except in Ireland, where the population relied on the potato crop, and where there was a famine in 1845–7). There seems to have been a decline in mortality during the late eighteenth and early nineteenth century in the UK. Historians disagree as to the possible reasons for this, but a better and more varied diet, improved medical treatment and fewer crop failures may all have been causes.

During the nineteenth century, there were huge differences between the health of working-class people and the better-off. There was a much greater chance of premature mortality if you lived in the unsanitary conditions of the growing cities. By 1880, of the population as a whole, three out of four people died under the age of 40, one out of two people died under the age of 20, and one in every four babies died in its first year (Adams, p. 170).

Table 7.1 The four stages of the UK's population growth

Stage	Years	Birth rate	Death rate	Population growth
1	to 1750	High	High	Slow, to 8 million
2	1750–1880	Stable	Falling	Fast, to 26 million
3	1880–1930	Falling	Falling	Slower, to 40 million
4	1930–90	Low	Low	Slow, to 57 million

Source: Townroe, C. and Yates, G. (1995) *Sociology for GCSE*, Addison Wesley Longman.

Table 7.2 The population* of the UK (in thousands)

	1961	1971	1981	1991	1992	1993	2031
England	43,561	46,412	46,821	48,208	48,378	48,533	52,435
Wales	2,635	2,740	2,813	2,891	2,899	2,906	2,977
Scotland	5,184	5,236	5,180	5,107	5,111	5,120	4,998
Northern Ireland	1,427	1,540	1,538	1,601	1,618	1,632	1,831
United Kingdom	52,807	55,928	56,352	57,808	58,006	58,191	62,241

* Data are mid-year estimates for 1961 to 1991 and 1992-based projections for 2031. See Appendix, Part 1: Population and population projections.
Source: Social Trends 25 1995 Central Statistical Office. Crown Copyright. 1995. Reproduced by the permission of the Controller of HMSO and the Central Statistical Office.

One result of the improvements in people's living conditions which followed both the Industrial Revolution in the nineteenth century and the setting-up of the welfare state is that people's life expectancy has increased. Gradually, the number of elderly people has grown as a proportion of the population as a whole; and as the birth rate has declined – due to factors which include contraception, which allows people to limit the size of their families – there are more older people and fewer younger people in the population.

Social Trends 25 reports that the dependent population (the population which is supported economically by those of working age, i.e. those under 16 and those over the pensionable age) now consists of a slightly rising number of children under 16 and a growing number of those over pensionable age – projected to reach just under 17 million people in 2036. The age structure of the population also varies between different *ethnic groups*. In general, ethnic-minority groups in the UK tend to have a younger age distribution than that of the population as a whole.

100 NOT OUT

Advances in medicine have led to a dramatic increase in the numbers of people reaching 100 years of age (known as centenarians). In 1951 there were 300 in the UK; by 1991 there were 4,390, all but 500 of whom were women. Centenarians, like Marie Shelley who celebrated her 105th birthday in 1977, receive a Telemessage giving congratulations from the Queen. The Queen Mother is 94, so maybe she will receive a Telemessage from her daughter in six years.

(The Guardian, 20 September 1994)

Ethnic and cultural diversity

There have been minority ethnic groups and small settlements of black people in the UK for several hundred years. In this sense, the UK has been a multi-ethnic society for a long period of time. However, since the 1950s there have been particular changes in the composition and size of the UK's black and Asian population. (See pp. 270–71 for further information on migration, and Thomson et al. 1995, Chapter 4, for ethnicity and race.)

The 1991 census was the first in the UK to include a question on ethnic group. *Social Trends* 25 shows that slightly over 3 million people (5.5% of the population) described themselves on their census returns as belonging to an ethnic-minority group. The proportion of the people who are in ethnic-minority groups varies from area to area. In 1991 the proportion of the population from ethnic minorities in rural areas was below 1%, whereas the proportions for most London boroughs and metropolitan districts were over 5%. Three in every five people from ethnic groups were under the age of 30, compared with two in every five for the population as a whole.

CHANGING STRUCTURES IN THE POPULATION

Demographic changes in families and households

We are often fascinated by the details of how life has changed over the generations in families and households with which we are familiar. However, we are unlikely to have sufficient personal experience of different families to enable us to see how and why patterns of family life, family size and family structure might be changing. For a clearer understanding of these changes, we need to consider historical and sociological research and the numerous studies which continue to be made into changes in household composition and kinship networks.

WHOM DO WE COUNT AS 'FAMILY'?

This apparently simple question is more important than it first appears. Our sense of duty, obligation and responsibility towards other family members arises partly out of *whom* we regard as 'close' family. How we expect these family members to behave towards us, and the level of physical, emotional and financial support we expect or hope family members to bestow, can be described as *kinship*.

> **ACTIVITY**
>
> Whom do you count as your family? Why do you include these family members? What does 'family' mean to you?
>
> Are there any other relatives besides parents and children living in your household? How does this situation compare with the experiences of previous generations in your household?

Some sociologists and historians suggest that, as industrialisation occurred in the UK, so close, mutually supportive families (involving kinship networks or large, extended family households – or both – that were essential to the survival of the rural family as a production unit) declined. Talcott Parsons has argued that an 'isolated nuclear family' is the typical family form in modern, industrial society because the need for binding obligations and duties towards other members of the family has disappeared. The state, it is argued, provides education, welfare, provision for old age and a basic level of financial security. Most important of all, members of families no longer need to work together to produce items such as food necessary for survival. Now, adults work for others, earning a wage and a status not determined solely by their role within the family.

If an 'isolated nuclear family' has emerged as the most common family type (not all researchers agree, as we shall see), with close bonds between spouses, parents and children but weaker bonds with wider relatives and the outside world, what might be some of the health and care implications?

- Our reliance on our immediate families for emotional and physical support and care in times of illness and need might serve to exert on the 'nuclear family' new kinds of pressure (can you say what these might be?)
- Writers such as Barrett and McIntosh (1980) have suggested that the nuclear family is 'anti-social'. By this they mean that family members become so wrapped up in family life that they neglect social contact with others. The single, the elderly living alone and lone-parent families can therefore feel excluded from a society which places so much emphasis on the 'cereal-packet' form of the family.

FAMILY DIVERSITY

Not all researchers agree that an 'isolated nuclear family' is the most typical form of family today. Some argue that to suggest that the extended family of the eighteenth century has simply been replaced by the nuclear family of the twentieth century is a grossly oversimplified picture of what has happened. Research by Michael Anderson (1980) indicates that there was a variety of household types in the pre-industrial period, which was not simply dominated by the extended family. The same may apply today. That is, a diversity of family types and structures seems to exist, with family members dependent upon each other to varying degrees. The conventional, two-parent, 1.8-children family, although it may still exist as a fairly common form, may present a misleading image if used to represent all families in the UK. The UK has the highest marriage rate and the second highest divorce and remarriage rate in Europe. This, coupled with the increase in young, single parenthood, means we are a nation with an increasing supply of step-, half- and 'almost'-relatives. Since the 1970s, these and other key demographic and social changes have meant that today's children and young adults are likely to experience different kinds of family life from those of their parents.

Three particularly significant trends in the family can be identified:

- fewer marriages, more cohabitation, more extra-marital births
- more divorce
- more lone-parent and 'reconstituted' families

These trends mean that individuals, as they move through the various stages of their lives (childhood, young adulthood, adulthood, old age) may experience differing forms of the family, of which the 'nuclear family' may be only one.

FEWER MARRIAGES, MORE COHABITATION, MORE EXTRA-MARITAL BIRTHS

The UK has the second highest marriage rate in the European Union; but, as in most other

Figure 7.2 A photo of the author's family circa 1915

European countries, there has also been a rise in divorce and cohabitation. Furthermore, marriages have fallen by almost 16% over the past 20 years, while divorces have more than doubled over the same period. The proportion of women aged 18–49 who are married has fallen steeply to 59% from 74% in 1979, with 29% single, 8% divorced, 4% separated and 1% widowed (OPCS, *General Household Survey* 1992).

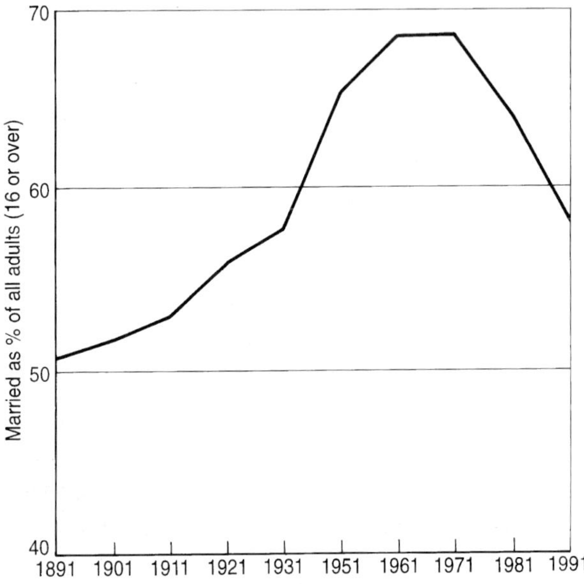

Figure 7.3 **The married population as a percentage of the whole adult population in England and Wales, 1891 to 1991**
Source: Factsheet 1, *Putting Families on the Map*, UN International Year of the Family 1994.

The *Survey* further indicates that nearly one in five unmarried people aged 16–59 in the UK are *cohabiting*. The peak age groups are 30–34 for males – with 33% of the unmarried cohabiting – and 25–29 for females – for whom the rate was 28%. Cohabiting prior to marriage is now more usual than not, but in general most couples appear either to marry or to break up after an average of two years 'living together'.

The average age at first marriage increased by about two years for both men and women between 1961 and 1991, to 27.4 years for men and 25.4 years for women. Teenage

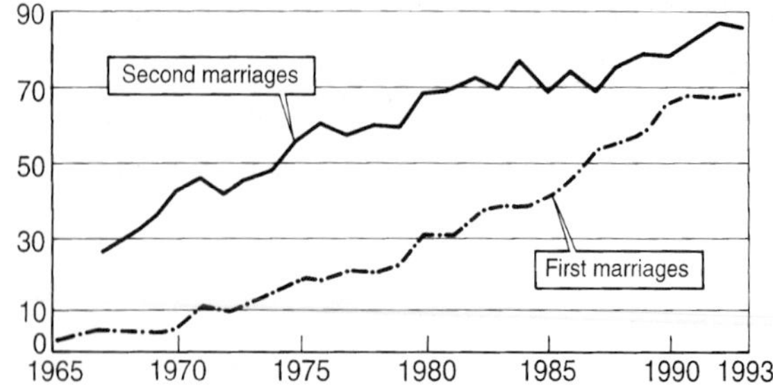

Figure 7.4 **Percentages of women who reported that they had pre-maritally cohabited with their future husband, by year of marriage, in the UK**
Source: The *Guardian*, 14 June 1995.

marriages are becoming less frequent – by 1991, only 2.2% and 8.3% of marriages involved respectively a teenage groom and a teenage bride.

Over a third of all marriages in 1991 were remarriages, where either or both members of the couple had already been divorced; 30 years ago this proportion was less than one in ten.

Seven in ten of all births in the UK take place within marriage, but since 1980 the number of children born outside marriage in the UK has risen dramatically: it represented three in ten of all births in 1991. The younger the mother, the more likely that she will be unmarried. However, 55% of births outside marriage in 1992 were registered by parents who both gave the same address – evidence that such births were occurring within stable relationships. The proportion of births outside marriage to teenage mothers has actually decreased over the period 1971–90, from 39% to 28%.

There were 160,000 legal abortions performed on women residents in England and Wales in 1992 – a fall of 7,000 from 1991 and of 14,000 from 1990. Rates of abortion fell for all age groups.

MODERN WOMEN WEDDED TO THE IDEA OF COHABITATION FOR LIFE

More couples are choosing to cohabit for life, rather than as a prelude to getting married, suggesting that the 'rush to marriage' that peaked

in the 1950s may go down as a quirk of British social history.

Growing numbers of women are continuing to cohabit after becoming mothers, as pressures to cement the relationship in a formal ceremony subside.

Fear of divorce, an aversion to the institution of marriage, and the high cost of traditional weddings are the most frequently-cited reasons for remaining legally single.

The research, published . . . by the independent Policy Studies Institute, shows that almost half of all conceptions take place outside marriage, and one in three women give birth while unmarried . . .

The author, Susan McRae, conducted interviews with 166 cohabiting mothers and a similar number of married mothers, who gave birth in 1988, and reviewed previous research. About 40 per cent of cohabiting mothers expected to marry partners at some stage; one-quarter thought that they might do, and just under one-third said they had no intention of marrying . . .

Fewer than half of 18–24-year-olds questioned in an earlier survey believe people should marry before having children.

(The Independent, *23 September 1993*)

ACTIVITY

Is marriage a dying institution? Why are more people choosing to cohabit with their partners rather than get married? Use these questions as the basis for a discussion or a debate.

MORE DIVORCES

There has been a rise in the divorce rate in the UK throughout this century. Before 1857 divorce was only available to the very rich who could afford a parliamentary divorce. In the year 1911 there were 580 divorces granted in England and Wales – this low figure a reflection of the difficulty people faced in satisfying the terms laid down for obtaining a divorce at that time. Until 1839 a separated wife had no right to access to her children, and only in 1873 could divorced women, for the first time, bring up their own children to the age of 14 (but even then, only if they were the 'innocent party' in the divorce). For more than 60 years after divorce was legalised, a wife could not divorce her husband for adultery alone. She needed to be able to cite other grounds such as cruelty. Husbands, however,

Table 7.3 Marriages, by type, in the UK (in thousands)

	1961	1971	1981	1991	1992
First marriage for both partners	340	369	263	222	222
First marriage for one partner only					
Bachelor/divorced woman	11	21	32	32	35
Bachelor/widow	5	4	3	2	2
Spinster/divorced man	12	24	36	35	36
Spinster/widower	8	5	3	2	2
Second (or subsequent) marriage for both partners					
Both divorced	5	17	44	45	47
Both widowed	10	10	7	4	4
Divorced man/widow	3	4	5	4	4
Divorced woman/widower	3	5	5	4	4
All marriages	397	459	398	350	356
Remarriages* as a percentage of all marriages	14	20	34	36	38
Remarriages* of the divorced as a percentage of all marriages	9	15	31	34	35

* Remarriage for one or both partners.

Source: Social Trends 25, 1995 Central Statistical Office. Crown Copyright, 1995. Reproduced by the permission of the Controller of HMSO and the Central Statistical Office.

could divorce their wives just for adultery.

There was a rapid rise in petitions for divorce in 1971 – due partly, however, to new divorce legislation (the Divorce Law Reform Act) – and divorce has continued to increase steadily since then. The vast majority of divorces are initiated by women. *Social Trends* 25 reports that over the past 20 years, divorces have increased sharply to 173,000 in 1992 – more than double the number in 1971.

ACTIVITY

Carry out further research into the divorce legislation of the past 100 years. In April 1995 the government produced a new White Paper on divorce law reform. The proposals in this would change the procedure for getting a divorce, taking away the concept of 'fault' in divorce but forcing couples to wait at least a year before they can get a divorce after the petition has been filed (doing away with the current three-to-six-month 'quickie' divorce based on adultery or unreasonable behaviour). What difference to the divorce rates do you think this proposed new legislation might make?

MORE LONE-PARENT AND 'RECONSTITUTED' FAMILIES

In 1992 the *General Household Survey* estimated that the number of families with children headed by a lone parent had risen to more than one in five. Of the 7 million mothers with dependent children in the UK in 1991, just over 1 million were lone mothers. The proportion of families headed by a lone father has remained at 1–2% of the total for much of the past 20 years. At present some two in three lone parents depend on social security.

Whilst the number of lone-parent families and children in those families has been increasing, this is not the whole picture. Just as lone-parent families are formed, so may they dissolve, through repartnership (marriage or cohabitation), the death of a parent or through the child becoming an independent young adult (Burghes 1994, p. 8).

Eight per cent of all families with dependent children are step-families. Some of these children will experience still further family disruption, since remarriages are more vulnerable to breakdown than first marriages.

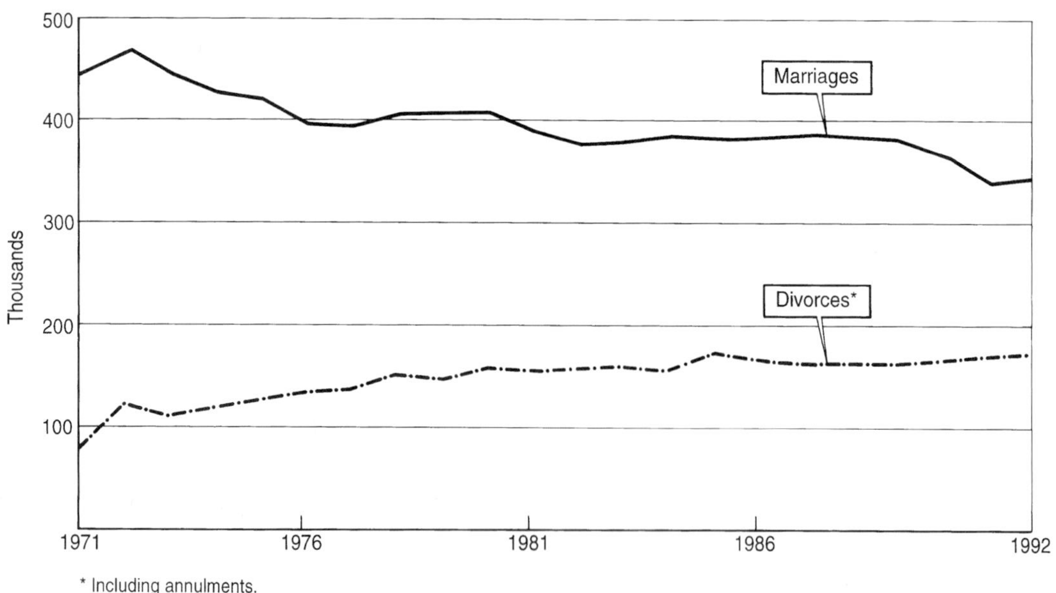

Figure 7.5 Marriages and divorces in the UK (in thousands)
Source: Social Trends 25, 1995 Central Statistical Office. Crown Copyright, 1995. Reproduced by the permission of the Controller of HMSO and the Central Statistical Office.

Table 7.4 Divorce, by duration of marriage, in the UK (in percentages)

	1961	1971	1981	1991	1992
0–2 years	1	1	2	9	9
3–4 years	10	12	19	14	14
5–9 years	31	31	29	27	27
10–14 years	23	19	20	18	18
15–19 years	14	13	13	13	13
20–24 years	14	10	9	10	10
25–29 years	21	6	5	5	5
30 years and over	21	9	5	4	4
All durations (= 100%) (thousands)	27.0	79.2	155.6	171.1	175.1

Source: Social Trends 25, 1995 Central Statistical Office. Crown Copyright, 1995. Reproduced by the permission of the Controller of HMSO and the Central Statistical Office.

ACTIVITY

1 While lone-parent families have become increasingly common in the UK, they are by no means a new phenomenon. Use historical sources to investigate the existence of lone-parent families at other periods over the past 150 years.

2 The rise in the divorce rate and an increase in the number of births outside marriage are two demographic changes which may help to explain the recent increase in the numbers of lone-parent families. What other reasons could there be?

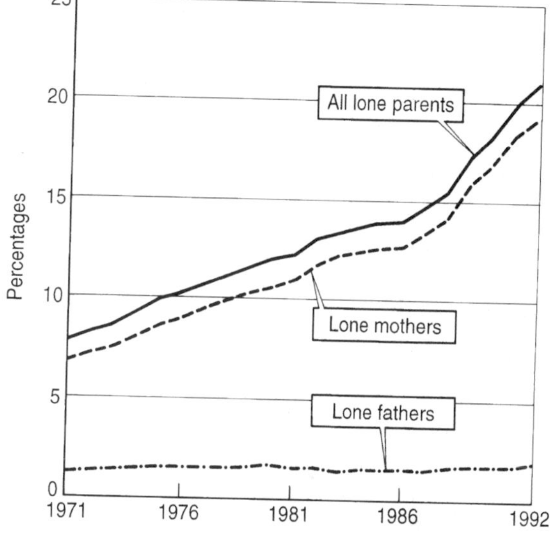

Figure 7.6 Families headed by lone parents as a percentage* of all UK families with dependent children

Source: Social Trends 25, 1995 Central Statistical Office. Crown Copyright, 1995. Reproduced by the permission of the Controller of HMSO and the Central Statistical Office.

Changes in households

Fewer than one in four households now conform to the traditional image of a married or cohabiting couple with children, according to the 1992 *General Household Survey*. More than a quarter of households in 1991 consisted of one person living alone – almost double the proportion in 1961 (*Social Trends* 24). Overall, the average household size has fallen from just over three people in 1961 to 2.5 people in 1991.

The average household size does however vary according to ethnic group, with white households containing fewer people on average than ethnic-minority households.

GENDER ROLES AND THE FAMILY: HISTORICAL DEVELOPMENT

During the period of the Industrial Revolution in the UK, great changes occurred to the domestic, social and working lives of men and women. There are many excellent

Table 7.5 'Best estimates' of the number of lone-parent families in the UK (in thousands)

Family type	1971	1976	1986	1991	1992*
Single mothers	90	130	230	440	490
Separated mothers	170	185	190	260	300
Divorced mothers	120	230	410	430	430
Widowed mothers	120	115	80	70	60
All mothers	500	660	910	1200	1280
All fathers	70	90	100	100	120
All lone parents	570	750	10101	1300	1400

* Provisional.
This chart is reproduced with permission of the editor of *Community Care*.

historical sources which students could consult for a fuller examination of gender roles in this period. The discussion here will concentrate upon changes in the second half of the twentieth century.

Sociologists observing family structures in the 1950s and 1960s noted that in settled, traditional working-class areas, the marital, parental and work roles of men and women were still largely segregated (separate from each other). Women took the main responsibility for childcare and housework, whether or not they also worked outside the home. Men were seen as 'breadwinners' and were almost excluded from the domestic sphere of the home, where mother–daughter ties were often very strong. This pattern of distinct and separate gender roles was reinforced by the postwar drive to give the returning troops employment and to rebuild the economy. Women were deliberately encouraged to feel that their 'natural' place was in the home, performing the 'housewife' role.

Studies since then have tried to document and explain structural and demographic changes which have occurred to these gender roles in the second half of the twentieth century. These include:

- changes in the participation by men and women in paid employment, which changes affect their roles within the family
- changes in perceptions of domestic and conjugal roles and responsibilities, and particularly in perceptions of 'parenting'

Gender, employment and the family

One key, long-term trend has been the dramatic increase, since the 1930s, in the level of married women's employment and participation in the labour force. In 1931 the census showed that 10% of married women were employed. By 1994 the number of women with jobs exceeded the number of men with jobs – albeit that out of the 30% of employees who work part-time in the UK, 80% are women.

Over the past 25 years it seems that each successive group of new mothers returns to paid work more quickly than the one before – a trend confirmed by the 1991 *General Household Survey* which showed that seven in ten children under five are being cared for out of the home or by nannies, after the number of working mothers increased by three-quarters in 10 years. Many working mothers with dependent children are still more likely to be working part-time than full-time, either through choice or through the lack of suitable or affordable child-care provision. Local authorities in the UK provide day-care facilities for just under 1% of under-fives. In 1991, only 1% of families with children under five used a workplace facility for childcare (Factsheet 3, *Families and Work*, UN International Year of the Family).

Other significant trends:

- While women's incomes are now clearly a major contribution to family income, they remain, on average, lower than men's. Women's hourly earnings were just 78.8% of men's earnings in 1992, although the gap has been narrowing in the past five years (ibid.)

- There has been a rise in the number of 'dual-worker' families. In 1973, in only 43% of couples with children were both partners in employment. By 1992, this figure had increased to 60%. In one in five of these families both parents worked full-time

ACTIVITY

1 What factors might account for the trends outlined above?

2 What impact might these changes be having on families?

Changes in perceptions of domestic roles and responsibilities

In 1973 Young and Willmott published a study called *The Symmetrical Family* based upon their research into London families in the 1950s and 1960s. In this study they argued that the rehousing policies of the 1960s, the increased affluence of young people and their greater geographical mobility as far as work opportunities were concerned meant that young people were more likely to set up home in small, nuclear-type families, at a distance from kin. This factor, combined with the greater opportunities for women to work, meant that the division of labour between men and women at home was changing. Husbands were becoming more 'home-centred', more likely to help with domestic work and more likely to share decision-making and financial resources with their wives. Young and Willmott argued that the developing form of the family in the UK was therefore a more democratic and 'symmetrical' unit, with the roles of husbands and wives becoming more similar.

However, evidence from the 1991 British Social Attitudes Survey showed that women continued to shoulder the main responsibility for work in the home in 75% of families. In 67% of households where both men and women work full-time, women are still mainly responsible for domestic duties. However, this may to some extent be a reflection of the much longer hours that men work outside the home. Women who work full-time are more likely to receive help from partners with cooking, cleaning and childcare, although women in part-time employment generally appear to combine the major share of household duties with paid work.

The research organisation Mintel published a study in 1994 (*Men 2000*) which found that 50% of married men left household chores wholly or mainly to women. In 1995, Mintel's 'Leisure Time' survey showed that women have less free time than men.

An understanding of the differences in hours worked in paid employment between men and women does help to throw some light on these trends.

HOURS OF WORK AND DAYS OF WEEK

British men work the longest hours in Europe and British women the second shortest (after the Netherlands).

- About one in five women with children worked just an 8–15 hour week in 1993
- Only one in 16 women usually worked over 48 hours per week, whereas as many as a third of their partners did so in 1992
- Nearly half of men and a quarter of women who were self-employed worked 49 hours or more a week, compared to 25% of men and 0.5% of women employees in 1992/93. (Self-employment itself has doubled in the last thirteen years)
- One in three men work a 6–7 day week, compared to just one in ten women

Clearly, the longer the hours that men spend in employment and the more often they work at weekends, the less time they have to spend with their families.

(Factsheet 3, Families and Work, *UN International Year of the Family)*

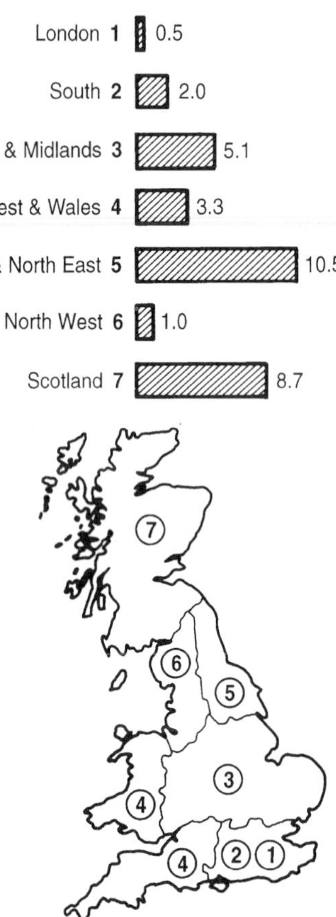

Figure 7.7 Graph showing how much less free time per week in hours is enjoyed by women compared to me
Source: The *Guardian*, 24 May 1995.

ACTIVITY

1 Do you think that people's perceptions of the roles of partners within families are changing? Why, or why not?

2 Is it more 'natural' for women rather than men to do housework and childcare? Why, or why not?

3 What financial, social and work-related problems might confront couples who did wish to share housework and childcare equitably?

4 To what extent does maternity provision in the UK enable men and women to share childcare?

Fertility and average family size

The birth rate (i.e. the number of live births per 1,000 persons of all ages in one year) in the UK has fallen steadily over the past 120 years. The average number of children per family in the 1860s was 6.16; by the 1930s, this had fallen to 2.06.

ACTIVITY

Using appropriate sociology or social and economic history texts, investigate some of the following reasons for this decline in average family size:

- the increasing availability of birth control
- the falling infant mortality rate
- economic factors – particularly the cost of raising children
- social factors such as feminism and secularisation

There has been a mini-boom in the number of births in recent years, which reached a peak in 1990 but has fallen slightly since. This was caused by the generation born in the 1960s 'baby boom' reaching their most fertile time of life. The number of births per year is projected to begin gradually falling from 1994, a decline which is likely to continue until the beginning of the next century when it is likely to rise again.

The Total Period Fertility Rate (TPFR) measures the average number of children a woman would be expected to have if she experienced the age-specific fertility rates of the year in question throughout her child-bearing life. In 1992 the TPFR was 1.80. In 1992, for the first time, a higher fertility rate was recorded for women aged 30–34 than for those aged 20–24, i.e. women in their early thirties were more likely to have a baby than those in their early twenties. The average age of mothers at childbirth, 27.7 years, was the highest since 1957.

The consequences of these trends are that fewer women are having babies, and that they are having them later in their lives. Only 20% of women born in 1947 were childless at 30; about 33% of women born in 1967 will still be childless when they reach that age. 20% of women now under 30 will remain childless if present trends continue. The average number of children born per women is now 1.54.

WORK BLAMED AS 1 IN 5 WOMEN EXPECTED NOT TO BEAR CHILDREN

An increasing number of women are not bearing children, with up to 20 per cent now expected to remain childless, according to a report published today.

The Family Policy Studies Centre Bulletin said projections suggested that about one in five women born over the past 30 years will remain childless – double the ratio for their mother's generation.

Poverty, the breakdown of relationships, inability to find a suitable partner and growing pressures of work and career were cited as reasons.

Figures last month showed more women delaying a family until their late 30s or 40s.

(The Guardian, *10 April 1995)*

Childcare provision

Mothers have primary responsibility for looking after their children in 96% of families in the UK. However, two-thirds of mothers with children under five use some additional form of care for their children.

The UN International Year of the Family Factsheet 4, *Families and Caring*, reports that two in five working mothers with children under five have their spouse, grandparents or friends to care for their children, which means that in many families parents work in shifts, with the mother fitting in her working hours around the father's. These additional care arrangements usually amount to 15 hours a week for working mothers with pre-school-age children, and five hours a week for working mothers with 5- to 11-year-olds.

Between 1982 and 1992 the number of registered childminders increased from 44,000, providing under 100,000 places, to 110,000, providing more than a quarter of a million places. During that same period private day nurseries also mushroomed, with the number of places increasing more than fourfold, but local-authority day-nursery places fell by 16%. Childminders still care for twice as many children as day nurseries.

ACTIVITY

1 Investigate the costs of childcare in the area where you live. How much does it cost per hour/day/week to place a child with
- a childminder?
- a private day nursery or playgroup?
- a workplace nursery or crèche?
- a private nanny or au pair, daily or live-in?

2 Is there any free, state- or local-authority-funded pre-school nursery or day-care provision in the area where you live?

3 Interview working women who use any of the forms of care above for their children. What proportion of their earnings do they spend on childcare?

The UN International Year of the Family Factsheet 4 suggests that many women are not working because they cannot find suitable childcare. Fewer lone mothers are working today than 20 years ago, mainly because these mothers have fewer practical and financial resources, which means that many cannot earn enough to cover the costs of childcare. However, since October 1994, lone-parent families (and some two-parent families who receive certain benefits) have been eligible for a weekly allowance of £28, which will help to offset the costs of childcare.

Table 7.6 Fertility rates, by age, in the UK

	Births per thousand women in each age group							Total period fertility rate*
	Under 20	20–24	25–29	30–34	35–39	40 and over	All ages	
1981	28	107	130	70	22	5	62	1.81
1986	30	93	125	78	25	5	61	1.78
1987	31	94	125	81	27	5	62	1.81
1988	32	95	125	82	28	5	63	1.83
1989	32	91	121	83	29	5	62	1.80
1990	33	91	123	87	31	5	64	1.85
1991	33	89	120	87	32	5	64	1.83
1992	32	86	118	87	33	6	63	1.81
1993	31	82	114	87	34	6	62	1.76

* The average number of children which would be born per woman if women experienced the age-specific fertility rates of the period in question throughout their child-bearing lifespan.
Source: Social Trends 25, 1995 Central Statistical Office. Crown Copyright, 1995. Reproduced by the permission of the Controller of HMSO and the Central Statistical Office.

Table 7.7 Childcare for children under five in the UK, 1991

Type of care	% of families with children 0–4
Unpaid family or friends	25
School/nursery school	25
Private/voluntary schemes	17
Paid childminder/nanny	11
Local authority scheme	7
Workplace facility	1
Total using care	64

Note: percentages add to more than the total because some respondents use more than one form of care.
Source: Factsheet 4, *Putting Families on the Map*, UN International Year of the Family 1994.

ACTIVITY

1 While there will not be any one 'ideal' form of childcare which will suit everyone's circumstances, investigate by interview or survey the kind of childcare which people would ideally prefer for their children.

2 Who, in families, tends to be responsible for making childcare arrangements and for paying for them?

3 Talk to childminders, nannies and nursery staff about their pay and conditions of work. Are they satisfied with these?

4 Investigate the government's proposal (in mid-1995) to provide vouchers to parents with nursery-age children with which they can 'buy' pre-school care for their 4-year-olds.

Informal carers

The *General Household Survey* estimated that in 1990, 6.8 million people in the UK had some caring responsibilities for sick, disabled or frail elderly people. This represents an increase of almost 1 million people since 1985. Of these carers, 1.4 million adults are caring for 20 hours or more a week. The main carers of older people are families themselves – in particular women, in their role as mothers and daughters. Men carers are most likely to be caring for a spouse. Nearly one in five carers is 65 or over, but nearly one in three carers (29%) who care for the sick, elderly or disabled for more than 20 hours a week also has children under the age of 16 to care for. (International Year of the Family Factsheet 4, *Families and Caring*.)

Mortality

The mortality rate refers to the number of deaths per 1,000 living members of a population per year (and infant mortality to the number of deaths of infants under one year old per 1,000 live births per year). Mortality rates are used to measure the health status of a population. If significant numbers of the population are dying prematurely for reasons other than war or an unexpected disaster, then there is a need to investigate the causes of this phenomenon.

From the late 1860s onwards, there has been a continuous national trend of falling mortality levels (infant mortality levels started falling steeply from 1900 onwards). Between 1861 and 1961, the death rate in the UK halved from 24 to 12 per 1,000, and life-expectancy increased. Why are people living longer today?

There is considerable debate about the possible reasons for this trend. Earlier historians often claimed that nineteenth-century advances in medical science, along with preventative public health measures, caused the fall in mortality. Thomas McKeown, in the 1970s, challenged this view by suggesting that the single main cause of mortality decline was a generally rising standard of living at the time. This meant that people could afford to eat larger quantities of more varied food because of rising wage levels. This then gave them greater resistance to disease. However, historians such as S. Szreter now suggest that McKeown's ideas fail to explain the persistence of high mortality rates in the growing urban areas of the UK in the nineteenth century. Although at this time people may have enjoyed higher wages and greater food consumption, the unsanitary conditions created in these growing cities overwhelmed the health benefits derived from more money and a better diet.

Mortality rates only really began to fall in the cities when the public health movement got under way and two Public Health Acts (1848 and 1875) were passed. These Acts ensured two essential facilities in towns:

- efficient waste-disposal systems
- adequate supplies of clean water

and they also helped to increase the number of medical officers of health in the country as well as other health professionals (S. Szreter, pp. 136–148).

At first sight, this debate about what may have reduced mortality levels in the second half of the nineteenth century may seem rather remote from health concerns today. However, the question about whether nutritional intake affects our long-term health and resistance to disease is an interesting one. How important is nutrition compared to other factors such as a clean environment and ready access to medical aid in affecting our long-term health and life-expectancy? Social changes in the production, retailing, marketing and consumption of food over the past 30 years mean that many of us are eating more processed and convenience food and higher levels of fat and sugar than is considered healthy. How are these changes likely to affect our long-term health?

A recent survey of the diet of pre-school children (the National Diet and Nutrition

Survey for children aged one and a half to four and a half) carried out by the Office of Population Censuses and Surveys for the Department of Health (HMSO 1995) found that today's children are taller than they were 27 years ago – a good indication that they are well-nourished – but that the majority eat a diet in which the 'wrong' foods are prominent. The foods eaten by the largest proportion of children were: biscuits, 88%; white bread, 86%; whole milk, 83%; savoury snacks, 78%; boiled, mashed and jacket potatoes and chocolates, both 74%: see Figure 7.9 on p. 268.

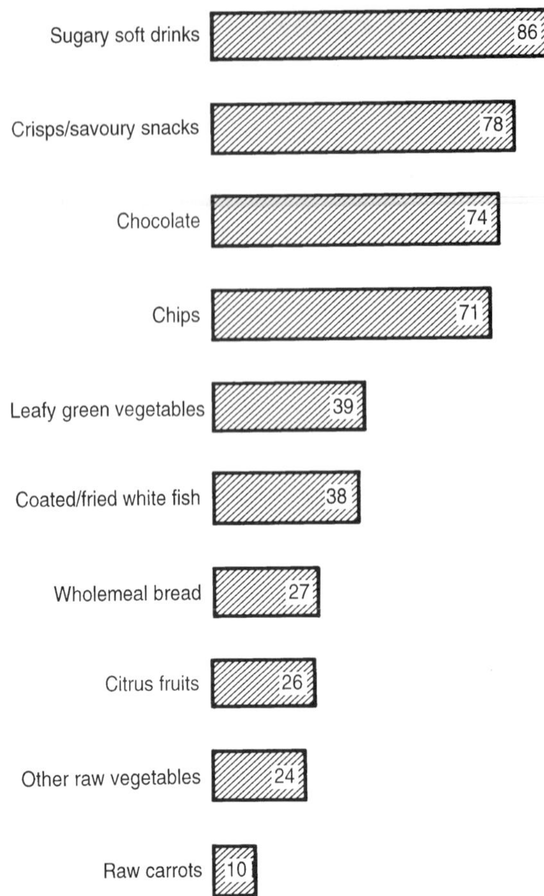

Figure 7.8 Percentage of children in a tested sample eating the listed foods, July 1992 to June 1993, UK
Source: The *Guardian*, 23 March 1995.

ACTIVITY

Do you think that trends in the diets of children today are likely to have any future effect on mortality levels? What other factors may also affect future mortality levels?

Today, the number of deaths in the UK is projected to rise from 658,000 deaths in 1993 to peak at 830,000 in 2051, when those born in the 1960s 'baby boom' will be in their eighties. The average life span is increasing by 10 years every decade: a boy born in 1996 can expect to live until he is 74, a girl until nearly 80.

Heart disease is now the largest single cause of death and the single main cause of premature death (although there has been a recent fall in the death rate from heart disease).

ACTIVITY

People are living longer on average. What possible advantages or disadvantages may arise as a result of this?

Morbidity

Of obvious interest to anyone concerned with health and social care are changes in the kinds of illnesses and diseases which people seem most likely to suffer from. In the 1850s, at the height of the Industrial Revolution in the UK, infectious diseases such as cholera, tuberculosis, typhoid, diphtheria, meningitis, polio and smallpox were a much greater danger to people's health than they are today – as was pregnancy and childbirth where complications were less easily treated. Morbidity rates concern the relative incidence of a particular disease in this country.

What kinds of illness and disease are most prevalent today? There is concern about three major groupings of illness:

1 'Lifestyle'-related illnesses (which nevertheless may have genetic components):
   - cardiovascular-disease disorders (heart attacks and strokes)
   - hypertension (raised blood pressure)
   - obesity
   - mental illness
   - alcohol-related illnesses
   - some cancers

2 Infectious diseases
   - meningitis
   - HIV/Aids
   - viral infections

3 Chronic illnesses and conditions
   - hearing impairment
   - cancers
   - asthma
   - respiratory illnesses
   - diabetes
   - degenerative diseases (those associated with ageing)

Some interesting trends here include:

- In 1991 the Department of Health's *Health Survey for England* found that around a quarter of both men and women interviewed in the survey reported having at least one cardiovascular disease in their life
- Just over one half of men and just under a half of women aged 16–64 in England had a Body Mass Index of more than 25, and so would be classed as overweight or obese
- Over the past 10 years, there has been a striking increase in hospital admissions and GP consultations for asthma. Asthma now affects 2 million people in the UK, half a million of them below the age of 16
- One person in three in England and Wales develops a cancer some time in their life, and cancer now causes one in four deaths
- For many years there has been a strong and consistent upward trend in the incidence of malignant melanoma of the skin (skin cancer) in England and Wales. Skin-cancer cases are currently increasing by 10 per cent a year

(Adapted from *Social Trends* 25 1995.)

ACTIVITY

Data and information about sickness and morbidity comes mainly from the OPCS's *General Household Survey* carried out annually. This has questions about short-term and acute as well as long-term and chronic sickness. Use a copy of the latest *Survey* results to investigate social-class and regional variations in morbidity and sickness rates.

Employment

Over the past 15 years in the UK, there have been enormous changes in the ways in which people work. Around 27 million people now make up the UK's working population, and some key trends are:

- Less than 50% of the working population in the UK has a full-time, long-term job with a traditional employment contract
- 1 million people have more than one job
- 6 million people (one-quarter of all those employed) have part-time jobs (8 out of 10 of these jobs are filled by women)
- Self-employment has more than doubled in the past 15 years. There are now 3 million people self-employed
- 1.5 million employees are in temporary jobs
- Shift-working is becoming more widespread
- Job-sharing is an alternative form of working which is becoming established in some areas of employment
- Homeworking and teleworking are growing forms of employment (but not to the large degree some people predicted). One million homeworkers (mainly women) are working long hours, with no sickness or pension entitlements, for an average of £1.28 an hour, according to a study carried out in 1994 (*Home Trusts* by Ursula Huws, for the National Group on Homeworking, 1994)

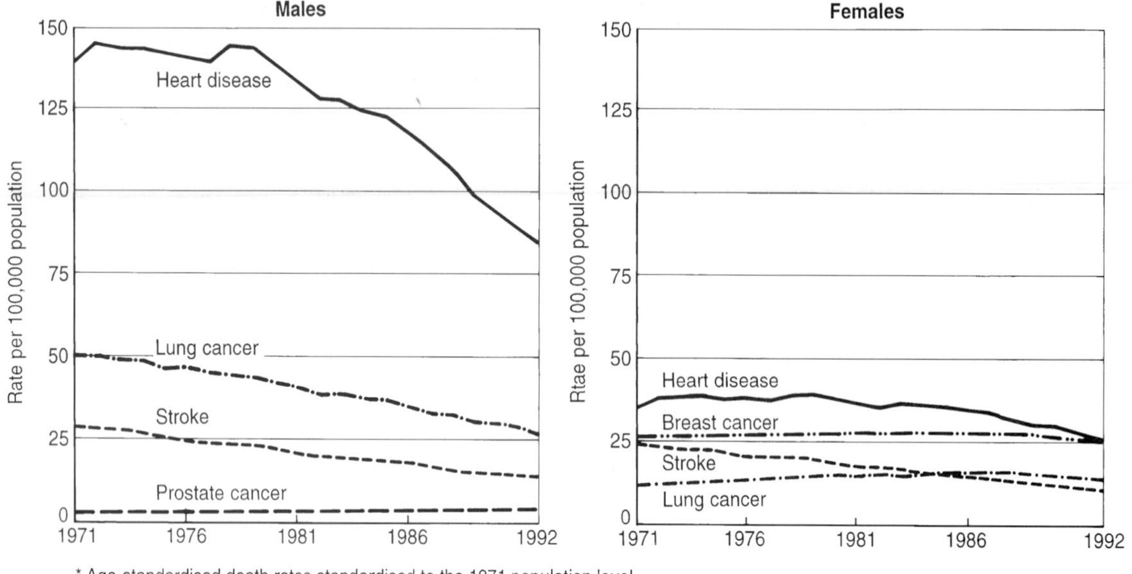

Figure 7.9 Death rates* for people aged under 65, by gender and selected cause of death, in England and Wales
Source: Social Trends 25, 1995 Central Statistical Office. Crown Copyright, 1995. Reproduced by the permission of the Controller of HMSO and the Central Statistical Office.

- Franchising, subcontracting and the use of consultants are ways in which organisations pay to get work done without themselves employing extra people

(Adapted from 'You've got to go with the flow' by Chris Brewster in the *Guardian Careers*, 22 April 1995)

ACTIVITY

1 What has caused these changes to people's patterns of work? Use the information above as the basis for a discussion about the causes and consequences of these changes.

2 Using historical sources, contrast these recent employment patterns with patterns of employment for men and women of different social classes during the nineteenth and early twentieth centuries.

Unemployment

Official statistics on unemployment have put the number of unemployed in 1995 at 2.7 million, although this figure is challenged by other people:

HIDDEN JOBLESS 'STANDS AT 2.3M'

Labour claimed yesterday that figures from the Department of Employment showed that nearly five million people were seeking jobs, compared with the official statistic of 2.7 million unemployed . . .

It based its claim on a parliamentary answer to Harriet Harman, the shadow employment minister, giving figures from the International Labour Organisation's tally of unemployed and 'economically inactive' . . .

But Philip Oppenheim, the Employment Minister, said that the group, which included some long-term sick, those who had given up looking for jobs and people who said they would work if they could find adequate childcare, had always existed and, at the end of the 1970s, was higher than in August last year.

(The Guardian, *7 February 1995)*

One of the most recent pieces of research into the pattern and nature of unemployment and the way it might be affecting men and women is a study carried out by the Employment Department. Based on data from the Spring-1993 Labour Force Survey, this research uses the International Labour Organisation's definition of unemployment:

> The International Labour Organisation (ILO) definition of unemployment . . . refers to people without a paid job, who are available to start work within the next two weeks and who had either looked for work in the four weeks prior to interview or were waiting to start a job they had obtained.
>
> Unemployment based on the ILO definition includes all those people who are actively seeking and available to start work whether or not they are claiming benefit.
>
> The ILO unemployment rate is the percentage of economically active people who are ILO unemployed.
>
> (Employment Gazette, *July 1994)*

The key findings of this research were as follows:

- Men's share of total unemployment has grown steadily in recent years: men composed 68 per cent of the total in spring 1993 compared with only 60 per cent in 1984
- The unemployment rate for married women (5.5 per cent) was less than half that for men and non-married women (both 12.3 per cent); this gap has widened considerably in recent years
- People who had lost or left their previous jobs made up a bigger proportion of the total unemployed (65 per cent in spring 1993 compared with 51 per cent in 1984)
- Some 13 per cent of the unemployed were returners to the labour market – down from 21 per cent in 1990 but similar to the 1984 level
- New entrants to the labour market (mostly young people) formed about 9 per cent of the unemployed total, down from 13 per cent in 1984 although a slight increase on 1990
- Self-employment was losing popularity as an option for unemployed people. Only 3 per cent (83,000) were seeking to become self-employed in spring 1993 – 10 per cent down on the year before
- Long-term unemployment as a proportion of the total unemployed was 42 per cent – up from 34 per cent in 1990
- Unemployment rates were three times higher for those previously in manual jobs than for those in non-manual employment
- Unemployment rates were highest in construction (20 per cent) and lowest in banking and finance (6 per cent)
- Unemployment rates rose faster for those with no or lower levels of qualification: in the year to spring 1993 the rate for those with no qualifications rose by 3 per cent, compared with 1.1 per cent for people with qualifications above A level

(Employment Gazette, *July 1994)*

ACTIVITY

Use the key findings listed above to answer the following questions and provide a basis for further research and discussion.

1 What are the differences in the unemployment rates for
(a) men
(b) married women
(c) non-married women?
Why might these differences exist?

2 What percentage of the unemployed were new entrants (mostly young people) to the labour market?

3 By what percentage has long-term unemployment as a proportion of total unemployment risen since 1990? What might account for this rise?

4 Which groups of workers are more likely to face unemployment? What reasons might exist for this?

5 To what extent does the possession of qualifications seem to affect the likely chances of being unemployed?

Migration

Changes in the movements of the population (either internally – within a country – or externally – into or out of a country) have always been of interest because of the social changes which accompany them. Changes in internal migration patterns in the UK over the past century are discussed later in this chapter. In general, there is a continuing trend for people to move out of Greater London, the west Midlands and the north-west. More people moved to the south-west, the rest of the south-east, the east Midlands and East Anglia than left those areas.

EXTERNAL MIGRATION

Movements of people into and out of the UK have occurred over the centuries. People have immigrated to the UK for a variety of reasons, which include:

- the chance of a better standard of living and paid employment
- refugee status – fleeing from persecution, danger, famine or religious wars in their own countries
- to join relatives already settled in this country

Emigration *from* the UK has been prompted by a similar range of factors:

- In the nineteenth century, white people from the UK emigrated to new lives in the old Commonwealth colonies such as Canada, Australia and New Zealand, or to parts of the world ruled by the British Empire, such as Africa, the West Indies or India
- In the twentieth century, emigration has often been prompted by the desire for a better or different lifestyle, e.g. in Australia, Europe or the USA

During the nineteenth century, more people emigrated from the UK than entered it. This remained the pattern until the period following the end of the Second World War. In the 1950s in the UK, there were large numbers of unfilled job vacancies in certain sectors of the economy. This labour shortage meant that employers started advertising the vacancies in countries such as Jamaica, Barbados, Pakistan and India. Many people in those countries had, under the 1948 Nationality Act, British-citizen status and were entitled to live and work in the UK. Attracted by the prospect of higher rates of pay and better living conditions than existed in their own countries, many people took up the changes offered, and there was a significant increase in immigration to the UK over the period 1950–60.

While there have been black people in the UK for many centuries, most black immigration into the UK has taken place since 1945. Their increasing numbers in the population rapidly became a focus for political controversies and tensions. A series of Immigration Acts were passed in the period 1962 to 1981 which made it increasingly difficult for black British passport-holders to immigrate to this country. As a result of these changes, the numbers of Asian and Afro-Caribbean immigrants to this country have steadily fallen. This trend has to be contrasted with the fact that because Britain is a member of the European Union, citizens of other member countries have an automatic right to work in the UK, and their immigration rights are *not* similarly restricted.

For further information, students are strongly advised to read an excellent account of migration patterns and race relations in *Sociology Themes and Perspectives* Haralambos and Holborn Fourth Edition Collins Educational 1995 London pp. 658–667.

ACTIVITY

1 Discuss the view that British immigration policy since the 1960s has been essentially racist.

2 Are there people in your class, school, college or neighbourhood who have experienced migration? What were their experiences?

The International Passenger Survey (IPS) is the main source of information on migration between the UK and other countries. It excludes migration between the UK and the Irish Republic, the movement of armed forces and their dependants, asylum seekers and others who enter the UK as visitors but subsequently qualify as migrants by staying for at least a year ('visitor switchers').

In 1992 IPS results seemed to indicate that more people left the UK than entered it. However, if allowances are made for asylum seekers, visitor switchers and movement to and from the Irish Republic, there was a net civilian *inward* migration of about 34,000 – lower than in previous years.

Richard Skellington and Paulette Morris have raised questions about the reliability of immigration statistics. For example, the IPS figures mentioned above are estimates based on only a very small sample of a few hundred interviews with people arriving in and leaving the country. Home Office statistics on migration tend to make detailed records of people immigrating to the UK but not of people emigrating. Skellington and Morris therefore suggest that

> the purpose of these [migration] figures is not to determine loss or gain of population through migration, nor is it to assist the allocation of resources for new immigrants, since the figures are concerned only with where people have come from, not where they may be settling. They are thus useless in ascertaining areas of the country where particular social or educational needs might arise.
>
> *(Skellington and Morris 1992)*

For a fuller discussion of this issue see Skellington and Morris 1992, p. 23.

People applying for and being granted asylum status still account for a significant proportion of immigrants each year.

LIVING STANDARDS, WEALTH AND POVERTY

Until recently, when considering social change over the past 150 years, there was a tendency to associate the UK in the nineteenth century with absolute poverty, the workhouse, beggars, alcoholism, destitution and a huge gap between the living standards of the rich and the poor, and the UK in the twentieth century with a series of reforms which represented progress, state responsibility for the poor, an increasing income equality and, at worst, relative poverty. But how can poverty be measured and defined? Is there less poverty today than in Victorian Britain? What social, economic, demographic and political changes and pressures now have an impact upon the nature and scale of poverty in the UK? Similar questions can, of course, be asked about 'wealth'. What is it? How can it be measured? Are people, on average, 'better off' than they were in the nineteenth century? How do people's incomes, savings, investments, inheritance and winnings affect their living standards? What differences exist between the income and wealth of various groups in the UK?

Towards the end of the nineteenth century, a number of researchers became interested in attempting to measure, explore and document the extent of poverty in the UK. Their interest was sparked by several factors including feelings of despair at worsening social conditions, a desire to expose the hypocrisy of those who clung to Victorian ideas of the Church, philanthropy and self-help, and a concern about what the working class poor might do if measures were not taken by the government to ease their condition. Some of

Table 7.8 Applications received for asylum (excluding dependants) and decisions*, by main geographical area of origin, in 1993 in the UK

	Europe and Americas	Africa	Middle East	Asia	Nationality not known	All applications
Applications received	5,280	10,295	1,520	5,175	100	22,370
Decisions* taken						
Recognised as a refugee and granted asylum	350	865	340	35	–	1,590
Not recognised as a refugee but granted exceptional leave	925	6,825	800	2,575	–	11,125
Refused asylum and exceptional leave	1,275	6,675	310	2,405	25	10,690
Applications withdrawn	470	470	160	805	15	1,925
Applications outstanding at end of year	13,275	20,675	2,550	9,195	15	45,805

* Excludes South East Asia Refugees. Information is of initial determination decisions, excluding the outcome of appeals or other subsequent decisions. Decisions figures do not necessarily relate to applications made in 1993.
Source: Social Trends 25, 1995 Central Statistical Office. Crown Copyright, 1995. Reproduced by the permission of the Controller of HMSO and the Central Statistical Office.

these early researchers used sophisticated statistical techniques to document poverty. Seebohm Rowntree studied poverty in York in *Poverty: a Study of Town Life* (1901), and Charles Booth's *The Life and Labour of the People of London* (1902), although subsequently criticised for some of its research methods, was a serious attempt to measure the extent of poverty in London. These studies confirmed each other's findings that just over a quarter of the populations of these towns could be said to be living in poverty. Rowntree's definition of poverty was based on the idea of a measurable subsistence poverty line below which one did not have the necessities of life. If a family fell below this line, then they were in *primary poverty*. If a family did have enough to live on but some of it was wasted, this was described as *secondary poverty* – a situation for which Rowntree did not always blame the poor, suggesting that their lives were so difficult that they could not be blamed for using some of their money to enjoy themselves or to relieve stress.

These two very important studies were followed by a number of other similar pieces of research into poverty at the beginning of this century. Many of these studies, while rich in statistical evidence, also contained detailed and graphic descriptions and observations of the circumstances of people's lives. Students investigating poverty in the UK today will find plenty of evidence for the influence of these two research traditions. There have been numerous large and small-scale research studies into poverty over the past 90 years. The findings of these remain the subject of considerable controversy: not everyone agrees with the way poverty is measured, with claims about the extent of poverty found, or with claims that poverty has increased over the past 20 years.

Chapter 4 of our first book covering the mandatory units for the GNVQ Advanced Course in Health and Social Care (Thomson et al. 1995) outlines and discusses some continuing inequalities in class, wealth and income in the UK. Students should be alert to the fact that there is a considerable body of literature on this subject: and that research often seems to throw up contradictory findings:

POVERTY CLAIM CHALLENGED

Claims that the poor have become poorer under the Tories were rejected yesterday by the independent Institute for Fiscal Studies.

While those in the lowest income bracket have less money today than the equivalent group in 1979, research suggests they are not the same people. Around half of the poorest 10 per cent escape from poverty each year, according to an analysis of 5,500 households in 1991 and 1992 . . .

Those people who managed to move out of the bottom tenth of the population, many of them pensioners, saw their incomes rise from £92 to £134 a week, while those who remained in poverty on average experienced a rise of £3 a week.

The worst-off group are those who entered poverty during the survey year, having average incomes of just £84 each week. They have often lost jobs or been divorced . . .

Separate research from the IFS also suggested that recent estimates of the gap between rich and poor have been too high. Most studies use measures of household income, but the Institute said that levels of spending could be a better guide. This is because the amount of cash coming in may be under-reported, especially by the self-employed, and some families may sustain their standard of living by dipping into savings or by borrowing . . .

(The Guardian, *25 May 1995)*

On the other hand, a survey by Department of Social Security statisticians of the period 1979–90/1, entitled *Households Below Average Income*, showed that the poorest families in the UK suffered a cut of 14% in their real income over this period, while the average household enjoyed an increase of 36%. The less well-off half of the population now receives only a quarter of the total income of the country, whereas in 1979 they received a third. Thirteen and a half million people (24% of the population), including 3.9 million children, are living on less than half the average income (reported in the *Guardian*, 1 July 1993).

ACTIVITY

Contrast the data in the two sources of information above. What differences emerge in the assessment of the distribution of wealth and income?

ACTIVITY

Descriptive accounts of poverty give an insight into the lives of the poor which statistics cannot. Contrast the following two accounts.

CHILDREN OF THE ESTATES LIVING IN STATE OF DESPAIR

There is a small boy in the playground, probably about eight years old, and he is crying while his young mother looks away. In a flat voice, she says: 'Shut your mouth.' He cries on. 'Shut your mouth'. He cries on. She turns and leans into his face. 'Shut your mouth or I'll slap you.' He shuts his mouth and starts to cry through his nose instead, and his mother looks away again.

The school doors have just opened for the day, and the children are arriving from every corner of the estate: out of the tower blocks with the spray-paint on the walls; past the empty houses with their windows 'tinned up' against the thieves; down the road where the young woman was murdered; round the corner and into the playground. Just about nobody arrives by car.

Outside the doors, it is chaos. A boy shows off the ear-stud he has been given for his birthday. A girl falls off the school wall and takes a cuff across the shoulder from her mother. Somewhere, a car alarm starts screaming. A mother in a dirty track suit shouts: 'Stop it off now' at the baby in her buggy. The boy loses his ear-stud and starts to scream . . . Then the parents start to drift away, the school doors close, and something rather strange begins to happen . . .

The poverty invades the school. You can see it in the fabric of the building, which has bars on its windows and a spiked fence around its grounds, none of which stops joy-riders careering around the playing fields at night, or intruders routinely robbing the building at weekends, leaving a trail of graffiti, syringes and broken windows behind them.

It touches the physical well-being of the children, who sleep in damp houses and turn up wheezing; who wake up to find no food in the house and come to school crying with hunger – in such numbers that seven months ago, the school started laying on breakfast. And it touches their personalities as they grow up in families which have collapsed under the weight of their hardship, spawning problems that are often bizarre, sometimes macabre, occasionally nightmarish, all of which amount to one overwhelming problem which presents itself each day to their head teacher: 'These children have no hope – they live in a state of despair.'

(The Guardian, *17 July 1995)*

We have reached the attic, and in that attic we see a picture which will be engraven on our memory for many a month to come.

The attic is almost bare; in a broken fireplace are some smouldering embers; a log of wood lies in front like a fender. There is a broken chair trying to steady itself against a wall black with the dirt of ages. In one corner, on a shelf, is a battered saucepan and a piece of dry bread. On the scrap of mantel still remaining embedded in the wall is a rag; on a bit of cord hung across the room are more rags – garments of some sort, possibly; a broken flower-pot props open a crazy window-frame, possibly to let the smoke out, or in – looking at the chimney-pots below, it is difficult to say which; and at one side of the room is a sack of Heaven knows what – it is a dirty, filthy sack, greasy and black and evil-looking. I could not guess what was in it if I tried, but what was on it was a little child – a neglected, ragged, grimed, and bare-legged little baby-girl of four. There she sat, in the bare, squalid room, perched on the sack, erect, motionless, expressionless, on duty.

She was 'a little sentinel', left to guard a baby that lay asleep on the bare boards behind her, its head on its arm, the ragged remains of what had been a shawl flung over its legs.

That baby needed a sentinel to guard it, indeed. Had it crawled a foot or two, it would have fallen head-foremost into that unprotected, yawning abyss of blackness below. In case of some such proceeding on its part, the child of four had been left 'on guard'.

The furniture of the attic, whatever it was like, had been seized the week before for rent. The little sentinel's papa – this we unearthed of the 'deputy' of the house later on – was a militiaman, and away; the little sentinel's mamma was gone out on 'a arrand', which, if it was anything like her usual 'arrands', the deputy below informed us, would bring her home about dark, very much the worse for it. Think of that little child keeping guard on that dirty sack for six or eight hours at a stretch – think of her utter loneliness in that bare, desolate room, every childish impulse checked, left with orders 'not to move, or I'll kill yer', and sitting there often till night and darkness came on, hungry, thirsty, and tired herself, but faithful to her trust to the last minute of the drunken mother's absence! 'Bless yer! I've known that young 'un sit there eight 'our at a stretch. I've seen her there of a mornin' when I've come up to see if I could git the rint, and I've seen her there when I've come agin at night,' says the deputy. 'Lor, that ain't nothing – that ain't.'

Nothing! It is one of the saddest pictures I have seen for many a day. Poor little baby-sentinel! – left with a human soul in its sole charge at four – neglected and overlooked: what will its girl-life be, when it grows old enough to think? I should like some of the little ones whose every wish is gratified, who have but to whimper to have, and who live surrounded by loving, smiling faces, and tendered by gentle hands, to see the little child in the bare garret sitting sentinel over the sleeping baby on the floor, and budging never an inch throughout the weary day from the place that her mother had bidden her stay in.

(Simms 1883)

SOCIAL PROBLEMS AND WELFARE PROVISION

The social changes described in the first part of this chapter have by no means eradicated problems such as poverty, unemployment, ill-health, homelessness and crime. Indeed, we enter a minefield when trying to look at the impact upon and the consequences for welfare provision of the relationship between social change and social problems. In negotiating a path through the evidence, we encounter more questions than answers, and some of these questions involve raising sensitive and difficult political issues. Later in this chapter, we shall examine the development and delivery of health and care services. We shall look at how such services are increasingly being provided in four different ways/sectors:

- as centralised services
- as localised services
- in a private sector
- in a voluntary and charitable sector

Students wishing to examine the response of each of these sectors to any social problem need to ask at least some of the following questions:

- What services does each sector provide, if any?
- What laws or legal rulings affect the ways in which provision can be made?
- What demographic or social changes have influenced the nature of the problem, or of the need?
- Why isn't all provision for that particular problem or need made by central government?
- What resources and funding are provided, and by whom?
- What gaps/inadequacies, if any, exist in this funding?
- What implications does this have for the social problem or the need in question?
- Can the social problem be adequately tackled by providing health and social care services, or are other changes in society required? What might these be?
- How do various agencies and organisations and their staff in the different sectors involved perceive both *their role* in alleviating this social problem and the nature of the problem or need in itself?
- Do they all agree on the nature, the definition and the causes of the problem or need?
- To what extent are some sectors of health and care provision working to 'plug gaps' in what they perceive to be inadequate or insufficient provision in other sectors?
- What is the public perception of the social problem or need? What range of attitudes and ideas exist in relation to this problem?

It would be unrealistic to expect you to review all the appropriate literature or carry out your own studies in an attempt to provide adequate answers to all these questions concerning any one social problem. However, consideration of such questions may equip you to enter the minefield mentioned above, understand and negotiate your way through the literature, ideas and evidence you come across, and emerge at the other side relatively unscathed and better informed about the way in which welfare services are changing.

The social construction of social problems

What is a 'social problem'? How are social problems defined? Who does the defining? Does it matter?

At first sight the answers to these questions may seem obvious. A social problem refers to an individual or a group of people who are behaving in ways unacceptable to others. For John Major, a social problem may mean 'offensive beggars:

PM ATTACKS 'OFFENSIVE' BEGGARS

John Major provoked an outcry last night when he said beggars were offensive and could drive tourists and shoppers away from cities. The law

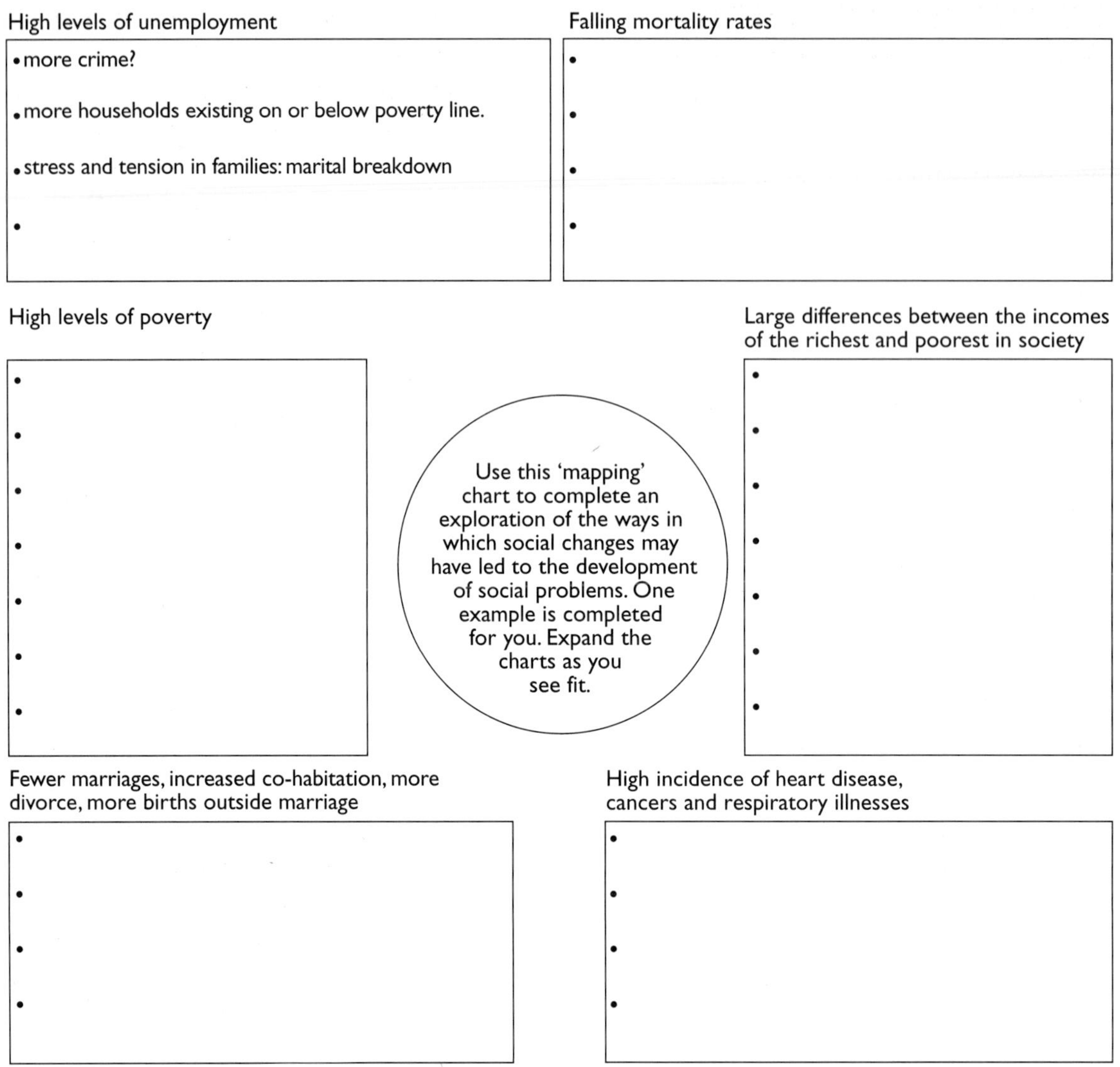

High levels of unemployment
• more crime?
• more households existing on or below poverty line.
• stress and tension in families: marital breakdown
Falling mortality rates
High levels of poverty
Large differences between the incomes of the richest and poorest in society
Use this 'mapping' chart to complete an exploration of the ways in which social changes may have led to the development of social problems. One example is completed for you. Expand the charts as you see fit.
Fewer marriages, increased co-habitation, more divorce, more births outside marriage
High incidence of heart disease, cancers and respiratory illnesses

Figure 7.10 An exercise relating the major consequences of social change to the development of social problems

should be used rigorously to deal with them.

'It is not acceptable to be out on the street,' the Prime Minister said. 'There is no justification for it these days. The problem about begging is as old as the hills.

'It is a very offensive problem to many people who see it.' In areas that depend on tourism 'it is damaging to everybody if that sort of activity continues. If people are in desperately straitened circumstances we have a social security safety net in this country which they can use.'

People should be 'rigorous' in reporting beggars to the police, he said, pointing out that they could be fined up to £1,000 and jailed for up to three years if they turned violent. 'I think the law should be used. It is there. It should be used. It is an offensive thing to beg. It is unnecessary. So I think people should be very rigorous with it.'...

(From an article in the Guardian, *28 May 1994)*

For some teachers it may be 'problem children'; for the victim of a burglary or a robbery it may be criminal behaviour; for someone recently made redundant it may be high levels of unemployment.

Is there any agreement about what can be defined as a social problem?

ACTIVITY

Using the following list, carry out the following four tasks:

1 Read the list and make a note of any of the items which you do *not* think represents a 'social problem' in the UK today.

2 For the rest, try to rank them in order of how serious a problem you think they are in the UK today.

3 Compare your list and rankings with those of others. What differences or similarities emerge in your ideas? Discuss these differences and similarities.

4 Are there any other 'social problems' which you think should be added to the list?

A Sectarian violence in Northern Ireland
B Homelessness
C Unemployment
D Racial violence
E Sexual inequality
F Juvenile crime
G Poverty
H Child abuse
I Domestic violence
J Illegal drug-taking
K Football violence
L Lone-parent families
M Video games
N Disability in old age
O Teenage pregnancy
P Working mothers

As the activity above will probably have demonstrated, there can be considerable difficulty in establishing any agreement over what a social problem is, let alone what may be the *causes* of that problem. Fifty years ago, William Beveridge identified 'five giant social evils' – want, disease, ignorance (lack of education), squalor and idleness (lack of employment) – as the key social problems of the 1940s. Are these still the five most important social problems today? Hulley and Clarke (1991) have suggested that there are two ways of approaching the explanation of social problems. On the one hand, they say, are claims that problems arise from the defects of particular individuals; on the other, problems can be seen as the result of particular patterns of social organisation.

Explanations of social problems based on the individual emphasise defects in the character, personality or behaviour of individuals which have affected their chances of progressing in life. These sorts of explanations often involve a search for an 'X' factor, something which distinguishes 'normal' people from those (the 'deviants') who are the cause of social problems; that is, those people causing social problems are felt to lack something which makes the rest of 'us' normal. These explanations tend also to see problems such as domestic violence, the abuse of children and mental-health conditions as essentially 'private troubles', to do with the failure of particular individuals and families.

Structural explanations of social problems, by contrast, emphasise inequalities in the distribution of wealth, income, power and life-chances in society. People's material conditions and power relations within institutions such as the family are analysed to show how problems may routinely arise. These explanations can attempt to show that the power to define 'normal' and 'deviant' behaviour is also unequally distributed in society. In other words, *ideologies* (sets of ideas or beliefs both about our society and about the places of ourselves and others within it) about what is normal can have a powerful effect on people's self-perceptions and behaviour.

Struggling to achieve normality as defined by 'majority opinion' can expose people to intolerable pressures. For example, a heroin addict may in fact be able to perform a professional job well but must always be under pressure to hide their habit because it is an illegal one. While resistance to dominant ideas about normality can be seen by others as rebellion and deviance, it also exposes the resisting individual to the risk of being labelled as, and subsequently treated as, deviant. For example, homosexual men who express physical affection to one another in public can risk abuse and attack for behaviour which, if it occurred between a heterosexual couple, would be viewed as normal.

Hulley and Clarke (1991) argue that individual explanations of social problems often carry more weight and are seen as closer to 'common sense' than structural explanations; and they are correspondingly more readily believed. However, they do recognise that people may use a variety of explanations, individual and structural, for social problems.

The study of social problems therefore involves looking at two processes:

- how social problems are caused, which will mean looking at explanations which take account of various social factors
- how social problems are socially constructed, which means looking at how dominant ideologies tend to 'lead' people into preferring individual rather than structural explanations for problems

To illustrate the social construction of social problems, we can refer to the notorious trial and conviction in November 1993 of Jon Venables and Robert Thompson for the murder of toddler James Bulger. The two 11-year-olds were sentenced to be detained 'at Her Majesty's pleasure'. Child murderers are extremely rare. Home Office figures show that since 1950, only two other children between the ages of 10 and 13 have been convicted of murder, with another two being convicted of manslaughter. The trial of the two boys amply demonstrated the search for an 'X' factor; what had caused these boys to deviate so far from 'normality' as to kill a toddler? The case was widely reported in the media in November 1993, and continued to be discussed for months afterwards. It became very much a public issue.

Individualist explanations for the murder focused upon:

- the personalities of the two boys, their IQs and mental capacities, along with the characteristics of their relationship with each other and their respective behaviour on the day of the murder. The judge in the case described the conduct of the boys as 'both cunning and very wicked' (*The Independent*, 25 November 1993). Detectives who interviewed the boys called them 'evil freaks of nature, who had killed for a buzz'. Detective Superintendent Albert Kirby of Merseyside police was reported as saying: 'There is no doubt that those two boys were wicked beyond anyone's expectation . . . they had a high degree of cunning and evil' (the *Guardian*, 25 November 1993)
- The personalities and characters of the boys' parents and families, and the fact that they came from broken homes and lone-parent families

Structuralist explanations for the murder focused upon:

- the social and economic backgrounds of the two boys and their families: the levels of social deprivation, unemployment and bad housing experienced by their families
- their alleged exposure to violent video films. The judge in the case suggested that 'I suspect that exposure to violent video films may, in part be an explanation' (*The Independent*, 25 November 1993)
- the lack of response from the 38 people who witnessed the boys with James Bulger, and the general failure of adult society to prevent the tragedy by detecting and dealing with the problems of these children before the murder occurred

Numerous theories for the reasons why these two boys committed murder were put forward by legal and medical experts, by psychologists and psychiatrists, by the police, by the judge on the case, by media witnesses of the trial and by the public. This must have been the most widely discussed criminal case in the UK for many years.

While you might find it useful to research and discuss this case in more detail, we concentrate here on the way in which it exemplifies the distinction between structuralist and individualist explanations for deviance and 'problem behaviour'. The tabloid press at the time clearly favoured individualist explanations, and the concern about these two boys prompted a wider discussion at the time about juvenile crime in general, its causes and solutions. The extent of the influence on the public of individualist as opposed to structuralist explanations is an important issue in this case, as 'what the public thinks' may be a factor in determining the release dates for these two boys. The Home Secretary in 1994, Michael Howard, said that before releasing prisoners serving life for murder (including child murders), a number of factors would be considered, including 'the public acceptability of early release' (the *Guardian*, 27 January 1994).

Social problems and social control

The relationship between social problems – however defined – and social control is a complex one. People defined as social problems are often seen as a threat to society. Their existence seems to challenge ideas of what is normal and thus assumptions about the ways societies should be organised. Several sociologists have noted how certain categories of people appear to arouse disquiet in others. Geoffrey Pearson (1983) has looked at how, since the 1850s, politicians, 'experts', the media and the public have regularly and repeatedly expressed 'respectable fears' about young people, delinquency, hooliganism and anti-social behaviour. The word 'hooligan' itself originated as a term to describe gangs of rowdy youths during the hot summer of 1898.

This is not to say that people do not have 'real' justifications for anxiety about the behaviour and attitudes of people in society, but rather that looking at the *public's response* to a social problem as well as at the problem itself can reveal concerns about what people believe should or should not change in a society. If a 'social problem' appears to have been in existence for a very long time but is talked about as if it were a new phenomenon or a worsening problem, then we need to ask questions about the extent to which it really is a problem or why measures taken to deal with it in the past have not succeeded.

Every society contains elements which attempt to impose and maintain control and social order. In the UK there are the formal structures of the law imposed by parliament and the agencies employed to ensure that the laws are obeyed, such as the police and the courts. There are also rules, formal and informal, in almost every social situation and organisation (such as families, schools and workplaces) which establish expected patterns of behaviour.

Some sociologists have suggested that society requires a certain amount of deviance (i.e. non-compliance with what may be accepted by others as 'normal') because it serves as a reminder to the rest of the society of what *should* happen; it draws the majority of society together against the 'deviants' and, in doing so, strengthens the bonds between people. Such functionalist explanations of deviance have been criticised by Marxists who have argued that certain elite or ruling groups in society will try to define as deviant any groups which appear to threaten the structure of that society and their dominant position within it.

ACTIVITY

'Travellers' are one category of people often regarded as a threat to 'normal' society. Investigate attitudes towards this group of people, or any other which you think is often viewed in a similar light.

The changing social factors which influence welfare provision

In Chapter 6 we considered the political and economic ideologies which shape social policy and welfare provision in this country. Many critics of welfare provision today argue that current social policies do not adequately seem to address (or acknowledge research into) the changing patterns of social life and social stratification in the UK. Whether or not this is a fair criticism is an issue students can explore in their own investigations into specific examples of welfare provision and social change.

Nevertheless, there is no doubt that governments have had to make some response to changing patterns of poverty, housing, education, health and employment, and we highlight these more fully on pp. 292–98. These responses have not always been planned. After the First World War in the UK, for example, social policy was dominated by a concern about unemployment as soldiers returned to civilian life and as the 1930s 'depression' hit the economy. Our next section, which considers the extent to which social stratification still affects access to welfare provision, takes up these issues in more detail.

Social stratification and welfare provision

Social stratification is a particular kind of social inequality. Haralambos and Holborn define it as:

> the presence of distinct social groups which are ranked one above the other in terms of factors such as prestige and wealth. Those who belong to a particular group or stratum will have some awareness of common interests and a common identity. They will share a similar lifestyle which to some degree will distinguish them from members of other social strata.
>
> *(Haralambos and Holborn (1995), p. 21)*

The resources of society (wealth, income, power, status, knowledge) are distributed differently and often unequally among these groups and 'layers' of society. There are many different ways in which it is possible to argue that society is stratified, and the theoretical debate can become quite complex. Students are advised to consult a mainstream sociology textbook such as the one quoted above for a fuller discussion of these debates.

As a starting point for discussion here, however, consult Figure 7.11. These diagrams are clearly oversimplifications of the ways in which stratification occurs in the UK. How would you modify, change and improve them to give a 'truer' picture of the ways in which resources are allocated unequally between different groups in our society?

As far as welfare provision is concerned, two questions arise:

- What is the impact upon the health and welfare of people of their position in the social structure?
- Does one's position in the social structure affect one's access to welfare provision? If so, how?

In exploring these questions, we will focus briefly on two examples: the position of women in the family and society, and the consequences for their health; and issues in access to health and care services for ethnic minorities in the UK. There are, however, many other issues which could be explored here. Do working-class people get a worse deal than other social classes from the health and social care systems in this country? Towards which groups in society are the most resources directed?

EXAMPLE 1: SOCIAL STRATIFICATION AND WOMEN'S HEALTH

In the 1970s, research such as Bernard's into women's experiences of marriage tended to see the roles women adopted within marriage, particularly the housewife role, as detrimental to women's health, especially if women were trying to combine paid employment with the major responsibility for housework and childcare. Studies of the 'wife's marriage' seemed to show that more wives than husbands expressed marital frustration and dissatisfaction, considered their marriages unhappy and initiated divorce proceedings. Compared to their husbands, wives appeared to suffer considerably more stress, anxiety and depression.

Sociologists such as Ann Oakley highlighted the housewife role and housework itself (rather than marriage as an institution) as the prime causes of women's isolation and oppression. Housework was seen to be repetitive and compulsive. It involved an endless cycle of cleaning, washing, cooking and looking after children. Bernard believed that 'being a housewife makes women sick'. She suggested that wives who did not work outside the home suffered from the highest rates of physical and mental illness.

Some studies seem to confirm these assertions. One in five women suffers acute stress or depression, according to a report in 1988 by the government's Women's National Commission. The report argues that women are twice as likely to suffer severe stress as men because they tend to be the buffers and absorbers of stresses in the other members of the family. Women cope by turning stress in on themselves, and this often leads to alcohol or cigarette addiction. Women are heavy 'consumers' of prescribed tranquillisers, and Hilary Graham (1984) argues that women show reluctance to be ill because of their role as 'carers' within the family. Research into the meaning of tranquillisers for women suggests that they are explicitly seen by women as a way of coping with their lives and with caring in particular.

However, while it is argued that women's experience of housework and childcare is isolating and stressful, it is also sometimes suggested that paid employment imposes an additional burden on women who still retain prime responsibility for these domestic roles. This appears to conflict with the idea that paid employment can be a positive influence on women's health.

In her study analysing data from the 1985–6 *General Household Survey*, S. Arber (1990) has attempted to explain these apparent contradictions. She tried to identify factors which would affect:

- women's health *status*, i.e. their long-term 'stock' of health, and
- women's health *state*, i.e. their present state of health

She concludes that women in disadvantaged

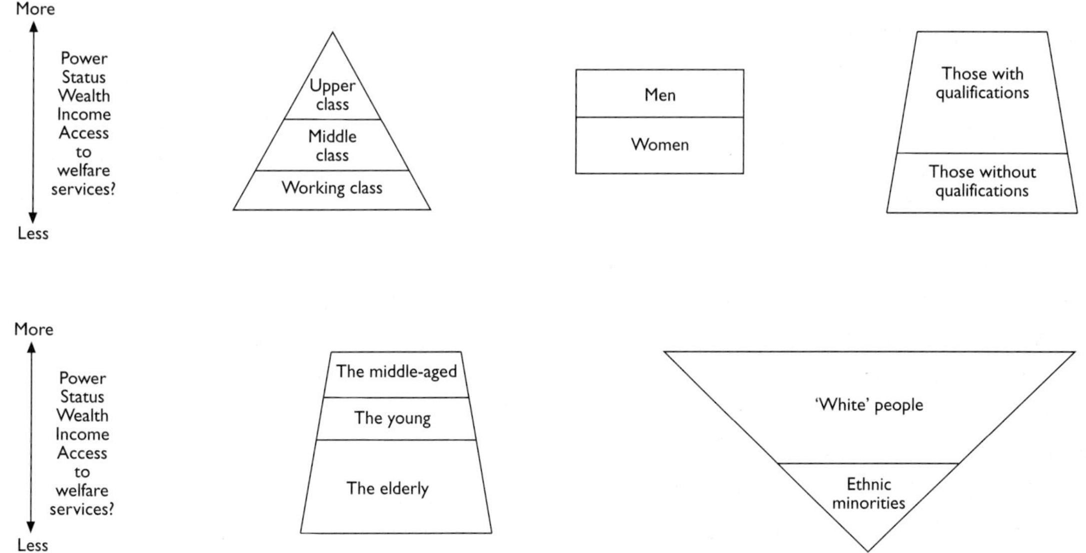

Figure 7.11 Simplified models of stratification in the UK (not to scale)

material circumstances are less likely to be able to cope with the stresses of fulfilling parental, domestic and full-time employment roles than women in more 'privileged' circumstances. More affluent women can use their greater financial resources to ease some of the burdens of housework and childcare (i.e. by buying in paid help), and are more likely to be in types of employment where there is likely to be some flexibility as regards hours worked, arrangements for leave and so on. Arber also argues that the extent to which the woman's partner contributes to the domestic division of labour will influence a woman's ability to manage the demands of a number of roles and the likelihood of role 'overload' and consequent poor health state.

There is also an increasing number of writers who now argue that a domestic role for women does not necessarily mean exploitation, stress and boredom. Yanina Sheeran argues that there is 'a marked reluctance to credit women with a powerful role at the core of family households, and to accept that many men are, for the most part, less visible peripheral beings, who may even be "managed" by a matriarch in some cases' (Sheeran 1993, p. 32).

SOAK IN BATH IS WORKING MOTHERS' ANSWER TO STRESS

A soak in the bath is the working mother's favourite way to relieve stress, a survey shows today.

Six out of 10 mothers find a soak the best way to relax, while a quarter said a drink is their choice. Making love appeals to only one in eight.

The nationwide survey by Gallup for *She* magazine covered 1,015 women, half working full-time and half part-time. Nearly a third had consulted a doctor about stress or a stress illness in the past five years. At least as many claimed to have a reduced sex drive. More than half said they overate. More than half suffered from anxiety or depression, with 40 per cent suffering insomnia. Two thirds of women said their lives were stressful. However, 93 per cent said they managed successfully, and more than three-quarters accepted stress as unavoidable.

Four out of five believed men lacked sympathy and understanding of their stress, and only half believed their partners helped enough at home.

(The Guardian, *1991)*

ACTIVITY

1 In what ways might women's role within society and the family contribute to their health or ill-health?

2 Investigate the ways in which women experiencing stress and tension might seek help for their problems. What services exist to help people in this situation?

EXAMPLE 2: ETHNICITY AND ACCESS TO WELFARE PROVISION

There is currently little published social-policy research about race and poverty, and official statistics on welfare issues rarely contain a breakdown by ethnic origin. For a useful summary of what does exist, see Chapter 6 of Carey Oppenheim's book *Poverty: the Facts* (Oppenheim 1993). Her analysis raises several issues which you may wish to explore in greater depth:

- Unemployment, low pay and poor working conditions are more likely to affect people from ethnic minorities in the UK than they are 'white' people
- There is some evidence to show that while people from ethnic minorities (especially Asian people) are less likely overall to claim benefits, black people and other ethnic-minority groups are more likely to claim unemployment benefit and family income supplement
- How far have racism and racial discrimination affected the delivery of welfare services and excluded ethnic-

minority groups from employment opportunities?
- To what extent have immigration policies disadvantaged people from ethnic minorities? The Immigration Act 1971 ruled that the wives and children of Commonwealth citizens could enter the UK only if a sponsor could support and accommodate them without recourse to 'public funds' such as income support, housing benefit and family credit

CHANGING VALUES AND WELFARE PROVISION

In this section we will look at the ways in which some of the social changes discussed in this chapter may have led to changing social values and attitudes and therefore to changes in the ways in which social problems may be seen.

Factors influencing social attitudes

For a fuller discussion of these theories and ideas, students are advised to refer to Chapter 4 of our first book, *Health and Social Care* (Thomson et al. 1995), which discusses the formation of attitudes through the process of *socialisation*. We all acquire particular ways of seeing both the world and the behaviour of others around us. However, social scientists are also interested in the ways in which certain sets of ideas and beliefs (*ideologies*) come to be more widely held, more popular and more taken-for-granted than others at particular times or among particular groups of people, or both. For example, have right-wing ideologies about the need for greater self-reliance and independence had a significant impact on peoples' own beliefs over the past 20 years?

One set of influences on our attitudes is the *mass media*. Over the past 50 years the forms and technologies of the mass media (newspapers, books, magazines, radio, television, video, cinema, advertising) have expanded and developed at such a rate that it would be unlikely that they had no influence at all on the formation of attitudes and opinions. However, there is considerable debate among social scientists as to the extent and form of that influence, and students are recommended to consult a media-studies or sociology-of-the-media text for a further elaboration of these arguments. There are, however, some relevant questions to be raised, if not answered, in relation to social change and welfare provision. For example:

- To what extent are our images of 'social problems' formed by the mass media? How might the processes involved in the selection and presentation of those images affect the way we view 'social problems' themselves and the solutions to those problems?
- What role do the media play in the creation of 'moral panics' over certain events or issues in society? What effects do 'moral panics' have on the policy-making process, and therefore on the provision of welfare services?
- What role do the media play in offering us a source of information and analysis about changes in social policy and welfare provision?
- What role may the media therefore play in raising people's expectations in relation to health and welfare services?

Another source of ideas and attitudes is our *education* and the *type and content of the schooling* we receive. Here again, there is great debate about the influence of such experiences. Can schools offer equal chances for educational achievement to all their pupils, regardless of their social and economic backgrounds? Can they compensate for inequalities in society? Do qualifications provide a route out of a poverty trap? Whose values and ideas do schools tend to reinforce?

Recent concern with standards and grades has led to questions being asked about the pressures exerted upon students in the current examination system and the consequent implications for their health and welfare. Is a competitive ethos in the best interests of students?

OUR GUILT FOR STUDENT'S SUICIDE

The remarks by the coroner after the tragic death of Charlotte Thompson (September 2) struck a chord with me. I had just spent time comforting my distressed daughter who 'only' got a B in GCSE Spanish after one year of study when others achieved grade A. She told me of girls at her academic, independent school complaining they had 'only got an A and not a starred A' in other subjects. The responsibility for this unhealthy pressure on young people lies with us all.

The Government introduced league tables which cause schools to expect high grades in order to maintain or improve their positions in the ratings. Universities must share responsibility for not making it clear to applicants that they are interested in the whole person and not just good grades. Schools must also realise that in colluding with league tables and publicising high grade achievers they risk making many pupils feel inadequate . . .

Finally, we parents must have the courage to recognise our children's limitations but be prepared to encourage them to realise their potential in other areas of their lives. If there is one thing the last 15 years have revealed it is that Oxbridge graduates do not necessarily have the intelligence to govern the country.

(The Guardian, *4 September 1994)*

Our political attitudes – how we vote, what parties we support and what ideas about the government and the running of the country we hold – depend not only on our social position in society – our class, our religion, the kind of housing we live in and our education – but also on how, and to what extent, various issues are taken up by the political parties. For example, there are different views about which is most important for society, controlling inflation or reducing unemployment. Working-class voters may be more likely to support parties that emphasise the reduction of unemployment as they are more vulnerable to it. Middle-class voters with relatively more secure jobs may prefer to see inflation brought down and vote accordingly. Teachers and nurses may have an interest in seeing more government spending on health and education, while business people who send their children to private schools may have an interest in lower taxes. Anthony Heath (1992) suggests that such voting patterns may also reflect people's values. People with radical, left-wing views on defence or welfare, for example, are unlikely to choose careers in business, where their views may be unpopular.

QUESTION

To what extent do you think that people are influenced in their political attitudes and voting behaviour by what the political parties say and do as far as health and welfare policies are concerned?

Economic factors may also influence our attitudes. The amount of money we earn and possess and our views about the spending of that money will inevitably influence our ideas about other people and how they acquire and spend money. Environmental factors, too, relate to all the others mentioned above. Where we live, the conditions we live in and the quality of our environment can all affect our view of the world.

Factors which might prevent the take-up of services provided

While attention is often focused on the inadequacies of services in meeting people's needs, another problem for health and social care workers is that of ensuring that the services which are on offer are

- known to potential users
- used as fully as possible
- used in the most productive and helpful way
- not monopolised by some groups at the expense of others

Activity

Imagine that you are setting up a new rape crisis and counselling centre in a small town. Decide what services you intend to provide. How could you go about ensuring that these services are offered to and used by those who might require them most?

What, then, might prevent people from using services provided?

1 If people do not know about their right to benefits and services, they cannot begin to start to claim them. The work of the Citizen's Advice Bureaux (700 offices in England and Wales) illustrates the enormous demand for information. In 1994 they received 1.8 million enquiries about social security, 1.77 million enquiries about debt and consumer rights, 840,000 about employment, 763,000 which were related to family or personal issues and 761,000 to do with housing.

   Some local authorities and charities employ welfare-rights officers whose sole job it is to ensure that people are better informed of their rights in relation to the welfare services.

Question

How could, in general, people be made better aware of the services and benefits on offer to them?

2 Where people have had no previous experience of particular health or social care professionals and organisations, the media can be an important source of information. However, it can also be a source of stereotyped ideas about services or providers, and may therefore be partly the reason why services are ignored. For example, social workers and teachers often get a 'bad press', and people may, as a result, be reluctant to contact social-services departments or, as adults, to return to education.

3 In a society where great stress is placed on independence and self-reliance, people may view the use of counselling, therapeutic and self-help/support groups with mistrust. They may fear the stigma of being labelled as 'someone with a problem' if people realise that they have sought help from others. They may simply not wish to involve others in their own affairs.

   Preferring to 'solve their own problems' may work perfectly well for some people but may force others into isolation, depression and even suicidal despair.

Activity

If you study in a college or a school which employs student counsellors, you may wish to invite a counsellor to talk to you about how they experience and try to overcome this problem.

4 The increasing use of charges for certain areas of health, education and social care services is a cause for concern. Prescription charges (which rose by 25p in April 1996 to £5.50 per item), charges for dental and eye treatments, and 'voluntary contributions' for school visits, music tuition, swimming lessons and special events in schools all mean that health and care services are no longer entirely free 'at the point of service' to users.

   A Consumers Association survey in 1995

found that just 64% of people now have all their dental care wholly or partly paid for by the NHS, compared with 80% in 1992. Only 60% of the UK's dentists are accepting new NHS patients. The survey also found that 41% of people who had not been to the dentist in the previous 18 months cited cost as the reason.

5 Although the overall number of people on hospital waiting lists began to fall in 1995, there are still over 1 million people on NHS waiting lists for treatment in England and Wales. In 1994 only 3,394 patients had to wait more than 18 months for treatment, according to the NHS Executive Committee's Annual Report. However, waiting lists often 'push' people into paying for private provision, and some commentators suggest that long waiting lists do promote greater use of the private sector in health. Indeed, income from private patients went up by 63% in the first three years of the NHS market, according to official statistics. Trust hospitals can now operate private pay-bed units, and NHS hospitals made £185.2 million from pay beds in 1993/4.

(Source: the *Guardian*, 4 May 1995.)

NHS CHIEF HAD PRIVATE OPERATION TO BEAT QUEUE

The head of the health care think tank which prompted the programme of hospital closures in London yesterday admitted he had paid for a private operation because the National Health Service waiting list was too long.

Robert Maxwell, chief executive of the King's Fund, said he had an operation for osteoarthritis of the knee at St Thomas's hospital, south London, which is being merged with nearby Guy's under the closure programme.

Mr Maxwell said he would have had to wait a year for NHS treatment. 'Many people are forced to have private treatment who do not wish it. My knee was serious enough an impediment to my work and I wanted to get it operated on as soon as possible . . .'

(From an article in the Guardian, *1 March 1995)*

On the other hand, the 1994 British Social Attitudes Survey found that public dissatisfaction with the NHS was falling sharply: the proportion expressing dissatisfaction with the NHS fell to 38% in 1993, compared with 47% in 1990.

6 Finally, excessive bureaucracy (long and complex forms and questionnaires to fill in, means-tested assessments, long waits for the results of assessments and interviews, problems and errors in the payment of benefits) is another reason why services may be less utilised than anticipated.

DISABLED 'TESTED LIKE WITCHES'

Disabled people in county Durham are losing appeals for social security benefits because they are managing to walk – to the appeal hearings.

With impeccably Kafkaesque logic, disability appeal tribunals sitting at Elvet House, Durham, are rejecting benefits claims from people who succeed in turning up to present their case.

Local welfare rights advisers say appellants have to find their way through a 100-yard obstacle course to reach the tribunal room. If they manage it, they are penalised for doing so.

'It's just like the medieval witch's test: if you floated, you were guilty,' said John Salisbury, head of Durham county council's welfare rights unit.

The tribunals are held in a ground-floor room at Elvet House, a 1950s building which accommodates several government agencies. But the route to the room is tortuous.

From the car park, where appellants only sometimes manage to park, the route is up a step or ramp, through two doors to reception, right turn through a door, down a long corridor and through a further door, left turn through a door, and, finally, right turn through yet another door into a waiting room. All doors are heavy fire doors, kept closed.

Rights advisers say the route is being regarded by tribunals as an unofficial and, they contend, unlawful test of the individual's mobility.

Disability appeal tribunals were introduced in 1992, when they were first held at Elvet House, and comprise three people, including a doctor . . .

(From an article in the Guardian, *7 February 1994)*

THE PROVISION OF WELFARE SERVICES

The first part of this chapter explored the factors which influence the ways in which governments formulate social policies in response to the needs people have for care, education and personal support; for the prevention and treatment of illness; and for financial and material help. This section will look at how, in practice, services are provided – or, using the current jargon, *delivered* – to people.

The phrase 'service delivery' suggests some process which is unproblematic, benign, efficient but rather impersonal, such as milk delivered daily to someone's door. In this section, one of the most important questions to bear in mind is whether this concept of service delivery is the most appropriate way to describe and assess the relationships which exist between

- those who formulate social policies
- those who have a practical or professional (or both) responsibility for the care, welfare, health, education, control or financial and material support of others
- those on the receiving end of such policies, i.e. the public

In asking questions about what methods or ways of providing services to people have been used, it is also helpful to try to stand back from what you read. If you were organising these services now, would you do so in the ways that have been attempted to date?

ACTIVITY

Most people are likely to have had some experience of being on the receiving end of health or care services. Almost all people will have had some formal education on this area.

1 Discuss one or two specific examples of health or education provision. These could be your experience of the services provided by your local GP surgery or a health clinic, or of taking GCSE examination courses, or of primary school.

2 What do you think are or were the best and the worst aspects of the service you are discussing? What was helpful and unhelpful about the physical facilities, the approach and behaviour of the staff, and the access to the service? If the service was compulsory (e.g. education), how did that affect your response to it? Make a list of points you come up with and then discuss your list with someone thinking about the same service. Did you find any areas of agreement or disagreement about the services provided?

3 What suggestions would you have for improving the services you are discussing? Do you think that there would be any problems in making those improvements?

We all have valuable personal experiences of some welfare services which we can use to evaluate those services. However, it does also help to have a wider understanding of the range of services provided, and of how they have developed and changed. Few people, even those working in health, education or care contexts, have a complete overview of all the services available to the public. There have been an enormous number of changes in the law, in social attitudes and trends, and in political areas, making it hard to keep up with developments in one particular area, let alone in others. A secondary-school teacher may therefore know a great deal about recent developments in the National Curriculum and the changes imposed by the most recent Education Acts, but may know less about the ways in which education in primary schools or the further-education sector is changing. Similarly, a nurse working in a large teaching hospital may be aware of the changes that the 1990 NHS and Community Care Act is having upon their work but be less clear about how it is also affecting the role of social workers.

ACTIVITY

In small groups, discuss what the advantages might be of gaining a wider knowledge of the ways in which social services are organised in this country.

You will probably come up with a broad range of ideas, but here are several to prompt further discussion:

- When you finally choose a specific career or job, your training may be relatively specialised. Taking a wider view of services at this stage may help you to decide what kind of work you might like to do and to gain an understanding of how that work relates to other forms of service provision
- In some health, care and education services, there is an increased emphasis on multi- or inter-agency working. Teamwork between groups of professionals is very common, and therefore it may help to have some understanding of the context in which other people work
- In many areas of health, education and care work, staff will at some point have to respond to requests for advice about other services which might help people, apart from the ones which they themselves provide. For instance, a teacher may have to refer a pregnant teenager to counselling and advice services. Knowing your way round the structure of health and care services in the UK may enable you to provide accurate and appropriate advice when asked
- If you are doing a work placement or a period of work experience as a part of your course, a knowledge of the wider structure of services may help you to appreciate how the department or organisation you are working with fits into a wider structure of services. You may have a better appreciation of the roles of the staff and of who controls and influences those services
- Services have developed in different ways in the UK, as the following pages will show. Having an overall view may make it easier for you to make judgements about and comparisons between services; good practice in some areas will highlight unhelpful approaches in others

Exploring the range of models and methods of welfare provision: the changing role of the state

Welfare provision in the UK has, as we have seen, had to respond to a large number of demographic and social changes. Fundamental social problems such as poverty, ill-health, unemployment and crime have not disappeared, although the ways in which they are experienced by people may have changed. The social relationships of class, gender and race still structure people's lives. The ways in which welfare provision is made today, however, are now also affected by political ideology, funding issues and technological change. New political ideologies since the 1970s (discussed fully in Chapter 6) have, at their base, an increasing concern about the cost of welfare services to the taxpayer and the state. To reduce this economic burden, more right-wing politicians have argued that:

- competitive markets should exist in the health and social care services
- public expenditure on these services should be cut
- the role of local authorities should be reduced, and that there should be more centralised control of services
- there should be a mixed economy of welfare, i.e. a mixture of private and public provision of services

The years of the Thatcher and Major Conservative governments from 1979 onwards have witnessed the practical implementation of many of these ideas. The pattern of welfare services provided in the UK today is thus radically changing, and in this section of the present book, we intend to provide you with ideas for exploring and investigating the range and types of social services in the UK. With social services taken in its most general sense, seven areas will be studied:

- personal social services
- health
- education
- youth services
- social security
- housing
- employment

A diagrammatic overview of current provision in each area will highlight recent relevant legislation. The section will then conclude with ideas and suggestions for further research. Social policy and welfare provision in the UK is constantly changing. The information provided in this book was accurate at the time of going to press, but you may need to check whether any changes have occurred or are likely to occur in the area you are studying.

The diagrammatic overview of each area mentioned above has been organised into four primary 'models' of the already-mentioned ways in which social services have come to be delivered in the UK:

- as centralised services
- as localised services
- as services provided by an independent, private sector
- as services provided through charities, the voluntary sector, non-profit-making organisations and other associations and agencies

(Refer also to the 'Useful Addresses' section at the end of this chapter in conjunction with these diagrams.) Brief descriptions of each type are given below.

CENTRALISED SERVICES

Central government departments, such as the Department for Education and Employment, and the Department of Health, and related agencies (such as the Benefits Agency) hold the purse strings on what can be spent on health, education and welfare; and levels of expenditure are decided by parliament. Each department is led by a government minister who is a member of the *cabinet*. The cabinet is a group of government ministers selected by the prime minister to form the senior executive 'advisory' group in running the country.

Centralised services respond to and implement parliamentary legislation on social policy, EU regulations and directives (see p. 223) and other parliamentary orders and regulations which arise from the legislation. Some of these centralised services and their related agencies run local, regional or area departments or organisations throughout the UK. Sometimes, provision in Scotland and Northern Ireland is separate but similar.

LOCALISED SERVICES

These, if not provided by regional or area organisations under the supervision of a centrally run service (such as the district and regional health authorities), have grown in response to the role and work of local government. In the first half of this century, local government was responsible for most of what social provision existed. 'Duties' were imposed on local authorities by parliamentary legislation which required them to provide particular services. Since 1945 local government has lost many of its health and care responsibilities (e.g. national assistance; hospitals and other health services) and gained new ones (e.g. for the personal social services). From the mid-1970s, there have been further attempts to limit the powers of local governments in some areas of welfare provision and to increase their powers in others.

Other localised services are those where charitable, voluntary and non-profit-making organisations have local networks, such as the national network of Citizen's Advice Bureau Offices. In some areas, specific services have established themselves in a particular locality and provide services to that locality only.

THE PRIVATE AND INDEPENDENT SECTOR

There have been private, profit-making providers of services in many areas of health, education and social care in the UK since the nineteenth century, and in some cases before that. What is currently of interest is the extent to which this private sector might be expanding and taking over some of the services traditionally provided by central or local government.

One key issue here is of course that private health, education and care services are available only to those who can afford to pay for them, either directly when requiring those services or through systems of insurance, such as private health-insurance schemes. Several interesting groupings of statistics indicate some current trends and developments in this area.

1 In 1992 there were 475,288 pupils attending 1,364 private, public and independent schools which were members of ISIS, the Independent Schools Information Service, in the UK. Eighty per cent of all independently educated pupils are in ISIS-member schools. For the previous eight years, there had been a steady growth in the numbers of pupils attending private schools, although this growth seems to have fallen off since 1992. Overall, the private sector educates approximately 7.5% of all school children in England and Wales; 4% in Scotland. However, these figures vary between age groups and different parts of the British Isles. For example, 10% of secondary-school children and nearly 11% of all children in the south-east of England are in the independent sector. Twenty per cent of sixth-formers (16–19-year-olds) are in independent schools (ISIS *Annual Census* 1992).
2 By 1989 the number of people in the UK covered by private health insurance was over 7 million, equivalent to 13% of the population. Private insurance mainly provides cover for a limited range of services such as non-urgent surgery. The majority of subscribers are in group schemes, especially those provided by companies as fringe benefits.
3 There has been an increase in the number of beds in private hospitals which can be run either by profit-making or by non-profit-making organisations. By 1988 there were around 200 private and voluntary hospitals. In 1986 over a quarter of hip-replacement operations were done privately.
4 There has been a rapid expansion in private residential and nursing-home provision for

Table 7.9 Areas of growth and decline in local-government control of social services

Growth

- Housing Benefit provision
- Social services departments

Decline

- Provision of housing
- Education

elderly people and other vulnerable groups. A change in the supplementary-benefit rules in 1983 enabled people being cared for in private and voluntary homes to receive higher levels of financial support. There is now a wide range and diversity in the private sector. As well as the examples mentioned above, this includes:

- hospices
- convalescent homes
- screening services
- complementary and alternative medicine
- services offering treatment with non-prescribed drugs

CHARITABLE, VOLUNTARY, NON-PROFIT-MAKING ASSOCIATIONS AND OTHER AGENCIES

There are now over 17,000 registered charities in the UK, most of them in the health, welfare and education fields. To qualify as a charity, an organisation must be for the relief of poverty, or for the advancement of education, or for the advancement of religion, or for other purposes beneficial to the community.

There is also a huge variety and range of voluntary services, some organised under umbrella national organisations, others very small and locally based.

One of the key issues facing charity and voluntary services is whether they should be involved in political campaigning – whether for or against government policies. Charities have increasingly entered into partnerships with central and local government, with the corporate sector, with industry and with the media. Charities and voluntary organisations are being urged to apply for contracts to supply services. The money they receive is thus increasingly coming from these contractual arrangements as well as from donations. Funded in this way, some are worried that they cannot 'bite the hand that feeds them', and that their independence may thus be under threat.

ACTIVITY

Models of delivery of social services: ideas for further research and investigation

1. Researching one of the seven sectors of service provision described in Figures 7.12–7.18 is an ideal activity for small-group work since the tasks can be divided up either
   - by one person taking responsibility for investigating one of the four models or areas of provision in that service in more depth and then pooling their information with others in the group to provide an overall picture, or
   - by one person taking an area of provision within a sector such as nursery education and looking at how each model of provision (central, localised, private, voluntary) contributes to the overall pattern of services, or
   - by the group investigating how the overall patterns of provision in any particular service are reflected in their own communities
2. A useful project for schools and colleges would be to ask students to investigate the patterns of service delivery in particular areas with the aim of building up resource banks of information for themselves and future students to use. Most of the organisations mentioned in this section of the book will provide some literature explaining their role and function. Updating such files of resources could be another useful task since legislation dates so quickly.
3. The diagrammatic overviews shown in Figures 7.12–7.18 provide only the bare bones of the overall picture, and they require 'filling in' and updating. An IT core-skills project might be to establish a useful database for this purpose.
4. Some of the information provided here only really applies to England and Wales. A similar exercise needs to be done to look at the specific range of services provided in Ireland and Scotland.

CENTRAL GOVERNMENT: STATUTORY SERVICES

The Department of the Environment Secretary of State: John Gummer (June 1994).

The Housing Corporation:
This organisation monitors housing associations and allocates government grants.

LOCALISED SERVICES

Local authorities provide housing for rent (council housing). They also have the primary responsibility for dealing with homeless people.

They are required to help homeless people in defined categories of 'priority need' e.g. families with young children, women expecting babies, the elderly or the ill.* Councils do not have to provide local authority homes: they may make arrangements for the homeless to be housed by a housing association, or to help them find a private-sector tenancy.

In 1992 local authorities in the UK secured permanent accommodation for 167,000 households.

Local authorities are responsible for the payment of housing benefit (HB). HB is paid to people who have a low income and who rent their homes. Council tenants have their rent account credited with the benefit: a rent rebate. Private tenants are paid a cash allowance: a rent allowance.

HB is a means-tested benefit: the amount received depends on income.

* This may change in 1996 if the Housing Bill 1996 becomes law.

THE PRIVATE, INDEPENDENT SECTOR

Around 70% of all housing in the UK is owner-occupied.
The private rented sector forms 10% of all homes.

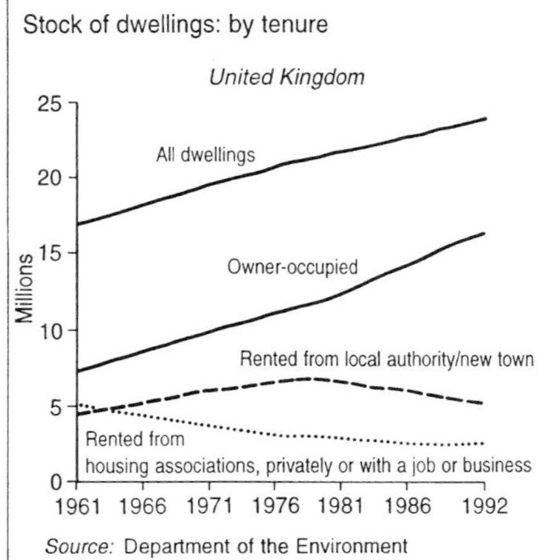

In 1991 there were over 639,000 vacant dwellings in England – just over three per cent of the total stock (*Social Trends* 1995).

In 1991 there were 36,607 repossessions of houses by building societies and banks.

VOLUNTARY SERVICES, CHARITIES, TRUSTS, AGENCIES, ASSOCIATIONS, NOT-FOR-PROFIT ORGANISATIONS.

Housing associations are organisations set up to provide low-rent accommodation for people with low incomes or with other needs. There are an enormous number and variety of housing associations, some very large, others very small.

By the 1990s, housing associations accounted for about 3% of all households.

There are many charities and voluntary organisations in this sector. Some well-known ones are:

- Shelter
- The Salvation Army
- Advisory Service for Squatters
- CHAR (Campaign for Homeless and Roofless)

Figure 7.12 Services in the housing sector

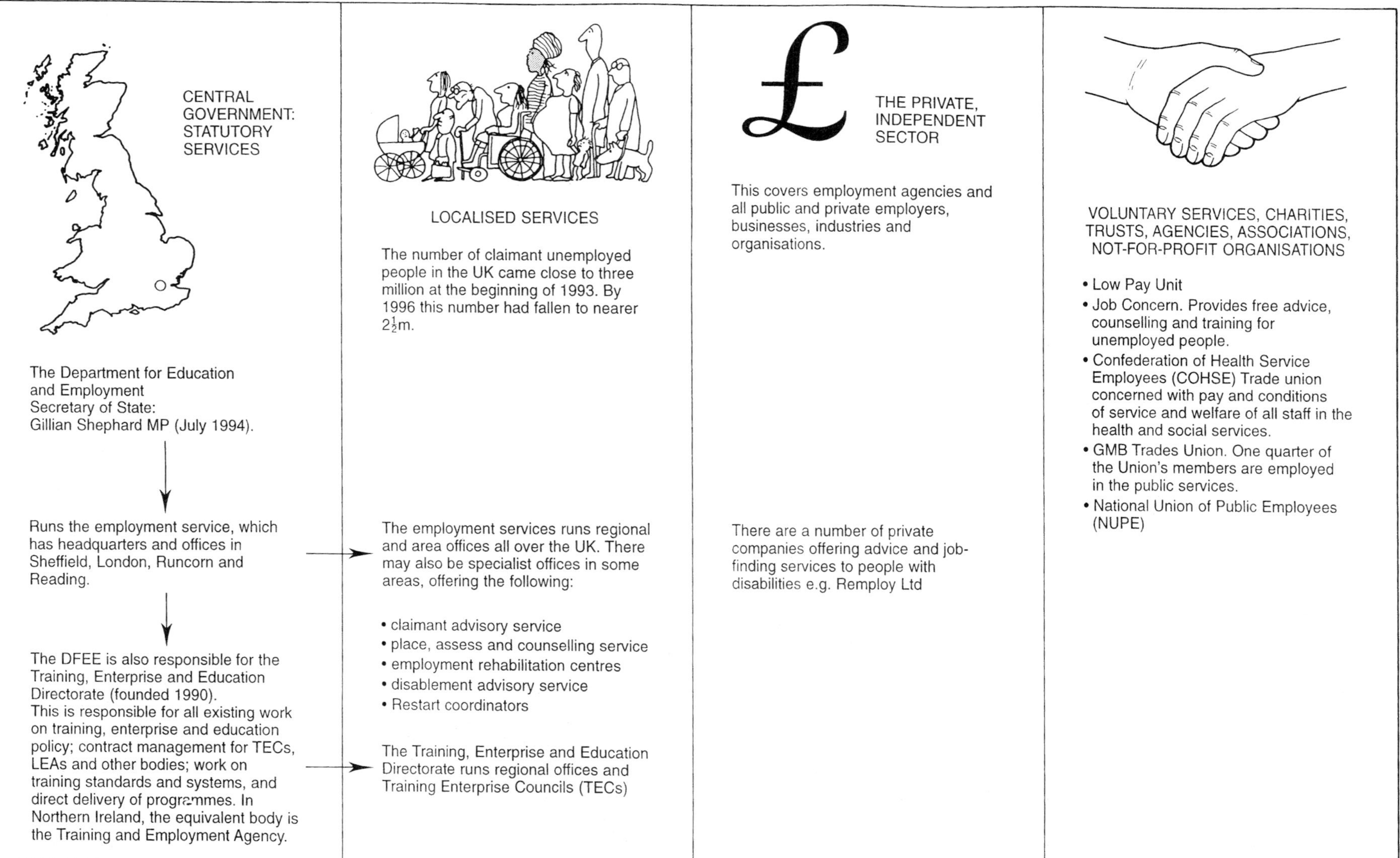

CENTRAL GOVERNMENT: STATUTORY SERVICES
The Department for Education and Employment
Secretary of State:
Gillian Shephard MP (July 1994).
Runs the employment service, which has headquarters and offices in Sheffield, London, Runcorn and Reading.
The DFEE is also responsible for the Training, Enterprise and Education Directorate (founded 1990).
This is responsible for all existing work on training, enterprise and education policy; contract management for TECs, LEAs and other bodies; work on training standards and systems, and direct delivery of programmes. In Northern Ireland, the equivalent body is the Training and Employment Agency.
LOCALISED SERVICES
The number of claimant unemployed people in the UK came close to three million at the beginning of 1993. By 1996 this number had fallen to nearer 2½m.
The employment services runs regional and area offices all over the UK. There may also be specialist offices in some areas, offering the following:
• claimant advisory service
• place, assess and counselling service
• employment rehabilitation centres
• disablement advisory service
• Restart coordinators
The Training, Enterprise and Education Directorate runs regional offices and Training Enterprise Councils (TECs)
£
THE PRIVATE, INDEPENDENT SECTOR
This covers employment agencies and all public and private employers, businesses, industries and organisations.
There are a number of private companies offering advice and job-finding services to people with disabilities e.g. Remploy Ltd
VOLUNTARY SERVICES, CHARITIES, TRUSTS, AGENCIES, ASSOCIATIONS, NOT-FOR-PROFIT ORGANISATIONS
• Low Pay Unit
• Job Concern. Provides free advice, counselling and training for unemployed people.
• Confederation of Health Service Employees (COHSE) Trade union concerned with pay and conditions of service and welfare of all staff in the health and social services.
• GMB Trades Union. One quarter of the Union's members are employed in the public services.
• National Union of Public Employees (NUPE)

Figure 7.13 Services in the employment sector

CENTRAL GOVERNMENT: STATUTORY SERVICES

The Department of Social Security Secretary of State: Peter Lilley MP (July 1994).

↓

Oversees the work of the Social Security Benefits Agency, (established 1991). This manages the delivery of social-security benefits which includes advice and information about benefits, handling claims, reviews and appeals; and arranging payments. It also provides staff for the

↓

Child Support Agency (CSA)(1993). This agency is responsible for the assessment of child-maintenance payments and their collection where requested. The powers of the CSA are held by the child support officers (CSOs), inspectors and other staff. The law gives the CSA wide powers to obtain information and to enforce payments.

LOCALISED SERVICES

Local authorities pay council-tax benefit (CTB): this is paid to people on low incomes to help them meet the full cost of the council-tax charge.

Local authorities may also run welfare-rights units or employ welfare-rights officers (or both): a service for people who may need help in applying for social-security benefits.

→ The Benefits Agency oversees the running of hundreds of local social-security benefits offices around the country. Some of these offices deal with all social-security benefits payable to claimants. In other areas, there may be additional specialised offices dealing with

- pensions
- national insurance
- income support
- resettlement
- appeals tribunals
- medical boarding centres (respiratory diseases)

→ runs regional offices.

£

THE PRIVATE, INDEPENDENT SECTOR

One of the biggest areas of the 'privatisation' of benefits in recent years has been in private pension plans and company pensions. More than two million people left the SERPS (State Earnings-Related Pension Scheme) scheme in recent years. Around 10 million employees rely on their employers for much of their income in retirement through company pension schemes.

VOLUNTARY SERVICES, CHARITIES, TRUSTS, AGENCIES, ASSOCIATIONS, NOT-FOR-PROFIT ORGANISATIONS

There are many advisory and voluntary organisations in this sector. These include:

- The Citizens Advice Bureaux. There are over 1,000 CAB offices in the UK, which provide a confidential advisory service and which monitor new legislation in this field. In 1992, the Bureaux dealt with 7.1 million new enquiries
- The National Claimants Federation
- The Disablement Income Group (DIG). This promotes the financial welfare of disabled people through a programme of advocacy, fieldwork, information, research and training
- Campaign Against the Child Support Act (CACSA)

Figure 7.14 Services in the social-security sector

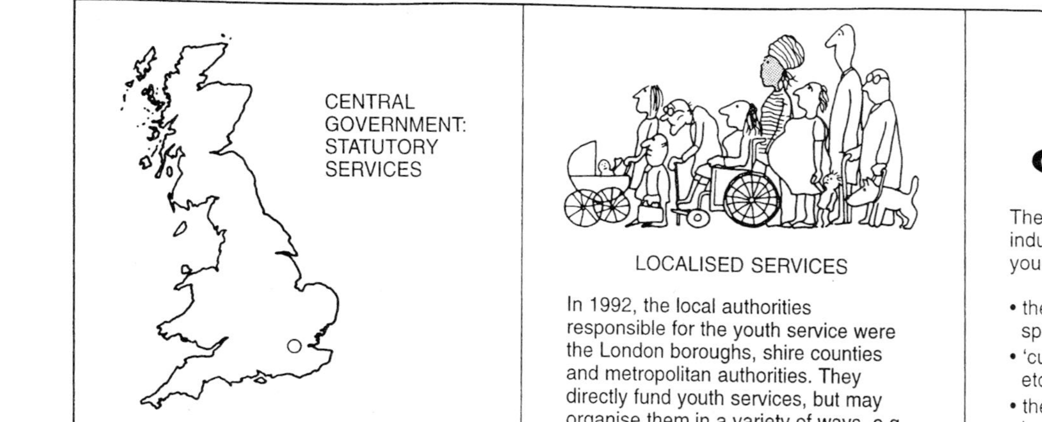

CENTRAL GOVERNMENT: STATUTORY SERVICES

A small unit, the Youth Service Unit – based in the Department for Education and Employment – supports the variety of local authority, voluntary and independent organisations. It implements policy and administers a grant scheme for national voluntary youth organisations

The National Youth Agency was founded in 1991. This agency is funded mainly by central government, and is meant to provide a focus for the youth service. It provides information and support for the informal and social education of young people. It offers curriculum materials, support in training, information and publishing services.

LOCALISED SERVICES

In 1992, the local authorities responsible for the youth service were the London boroughs, shire counties and metropolitan authorities. They directly fund youth services, but may organise them in a variety of ways, e.g. through either

- a youth service or youth and community service, or
- a community education service, or
- the recreation and leisure department

Services might include

- local-authority-run clubs and projects
- support for the voluntary sector
- outreach youth workers
- youth services in schools and colleges

The majority of youth workers work part-time: paid or unpaid. There are approximately 4,500–5,000 full-time youth workers employed by local authorities, and a further 700 officers and advisors. Paid part-time workers form the equivalent of 31,500 full-time workers. There are around ½ million volunteer youth workers, some of whom are young people.

All have local area groups and networks.

THE PRIVATE, INDEPENDENT SECTOR

There are, of course, many private industries and services which cater for young people. Included here are

- the major music, fashion, media and sports industries
- 'cultural' industries (books, art, theatre etc.)
- the leisure, travel and tourist industries

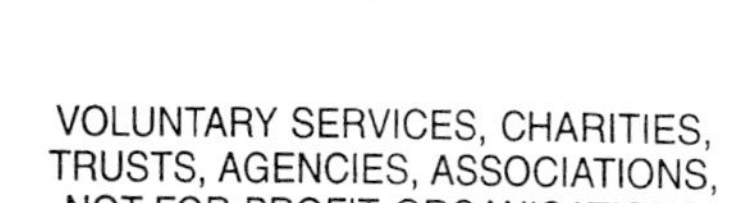

VOLUNTARY SERVICES, CHARITIES, TRUSTS, AGENCIES, ASSOCIATIONS, NOT-FOR-PROFIT ORGANISATIONS

Some examples here include:

- The Brook Advisory Centres. A charity which aims to prevent and mitigate the effects of unwanted pregnancy by educating young people in the matters of sex and contraception. It offers individual advice and counselling.
- British Youth Council. National forum for young people in the UK: aims to advance their interests and views

A number of local authorities are looking at ways of devolving their spending on youth services to voluntary service providers, through the establishment of trusts, contracts and service agreements

- National Association of Young People's Counselling and Advisory Services (NAYPCAS). This is a coordinating body for services which aim to provide information and support to young people.

Scout Association
Girl Guides Association
Youth Clubs UK
National Association of Muslim Youth

Figure 7.15 Services in the youth-service sector

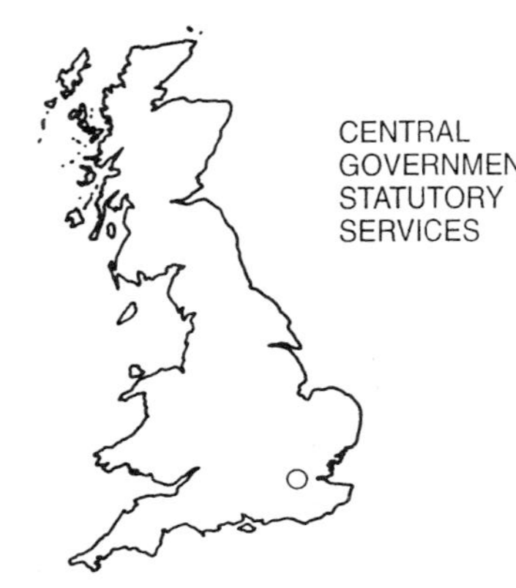

CENTRAL GOVERNMENT: STATUTORY SERVICES

The Department for Education and Employment
Secretary of State for Education: Gillian Shephard MP
In Scotland, the Education Department is part of the Scottish Office.

OFSTED (Office for Standards in Education) began work inspecting schools in September 1993.

The Secretary of State for Education appoints all or most members of the following bodies

- The Higher Education Funding Council funds the universities and other HE institutions.
- The Further Education Funding Council funds the further-education and sixth-form colleges
- The Funding Agency for Schools funds the grant-maintained schools (nearly 700 by the end of 1993)
- The Schools Curriculum and Assessment Authority
- National Council for Vocational Qualifications

LOCALISED SERVICES

The education departments of local authorities or county councils will typically run*

- an HQ or central offices under the direction of a chief education officer (and deputies or assistants)
- all maintained schools in the area:
  nursery
  infant
  junior
  middle
  secondary
- special schools (day and residential)
  special units
  schools psychological service
  special needs advisory and support team
  hearing impaired units
  multi-cultural resource centre
  teachers' centres
- adult education
- educational welfare services

* These services will vary from authority to authority

In 1990/91, there were 508,000 full-time teachers and lecturers in schools in the UK (maintained and non-maintained).

THE PRIVATE, INDEPENDENT SECTOR

In 1994, a total of 586,695 pupils attented 2,431 independent schools in England, Scotland and Wales.
There were 96,909 boarding places in independent schools (compared with approx 5,000 in local authority schools). Some 12,000 boarding places in independent schools are taken up by children of service families, who are frequently moving about this country and abroad.

Fees per term can be in the following ranges:

	Prep schools	Senior schools
Boarding	£2,000–£3,000	£2,500–4,200
Day	£800–2,100	£1,200–2,900

The assisted places scheme funds over 27,000 pupils to attend private/independent schools, with some of these schools receiving over £1 million in government money.

City Technology Colleges:
15 established by 1993. Originally intented to be financially sponsored by private companies, now government and/or local authorities (such as the London Borough of Wandsworth) provide considerable financial support.

There are more than 400,000 playgroups in places in the independent sector.

VOLUNTARY SERVICES, CHARITIES, TRUSTS, AGENCIES, ASSOCIATIONS, NOT-FOR-PROFIT ORGANISATIONS

There are hundreds of small organisations in this sector. Three examples are:

- The Helen Arkell Dyslexia Centre
- The National Association for Special Educational Needs (NASEN)
- The National Campaign for Nursery Education

Figure 7.16 Services in the education sector

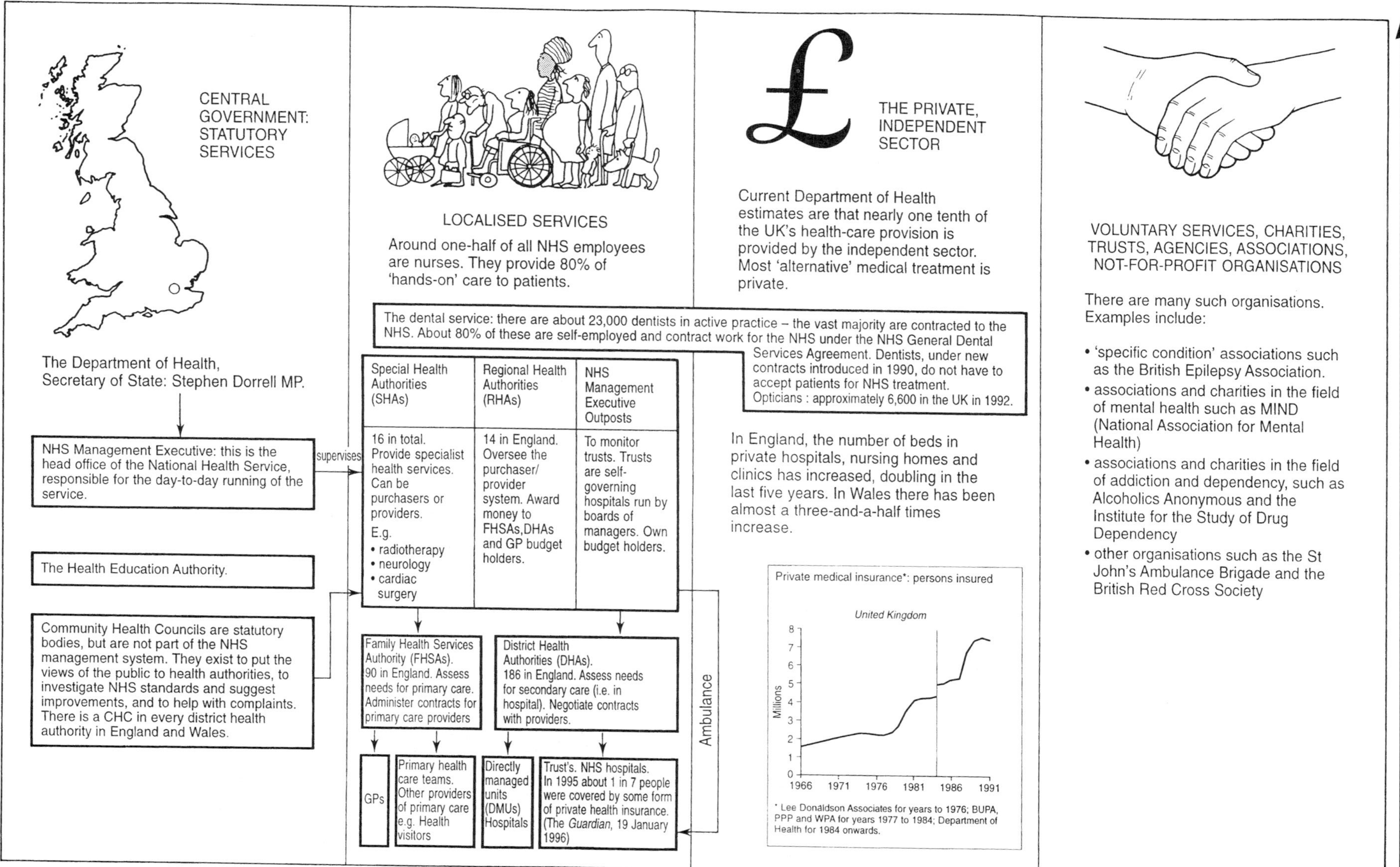

Figure 7.17 Services in the health sector

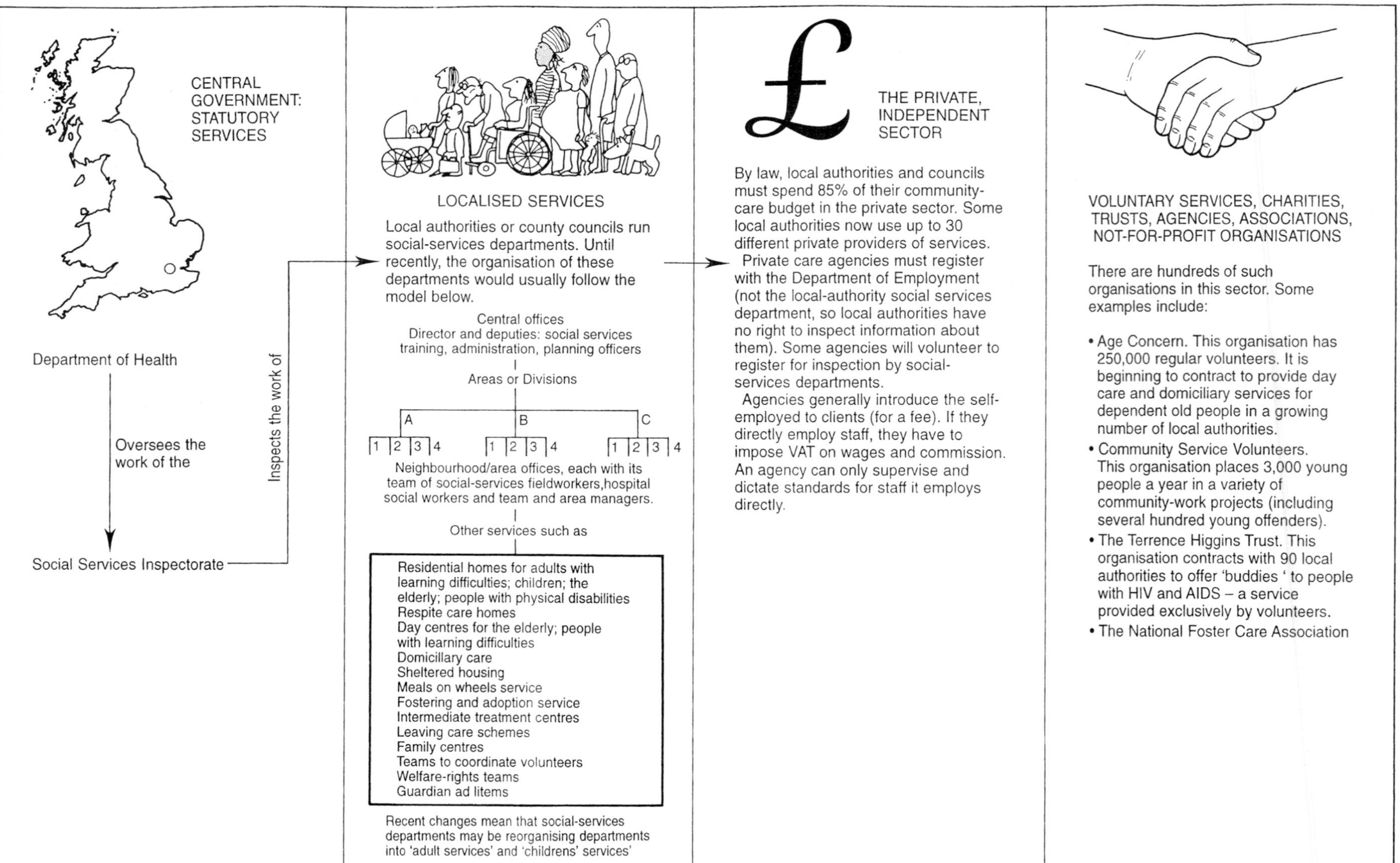

CENTRAL GOVERNMENT: STATUTORY SERVICES
Department of Health
Oversees the work of the
Social Services Inspectorate
Inspects the work of
LOCALISED SERVICES
Local authorities or county councils run social-services departments. Until recently, the organisation of these departments would usually follow the model below.
Central offices
Director and deputies: social services training, administration, planning officers
Areas or Divisions
A
B
C
1 2 3 4
1 2 3 4
1 2 3 4
Neighbourhood/area offices, each with its team of social-services fieldworkers,hospital social workers and team and area managers.
Other services such as
Residential homes for adults with learning difficulties; children; the elderly; people with physical disabilities
Respite care homes
Day centres for the elderly; people with learning difficulties
Domicillary care
Sheltered housing
Meals on wheels service
Fostering and adoption service
Intermediate treatment centres
Leaving care schemes
Family centres
Teams to coordinate volunteers
Welfare-rights teams
Guardian ad litems
Recent changes mean that social-services departments may be reorganising departments into 'adult services' and 'childrens' services'
£
THE PRIVATE, INDEPENDENT SECTOR
By law, local authorities and councils must spend 85% of their community-care budget in the private sector. Some local authorities now use up to 30 different private providers of services.
Private care agencies must register with the Department of Employment (not the local-authority social services department, so local authorities have no right to inspect information about them). Some agencies will volunteer to register for inspection by social-services departments.
Agencies generally introduce the self-employed to clients (for a fee). If they directly employ staff, they have to impose VAT on wages and commission. An agency can only supervise and dictate standards for staff it employs directly.
VOLUNTARY SERVICES, CHARITIES, TRUSTS, AGENCIES, ASSOCIATIONS, NOT-FOR-PROFIT ORGANISATIONS
There are hundreds of such organisations in this sector. Some examples include:
• Age Concern. This organisation has 250,000 regular volunteers. It is beginning to contract to provide day care and domiciliary services for dependent old people in a growing number of local authorities.
• Community Service Volunteers. This organisation places 3,000 young people a year in a variety of community-work projects (including several hundred young offenders).
• The Terrence Higgins Trust. This organisation contracts with 90 local authorities to offer 'buddies ' to people with HIV and AIDS – a service provided exclusively by volunteers.
• The National Foster Care Association

Figure 7.18 Services in personal social services

Welfare provision and the role of the state: an illustrative example

To what extent is the state (the government) still:

- the main provider of health and care services
- concerned to provide health and care services to all those in need (i.e. universalistic provision)?

A key example of the move away from the universalistic provision of services is illustrated by 'community care' policies. You will be familiar with these from your study of the Mandatory Units for GNVQ Advanced Health and Social Care. Here you have an opportunity to explore the issues in more depth.

'COMMUNITY CARE' POLICY

The implementation of the NHS and Community Care Act 1990 signalled the firm commitment of the Conservative government towards 'care in the community'. Put simply, this policy means that there is an attempt to look after the elderly, the mentally ill and people with disabilities and learning difficulties in the 'community' rather than in hospitals, psychiatric institutions or other 'homes'. Care organised in this way is argued to be less expensive to the government and less damaging to the individuals involved. There have been many interesting studies of the effects of 'institutionalisation' on long-stay patients in hospitals and homes, most of which tended to argue that such incarceration damaged the health and well-being of patients. It has thus been argued that people could best be treated within a 'community context'.

Under the NHS and Community Care Act, social workers are meant to assess an individual's needs for care and then put together a 'package of care' (see pp. 87–88) which might mean buying in private and voluntary services, as well as state-run services, to meet these needs. Under this Act too, some people have to contribute financially to their own care, using savings to finance long-term care in residential or nursing homes, for example. Many councils charge for services such as home helps and day-care centres. However, one of the most recent issues in this debate is at what point in the treatment and care of an individual 'care in the community' should begin and free, medical, acute NHS care should end.

There have also been attempts to define what exactly appropriate 'care in the community' might be for psychiatric patients, particularly those with no income, job or even home. This issue was highlighted when in 1993 Christopher Clunis, a schizophrenic, killed a stranger, Jonathan Zito, at Finsbury Park Station, North London. Jayne Zito, the dead man's widow, called for improved community care for psychiatric patients, and an inquiry was launched into the affair. In March 1994 Virginia Bottomley, the health secretary, admitted that there may be too few hospital beds for psychiatric patients in certain parts of London.

The Government was under pressure last night to plough more money into mental health care after shortage of hospital beds was identified as an important issue by the official inquiry into the killing of Jonathan Zito by Christopher Clunis, a schizophrenic.

The finding came within 24 hours of another inquiry report which found that overcrowding of psychiatric wards in north-west London might have contributed to the deaths of 14 patients over 20 months . . .

Jean Ritchie, QC, who led the [Clunis] inquiry, said that as wards were typically running at capacity of 120 per cent, with a fifth of beds occupied by two patients every day, it seemed that at least 20 per cent more beds were needed. 'We are concerned that such a need may be reflected in every inner-city area in the country,' she and her colleagues said.

Virginia Bottomley, the Health Secretary, yesterday announced an extra £10 million for community-based mental health services in London in 1994–95. But none of this money will go towards beds of the type specified by the inquiry team.

Mr Clunis stabbed to death Mr Zito, a stranger, as he waited for an Underground train at Finsbury Park in December 1992 ...

The inquiry found he had been left free, untreated and in a homicidally deluded state, because of a series of errors by doctors, social workers and police, aggravated by shortage of resources and poor understanding of mental illness.

'In our view, the problem was cumulative; it was one failure or missed opportunity on top of another,' the team said.

The report says care in the community is the right policy for the majority of people with mental illness. But it calls for better supervision of patients in the community and a toughening of plans to monitor those considered a risk to themselves or others. Discharged patients should have a 'befriender' to ensure treatment . . .

The fundamental problem emerging from the report, Mrs Bottomley said, was of a 'number of people all trying to help and care for Christopher Clunis, but doing so in isolation from one another' . . .

(The Guardian, *25 February 1994)*

Finally, there is also the question of whether the community-care policy is doing anything to improve the lot of carers. A survey of 426 carers by the Carers' National Association found that more than a quarter had not heard of the community-care system, and that three-quarters said that there had been no assessment of the needs of the person they look after. Carers expressed worries that there are not enough support systems in the community for them – not enough cheap access to respite care, for example.

The management of the 'caring services' in the UK

In Chapter 6, it is argued that a managerialist, marketplace ideology of social policy is affecting the ways in which services to people are being planned and justified. This ideology is also affecting the ways in which policy-makers, workers and the public are being encouraged to assess the value and effectiveness of these services. Alongside this have come changes in the language used to make such judgements. In this section we will look critically at these changes, asking the following questions:

- What measures of effectiveness are currently being used?
- What are these measures attempting to monitor, and why?
- Are these measures appropriate or useful?
- Does everyone agree that these measures should be used?

There is always more than one perspective on the effectiveness of a service. Whose perspectives have the most influence on the actual delivery of that service?

Activity

The following are two examples of service users:

1 Maria visits the local GP surgery with her 1-year-old child who is crying uncontrollably and is very distressed. The child has a temperature. Maria has no appointment and is asked to wait until a time is available when the doctor can see her. This takes nearly 20 minutes.

2 David and John are wheelchair-users, and although enrolled at an further-education college to take GNVQ courses, can only attend classes on the first and second floor of the college if they use the goods lift to travel up and down. There is no other access to these floors for wheelchair-users.

For each of the cases above, discuss how effective the service provided was from

- the point of view of the users
- the point of view of the staff
- the point of view of those planning, administering and providing the service

(a) What differences in perspective emerge?
(b) In what possible ways could the effectiveness of the services provided be measured?
(c) What problems might arise in doing this?
(d) Are there any improvements which could be made to these services (from all points of view concerned)? What would these be? Would they cost more money? How could they be paid for? What changes would have to take place to allow the improvements to occur?
(e) Could the service-users themselves have done anything to improve the services they received?

Services to people are not provided in a vacuum. They are a response to a perceived need, requested or not. *Why* people may need or request services from others is therefore an unavoidable question, and judgements about the effectiveness of service delivery cannot be separated from views about why the service was necessary in the first place, who needed it and in what circumstances, and how they responded to the service offered.

Against the background of these wider issues, we need to consider the measures of effectiveness which current social policy-makers are proposing. Most of these have developed within a political climate which, as we have seen, has claimed that:

- the welfare state is costing too much, and that levels of state spending must be reduced
- the welfare state encourages dependence and lack of self-motivation. People, it is argued, should be encouraged to take responsibility for their own and their families' health and welfare
- workers in health, education and social services should increasingly be working to manage the provision of health, education and care to others *by* others (especially the private-sector and voluntary agencies), and by people for themselves
- 'market forces' and 'business values' should determine the kind of services provided

In this new political climate, certain ideas, borrowed from private industry, have now become common in managing welfare services. These are discussed below.

PERFORMANCE INDICATORS

Performance indicators are an attempt to set targets of achievement which can then be used to measure changes in meeting those targets over periods of time. They can also be used to attempt to measure the performance of one organisation against what is achieved elsewhere.

For example, the performance of a company which manufactures washing machines can be indicated by how many washing machines are sold in any given year. In 1996 a 'target performance' of 30,000 washing machines sold may be set. In 1997 the company may well sell 35,000 machines, thus exceeding and improving its performance in comparison with the previous year.

In their simplest form, performance indicators are the goals or targets set by an individual or an organisation which, for them, indicate an effective or successful level of performance by that individual or organisation. Performance indicators in the National Health Service were first published in 1983 and covered clinical services, finance, manpower and estate management. Their introduction into the NHS and other care and education contexts, including the criminal-justice system, has been highly controversial. Some of the debates surrounding their use will be explored below.

Debate 1

Performance indicators will make service providers more accountable to the public, who, through income and council tax, pay for these services. The statistical information gathered in measuring performance should allow the public to judge more effectively whether their money has been well spent and whether the providers of services are doing their jobs competently.

It is in these terms that the government has encouraged the use of performance indicators and targets in selected areas of public service. One example, from education, will illustrate the very different views on this issue.

In education, the government has introduced a Parent's Charter which means that all schools now have to publish their National Curriculum test and public examination results. This, it is considered, will help parents make the best choices for their children, and will encourage all schools to do better (Department for Education 1992).

National Curriculum tests, taken at ages 7, 11 and 14 (Standard Assessment Tests or SATs), have been phased in since 1991. In 1995 tests for 11-year-olds were introduced for the first time. Parents should also now receive an annual report from their child's school, which must contain the results of the National Curriculum tests, if the child has taken them, as well as other information.

In addition, in 1993, the Secretary of State for Education was given wide general powers by parliament to collect data from schools, including attendance rates. Schools were already obliged to report attendance rates to local education authorities, and in November 1993 the government required these rates to be published in national 'truancy league tables'.

In effect, then, it would be true to say that the main indicators through which the government intends the performance of schools and their pupils to be judged and compared are currently:

- national examination results
- national test results (at 7, 11 and 14)
- attendance rates

However, the implementation of the Parent's Charter has not been straightforward due to opposition from teachers and parents. The national 'league tables' of examination results have now been published for four years (since 1992) at the time of writing. Yet, the national testing of children at ages 7 and 14 and the subsequent publication of national test results was affected in 1993 by the three largest teaching unions voting to boycott work relating to National Curriculum assessments. Various pressure groups and interest groups representing parents also campaigned against the tests. Few schools, in the end, carried out the tests at 7 and 14 in 1993, making the publication of national tables pointless.

Teachers objected to the tests for various reasons:

- They argued that using test results as indicators of the performance of schools and students was misleading because schools in poorer or inner-city areas with higher numbers of children from families in poverty could not be fairly compared with schools in wealthier, more middle-class areas. This raises the question of exactly what an appropriate performance indicator could be in education. Should such indicators vary from school to school?
- They claimed that the tests at 7 and 14 wasted class teaching time and were overlong and overcomplicated to carry out. They suggested that the tests did not tell the class teacher of 7-year-olds much that they did not already know and that they put teachers under an excessive workload in administering, marking and recording the results of the tests
- English teachers in particular suggested that the content of some of the tests at 14 forced teachers into boring, routine and dull teaching methods to prepare their students for the tests

Some parents agreed with the teachers' concerns, but also argued that:

- the element of competitiveness and comparison of results (children are awarded different levels of performance) was unhelpful and divisive for children as young as 7 and stressful at 14 years of age

In response to some of these concerns, a review of the National Curriculum was initiated in 1993 by the government's curriculum and advisory body, headed by Sir Ron Dearing. The subsequent Dearing Report suggested some simplifications of the testing procedures. While the 1994 tests for 7- and 14-year-olds were once again boycotted by teaching unions, and the government's plans for attendance 'league tables' were altered, the 1995 tests were carried out with little opposition.

PATTEN BACKS DOWN ON TRUANCY RATES

John Patten staged another retreat yesterday over school league tables by dropping a controversial indicator of truancy rates.

The Education Secretary also indicated that new ways of measuring long-term school performance now had a higher priority than tables of raw results of 11-year-olds in tests that will be compulsory from next year.

Schools will also be required to list weekly teaching hours, along with GCSE, A level and vocational exam results, although research into whether more teaching improves results has yet to be completed ...

Last year, the Government published for the first time two indicators of truancy – figures indicating the percentage of children who had been absent without leave for at least half a day and the percentage of teaching time lost through pupils' absenteeism.

These appeared to show that one in eight pupils had truanted at least once, although percentages of overall teaching time lost were small – about 1 per cent in secondary schools.

Now area-by-area records in primary schools and school-by-school details in secondary schools will list separately overall teaching time lost for authorised and unauthorised absences. But there will be no pupil absentee figures.

Teachers had complained that the figures were inaccurate because schools interpreted unauthorised absence in different ways ...

(The Guardian, *8 June 1994)*

ACTIVITY

1 Using the extract above, answer the following questions:
- Which new ways of measuring long-term school performance are being suggested by John Patten?
- Which two indicators of truancy did the government publish in 1993?
- Why might pupil absence records in schools be inaccurate?
- How does Mr Patten hope schools will use the National Curriculum test results?
- Explain what is meant by the last sentence of this article

2 People have very different views about the usefulness of these performance indicators in education. Explore the debate in more depth by:
- carrying out a small-scale survey of attitudes towards the test and truancy league tables
- interviewing teachers/parents and representatives from the major political parties: are parents beginning to use the examination, test and truancy league-table results to choose schools? Have parents total freedom to choose the schools they want for their children? Do parents and teachers feel that education could be measured in other ways besides these? Can educational achievement be measured at all?
- conducting further research into the current situation regarding the dispute between teachers, parents and the government. Are the tests being carried out in schools near you? Are they changing?

3 In July 1994 the government published the first NHS hospital league tables of performance. Find out more about these. Look at what was measured and what the professional and public reaction was to these tables.

Debate 2

Performance indicators are useful because they make workers do their best, most productive work.

This is another common justification for the use of performance indicators. The Audit Commission Report *Trusting in the Future* (1994) examined the cost of treating patients in different hospitals and suggested that productivity is maximised if staff are well informed; clear about and able to carry out what is expected of them; well-motivated; and given feedback on how they perform. The report suggests that where staff work productively (and are absent less), the cost of treating patients can be less.

The suggestion here is that the use of clear performance indicators can help staff working in health and care contexts to know exactly what they are working towards. It should, in theory, help them to plan and complete work more effectively. On the other hand, it can be argued that performance indicators can be used to exert more centralised, government or management control over workers and services. There is also the problem that while it might be relatively straightforward to exhort a worker to sell, say, an extra five package holidays to Spain per month worked, there may be factors influencing how well a patient recovers from an operation or how well a child does in a test which workers in these services feel are completely outside their control. They may also feel that the time and financial resources needed to achieve 'target performances' are not available.

ACTIVITY

It will not have escaped your notice that the way you are assessed on the GNVQ Health and Social Care course reflects attempts to set out exactly what you should be learning and how 'evidence' of your work can be provided. The 'performance criteria' in use on your course define what is required to achieve 'competence' in a particular piece of work. Usually, evidence of competence has to be gathered as assignments, assessments, evidence of prior learning and test results.

1 What are your views of this method of assessing your work?

2 Interview workers in health and social care contexts whose work may already be assessed by performance indicators. What are their views of these procedures?

Debate 3

Performance indicators will improve services to people because the public will demand better performance from inadequate providers of services; and workers will be able to achieve more because of greater clarity about their roles.

The questions which can be raised in response to this claim are:

- Will the public demand better services?
- How can they do this? What complaints procedures exist?
- What happens if targets are not met?
- The Citizen's Charter places emphasis on responsiveness to customers or users of services, but how might this apply, for example, to the 'users' of the criminal-justice system, since offenders do not exactly 'choose' the services of the police, the courts, probation officers or prisons?

The Patient's Charter, introduced in 1992, laid down that hospitals would have to publish details of their official 'waiting lists' for treatment. It also set a target specifying that in non-urgent cases patients would have a maximum waiting time of 18 months.

NHS WAITING LISTS REACH RECORD HIGH

Hospital waiting lists in England grew by 7.1 per cent in the third year of the National Health Service market to a record high of almost 1.07 million people, government figures showed yesterday.

The number waiting more than a year rose by 14.2 per cent to 64,660, according to the figures – released by the Department of Health ...

Ministers were also able to point to a fall of 9,831, or 13.2 per cent, over the same three-month period in the number waiting more than a year. Dr Brian Mawhinney, Health Minister, said the time people had to wait for treatment was continuing to improve. 'The facts are that of patients seeking admission, half are admitted to hospital immediately, three-quarters wait no longer than three months and 98 per cent are admitted within a year.'

The figures show that the total number of people on waiting lists rose from 992,324 in March 1993 to 1,065,349 in March this year. Of these, 64,232 had been waiting between one and two years and – in breach of the Patient's Charter – 428 more than two years ...

David Blunkett, the shadow health secretary, described the figures as disgraceful. They did not take account of an estimated 2 million patients waiting for their first out-patient appointment before they could join an official waiting list.

(The Guardian, *7 May 1994)*

ACTIVITY

1 Contact the administration department of your nearest hospital to see if it publishes information related to current waiting lists for treatment. How easy was it to obtain this information?

2 What ways exist of making comments and complaints about services in health and care contexts?

3 *Leafylane Youth Club*
Leafylane Youth Club is a run-down and underused club housed in a converted old house on a council estate located five miles from the centre of a large industrial town. There are three full-time and two part-time staff employed as youth workers by the local authority, and the club opens every evening, except Sundays, from 4.00 pm to 10.30 pm.

A new coordinator has been employed to run the club, and she intends to tackle some of the current problems the club faces. These include:

- Facilities and resources are limited; many are old, out-of-date and broken
- Few girls attend the club. Those who do tend to be very passive; it is mainly the boys who participate in and dominate activities
- Although there are many families from different ethnic backgrounds on the estate, it is mainly white young people who attend the club
- Nearly all the evening activities are based inside the club buildings as there are no outside facilities. The members seem reluctant to take part in organised activities in the wider community or to go on visits further afield
- Attendance at the club has been falling gradually over the past three years. There is a growing drug culture on the estate outside the club

At her first meeting with the other youth workers, the new coordinator asks her staff to begin to work with her on an overall plan to improve the youth club. She tells them that the local authority has promised the club an additional grant of £20,000 this year and double that the next if, by the end of the current financial year:

- the club has set itself a list of performance indicators and targets to be achieved
- it can show that it has met 90% of those targets within the year

Role-play this meeting. Could you set performance indicators and targets for this club? What might they be? What problems in setting and achieving these targets could you anticipate?
NB: If you could invite a youth worker in to work on this exercise with you, it would be valuable to have their view.

STANDARDS

The concept of standards has been a particular issue in education since the early 1970s, when it first began to be associated with attempts to measure an increase or decline in literacy, numeracy and educational achievement as indicated by examination results. As part of a 'New Right' critique of comprehensive schools and progressive education, it has also been used to refer to a perceived decline in moral standards (on the part of students *and* teachers!), in discipline in schools and in pupil attendance at school.

The term 'standards' is now being increasingly used also in social services and health contexts, where it has much more in common with the concept of performance indicators. Many of the debates about the use of performance indicators therefore also apply to the use of standards. The following extract gives details of the standards set for the Benefits Agency.

STANDARDS OF SERVICE

The Secretary of State sets annual performance targets for the Agency covering benefit clearance times, accuracy, customer satisfaction and financial recovery (overpayments and fraud detection). The Agency also sets internal targets after consultation with Ministers. These are included in a national *Business Plan* which is published every March. The targets are important as they are intended to set minimum standards of service – for example, that IS claims should be dealt with within five working days. They also influence both national and local service priorities. The Agency is required to publish a *Customer Charter* setting out performance targets and service commitments as well as including information about the Agency, such as the procedure for complaints. Copies are available from your local office or from the Agency's HQ in Leeds.

Districts are also required to produce their own business plan setting out targets and objectives for the year. A local version of the *Customer Charter*, called a 'customer service statement', should be published containing service commitments to at least national standards. Benefit clearance time targets should be displayed in office waiting rooms.

(Child Poverty Action Group 1994, p. 5)

In the area of personal social services, the Social Services Inspectorate (SSI) at the Department of Health now sets standards for social-work practice based on:

- existing legislation, e.g. the Children Act 1989
- government regulations and guidance
- current professional understanding (based on research and professional experience) of what constitutes good social-work practice and management of services, and of what constitutes good quality services (see SSI 1993)

By the term 'standard' the SSI means the quality of performance which is required in the management and delivery of social services, if service provision is to accord with Department of Health policy and practice guidance. Standards cannot be fixed or immutable, particularly in the child-protection field where different approaches to policy and practice are continually being developed and evaluated.

The SSI also uses the concept of *criteria*.

These are similar to the 'performance criteria' in your GNVQ syllabus and are the statements of expectation about whether the performance meets the required standards.

In *Evaluating Performance in Child Protection* (1993) the SSI sets out a framework of standards and criteria for use by social workers and social-services departments. This framework explains what the departments should be providing. Two of these are reproduced here:

1 *Standard*

The Social Services Department publishes advice for the general public, professionals and anyone caring for a child, indicating whom to contact if they have concerns about a child being abused or harmed.

Criteria

- The SSD publishes advice about who to contact when a child is thought to be, or is, at risk of suffering significant harm
- The advice is clearly written in a style, language and medium which ensures that the information is accessible to children, anyone caring for a child and members of the general public

2 *Standard*

The SSD has a clearly written, comprehensive child-protection policy.

Criteria

- The child-protection policy is an integral part of the SSD's childcare policy, is consistent with Area Child Protection Committee (ACPC) policy, and is formally endorsed by the Social Services Committee
- The policy is based on current statutes and related regulations and guidance
- The policy is based on current knowledge, practice developments and research findings about what constitutes a quality child-protection service
- The policy takes account of the responsibilities of other agencies involved in child-protection work
- The policy addresses all the key aspects of the child-protection process, including services to families and the provision of therapeutic facilities
- The policy states the SSD's commitment to the delivery of services which are anti-discriminatory and sensitive to the needs of children and their families
- The policy takes account of the views of consumers of the service
- The policy is written in a language and style which can be understood by social-service professionals, other staff in the SSD, users, carers and members of the public
- The policy states that all children whose names are on the Child Protection Register should have an allocated key worker
- The policy is regularly reviewed and revised to take account of new developments in child-protection services and of any changes in legislation, regulations and guidance

Activity

1 Contact your local social-services department and ask them if they
  - publish advice on who a member of the public should contact if they have concerns about a child being abused or harmed
  - publish a child-protection policy available to the public

  Ask for copies of these documents and, if they are available to you, check their contents against the criteria mentioned by the SSI above; e.g. are they written in an accessible, clear style?

2 Not all social-services departments will have achieved all the standards set out by the SSI. Some will have selected from the framework ones they feel are more important to work on than others. Invite a speaker from the local SSD willing to discuss with you how standards are being taken up by their department.

CONSUMER CHOICE

Consumer choice is another term borrowed from industry which is increasingly being promoted in the context of health, care and education. In theory, this means that instead of health authorities, social-services departments and education departments providing services and then clients, patients and students being allocated those services according to what is available, the needs or choices – or both – of 'service users' should be identified and services tailored to their demands, requirements and concerns. It has been argued by Conservative governments that allowing care and health organisations to be organised more like businesses, competing in the market for customers, will encourage those organisations to respond more closely to 'what people want' since people will be able to pick and choose between the services offered.

In education, Conservative governments since 1979 have argued that there should be a greater choice and diversity in the types of secondary school which parents could choose for their children: grant-maintained, City Technology College, grammar, voluntary-aided, magnet, secondary–comprehensive, selective and non-selective, private.

ACTIVITY

To what extent is a variety of secondary schools available to all parents and their children in the borough or county where you live?

In April 1987 the government issued a White Paper, *Promoting Better Health*. It focused on

- improving standards of general practice
- increasing the emphasis on health promotion
- giving consumers more choice

The government argued that the way to meet these objectives was to stimulate some degree of competition between GPs and to offer them some financial incentives to improve their work. As a result the new GP contract was introduced in 1990. This allows GPs to hold their own budgets and, in theory at least, is intended to allow GPs and other health professionals to make more choices on behalf of their patients over what treatments or services can be bought for them.

Some patient consumer and advocacy groups have suggested that, if this is to be the case, patients need to be much better informed about the quality and success rates of different treatments at hospitals, health centres and clinics.

In June 1993 the Department of Health published for the first time 'league tables' of the numbers of cancelled operations and the time patients have to wait in accident and emergency departments before treatment. These statistics also include ambulance waiting times and the numbers of patients not admitted or seen within one month of having an operation cancelled at the last minute.

PATIENT GROUPS WANT LEAGUE TABLES OF HOSPITAL DEATH RATES PUBLISHED

League tables of hospital death rates should be made available to the public, and medical culture should be changed so that doctors do not feel threatened by well informed patients, researchers and patient groups said yesterday.

Far more information about medical advances needs to be given to patients, and they should be encouraged to ask questions about treatment options, the groups said.

Rabbi Julia Neuberger, chairman of Camden and Islington community health services, in London, said that despite the difficulties in comparing like with like, and taking account of the different mix of patients, there was still a case for publishing mortality league tables to give patients a better idea about good and bad hospitals.

Speaking at a conference in London organised by the King's Fund Centre, the health research organisation, Rabbi Neuberger said Britain should move towards a more American model of the doctor–patient relationship, where it was assumed the patient would participate in questions about treatment.

'The assumption in America is that patients will be given detailed information about their treatment. They will ask questions, and if they don't like what they hear they will get more information. We need to find better ways to train patients in this country to ask questions . . .'

Information leaflets and 'effectiveness bulletins', giving consensus views by doctors on the most effective treatments for various conditions, could be made available, and patients should be encouraged to ask why they were getting treatment which differed from this . . .

(The Guardian, *10 November 1993)*

ACTIVITY

Read the extract above. What problems might arise if the public tried to consult league tables of hospital mortality rates?

COST-EFFECTIVENESS

The notion of cost-effectiveness is an economic term which is increasingly becoming a part of everyday speech. To make something cost-effective simply means to ensure that the maximum financial profit or minimum financial loss is achieved by any organisation, industry or individual selling or providing a product or a service. For example, it will not be cost-effective to take a job as, say, a nursery nurse if the costs of accommodation, bills, travel, taxes and daily living exceed the annual wage. The 'costs' of doing the job have to be weighed against how effective the wage is as income.

The income or funding of health, education and social services is generally limited by a number of factors, and financial resources are not infinite. For some people the way in which the idea of 'cost-effectiveness' has been applied in these areas is simply a euphemism for further 'cuts' in financial resources: the 'least-cost' method of achieving a particular objective. However, 'cost-effectiveness' may be justified as a way of conserving scarce resources and avoiding unnecessary expenditure or waste.

Several issues and problems do, however, arise when trying to apply cost-effective measures to health, education and care contexts. Some of these will be considered below.

1 Short-term gains in cost-effectiveness have to be weighed up against the possible long-term consequences of measures taken. For instance, a school managing its own overall budget may try to employ more 'beginning', newly qualified teachers in preference to older, more experienced teachers who would cost more in wages. Hence the school may, in the short term, save money from its overall wages bill. This saving would need to be measured against the following possible longer-term consequences:
   - The loss of effective teaching and leadership from more experienced staff could lead to a decline in examination results at the school. Fewer prospective students then apply to the school as its popularity falls
   - As the 'roll' of the school falls, the school attracts a lower annual budget and may be forced to make teachers redundant
2 Cost-effective measures in one part of a service may drive up costs in another, as the following extract suggests.

GPs URGED TO SAVE £425m ON DRUGS BILL

Family doctors give their patients too many drugs and the wrong types of drugs because they spend too little time seeing them, the Audit Commission says today in a report calling for more rational prescribing.

Patient care could be improved and the National Health Service could save £425 million a year if all general practitioners prescribed as well as 50 medical practices studied by the commission, the report concludes.

The report will anger drugs companies. They point out that GPs write far fewer prescriptions than their counterparts in most other European countries, as much as five times fewer than in France, and they maintain that good prescribing can save NHS money by keeping patients out of hospital . . .

Drugs prescribed by GPs cost £3.6 billion in England and Wales in 1992/93, 10 per cent of the NHS budget. The bill is growing at an annual rate of 14 per cent and ministers are seeking ways to curb it.

The commission says the basic problem is that GPs spend too little time with their patients. Inadequate consideration may be given to a case, or alternative treatments, and a doctor under pressure may find it quicker to write a prescription to end a consultation.

Previous studies have shown that GPs who spend an average of 10 minutes or more with a patient prescribe fewer antibiotics, the report says. Doctors can make more time for patients by delegating to other members of the health team, keeping accurate and computerised records and seeing fewer drug company representatives . . .

The Royal Pharmaceutical Society welcomed the report, but the Association of the British Pharmaceutical Industry said the commission's recommendation would disadvantage patients, impose unnecessary restrictions on GPs and drive up health care costs.

(The Guardian, *8 March 1994)*

ACTIVITY

Read the article above and use it to answer the following questions.

1. What does the Audit Commission mean by 'more rational prescribing'?
2. How does it suggest that more rational prescribing could cut costs in the NHS?
3. What arguments can you think of for and against the Audit Commission on this issue?

3 Cost-effectiveness measures sometimes indicate that a service could be improved by money being spent on it in different ways from the current arrangements. Money could be 'switched' from one area or aspect of a service to another without any overall increase in funding being needed.

For example, at present, family doctors have a contractual obligation with the Department of Health to provide 24-hour care, 365 days a year, to their patients. This means that they have to ensure that an emergency and night call-out service is provided. Some GPs argue that up to 60% of emergency call-outs do not justify a home visit. They suggest that dealing with 'trivial' problems may hamper them in attending to genuine emergencies. They may also be tired the next day when seeing patients in the surgery. They argue that it is therefore not 'cost-effective' to expect them to be on 24-hour call. Some doctors would like to see emergency night centres set up where patients could obtain out-of-hours care. Others have suggested that services could be better paid for if fines, removal from GP lists and loss of the right to visits at night and weekends were used to deter patients who demand home visits for 'trivial' reasons.

4 Finally, the issue of cost-effectiveness is at the heart of the debate over 'health care rationing' – i.e. who makes the day-to-day decisions over the allocation of scarce resources, and on what basis. The problem here is that it is not always clear to the public in what ways and for what reasons health and social services are offered to some people and not others. The public often assume that in health care at least, everything possible will be done to relieve suffering and save lives. But in practice *decisions* are taken about whether certain services are 'cost-effective'. For example, in 1994 hospital consultants in Manchester and Leicester said that they will not offer non-urgent heart-bypass operations to heavy smokers.

For further information on 'QALYs', the 'quality-adjusted-life-years' system used in some hospitals to try to work out the cost-effectiveness of various different treatments, see Chapter 5, pp. 165–168.

QUALITY AND CONSISTENCY

Another unavoidable 'buzz word' of the 1990s in public services is 'quality', a term borrowed from a particular form of management theory used in industry. 'Total quality management' or 'quality management systems' refers to the idea that the services provided or products made by any organisation can be improved if all the people working in that organisation are:

- fully committed to the organisation
- involved in, aware of and able, to the best of their ability, to implement all the procedures and processes necessary in that organisation to produce the service or product

If management can ensure that this is the case by monitoring the systems used in their organisation, this is meant to result in a situation whereby, regardless of who actually carries out the necessary tasks, the user consistently receives the required service without errors or problems occurring. Monitoring systems involve knowing who is doing what tasks, and by when, and who is using which methods. Management information systems (usually computerised) are now used by many organisations in health and care contexts to supply such information. The aim is to improve the 'quality' of the service by raising standards and achieving greater efficiency.

Therefore, 'quality assurance' procedures in workplaces are intended to:

- describe and evaluate the work people in that organisation do
- assess the 'performance' of that work, with a view to seeing if it can be improved, sometimes through 'appraisal' schemes

ACTIVITY

An obvious problem with the concept of 'quality' is that different people will have very different definitions of what it might mean. What does it mean to you and others in your class or group? Brainstorm the word and discuss the different ideas which emerge from your discussions.

ACTIVITY

1 Imagine that you have been asked to set standards for higher-quality work in teaching and lecturing in your institution. Before trying to do this, you decide that it will be necessary to take a closer look at some aspects of the work that teachers and lecturers do.

Today you are focusing on one of three aspects of the work that teachers do
- setting and assessing students' work
- tutorial work
- classroom teaching

Choose one of these areas to investigate.

2 With the permission of the teacher involved, interview a member of staff to find out exactly what duties and obligations they have in their chosen area (e.g. how many classes do they teach in a week? How many assignments do they write? How much time is spent preparing for tutorials? etc.). Find out what the teacher's own perceptions are of their ability to perform these tasks.

Ask the teacher about how they see their own role in relation to the organisation as a whole. How would this teacher interpret the idea of quality in relation to their own work? What would they see as good or poor quality work?

The overall aim of the interview with the teacher is for you to find out as much as you can about the work the teacher does.

3 Again, with permission, ask if you might observe that teacher in, for example, assessing students' work or giving a tutorial or a lesson.

4 Based on what you have learnt in 2 and 3 above, now try to draw up a list of six or seven standards which you think would be useful goals for your institution if it were trying to improve the quality of teachers' work. Remember here that you are not commenting directly on the particular work of the teacher you have observed but using what you have seen to give you ideas for good practice. For example, you might think that one stated aim or goal of your institution should be that good quality teaching would involve returning marked coursework assignments within three weeks of their being handed in.

5 Discuss your list with the teacher you interviewed. What advantages and disadvantages would they see in trying to adhere to the standards which you have come up with?

ACTIVITY

Investigate the use of British Standard 5750 (BS5750), an internationally recognised standard for quality systems which some public services are using. More information is obtainable from the British Standards Institution (see the 'Useful Addresses' section at the end of this chapter).

Other issues in the provision of services

The key issues which have had an impact on the way services are provided are:

- changing patterns in the administration and staffing of those services
- the resourcing of those services

ADMINISTRATION AND STAFFING

Since the mid-1980s, in all social, health, education and care services, there has been an encouragement and active creation of management posts and roles. These managers have essentially had the task of implementing the social legislation of the 1980s and 1990s in their organisations and institutions. In some services, personal social services in particular, those people promoted into lower- or middle-management posts have often previously been practitioners with limited or no previous 'management training'. Their new roles have left them with little direct work with clients or 'service users' and have meant learning a new managerialist bureaucratic ethos.

On the other hand, at the higher management end of the organisation of health and care services, there has been a trend to appoint people to the most senior posts who have had no previous direct experience of that particular care service but may have had previous industrial and management experience. A survey for the Department of Health, reported in the *Guardian* on 10 June 1994, showed that fewer than one in five top managers in the NHS has a background of medicine, nursing or any other clinical specialism.

These trends have caused some problems. First, not all newly appointed lower and middle managers in social and care services agree with the social-policy changes of the 1980s and 1990s; they find themselves attempting to implement policies with which they are not wholly comfortable and with which many of their staff also disagree. This has been one of the key themes in the BBC TV programme *Casualty*.

Second, the pay of some higher managers and executives, particularly in the NHS, has increased relatively faster than that for most other NHS employees. A report in 1993 by Income Data Services showed that, on average, the chief executives of trust hospitals had received 9% pay rises over the previous year, with some getting 33%. The pay increases of most public-sector workers, on the other hand, were limited to 1.5% over the same period.

ADMIN IN THE 'NEW LOOK' NHS COSTS EXTRA £1.5bn

The National Health Service employs 36,000 more managers and clerks but 27,000 fewer nurses than it did before the Government started to introduce market-style changes, official figures disclose today.

Analysis of the figures by a Labour MP suggests that the service has spent, cumulatively, an extra £1.5 billion on bureaucracy over and above what would have been necessary to sustain the numbers of managers and administrative and clerical staff employed in 1989 . . .

[T]he number of NHS managers rose from 6,091 in 1989/90 to 20,478 in 1992/93 – an increase of 236.2 per cent. In 1992/93 alone, the number rose 22.1 per cent.

Over the same period, administrative and clerical (A&C) staff rose from 144,582 to 166,363 – a 15.1 per cent increase. The rise in 1992/93 alone was 5.6 per cent. Taking together managers and A&C staff, the rise over the whole period was 36,168 or 24 per cent.

By contrast, the number of nursing and midwifery staff, expressed as whole-time equivalents, fell by 27,235 from 508,341 in 1989/90 to 481,106 in 1992/93 – a drop of 5.4 per cent, with a drop of 13,410 or 3.4 per cent in 1992/93 alone.

Ministers have responded to previous figures on staffing changes by arguing that some increase in management numbers was necessary to beef up the NHS in areas where it was weak, particularly finance. But they have said some of the rise, and some of the fall in nursing numbers, is explicable by reclassification of senior nurses as managers . . .

(The Guardian, 9 December 1993)

ACTIVITY

Using the article above, answer the following questions

1 According to the official figures, how many NHS managers existed in 1989/90? How many existed in 1992/93? What percentage increase does this represent?

2 Over the same period, 1989/90–1992/93, by what percentage did the numbers of administrative and clerical staff in the NHS rise?

3 Over the same period, 1989/90–1992/93, by what percentage did the number of nursing and midwifery staff fall?

4 How do Conservative Party ministers explain these figures?

5 To what extent do these figures support the suggestion that there is an increasing emphasis on management in the health profession?

6 Is an increasing emphasis on the role of managers in the health and care services a good or bad thing?

ACTIVITY

Investigate the apparent growth in 'managerialism' in any institution with which you are familiar or can make contact. For example, in your school or college, arrange to interview anyone in a management position such as a head teacher, a manager of a curriculum section or a head of department. What changes have occurred to their jobs in the past few years? What has been their response to these changes? Do they think that students are getting a better service from the education system? What training in management have they had? Was it useful? Why?

MEDICAL ADVANCES
Transplant surgery; 'Keyhole' surgery; Laser treatments e.g. for eye operations; Genetic testing/screening; Ultra-sound scanning; Infertility treatments; Artificial hip/knee/joint operations; Drug treatments; Intensive care facilities

COMPUTERISATION
Of files, data, medical and other records of service users; Use of Compuserve and the Internet – databases and bulletin boards; Use of e-mail; Of research methodology and results – analysis in medicine, health and social care; Use of computer programmes for medical diagnosis e.g. magnetic resonance imaging (MRI); Electronic bar codes may be introduced on NHS prescriptions
Example:
The Samaritans can now be contacted by electronic mail on jo@samaritans.org. They are linked up with the worldwide Internet computer network and receive four or five e-mail messages a day, from around the world.

COMMUNICATION NETWORKS
Use of video cameras (CCTV) for security electronic 'tagging' of offenders; Use of private electronics companies to provide 'bedside entertainment systems i.e. TVS' in hospitals; Use of video link-up systems
Example:
A regional Fire Brigade uses video cameras to film onlookers at fires in order to identify potential arsonists.

Figure 7.19 Ways in which new technology affects health and care services
Source: The *Guardian*, 9 April 1994 and 8 March 1995.

The impact of technology upon welfare provision

Figure 7.19 indicates the growing number of ways in which changes in technological expertise can affect health and social care services in the UK. While there is no space here to describe and investigate all these in detail, it is possible to discuss some selected examples.

1 *Medical advances.* There is much dispute about the cost, effectiveness and efficiency of many new technological innovations in medicine. This has especially been the case with transplant surgery, where 'failures' in extremely expensive operations and the shortage of organs for donation often attract a great deal of media and public attention. However, Rob Baggott argues that new technology can be both efficient and effective. For example, minimally invasive therapies (MITs) such as lithotripsy – the crushing of stones, such as those found in the kidney or gall bladder, by using ultrasound waves – can often be relatively quick treatments which reduce hospital stays for patients and lower the likelihood of post-operative infection (Baggott, p. 59).

2 *Computerisation.* Most of us will be familiar, by now, with seeing a computer screen at the desk of our GP's surgery. There can be few health and care organisations in the country which do not use computers for filing, databases, service-user records and internal communications.

One of the world's largest computer bulletin boards, Compuserve, has become a means of swapping messages and experiences about health and care. Compuserve has 2,000 or so general databases which include specialist medical/health services such as those for diabetes, cancer, disabilities and general health and fitness. Compuserve believes these forums can, for example, provide answers to basic questions, for which patients with rare illnesses would otherwise wait months. In one case, doctors in the cancer forum diagnosed a rare cancer before the patient's own physicians had confirmed that diagnosis (the *Guardian*, 1 February 1994).

3 *Communication networks.* The increasing use of

video cameras for security in public buildings and city centres is another focus for debate. In 1994 just over 50 local authorities purchased closed-circuit-television (CCTV) systems for high streets, and they are now in place in 90 cities and towns in the UK. In Newcastle city centre in one year, the crime rate fell 19%, and there were 400 arrests directly as a result of CCTV. However, questions have been raised about who has access to the camera monitors and the tapes. How are these people trained? If the tapes are used in courts, there is always the danger of misidentification from poor-quality recordings. It may also be possible that police forces will see the installation of tapes in public areas as a cheaper way of 'policing' those areas than employing police officers 'on the beat'.

A different use of video technology involves the use of video link-ups, an example of which exists in a clinic based at the South Westminster Centre for Health in London. This has a hospital video link with consultants in the Royal Victoria Hospital in Belfast. The video link allows nurses with any difficult cases at the clinic to see the consultant and to show them the patient's injury. The nurses use a camcorder with added light to improve the picture.

ACTIVITY

1 Organise a visit to a hospital, a GP practice, a social-services department or other health and care organisations to investigate the use of new technology.

2 Choose a number of examples of the use of new technology illustrated in Figure 7.19. Carry out further research into their use, and explore people's perceptions of their desirability.

3 Explore the ethical dilemmas raised by these new technologies. Among questions which you may want to raise are:
- If new technological innovations are made, who should have access to them? Can often-expensive treatments, facilities and services be made available to all people who need them?

4 Read the following extract and answer the questions below:

WOMAN IN LABOUR SENT ON 84-MILE DASH FOR INTENSIVE CARE COTS

A woman in premature labour with twins was sent on an 84-mile dash by ambulance across three counties because all the hospitals nearer her home were full, it was disclosed last night.

Karen Riordan, aged 31, was shuttled from Bristol to Exeter, across Avon, Somerset and Devon, with a midwife at her side after being told all incubators were booked up. Nurses telephoned at least five other hospitals before eventually finding the spare intensive care cots . . .

Just 13 hours later, Mrs Riordan gave birth to healthy daughters, Naomi and Lily. They were transferred back to Bristol on Wednesday and given a room of their own. . .

A Bristol and District NHS Trust spokeswoman, Theo Wood, admitted no incubators had been available. She said: 'We very much regret that Mrs Riordan had such an unpleasant experience . . .

(*The Guardian, 28 March 1995*)

- Do some new medical advances (e.g. 'key-hole' surgery) have unwanted and damaging side-effects?
- Does medical technology increase the power of the doctor over the patient to the extent that the doctor is confirmed as the 'expert' and the patient loses control over the interpretation and treatment of their condition?

- Does office computerisation increase the efficiency of health and social care workers?
- Could the increasing availability of medical and social information on computer systems allow people more freedom to help themselves?

Recent changes in society: contemporary welfare provision

How have the changing patterns of welfare provision affected service users in the UK? In this final section, one example of a group of people in need will be considered – the homeless – although students should be aware that they could choose any appropriate group for a similar study (e.g. the unemployed, the elderly, the poor, teenage smokers). Students may wish to try to assess how successful the current provision of services, healthcare advice or material (or both), and financial support appears to be for their chosen group. In doing so they may find it useful to consult the government's own Health of the Nation targets set in 1992.

FAT AND FAGS FAIL HEALTH TARGET TESTS

The Government is failing to meet two targets to make Britain healthier, as teenage smoking is rising and the number of obese people continues to increase, a Department of Health report published yesterday shows . . .

The second report looking at progress towards meeting the Health of the Nation targets shows that although smoking rates are generally declining, this is not true in young people aged 11 to 15. The target was for smoking rates in that age group to fall by last year from 8 per cent in 1988 to 6 per cent. The report shows the rate is about 13 per cent for girls and 10 per cent for boys.

On obesity the target is to reduce the percentage of obese men and women by a third by 2005 – from 7 per cent of men to 6 per cent, and from 12 per cent of women to 8 per cent. The report shows that in 1980, 8 per cent of women were obese, but by 1993 this had risen to 16 per cent. In 1980, 6 per cent of men were obese, and by 1993 13 per cent.

However, between 1993 and 1994 heart disease in the under-65s fell by nearly 11 per cent, strokes in the under-65s fell by 6 per cent, suicides dropped by 6 per cent, accidents in the under-15s fell by 10 per cent and for those above 65 by 11 per cent.

The report also shows under-age pregnancies at the lowest recorded rate for 10 years, standing at around 8 per 1,000 girls aged 13 to 15. Gonorrhoea rates, seen as 'proxy' for other sexually transmitted diseases including HIV, fell by 24 per cent in 1992 and a further 17 per cent in 1993 – now standing at 11,803 a year, or 38 per 100,000 of the population . . .

(From an article in the Guardian, *20 July 1995)*

Homelessness

ACTIVITY

1 What is homelessness? What images or associations come to mind when you think of 'the homeless'? Make a note of these.

2 Have you, or anyone you know reasonably well, ever had any personal experience of homelessness? You may be willing to talk to others in your class about this.

3 If you or others you know well have not had any personal experience of homelessness, where do the ideas/associations you wrote down for question 1 come from?

4 Do you see homelessness as a social problem? Why, or why not?

You may wish to compare your answers to

the questions above with the following list of types of 'the homeless' (taken from Skellington 1993).

1 people literally without a roof over their head, including those regularly sleeping rough, newly arrived migrants, victims of fire, flood, severe harassment or violence, and others;

2 people in accommodation specifically provided on a temporary basis to the homeless (hostels, bed and breakfast accommodation, etc.);

3 people with insecure or impermanent tenures: this includes other ('self-referred') hotel or bed-and-breakfast residents, licensees and those in holiday lets, those in tied occupation who change job, tenants under notice to quit, squatters and licensed occupiers of short-life housing, and owner-occupiers experiencing mortgage foreclosure;

4 people shortly to be released from institutionalised accommodation, including prisons, detention centres, psychiatric hospitals, community or foster homes, and other hostels, who have no existing alternative accommodation or household to join;

5 households which are sharing accommodation involuntarily;

6 individuals or groups living within existing households where either (i) relationships with the rest of the household, or (ii) living conditions, are highly unsatisfactory and intolerable for any extended period;

7 individuals or groups living within existing households whose relationships and conditions are tolerable but where the individuals/groups concerned have a clear preference to live separately, including cases where the 'potential' household is currently split but would like to live together

Would you agree that all the categories included in this table should fall under the category 'homeless people'? Why, or why not?

HOW HAS HOMELESSNESS BECOME A SOCIAL PROBLEM?

In the previous section of this chapter we looked at how social problems may be socially constructed, and at how they may be caused. It should now be clear that any explanations of homelessness cannot easily be separated from ideas about what kinds of home should be available to people and how people should pay for them.

ACTIVITY

With which of the following views do you agree or disagree? Discuss and debate your ideas with others.

1 Housing is a basic human need, and should be a human right.

2 The government, or state, should be responsible for the building, the supervision and the subsidy, for those in need, of the majority of housing in this country.

3 There should be a mixture of housing available to people, including
- state-subsidised housing
- a private rented sector
- owner-occupied housing
- housing associations

4 Most people should aim to own their own homes: owner-occupation means that people will take more care of their homes.

5 People should work hard to earn the right to buy a good home.

Since 1979 the policy of Conservative governments has been to encourage owner-occupation and discourage council housing; in other words, it has found ways to encourage a particular relationship between people and their homes, one based on the requirement (for most people) to borrow large sums of money (a mortgage) from financial institutions such as banks and building societies to pay for the cost of buying a home. The loan must be repaid in full, plus interest, before people can truly be said to 'own' their own home.

The emphasis on the desirability of this kind of tenure has influenced current government thinking about homelessness. Skellington (1993) suggests that the Poor Law established the perception of the homeless as undeserving and feckless: the workhouse accommodation provided was to be of the most basic and punitive kind, to discourage such traits in others. From the 1940s to the 1970s, despite evidence that homelessness was primarily caused by housing shortage rather than personal inadequacy, governments, argues Skellington, failed to take any specific action on the issue.

However, in 1977 the Homeless Persons Act was passed, giving local authorities a statutory responsibility for housing the homeless. The Act defined homelessness as 'the lack of secure accommodation free from violence or the threat of violence'. Under this Act four categories of people could ask to be housed by local authorities:

- the homeless as defined in the Act (or those threatened with homelessness within 28 days)
- people in a priority-need group, such as families with children, pregnant women and emergency cases
- people classified as intentionally homeless within the meaning of the Act
- people who had a local connection with the district

The problems with this Act were that:
- the duty to secure accommodation did not extend to 'non-vulnerable' single adults and young people
- violence or threatened violence from people outside the home was not an acceptable reason to ask to be housed or rehoused
- there was no right of appeal
- the wording of the Act was vague and ambiguous, which led to different local authorities interpreting it in different ways
- the legislation defined homelessness to mean lack of *accommodation* rather than the lack of a *home*, thus concealing the housing needs of large numbers of people, e.g. people living in their parents' households or those wanting to leave a failed marriage
- the wording of the Act tends to reinforce a distinction between a 'deserving' and an 'undeserving' poor

The Act thus left unanswered two important questions: who are the homeless? How many homeless people are there in the UK? It is important to ask questions such as these because they illustrate how the nature and extent of a 'social problem' can be disputed. Official statistics on homelessness obviously use the definitions contained in the Act, and may therefore obscure the 'true' extent of the problem. Skellington argues that many of the official statistics collected on homelessness make it difficult to analyse homelessness by gender or to assess the numbers of the long-term homeless. A report from the Association of London Authorities published in September 1994 shows that in London the figures for the homeless living in temporary bed-and-breakfast and hotel accommodation are lower now than at any time in the last 10 years because some councils at least have begun to lease out to homeless families, on a temporary basis, newly converted, housing-association, private rented or other properties while they wait for more secure accommodation, but the total number of homeless families in temporary accommodation in the capital is now 34,000, or about 80,000 people, over 30,000 of whom are children. Eight years ago the total was half that figure. Households in temporary accommodation in London account for 60% of the national total (the *Guardian*, 2 September 1994).

WHY DO PEOPLE BECOME HOMELESS?

Looking first at individualist explanations for homelessness, i.e. those which emphasise the particular circumstances of the individuals involved, Skellington (1993) gives the following evidence based on data from the Department of the Environment:

- In the majority of cases, the reason cited for homelessness was that parents, friends or relatives were no longer able or willing to accommodate people
- Other important factors were: relationships with a partner breaking down; the loss of an owner-occupied home; eviction from a privately rented home

Compared to the 1960s, homeless households are less likely to result from eviction by landlords and more likely to be the result of repossession as a result of mortgage payment arrears. There has also been a growth in the numbers of marital and family disputes, which can also be a cause of homelessness. Domestic violence and child abuse are further important factors. Finally, there is the drift into homelessness from institutional life (from psychiatric hospitals in particular). As many as 40% of homeless people have suffered some form of mental illness.

Structural or underlying explanations for homelessness tend to emphasise the following points:

- Since the 1970s the combined effects of job loss and insecurity, reduced entitlements to benefits, higher rents and poverty have made more people vulnerable to homelessness
- Young people were particularly affected by this when, in 1988, their entitlement to benefits was altered
- There is a continuing shortage of owner-occupied and rented housing for poorer sections of the community

ACTIVITY

Use the various explanations for homelessness above as a starting point for further research into this issue. Questions which you may wish to explore in more detail are:

1 What are the latest policies which central and local governments are proposing in connection with the issue of homelessness? How is the changing pattern of welfare provision affecting the way homeless people are treated?

2 What do organisations, such as Shelter, which campaign on behalf of the homeless think should be done to solve or alleviate the problem?

3 Have the homeless themselves got a voice in this policy-making process? (The growing circulation of the publication *The Big Issue* in London and other major cities could provide some helpful material here.)

4 Are black and ethnic-minority groups more vulnerable to homelessness than other groups in society? If so, why?

5 How does homelessness affect people's lives?

THE ISSUE

- campaigns on behalf of the homeless
- highlights the major social issues of the day

- gives homeless people the chance to make an income
- increases the opportunity for homeless people to control their lives
- allows homeless people a chance to voice their views and opinion

THE CONCEPT

The Big Issue is sold by homeless and ex-homeless people who buy the magazine for 30p and sell it to the public for 70p. All vendors receive training, sign a code of conduct and can be identified by *Big Issue* badges. *The Big Issue* is sold in London, Scotland, the North West, Bath, Brighton, Birmingham, Bristol, Ireland and Cardiff.

The Big Issue also provides housing, training and employment initiatives to help the homeless off the streets. *The Big Issue* subsidiary 'Making it' will employ ex-vendors in the development and marketing of commercial products.

The Big Issue is funded through advertising, business sponsorship and sale. All profits go back into helping homeless people.

(The Big Issue, *18–24 March 1996)*

QUESTIONS

1 Taking one or more 'social problems' such as poverty, homelessness, unemployment or crime, explore a range of ways in which, since 1850, these problems have been defined, described and explained. Use historical, contemporary and sociological sources to analyse a variety of differing political and theoretical perspectives on these issues.

2 Taking the social problem(s) you have analysed in 1, examine major social changes since 1850 which may have contributed to the existence of this (these) problems.

3 For the social problems analysed in 1 and 2, identify and describe what welfare provision exists to alleviate this (these) problem(s)
(a) nationally
(b) locally.

4 Arrange to interview a health or welfare worker whose work involves making provision for people affected by the social problem(s) you have analysed. What have they noticed about
(a) changing public, professional and political values and attitudes towards the provision of these services?
(b) patterns of 'take-up' of these services?

REFERENCES AND RESOURCES

Adams, C. (1982), *Ordinary Lives – A Hundred Years Ago*. London: Virago.

Anderson, M., (1971), *Sociology of the Family*, 'Family, Household and the Industrial Revolution'.

Anderson, M. (1980), *Approaches to the History of the Western Family 1500–1914*. London: Macmillan.

Arber, Sara (1990), 'Opening the "Black Box": Inequalities in Women's Health', in P. Abott and G. Payen, eds, *New Directions in the Sociology of Health*. Basingstoke: Falmer Press.

Audit Commission (1994), *Trusting in the Future*. London: Audit Commission

Baggott, R. (1994), *Health and Health Care in Britain*. New York: St Martin's Press Inc.

Bernard, J. (1976), *The Future of Marriage*. Harmondsworth: Penguin.

Booth, C. *Life and Labour of the People in London*, 17 vols. (1902–4).

Brown, Tony (1993), *Understanding BS5750 and Other Quality Systems*. Aldershot: Gower.

Burghes, Louis (1994), *Lone Parenthood and Family Disruption: The Outcomes for Children*. London: Family Policy Studies Centre.

Cahill, Michael (1994), *The New Social Policy*. Oxford: Blackwell.
CANST (199?), *Digest of Social Legislation*. London: Citizens Advice Notes Service Trust.
'Characteristics of the ILO Unemployed' (1994), *Employment Gazette*, July.
Charities Digest 1994. London: Family Welfare Association.
Choice and Diversity: A New Framework for Schools, Cm. 2021. London: HMSO.
DFE (1992), *Education into the Next Century*. London: Department for Education.
Family Policy Studies centre: all publications.
Field, D. (1992), 'Elderly People in British Society', *Sociology Review*, vol. 1, no. 4, April.
Giddens, Anthony (1995), *Sociology*, 4th edn, Cambridge: Polity Press.
Graham, H. (1984), *Women, Health and the Family*. Brighton: Wheatsheaf.
Haralambos, M. and Holborn, M. (1991), *Sociology: Themes and Perspectives*, 4th edn. London: Collins Educational.
Heath, A. (1992), 'Social Class and Voting in Britain', *Sociology Review*, vol. 1, no. 4, April.
Hulley, Tom and Clarke, John, 'Social Problems, Social Construction and Social Causation', in M. Loney *et al.*, *The State or the Market: Politics and Welfare in Contemporary Britain*, 2nd edn, London: Sage.
ISIS (1992), *Independent Schools Information Service Annual Census*. London: ISIS.
Keating, P. (ed) (1976), *Into Unknown England 1866–1913 – Selections from the Social Explorers*. Glasgow: Fontana.
McGlone, Francis (1992), *Disability and Dependency in Old Age: A Demographic and Social Audit*. London: Family Policy Studies Centre.
McKeown, T. (1976), *The Modern Rise of Population*. London.
National Youth Agency (1992), *What is the Youth Service?* London: National Youth Agency.
Oakley, Ann (1974), *Housewife*. London: Allen Lane.
O'Donnell, M. and Garrod, J. (1990), *Sociology in Practice*. Walton-on-Thames: Nelson.
Oppenheim, Carey (1993), *Poverty: The Facts*. London: Child Poverty Action Group.
Parsons, T. (1959), *The Family: its Functions and Destiny*. New York: Harper and Row.
Pearson, Geoffrey (1983), *Hooligan: A History of Respectable Fears*. Basingstoke: Macmillan.
Rowntree, B.S. *Poverty: A Study of Town Life* (1901).
Sheeran, Yanina (1993), 'The Role of Women and Family Structure', *Sociology Review*, vol. 2, no. 4, April.
Skellington, R. (1993), 'Homelessness', in R. Dallos and E. McLaughlin, eds, *Social Problems and the Family*. London: Sage.
Skellington, Richard (with Paulette Morris), *'Race' in Britain Today*. London: Sage.
Slattery, Martin (1989), *Urban Sociology*. Ormskirk: Causeway Press.
Social Services Inspectorate (1993), *Evaluating Performance in Child Protection*. London: Department of Health/HMSO.
Social Trends 25 (1995). London: HMSO.
Szreter, S. 'Mortality and Public Health 1815–1914' in Digby, A., Feinstein, C. and Jenkins, D. (eds) *New Directions in Economic and Social History* vol. II. (1992). London: Macmillan.
Thomson, Hillary *et al.* (1995), *Health and Social Care*. London: Hodder and Stoughton.
Tissier, Garry (1993), 'Not in our Backyard', *Community Care*, 26 August.
Townroe, C. and Yates, G. (1995), *Sociology for GCSE*. Harlow, Essex: Longman.
UN International Year of the Family, Factsheets 1–5: 1 *Putting Families on the Map*; 2 *Families, Poverty and Resources*; 3 *Families and Work*; 4 *Families and Caring*; 5 *Parents and Families*.
Young, M. and Wilmott, P. (1975), *The Symmetrical Family*. Harmondsworth: Penguin.

USEFUL ADDRESSES

Advisory Service for Squatters
2 St Paul's Road
London N1
Tel.: 0171 359 8814

Age Concern
Bernard Sunley House
60 Pitcairn Road
Mitcham
Surrey CR4 3LL
Tel.: 0181 640 5431

Alcoholics Anonymous
General Service Office
PO Box 1
Stonebow House
Stonebow
York YO1 2NJ

British Epilepsy Association
Ansley House
40 Hanover Square
Leeds LS3 1BE
Tel.: 01532 439393

British Red Cross Society
9 Grosvenor Crescent
London SW1X 7EJ

British Standards Institution
Quality Assurance Business Development
PO Box 375
Milton Keynes MK14 6LL

British Youth Council
57 Chalton Street
London SW11 1HU
Tel.: 0171 387 7559

Brook Advisory Centres
Central Office at:
9 York Road
Edgbaston
Birmingham B16 9HX
Tel.: 0121 455 0491

Campaign Against the Child Support Act (CACSA)
London: 0171 837 7509
Bristol: 01272 426 608
Manchester: 0161 344 0758

CHAR (Campaign for Homeless and Rootless)
5 Cromer Street
London WC1H 8LS
Tel.: 0171 833 2071

Child Support Agency
Millbank Tower
21–24 Millbank
London SW1 4QU

Child Poverty Action Group
1–5 Bath Street
London EC1V 9PY

Citizens Advice Bureaux
Myddleton House
115–23 Pentonville Road
London N1 9LZ
Tel.: 0171 833 2181

Citizens Advice Notes Service Trust
1 Stockwell Green
London SW9 9HP

Community Care
Room H320
Quadrant House
Sutton
Surrey SM2 5AS

Community Service Volunteers
237 Pentonville Road
London N1 9NJ
Tel.: 0171 278 6601

Confederation of Health Service Employees (COHSE)
Glen House
High Street
Banstead
Surrey SM7 2LH
Tel.: 01737 353322

Department for Education
Sanctuary Buildings
Great Smith Street
London SW1P 3BT
Tel.: 0171 925 5000

Department of Employment
Caxton House
Tothill Street
London SW1H 9NF
Tel.: 0171 273 3000

Department of the Environment
2 Marsham Street

London SW1P 3EB
Tel.: 0171 276 0900

Department of Health
Richmond House
79 Whitehall
London SW1A 2NS
Tel.: 0171 210 3000

Department of Social Security
Richmond House
79 Whitehall
London SW1A 2NS
Tel.: 0171 210 3000

Disablement Income Group (DIG)
Millmead Business Centre
Millmead Road
London N17 9QU
Tel.: 0181 801 8013

The Helen Arkell Dyslexia Centre
Frensham
Farnham
Surrey GU10 3BW
Tel.: 01252 792400

Family Policy Studies Centre
231 Baker Street
London NW1 6XE

GMB Trades Union
22–24 Worple Road
Wimbledon
London SW19 4DF
Tel.: 0181 947 3131

Health Education Authority
Hamilton House
Mabledon Place
London WC1H 9TX
Tel.: 0171 383 3833

Housing Corporation
149 Tottenham Court Road
London W1P 0BN
Tel.: 0171 387 9466

Independent Schools Information Service
56 Buckingham Gate
London SW1E 6AG

Institute for the Study of Drug Dependence
1–4 Hatton Place
London EC1N 8ND
Tel.: 0171 430 1991

Job Concern
37 Sunshine Way
Mitcham
Surrey CR4 3HQ
Tel.: 0181 685 0925

Low Pay Unit
27/29 Arnwell Street
London EC1R 1UN
Tel.: 0171 713 7616

MIND (National Association for Mental Health)
22 Harley Street
London W1N 2ED
Tel.: 0171 637 0741

National Association of Young People's Counselling and Advisory Services (NAYBCAS)
Magazine Business Centre
11 Newarke Street
Leicester LE1 5SS
Tel.: 01533 558763

National Association for Special Educational Needs (NASEN)
York House
Exhall Grange
Wheelwright Lane
Coventry CV7 9HP
Tel.: 01203 362414

National Campaign for Nursery Education
23 Albert Street
London NW1 7LU
Tel.: 0171 387 6582

National Claimants Federation
PCU
PO Box 21
Plymouth PL1 1QS

National Foster Care Association
Leonard House
5–7 Marshalsea Road
London SE1 1EP

National Union of Public Employees (NUPE)
Civic House
20 Grand Depot Road
Woolwich
London SE18 6SF
Tel.: 0181 854 2244

National Youth Agency
17–23 Albion Street
Leicester LE1 6GD
Tel.: 01533 471200

Remploy Ltd
415 Edgware Road
Cricklewood
London NW2 6LG

Salvation Army
Territorial HQ
101 Queen Victoria Street
London EC4P 4EP
Tel.: 0171 236 5222

Scottish Office
New St Andrew's House
St James Centre
Edinburgh EH1 3TG
Tel.: 0131 556 8400

Shelter
88 Old Street
London EC1V 9HU
Tel.: 0171 253 0202

Social Security Benefits Agency
Quarry House
Quarry Hill
Leeds LS2 7UA
Tel.: 01532 32400

Social Services Inspectorate
Wallington House
133–155 Waterloo Road
London SE1 8UG
Tel.: 0171 972 2000

St John's Ambulance Brigade
1 Grosvenor Crescent
London SW1X 7EF
Tel.: 0171 235 5231
Sustrans – Paths for People
35 King Street
Bristol BS1 4DZ
Tel.: 01272 268893

Terrence Higgins Trust
52–54 Gray's Inn Road
London WC1X 8JU
Tel.: 0171 831 0330

UN International Year of the Family
UK Office
Yalding House
152 Great Portland Street
London W1N 6AJ

INDEX